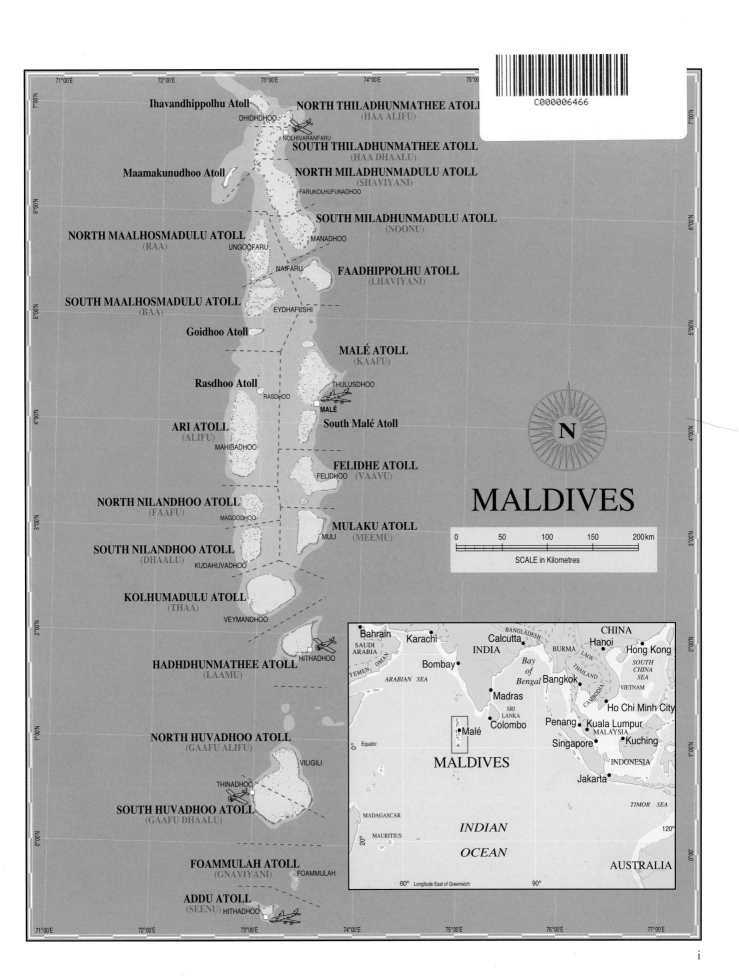

# MALDIVES

Ihavandhippolhu Atoll

**NORTH THILADHUNMATHEE ATOLL**
(HAA ALIFU)

DHIDHDHOO

NOLHIVARANFARU

**SOUTH THILADHUNMATHEE ATOLL**
(HAA DHAALU)

Maamakunudhoo Atoll

**NORTH MILADHUNMADULU ATOLL**
(SHAVIYANI)

FARUKOLHUFUNADHOO

**SOUTH MILADHUNMADULU ATOLL**
(NOONU)

**NORTH MAALHOSMADULU ATOLL**
(RAA)

MANADHOO

UNGOOFARU

NAIFARU

**FAADHIPPOLHU ATOLL**
(LHAVIYANI)

**SOUTH MAALHOSMADULU ATOLL**
(BAA)

EYDHAFUSHI

Goidhoo Atoll

**MALÉ ATOLL**
(KAAFU)

Rasdhoo Atoll

THULUSDHOO

RASDHOO

**MALÉ**

**ARI ATOLL**
(ALIFU)

South Malé Atoll

MAHIBADHOO

**FELIDHE ATOLL**
FELIDHOO    (VAAVU)

**NORTH NILANDHOO ATOLL**
(FAAFU)

MAGOODHOO

**MULAKU ATOLL**
MULI    (MEEMU)

**SOUTH NILANDHOO ATOLL**
(DHAALU)

KUDAHUVADHOO

**KOLHUMADULU ATOLL**
(THAA)

VEYMANDHOO

HITHADHOO

**HADHDHUNMATHEE ATOLL**
(LAAMU)

**NORTH HUVADHOO ATOLL**
(GAAFU ALIFU)

VILIGILI

THINADHOO

**SOUTH HUVADHOO ATOLL**
(GAAFU DHAALU)

**FOAMMULAH ATOLL**
(GNAVIYANI)    FOAMMULAH

**ADDU ATOLL**
(SEENU)    HITHADHOO

N

0    50    100    150    200km

SCALE in Kilometres

## Inset map

Bahrain
SAUDI ARABIA
YEMEN    OMAN
Karachi
ARABIAN SEA
Bombay
INDIA
BANGLADESH
Calcutta
BURMA
Bay of Bengal
Madras
SRI LANKA
Colombo
Malé
**MALDIVES**
Equator
0°
MADAGASCAR
MAURITIUS
20°
60°    Longitude East of Greenwich    90°
INDIAN OCEAN
CHINA
Hanoi
Hong Kong
LAOS
THAILAND
Bangkok
SOUTH CHINA SEA
CAMBODIA
VIETNAM
Ho Chi Minh City
Penang
Kuala Lumpur
MALAYSIA
Kuching
Singapore
INDONESIA
Jakarta
TIMOR SEA
120°
AUSTRALIA

i

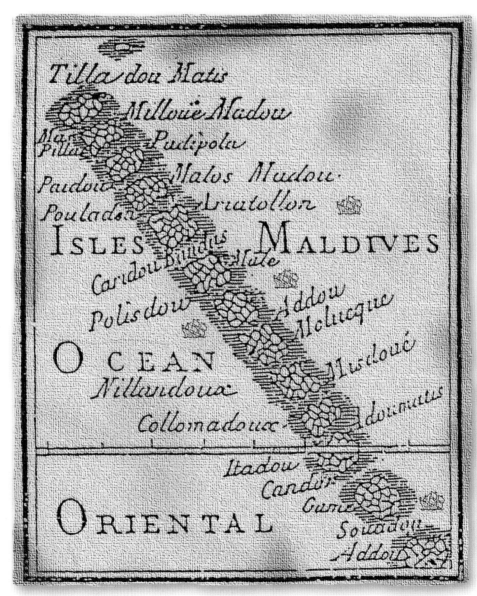

Isles Des Maldives, 17th Century. Early European charts were based on Arab charts and show the Maldives archipelago running in a north-west to south-east direction. This indicated that atolls in the south were more distant from the Arabian coast.

# Dive Maldives

## A guide to the Maldives Archipelago

### 3RD EDITION

**TIM GODFREY**

Atoll Editions
PO Box 113
Apollo Bay Victoria 3233 Australia.

Fax (+61) 3 52376332
www.atolleditions.com.au
Email: info@atolleditions.com.au

First published in 1996 by Atoll Editions
Second edition: 1998
Third Edition: 2006

National Library of Australia
Cataloguing-in-Publication entry
Godfrey, Tim
    Dive Maldives: a guide to the Maldives Archipelago.
    ISBN 1 876410 84 1.
    1. Deep Diving – Maldives. I. Title.

Typeset in 10pt Garamond by Atoll Editions
Cover design by Narelle McDonald
Finished Art & Production by munchdesign.com

## FOREWORD & ACKNOWLEDGEMENTS

The third edition of Dive Maldives builds on the previous two editions and contains another 28 pages with maps, island information and diving details on four more atolls. The opportunity to dive and explore these exciting new areas comes with the opening of new resorts in previously undeveloped atolls and their servicing by seaplanes, the expansion of air services to regional airports and the widening network of safari boat cruises. The Maldives continues to fascinate divers and as the island republic recovers from the 2004 Tsunami, tourism will undoubtedly play an increasingly important role in the ongoing recovery and development of the atolls.

There are many people and organizations that have contributed to the success of this publication over the years. To all of them I owe my grateful thanks. These include:
Novelty Printers and Publishers, Sea Explorers Associates, Euro Divers Maldives, Voyages Maldives, Maldivers, Kabeela Maldives, Hazash Enterprises, Island Breeze Maldives, Najaah Artpalace, DIVE Magazine, Tony Backhurst Scuba Travel, Maldivian Air Taxi, Island Aviation Services, Dhiraagu, Ministry of Transport and Civil Aviation, National Centre for Linguistic and Historical Research, Ministry of Atolls Development, Ministry of Tourism.

Also the following: Dave Doppler, Charles Anderson, Ahmed Shiam, Karen & Todd Rempel and Cinzia Mariolini for their kind assistance. Ruud Paesie for his maps of Fotteyo, Vattaru Kandu, Rakeedhoo, Mulaku Kandu, Dhigali Haa and Filitheyo Thila; Petra Hellmann for her maps of Fushivaru Thila, Kuredu Express and Shipyard; Saskia Nieuwkoop for her maps of Broken Rock; Anders Fagh for his map of Miyaru Thila; and Doris Wolf for her map of Boduhithi Thila.

I am grateful to the staff at resorts and dive schools at which I stayed and divers who helped in any way possible.

I would particularly like to mention Rudie Kuiter (Photo Guide to Fishes of the Maldives), Neville Coleman (Marine Life of the Maldives) and Sally McPhee who have provided their expertise as taxonomists and photographers to give readers a closer look at the marine life in the Maldives.

Mohammed Ibraheem Loutfi (since deceased) generously granted his time and knowledge towards making the geographical and historical notes in this book as accurate and informative as possible.

For the production of this book I am indebted to: Chris Crook for country and atoll maps. Jim Darby and Dianne Parsons for editorial advice and corrections, Kenneth Yendell for book design and Narelle McDonald for book layout and cover design.

All photographs are by Rudie Kuiter except the following:
**Adam Ali:** page 99.
**Adrian Neville:** page 7, 57 all, 59, 84 top, 108, back cover left.
**Ahmed Nazim:** page 147 middle, 149 bottom.
**Andrew Kennedy:** page 120 middle.
**Antonio Frisca:** page 115 all pics, 117 top.
**Brian Knutson:** page 29 middle.
**Brigitte Schmpera:** page 169 top and bottom right.
**Federico Fiorillo:** page 76 bottom, 89 bottom right.
**Infoterra:** page 153.
**John Callahan:** page vii, page 22 left.
**Kimmo Hagman:** page 120 bottom.
**Musthag Hussain:** page iii, 1 top, 17 top, 39 top, 47 left, 85 bottom, 87, 100 bottom, back cover right.
**National Centre for Linguistic and Historical Research:** page 151 all.
**Neville Coleman:** page 137 top, 139 bottom, 149, 157 bottom left and right, 167 all, 168 all.
**Oliver Clarke:** page 122.
**Spaceimaging:** page x, 19, 25, 42 centre.
**Sigurd Schjoett:** page 58, 74 all, 91 left, 93, 119, 120 top.
**Simon Rogerson:** front cover, 54, 61 bottom left and centre, 63 bottom right, 65, 67 bottom, 81 bottom, 84, 85 top, 96 bottom, 103, 147 bottom, 156 bottom, 157 top inset, 165 bottom left and right.
**Tim Godfrey:** page 11, 13 left and right, 17, 22 right, 23 all pics, 24, 31 top, 34 top, 45 top, 48, 52 top left, 91 right, 107, 109, 116, 127, 128 top, 130, 131 top, 133, 134 all pics, 135 all pics, 136, 143 all, 144 all, 154, 159, 160 all, 161 all, 169 left.
**Udo Kefrig:** page viii, 1 bottom, 14, page 27 all pics, 44 bottom, 47 top, 69, 82 all pics, 89 bottom left, 96 top, 131 inset, 157 top.
**Voyages Maldives:** page 17 bottom.

# Contents

# How to use this book

The maps in this book are divided into three types: atoll, region and site maps. The atoll maps show the resorts in blue type with traditional island names in brackets. Also shown are uninhabited islands, reefs, Protected Marine Areas, channel names, and some of the well known dive site locations. The region maps show the same features but in more detail with all the dive site locations as described in this book. The dive site maps show the topography and features of underwater reefs and are useful references for divers.

Those dive sites illustrated by a map contain a general introduction describing their location, depth, fish life, coral growth and features. The fish life is generalized as being either **average, above average or abundant** and coral growth is either **poor, good, very good or excellent**. The maps include the approximate scale of the site, depths and location of reef features, such as caves, overhangs, saddles and canyons and also the approximate location of commonly seen fish and other marine life.

At the back of the book is an index of fish, dive sites, and diver information. They can be used as a quick reference for finding information on any one of these particular subjects. The fish names and identification are based on **Photo Guide to Fishes of the Maldives**, by Rudie Kuiter and invertebrate names are based on **Marine Life of the Maldives**, by Neville Coleman.

All dive sites are given a rating between ★ and ★★★★. The star rating is based on the experience level recommended to dive the location. They are:

★      Beginners. Easy diving, less than 20 metres, no/little current, not much swimming.

★★      Beginners. If conditions are suitable. General diving, not totally protected from current.

★★★      Advanced divers. Diving prone to strong currents. Greater depth.

★★★★ Experienced divers. Diving prone to strong currents, deeper dive. More difficult conditions.

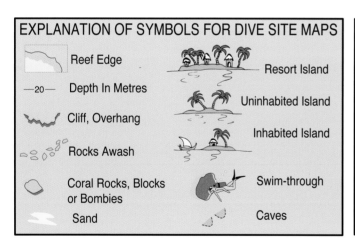

## EXPLANATION OF SYMBOLS FOR DIVE SITE MAPS

- Reef Edge
- —20— Depth In Metres
- Cliff, Overhang
- Rocks Awash
- Coral Rocks, Blocks or Bombies
- Sand
- Resort Island
- Uninhabited Island
- Inhabited Island
- Swim-through
- Caves

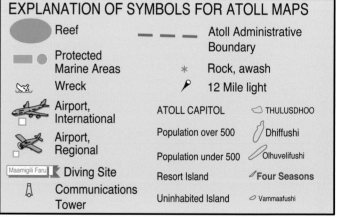

## EXPLANATION OF SYMBOLS FOR ATOLL MAPS

- Reef
- Protected Marine Areas
- Wreck
- Airport, International
- Airport, Regional
- Maamigili Faru ⟓ Diving Site
- Communications Tower
- — — — Atoll Administrative Boundary
- * Rock, awash
- ⌐ 12 Mile light

| ATOLL CAPITOL | THULUSDHOO |
| Population over 500 | Dhiffushi |
| Population under 500 | Olhuvelifushi |
| Resort Island | Four Seasons |
| Uninhabited Island | Vammaafushi |

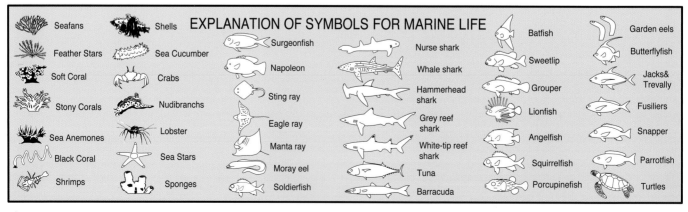

EXPLANATION OF SYMBOLS FOR MARINE LIFE

- Seafans
- Feather Stars
- Soft Coral
- Stony Corals
- Sea Anemones
- Black Coral
- Shrimps
- Shells
- Sea Cucumber
- Crabs
- Nudibranchs
- Lobster
- Sea Stars
- Sponges
- Surgeonfish
- Napoleon
- Sting ray
- Eagle ray
- Manta ray
- Moray eel
- Soldierfish
- Nurse shark
- Whale shark
- Hammerhead shark
- Grey reef shark
- White-tip reef shark
- Tuna
- Barracuda
- Batfish
- Sweetlip
- Grouper
- Lionfish
- Angelfish
- Squirrelfish
- Porcupinefish
- Garden eels
- Butterflyfish
- Jacks & Trevally
- Fusiliers
- Snapper
- Parrotfish
- Turtles

*The Maldivian dhoani is a decorative, durable craft designed for efficient shallow water sailing*

*Whale Shark,* Rhincodon typus

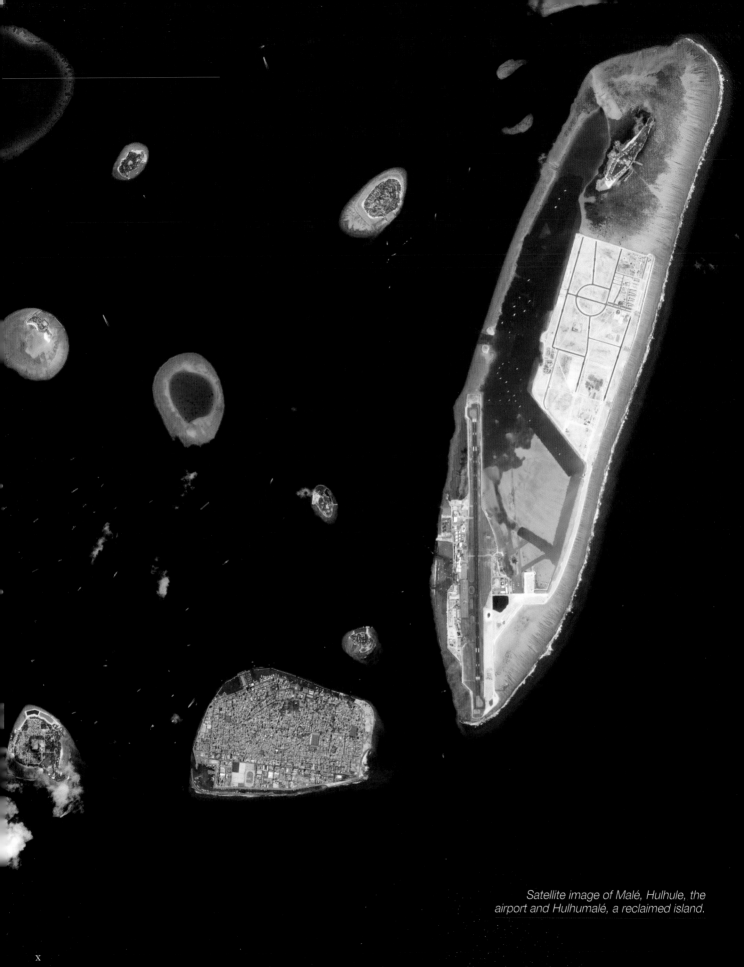

*Satellite image of Malé, Hulhule, the airport and Hulhumalé, a reclaimed island.*

# Introduction

*One of the great attractions of the Maldives is the seemingly endless number of top-quality diving options. When combined with its unique islander lifestyle, it is not surprising that divers are lured back again and again to this Indian Ocean archipelago.*

Early mariners said the islands were so numerous and the channels so narrow that the ships' yards touched the trees of islands on either side. Underwater, the reefs are more abundant. Divers can swim away from one reef and no sooner lose sight of it, than find another one looming up ahead, like a mirage, until it becomes clearly distinguishable.

Despite their proximity, each dive site has its own character and mood, just as the currents that are born of them display their own temperament and behaviour. The outside reefs are defiant, like fort walls; solid and impenetrable. They spurn the seething water before them and temper its forces with a solid barrier of battle hardened coral.

The *kandus,* or channels, are more assertive, like the gates of a fort, steering the restless currents through their narrow openings, forcing them against jagged walls and into crevices and caves where the first filtering of nutrients takes place. The currents bounce back fighting, forming eddies and swirling streams before being funnelled, exhausted, into the more placid interiors of the atoll.

In the channels, divers can find caves and overhangs full of soft coral, a wide range of invertebrates, gorgonians, and sponges. There are also canyons and on the outside corners are steep drop offs. At these impressive sites, vast schools of fish feed in colliding waters.

*There are many wrecks on the reefs of the Maldives. Most are encrusted with coral but some parts remain exposed. The anchor of the SS Sea Gull lies on the reef top at Gaafaru Falhu.*

*A typical underwater sight: a diver observes a magnificent display of soft corals and other invertebrates at a 'thila' in North Malé Atoll.*

Across the channels and within the atolls are the *thilas.* Mysterious and secretive, they are sentinels of rock that spring from the ocean floor to within a few metres of the surface, splitting and trapping the currents as they pass, causing surprise and confusion. These thilas act like magnets for marine life and provide a spectacular change of scenery.

Around some thilas and reefs are large coral rocks, that can be used like compass points to direct divers away from the reef, perhaps to another one, and safely back home. There are many reefs inside the atolls. They are often exposed at low tide and form the body of the atoll. They are restful sites, pretty to look at, and always available.

Above the water is the vast collection of islands, reefs, and sandbars that make up this rich and historically unique nation. No diver can fail to be impressed by the formation of the islands and the way in which the people have adapted to them.

The isolation of the islanders from the rest of the world has left an intriguing history which is still being unravelled. Stepping ashore in the capital Malé just 20 years ago was, for westerners, like stepping into a time warp. Fishing dhoanis were tied off to old cannons strewn along the sandy waterfront. At the tea houses on Marine Drive, a foreign face drew inquiring glances.

Today, every resort has access to a diving centre, and visiting divers are the mainstay of the Maldivian economy. Changes to the marine environment from fluctuating weather patterns, the influx of tourists, a rapidly expanding local population, commercial fishing pressures and the development of new resorts in the outer lying atolls, is inevitable. Keeping those changes in context will be the challenge of the next decade.

# Chapter 1 - Coral Reefs of the Maldives

*The atolls of the Maldives form the central part of a great underwater mountain range stretching for over 2000 km from the Laccadives Islands, in the north, to the Chagos Islands, in the South.*

## GEOGRAPHY

The Maldives cover an area of 90,000 sq. km and lie between Latitude 7° 6' 30" N to 0° 42' 30" S, and Longitude 72° 32' 30" E to 73° 46' 15" E. Estimates of the number of islands differs, depending on the definition of an island. Officially there are 1190 islands having some form of vegetation on them, whether grass or bushes or trees. Of this number 991 are uninhabited and 199 inhabited.

Unofficially there are 1120 islands, but the actual number varies from one year to the next as islands are continually being washed away and new ones formed. The islands are divided into 26 geographic atolls. Minicoy is the 27th atoll but it was linked to India in 1753 during the time of Sultan al Mukarram Mohamed Imadudeen III (1750 – 1757 AD). For convenience, these atolls are divided into 19 administrative groups and named according to the letters of the Maldivian alphabet. In the resort atolls, Felidhoo Atoll is now referred to as Vaavu, Ari Atoll as Alifu, Malé Atoll as Kaafu, Faadhippolhu Atoll as Lhaviyani, South Maalhosmadulu Atoll as Baa and Addu Atoll as Seenu.

## FORMATION

Charles Darwin proposed that the atolls of the Maldives developed as the mountain range gradually subsided into the sea or sea levels rose. The fringing reefs surrounding these mountains built up and became more distant from the centre of the range until there was nothing left but a circle of reefs enclosing a lagoon, called an atoll.

During a seismic survey by Esso in 1980, a well sunk near Bandos concluded that a volcanic base lay beneath 2100 metres of limestone, supporting the subsidence theory of Darwin.

Coral reefs are created by a tiny animal, called a polyp, which secretes a hard limestone skeleton and provides the reef framework. Fragile branching coral may grow between 20 to 30 centimetres per year, while massive boulder-shaped coral may grow only a few millimetres per year. Coralline algae, which thrives in areas exposed to wave action and places too deep and dark for the coral, cement the framework of dead and broken coral together forming a solid limestone base.

The type and shape of the reef developed depends to a great extent on the depth and shape of the ocean floor, the currents, the recent geological history of the area and degree of exposure to wave action. Yet coral reefs have not always existed as they do today.

During the ice ages, falls in sea-levels forced reef building coral away from the reefs to colonise new areas. At the same time, reefs were left high out of the water. The limestone reefs were readily eroded by fresh water and this led to the formation of caves and canyons of all shapes and sizes. After they were again flooded by the sea, marine life re-established itself and layers of coral and coralline algae continued to grow upon the eroded gutters and valleys. These eroded substrata largely govern the shapes of modern reefs. Today, many of these features remain submerged providing divers with spectacular natural attractions.

## ORIGINS

The names of atolls, islands and coral reefs of the Maldives have a curious mixture of spellings, resulting in many simplifications to make names more readable. In some cases, original meanings of words have also been changed. For instance, the word atoll is the only word in the English language of Dhivehi origin, coming from the word *atholhu*. The Oxford definition of an atoll is a 'ring-shaped coral reef enclosing a lagoon.' However, an *atholhu* is an administrative district, sometimes covering more, or less, than one 'atoll'.

Different maps of the Maldives rarely have the same spellings. On some, Ihavandhippolhu Atoll, at the very north of the Maldives, is sometimes named Ihavandiffulhu Atoll. The original meaning of *polhu* is portion, and refers to the upper portion of islands in the Maldives; whereas *fulhu* is the name of a person. Felidhe-Atholhu is the old name of the atoll now called Felidhoo Atoll. It is sometimes abbreviated to Felidhu Atoll. Likewise Nilandhe-Atholhu is an old atoll name which is also called Nilandhoo Atoll. Huvadhoo Atoll in the south is sometimes named on maps as Suvadiva Atoll, which is another more recent name and Goidhoo Atoll is also called Horsburgh Atoll.

Island names can often be traced to a particular characteristic of an island. For instance, Thundufushi is an island in Ari Atoll. *Thundu* means edge, or point, and this island lies on the eastern point of the reef. Other island names refer to an incident that may have occurred there. Dhehasanu Lonu Bui Huraa, is an island in Ari Atoll and is an old name meaning 'two [men named Hasan] drink salt water island'. Other islands and reefs are old words of Sinhalese origin. Names like Lankanfinolhu, Vihamanaafushi and Furanafushi are examples.

Reef names, too, can have interesting origins. Himmiyafaru, in north west Malé Atoll, can tell fishermen much about the reef. *Himmi* means the gap between two objects and in this case the reef is divided in two parts by water. Another reef with a story is Koonimasfaru, in the north of Malé Atoll. *Koonimasfaru* means spoiled fish reef. It is widely believed that a whale was caught inside the lagoon and became stranded and died when the tide receded. The resultant smell is said to have drifted across to the island of Gaafaru, thus giving the reef its name.

Many islands, like Vihamanaafushi, Velassaru, and Medhu Finolhu, have adopted new names since the arrival of tourism. They are now called Kurumba Village, Laguna Beach Resort and Reethi Rah Resort respectively, but many locals still call them by their traditional names.

There are many words in Dhivehi used to describe an island. A *fushi* is a big island usually on the outside reef of the atoll. Meerufenfushi, Kandoomafushi, and Farukolhufushi are examples. A *finolhu* is an island with few or no coconut trees. Islands like Dhigufinolhu, Kanifinolhu and Eboodhoofinolhu

have grown in size since early times but have retained their names, despite having many more coconut trees. *Dhoo* and *Huraa* are other words for an island and *le*, as in Malé, is a contraction of the sanskrit word *liu*, meaning island.

Reefs are usually called farus or falhus. A *faru*, is a reef partially exposed at low tide and a *falhu* is often a reef encircling a lagoon, sometimes with one or more islands inside. *Gaa* and *haa* are other words used to describe coral reefs. A *giri*, is a name for a small patch of coral close to the surface. Most island resorts have their own bodu giri (big reef), and kuda giri (small reef). A *thila*, is a coral reef usually a few metres below the surface. Many dive sites, such as Okobe Thila, Nassimo Thila and Miyaru Thila, have names that indicate the presence of such a reef formation. The channel between two reefs is called a *kandu olhi* in Dhivehi but is simply called a *kandu*. There are many other names describing the natural features of the islands which the curious traveller will come across, but it is *maa kandu* – the big sea outside the atoll – in which most divers will discover the real attraction of the Maldives.

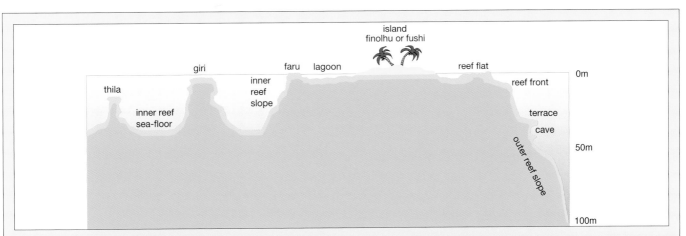

The outer reef slope of the atolls are generally distinguished by greater depths and increased clarity of water. The visibility may exceed 50 metres. Looking down the reef slope, the coral communities change rapidly with increasing depth. At depths greater than 20 metres, wave surge is non-existent and extensive coral growth may occur to depths of 50 metres and more. Light availability is the main factor limiting the range of the coral here.

The upper parts of the outer reef slope may be affected by wave action, restricting the growth of more delicate plate coral. Coral growth can be wiped out in a single freak storm in this zone. In areas less exposed to wave action, extensive stands of staghorn acropora can dominate. A great variety of fish life occurs among the coral in this zone.

The reef front is the part of the reef which takes the full force of the ocean swells. The coral here tends to be gnarled and stunted as a result of the pounding by waves.

The reef flats can range in width from a few metres to a few kilometres. Rainwater can damage or completely destroy the coral in this zone if heavy or cyclonic rainfall coincides with very low tides.

Lagoons with good circulation of water may have large stands of branching acropora growing on the sand. Lagoons can trap many fish varieties as the tide recedes.

On the inner reef slope, coral growth may be rich if the slope is not too steep. Steep or vertical slopes may be bare. Many interesting caves, overhangs and gullies can occur in this zone. The atoll floor consists mostly of sand and rubble and is usually at a depth of between 30 to 50 metres. Rising from the floor are the giris and thilas. The giris nearly reach the surface, whereas the thilas lay below at depths between five and 15 metres.

# Climate

The Maldives have a tropical climate with warm temperatures year round and a great deal of sunshine. During a 24-year period between 1967 – 1990, the hottest month on average was April, with a maximum monthly mean temperature of 31.5° C and a minimum of 26.5° C. The coolest month was December, with a maximum monthly mean temperature of 29.8° C and a minimum of 25.3° C.

There is considerable variation in climate between the northern and southern atolls in the Maldives. In the south the rainfall is greater but so are the number of rain days. Showers are not as heavy as in the north. There are greater extremes of temperature in the north also, as the seasons are more evident further away from the equator.

**Monsoons**

| | |
|---|---|
| December – April | NE Monsoon |
| April | Transition period |
| May-November | SW Monsoon |
| November | Transition period |

The weather is determined to a large extent by the monsoon circulation. Each year there are two monsoon seasons, the north-east monsoon *iruvai* and the south-west monsoon *hulhangu*. The prevailing winds, which can become quite strong, are from the SW-W-NW during the south-west monsoon and N-NE-E during the north-east monsoon.

The north-east monsoon brings the driest period, the air having a comparatively short sea track compared with that during the remainder of the year. There is generally little cloud except in the south. The relative humidity at this time is only 5% lower than during the south-west monsoon, but this lowering is enough to make a considerable difference to comfort.

The hot season is in March and April. Frequent light winds from the north east and variable sea breezes are experienced. In April, calm, windless days are more likely to be experienced than at any other time of the year. The transitional period between monsoons begins in April and by the end of May the winds are predominantly W-SW. A fortnight of strong winds and rain usually ushers in the change of seasons. Occasionally the tail end of cyclones from the Bay of Bengal are felt during this period.

The wet season is from June to September when the south-west monsoon is firmly set. Gales and moderate to rough seas are common during this season. Cloudy days are more frequent.

November is again a transitional period. During October, days of light winds are experienced more frequently and by the end of November, winds have shifted from W-NW to N-NE. The effects of cyclones from the Arabian Sea can be experienced during this period. The first month of the north-east monsoon,

December, is typically rough with strong winds and rain. The monsoon gradually travels down the Maldives from the north and is ushered in by a fortnight of very strong winds from the north east with heavy rain squalls.

Because the Maldives is in the equatorial belt, severe tropical storms and cyclones are extremely rare events. But whenever cyclones form in the Bay of Bengal or Arabian Sea, the spiralling feeder band clouds appear over the Maldives and cause spells of rain and showers. The weather in the north may deteriorate considerably as a result, but there is little effect on the southern islands as it is almost impossible for low pressure areas to develop within 5° of the equator.

There are some useful guidelines for predicting the weather. There is not a lot of variation in relative humidity but if it is 85% or above, there is a strong chance of rain or showers. If it is between 80% – 85% there is a chance of a change in weather to wet. If it is 90% or above, there will be rain and storms. When below 80%, the general weather should be mainly fine.

If the barometer drops to 1005 or 1004 (mean reading usually 1009) then bad weather is likely to occur at any time. If the barometer drops to 1003 actual, the lowest limit, galeforce winds, heavy rain with thunderstorms and rough seas will result. In some situations, there may not be a drastic drop in pressure for a change in weather to occur. This could be due to a tailcloud band of a tropical cyclone originating in the Bay of Bengal, Arabian Sea or South Indian Ocean, or due to excessive heating over the equator, where large convective clouds can develop bringing heavy showers with gusty winds. In these situations the pressure can be as high as 1012.

Ocean water temperatures rarely vary beyond 27 – 30° C although thermoclines can sometimes be experienced at depths below 20 metres. During hot periods, water temperatures inside the lagoons increases measurably, influencing water temperatures inside the atolls. During these periods most divers are comfortable diving without a wetsuit, although those of slight build may shiver a little. During overcast periods with wind and rain squalls, it is wise to carry extra clothing on the boat after a dive. Lycra and 3mm wetsuits are popular in tropical waters but some divers prefer a 5mm suit if doing more than one dive a day. In April 1998, water temperatures rose to abnormally high levels causing widespread coral bleaching with reports of up to 80-90% of shallow water corals dying. Coral reefs are now being closely monitored to assess their recovery. With 2004 estimates of sea-level rises varying considerably, there is great concern about the capability of coral reefs to keep up with such a rapid change. Abnormal monsoon seasons have also been experienced in recent years.

# Currents

"Currents run for six whole months, each way. If a vessel happens to be at the northern extremity of the islands it is no great matter, for then it is only carried to Cochin, on the coast of India, or thereabouts, about a 150 leagues distance, or to some of the islands on that coast. But if they cannot make the islands of Ceylon, they are carried to Sumatra, a distance of about 500 leagues; and if ill-luck has it that these currents carry them away at the close of the monsoons, and before they make land anywhere, they are caught in the other current; as often happens, they are infallibly lost, as I have seen in a number of cases, when they were expecting to make land every night, and were without water and provisions. If the current carries them to the west, they are borne straight to the Arabian coast, which is much further off than that of Sumatra; but most often they are dead before they get there."

*Francois Pyrard, Maldives, 1602 – 1607.*

The currents of the Maldives are notorious for their strength. For this reason early traders in the Indian Ocean were extremely cautious when in the Maldives region. Many ships by-passed the Maldives to the north and south when they had no reason to visit, others took on local pilots to steer them through the maze of reefs and their treacherous currents.

The exposure of the Maldives to the vast Indian Ocean ensures that an immense body of water is constantly flowing across the plateau on which these atolls are built. Oceanic currents are largely influenced by the direction of the trade winds and are of great strength. Currents in the channels near Malé have been recorded at four knots or more. Inside the atoll, current speeds are more settled and leisurely dives are more the norm. Tidal currents, which flow according to the height of the tide and the direction of the prevailing winds, are said to be much weaker than oceanic currents, though they cause velocity variations in the flow.

Early Arab navigators studied the patterns of these oceanic and tidal currents to help them determine their position. When in the vicinity of the Maldives they observed changes in current direction and surface patterns as the ocean's waters confronted the great underwater barriers of the Maldive archipelago.

On the eastern side of Malé Atoll, currents predominantly flow into the atoll when the north-east monsoon is firmly set and flow outside during the south-west monsoon. The opposite applies to the western side of the atoll. This is by no means the rule, as changes in wind direction and tides can offset the influence of the oceanic currents. If the winds ease off for a few days, then currents are more likely to flow both in and out of the channels.

During the seasonal transition months of April and November, when the wind direction and oceanic currents are less predictable, current is more likely to be influenced by the tides and similarly flow both in and out of the channels.

At atoll passages, current streams can be quite irregular due to the islands, reefs and sandy shoals. Most dhoani captains show great skill in reading the direction of the current and take great pride in their knowledge of the ocean. If you ask: *"Oi othee kon thaakah?"* (which direction is the current going?), they will usually wave their hand and say: *"mee a taa"* (this way), or *"eh a taa"* (that way).

Usually they can tell the current direction by the tiny wave patterns on the surface. If there is no wind, the current forms ripples that bend around stationary objects, like the reef, in the direction of flow. The captains can also tell current direction by the shape of the ripples and the movement of the dhoani. If the current is flowing against the wind, then the surface appears more choppy than if the current is flowing in the same direction as the wind. If there is very little, or no current, and the captains don't know its direction, they will usually guess one way or the other, otherwise lose face. For this reason, it is always advisable for the divemaster to enter the water and check if in doubt. It is better to be sure, and dive on the best point, than miss the point altogether.

## CLIMATOLOGY OF MALDIVES

| | Jan | Feb | Mar | Apr | May | Jun | Jul | Aug | Sep | Oct | Nov | Dec |
|---|---|---|---|---|---|---|---|---|---|---|---|---|
| **RAINFALL (mm)** | 119 | 58 | 69 | 128 | 222 | 194 | 210 | 194 | 200 | 235 | 211 | 193 |
| **SUNSHINE (hr/day)** | 8 | 9 | 9 | 8 | 8 | 7 | 7 | 7 | 7 | 8 | 8 | 8 |
| **MAX. TEMPERATURE (°C)** | 31 | 31 | 32 | 32 | 31 | 32 | 31 | 30 | 30 | 30 | 30 | 30 |
| **MIN. TEMPERATURE (°C)** | 25 | 25 | 25 | 26 | 26 | 25 | 25 | 25 | 25 | 25 | 25 | 25 |
| **RELATIVE HUMIDITY (%)** | 78 | 77 | 76 | 77 | 79 | 80 | 80 | 80 | 80 | 81 | 81 | 80 |
| **WIND SPEED (mph)** | 10 | 9 | 8 | 8 | 12 | 13 | 12 | 12 | 12 | 12 | 9 | 9 |
| **CLOUD COVERAGE (oktas)** | 5 | 4 | 4 | 5 | 5 | 6 | 6 | 6 | 6 | 6 | 5 | 5 |

Source: Department of Meteorology Calendar 2006

# Diving safety

Drift diving is the most common type of diving in the Maldives. It is easy and safe when conducted properly and gives divers the opportunity to see more fish life, coral and rock formations than could otherwise be seen. The outside reefs and channels are the staging points for these thrilling dives but care should be taken when diving in a current.

Diving with an ingoing current is generally safer than an outgoing current. If there is a strong current flowing out of the atoll, divers should take extreme care. At these times divers need to stay close to the reef and shallow on the outside corners, then swim across the reef corner away from the main current flow to the lee of the reef.

The channel entrances often have protruding ridges that extend well out into the channel on the outer rim of the atoll at between 20 and 30 metres. Inside the atoll, the water often deepens to 40 metres. With an ingoing current, the channel corners are a favourite place to hold dead reef and watch sharks and pelagics feeding and congregating in the open water.

It is an exciting and memorable spectacle but at certain times, such as during spring tides, it is not always advisable to dive these locations - especially for novice or inexperienced current divers, or those with cameras or physical limitations. As the currents swirl round the outer wall and into the channel, they form eddies, whirlpools, and downward streams that can rapidly and unexpectedly take divers away from the reef and downwards into deeper water. The danger of panic is increased when divers become separated and find their pressure gauge rapidly approaching the red as they gasp to maintain control and positive buoyancy.

At all times divers should stay close to the reef and be prepared to take hold of it to claw their way back up to more shallow depths and protected waters. If caught in open water, divers should inflate their jacket, closely monitor depth and contents gauges, and make a controlled open water ascent.

Current diving can be exciting, but care should be taken at all times or a dive can quickly turn into a disorganised and frightening event. Currents can change rapidly in strength during a dive and sometimes the dive may have to be aborted in the interests of diver safety. A knowledgeable divemaster and competent boatmen are required at all times.

## GUIDELINES

A few basic guidelines can make a dive safer and more enjoyable when diving in a current.

- Ensure you check your equipment and your buddies so you can begin your dive immediately.
- Do not stay too long at the surface when you begin your dive.
- Descend quickly to the reef.
- Never try to swim against a strong current. Stay close to the reef using your hands if necessary to pull yourself along (hold only dead coral and look before grabbing the reef).
- Never dive alone and follow the buddy system procedures.
- The visibility is usually good so do not underestimate the distance.
- The maximum depth is not to exceed 30 metres.
- Make all your dives no-decompression dives.
- If you should not see your boat after surfacing, a surface balloon, or 'parachute' makes you visible from a distance. This is a mandatory accessory for each group of divers at most dive schools. Inflate your parachute if a long way from the boat or making an open water safety stop.

# Tides

For divers, the effect of tides is important as they can determine the strength and direction of currents and make shallow water navigable.

Slack water at high or low tide is usually the easiest time to dive, but not necessarily the best. Depending on the season, divers can take advantage of a rising tide and clear water flowing into the atoll to make, for instance, a drift dive through one of the channels.

Spring tides occur between one and three days after a new or full moon and neap tides occur just after the first and third quarters of the moon. During neap tides, the influence of the sun and moon are working against each other, resulting in a minimal tidal range. The approximate times between successive high tides is 12 hrs 25 mins and the interval between spring and neap tides is about 7 1/4 days.

During spring tides, the range is between about 88 cm and 110 cm and during neap tides the range can be as little as a few centimetres. Variations of just a few centimetres can make an immense difference to the strength of tidal currents.

The height of the tide is also affected by the weather. Winds from different directions influence the raising and lowering of the water level and situations of high sea levels on the outside of the atolls are caused by storm surges and wave set-up. The water also stands higher with a low barometer, to what extent is uncertain.

The times of low and high water must not be considered to coincide with the times of slack water and change of current direction. Inside the atolls, water often runs in or out long after the tide has turned. Precise and long term data on tidal range and patterns of flow do not exist. Tidal gauges have operated in Malé since 1988 and data collected is now being used to predict tides.

# Protected Marine Areas

On World Environment Day, June 5, 1995, the Government of the Maldives announced the establishment of 15 Protected Marine Areas within the major tourist atolls. This is the first step in protecting popular dive sites from the detrimental effects of over-fishing, coral mining, anchor damage and rubbish.

Awareness of the need for Protected Marine Areas was brought about initially by unrestricted shark fishing, especially at world renowned dive sites such as Fish Head (Mushimasmingili Thila) and Lions Head. In 1995 – 1996 shark fins were fetching up to US$70/kg, so there is great incentive for fishermen to meet the growing demand. The number of sharks at some dive sites today is less than they were just a few years ago and over-fishing, if unchecked, poses long term problems for the diving industry.

In the past few years, the number of people entering the aquarium industry has increased and the business is expanding rapidly. Many divers visit the Maldives especially to record and photograph the small and beautiful fish that find their way into private fish tanks. Since most of these fish are taken from areas close to Malé, this industry, also, could be in direct conflict with the recreational diving industry. Steps have been taken to introduce a quota system for those species that are considered rare in the Maldives and it is hoped that these measures will help protect existing aquarium fish stocks.

In 1993, the grouper fishing industry started and in 1995 it took off with alarming intensity. With a big demand for grouper, especially in Asia, and high prices being paid for their delicate flesh, private exporters have been quick to exploit the opportunity. Currently, local fishermen can fish without restriction on numbers and sizes to fill the demand of Asian markets. Live grouper are shipped monthly to Asian markets and ice-chilled grouper are air-freighted to Singapore.

The reefs surrounding Guraidhoo and Kandooma are one of the diving highlights in South Malé Atoll. The two channels to the south of Guraidhoo (left of picture) have been declared Protected Marine Areas.

Experienced long-term divers believe grouper and other fish stocks on many reefs of the tourist atolls have been affected by over-fishing. Many resorts themselves allow fishing at dive sites and must share the blame. Controls on grouper fishing are now being looked at and a possible remedy in the future is envisaged.

At the beginning of 1995 the giant napoleon fish, or hump-headed wrasse, was starting to make an appearance in the chilled export bins bound for Singapore. With fisherman receiving up to US$50/kg for the napoleon, the big fish were being hunted mercilessly. However, following protest from all quarters, the government has now totally banned the export of napoleon fish.

Sea-cucumbers have been overfished in the past and a ban on scuba diving for them, now in force, is expected to allow deeper ones to regenerate. Sea-cucumbers are regarded as the vacuum cleaners of the ocean floor and the consequences of their removal from the eco-system is not fully known.

Collecting black coral for jewellery has been banned from January 1, 1995 and coral mining for building purposes has been restricted to certain areas to protect the existing reefs and to give them a chance to keep up with predicted sea-level rises.

Imported turtle products have been banned and a total ban on turtle collecting has taken effect. Tourists are now being made aware that their purchase of jewellery or gifts made from turtle shell are a threat to the turtle population. Purchase of shark jaws is also discouraged.

Giant clams were collected without restriction until 1991 and their absence on the reefs is often overlooked. The export of clam meat has been banned but large quantities of shells remain.

Anchor damage at dive sites, especially thilas, was considerable in the past but most people are now aware of the damage anchors cause to the coral and adopt different diving techniques. If a line has to be secured at a site, then it is up to the divemaster to dive down and tie a rope rather than use an anchor. However, damage to the coral from divers, especially inexperienced divers in a current, continues to be a cause for concern. It is most frustrating for caring divers to witness degradation of the reefs through neglect. Every divemaster should restrict diving at sensitive sites to the ability of their least-able diver.

Rubbish is a general problem not confined to dive sites. It is one of the most visible signs of human impact and one of the most difficult problems to control. Rubbish is often seen on the open seas and washed up on the reefs of some resorts and uninhabited islands.

Rubbish comes from several sources. Tourist consumption leaves tons of rubbish to be disposed of. All resorts are now required to have compactors and incinerators but these are not always used. Maldivians have traditionally thrown all their waste materials, mostly coconut products, into the ocean, but with increased wealth and the availability of packaged goods, many of those wastes are being disposed of in the same way. On some inhabited islands, rubbish is dumped on the edge of the island only to be washed away on the high tide.

Malé, with a transient population of more than 80,000 people, now disposes its rubbish burden at Thilafushi, a newly created island – and one of the fastest growing – near Villingili. In the past, much of Malé's rubbish went into the sea off the island capital, but with an increased environmental awareness divers have removed much of the rubbish during cleanup days. However rubbish disposal on outlying inhabited islands continues to be a clearly visible problem.

The number of safari boats has increased exponentially in the past 10 years and disposal of rubbish from the boats is another cause of the problem. Many tourists give little thought to what happens to their waste products. In some cases, these are conveniently and quietly disposed of at night or while guests are diving. Some rubbish, such as crushed cans and food scraps can be disposed of at sea outside the atolls, but all other rubbish, such as plastics, containers and batteries should be returned to Malé and disposed of at the harbour in the correct manner.

The most effective way to clean up rubbish is to write letters of complaint and send photos to tour operators or the tourism ministry if abuses occur. In that way we may eventually see rubbish-free waters.

In October 1999, the Maldives Government announced the expansion of the system of Protected Marine Areas. Nine of these sites have been confirmed and the locations are shown on the maps.

## PROTECTED MARINE AREAS

## MANAGING THE MARINE ENVIRONMENT

Divers visiting tropical waters for the first time should realise that correct buoyancy control is the most important skill to learn for the protection of the marine environment.

Photographers need to pay special attention – responsible underwater photography over live coral requires divers to photograph while maintaining correct buoyancy control.

Divers should be careful not to kick or break the coral with their fins and to hold only dead coral.

Fish feeding at dive sites is discouraged as this upsets their natural feeding habits.

Divers are often tempted to chase or touch the fish, mantas and turtles but this makes them frightened and less inclined to return. Handling fish like grouper and moray eels, may remove the slime coating the skin, leading to infection of the fish.

Divers are not allowed to harpoon fish, collect lobsters, coral or shells (dead or alive) or any other animal. Lobsters are often available from the resort menu – but every lobster eaten is one less to be seen under water.

Shells and coral jewellery can be purchased at some boutiques and inhabited islands but many people take a dim view of this practice as it works against the protection of the marine environment.

Fishing at all dive sites should be discouraged and anchor dives should not be made.

# Indian Ocean Maritime History

## THE ARAB TRADERS

The Maldive Archipelago lies across the direct sea route between Southern Arabia, Sri Lanka and the Far East and was a formidable barrier to early Indian Ocean maritime traffic. The early Arab navigators were among the first traders to visit the Maldives, using Malé as a stopover on the return route from Southeast Asia.

On the outward journey from Southern Arabia during the violent and unpredictable south-west monsoon, the Arabs generally sailed north east across the Arabian Sea towards Diu, South India, then down the Malabar coast and past the southern most tip of Sri Lanka. They then worked straight across to Aceh in Sumatra, thereby avoiding the Maldives.

For the return journey, the north-east monsoon was less fierce, allowing the option of taking the more direct and faster route through the Maldives. Speed meant greater profits for the merchants and moreover, stopping at Malé gave the traders another port of call so they could trade in products like dried Maldives fish (for which the archipelago was famous) and the cowries that gave the islands their name: *Diva Kudha* (Cowrie Islands).

This journey involved considerable risk. Although the Arabs were recognised as skilled navigators, they still had to negotiate the myriad reefs of the Maldives. At the time of the Arab Suleiman (ninth century), Arabs were aware of most of the atolls in the north and were trading at least as far south as *Dhibat al-Mahal*, Malé.

Early Arab maps of the archipelago show the islands running away to the south east towards the southern end of the Maldives, an indication that the atolls to the south were more distant from the Arabian coast and less frequently visited. According to Arab historians none of the various passages through the islands are mentioned in the early texts, except for a *"wide strait"* between Suvadiva and Hadhdhunmathee Atolls, being the One-and-a-half-degree channel.

Despite having little surety in the way of charts, the Arabs dominated trade in the Indian Ocean from at least the ninth century up until the arrival of the Portuguese in early 16th century. Part of the reason for this success can be attributed to their skill at navigating their way through the Maldives.

Duarte Barbosa, a Portuguese soldier who served in the East between 1501 – 17, says of the Arab traders:

Many ships of the moors which pass from China, Maluco, Peegu, Malaca, Camatra, Benguala and Ceilam, towards the Red Sea touch at these islands to water and take in supplies and other things needful for their voyages. At times they arrive here so battered that they discharge their cargoes and let them go to the bottom. And among these isles many rich vessels of Moors are cast away, which crossing the sea, dare not through dread of our ships finish their voyage to Malabar.

## CHINESE TRADE WITH THE MALDIVES

The Chinese had trade relations with countries of the Indian Ocean from an early date but it wasn't until 1405, when the first of several enormous naval expeditions to the Indian Ocean was launched, that the Chinese influence in the region was extended.

Seven spectacular expeditions under the control of the grand eunuch, Cheng Ho, were despatched to the 'Western Ocean' over a 20 year period making China the most important state in the orient. On each occasion, Cheng Ho commanded thousands of government soldiers and more than 100 ocean-going vessels. The largest expedition, the first, comprised over 300 ships and nearly 28,000 men. Cheng Ho's largest ships were estimated to be 300' long and 150' broad ranging from nine-masted 'treasure ships' to three masted escort vessels.

The treasure ships brought back "cargoes" including elephants tusks and rhinoceros horns, strings of pearls, aromatics and incense. To pay for these luxuries, the Chinese exported gold, silver and copper, rice and grains, silks and porcelain. The porcelain was originally sent as ballast for the light, valuable silk stuffs, but quickly created its own market.

Altogether more than 30 countries in the Indian Ocean were visited by the Chinese on these expeditions, as well as ports in the Persian Gulf, the great markets of Aden and Mecca, and centres such as Mogadishu on the coast of Africa. The Maldives was one of the countries visited, although it is not certain on which occasions. They were most likely visited in the course of the fifth, sixth and seventh and definitely the fourth (1413 – 15) expeditions. Delegations from each country were sent back to China including an ambassador from the Maldives who was returned on a later expedition.

The Chinese map, the *Mao K'un* map, illustrates that the Maldives was an important stopover for Chinese shipping. Sailing directions from Malé to Mogadishu on the coast of Africa suggest that some voyages were made by way of the Maldive Islands.

Some places in the Maldives mentioned in this map include Hadhdhunmathee Atoll, Mulaku Atoll, Malé or Sultan's island, and Faadhippolhu Atoll.

The Maldive islands were known to the Chinese as the 'Liu Mountains' (although the islands are around three metres high, any land above sea-level may be designated a mountain) and the islands were held in superstitious awe. In *The Overall Survey of the Ocean's Shores*, Ma Huan wrote:

> Tradition says that there are more than 3,000 Liu. This place is in truth the so-called 'Three thousand weak waters'. The inhabitants all dwell in caves; they know nothing about rice and grain, [and] they only catch fish and shrimps to eat; they do not understand wearing clothes, [and] they use the leaves of trees to cover themselves in front and behind. If favourable winds and waters are met with, when the ship's master loses his bearings and the rudder is destroyed, ships passing these liu drift into ebbing waters, gradually become uncontrollable, and sink; [and], as a general rule, when you travel by ship it is always right to avoid these [islands].

## MALDIVIAN TRADERS

Being at the crossroads of the Indian Ocean, the Maldivians themselves were trading among the great ports of the time from the coast of Arabia in the west and India in the north to Sunda (Java) in the east.

Tome' Pires, in his *Suma Oriental* of 1515, says Maldivians were among the traders at Malacca. He also tells us that the port of Bantam in the kingdom of Sunda (Indonesia) was trading with the Maldive Islands *"because they can get from Sunda to the Maldives islands in six or seven days"*.

The Maldivian sailors were well travelled and their knowledge of other countries in the region, as well as their own, impressed western mariners. In 1529, the French brothers Jean and Raoul Parmentier arrived in the Maldives at Foammulah and enquired of the chief priest their true location. To this point the priest was able to answer their question and moreover, *"this chief priest showed the captain in what quarters lay the countries of Adan, Persia, Ormus, Calicut, Zeilan, Moluque and Sumatra, and proved himself to be both learned and well travelled"*.

Maldivians were unafraid to travel great distances using only basic instruments for navigation. In 1835, as recorded in *The Asiatic Journal* a Maldivian boat which had its mast, rigs and rudder destroyed by a storm while sailing to Malacca, was found in Southern Burma after drifting for one and a half months.

> It was built of wood from the coconut tree, without one single iron-nail. In the poop was a sheltered cabin, and in the bow was a kind of deck made of woven strawmats, to hinder water from entering. It is indeed a miracle that such a boat, without any strength, and with a strawmat as sail can cross any ocean. These Maldivian sailors, with a compass made by a black-smith, and a sea-chart that just informs about their own archipelago and the place in the Bay of Bengal where they go for trading, and finally an instrument of wood in the shape of the letter 'T', to be used to determine their latitude, they really can find their way.

On some islands were schools for teaching navigation where they make and repair nautical instruments such as the astrolabe and quadrant. In the *Indian Ocean Directory*, 1834, Commander Moresby wrote:

> On one occasion I was much surprised in seeing a wooden sextant very neatly made by them; the glasses and telescope had been fitted from old instruments; they copy our nautical tables, generally using our figures, and translate the rules in our navigation books into their own language.

In their own territory, Maldivian knowledge of the islands was unsurpassed and critical for many foreign ships wishing to pass through the archipelago. The Maldivians had their own charts with all the rocks and dangers marked. Captains in the early 16th century who found themselves approaching Maldivian waters by mistake, either for lack of wind or through bad steersmanship, were advised to send a skiff ashore to fetch a native pilot who could guide the ship into one of the navigable channels between the islands, and, until the pilot came aboard, to stand off at some distance from the shore. In 1780, Frenchman Jean Laharpe wrote:

> Inside every atoll, full of reefs and shoals, the navigable passages are so dangerous, that the inhabitants do not sail them during the night, even if the sea is always calm. In daytime the boats are numerous, but in the evening, even if the weather is fine, tradition says that they go ashore or they go to anchor. The Maldive people are maybe the world's best sailors but the seamen's skills do not prevent numerous shipwrecks.

## THE ARRIVAL OF THE PORTUGUESE

The Portuguese arrived in the Indian Ocean at the close of the 15th century, and were quick to examine every trading link as they set about conquering trade.

It wasn't long before the Maldives came under the microscope, chiefly for its coir, the outside fibre of the coconut shell which was used for ship's rigging and cables and was an important trading item. An anonymous Portuguese geographer wrote before 1505:

> These ropes are used in all India because there are no better ropes to be found outside these islands. They do not decay in the sea water and are of great commercial value for the islands, as 12 – 15 ships every year go to Calecud and Cambaya and these ships never take anything else but these ropes.

Tome' Pires identified all the major ports and their trading partners from Aden – the key seaport of Arabia – to the heavily fortified centre of Goa, on the west coast of India, to Malacca, a city *"that was made for merchandise, fitter than any other in the world"*. Since Malé was one of the strategic ports in the trading link that straddled the Indian Ocean, the Portuguese set about forcibly controlling the trade which passed through her.

## ENCOUNTER WITH THE MALDIVIANS

One of the first encounters between the Maldivians and the Portuguese invaders was in 1503 near Calicut, between the Portuguese Captain Vincente Sodre and his caravels and four ships from the Maldives.

In his account of Sodre's expedition, Gaspar Correa informs us that the four ships were loaded with coconut ropes, dried fish, silk cloths and cowries, which were used as coins in Bengal. On board were many Moorish merchants from Calicut who went over to the Maldives to barter with salt, cooking-pans, rice and silver, as these commodities were not to be found on the islands. At the time, the Portuguese were involved in a dispute between the Raja of Calicut who was at war with the Portuguese. Correa wrote:

> Captain Sodre seized the Gundra ships and the cargo, and ordered the Maldivian Captains to point out the Moors from Calicut, and if not, Sodre would burn them all together. This scared them and they gave the Calicut Moors up. All these Moors were tied by their hands and feet and thrown into one of the Gundra ships, which had already been emptied of its cargo. Oil was poured over the men and the ship and then all was put to fire.

## PORTUGUESE TAKE MALÉ

The first intrusion of the Portuguese in the Maldives occurred in December 1518 when a flotilla carrying 120 men under the command of Joao "scent money" Gomes, was despatched to Malé. Gomes took Malé and fortified part of the island with guns and proceeded to rob and harry the islanders. The Maldivians obtained help from a powerful Cochin merchant turned pirate, Pata Marakkar, who in 1521 sent 12 well manned Malabar paraos, that surprised the Portuguese, sinking one carevella and capturing the other six. All the Portuguese were killed and the islanders were freed from occupation.

No further attempt was made to capture Malé until the reigning Sultan Hasan IX abdicated the throne following a palace revolution, which brought his cousin Ali VI to the throne. Hasan departed secretly to Cochin where he took refuge with the Jesuits and became a Christian. He requested from the Viceroy of the Indies at Goa to retake Malé and in 1557, an armed Portuguese force set out to conquer Malé. Their mission was unsuccessful and they were forced to retire, losing four ships and many men.

The next year they returned with a stronger force and took Malé, and for the next 15 years (1558 – 1573) a governor was appointed by the Portuguese to rule in the name of the Christian King.

The retaking of Malé by the Maldivians is enshrined in folklore. In 1573, two brothers from a noble Maldivian family, the elder of whom was Muhammad Bodu Thakurufaanu, later to become Sultan Ghazi Muhammed, led a group of rebels who captured the fortress at Malé and killed the entire Portuguese garrison. This event marked the end of any real influence of the

*Many artifacts of historical interest lie buried or beneath the sea. In 1992, a collapsed seawall on Malé revealed a number of cannons, remnants of the bastions which once lined the waterfront of Malé.*

Portuguese in Maldivian affairs, although there were attempts to retake Malé in 1632 and 1649.

Bodu Thaurufaanu's famous vessel *Kalhuohfummi,* which was built for the purpose of fighting the Portuguese, was wrecked on the reef of Koluvaariyaafushi, Mulaku Atoll, and the remains are believed to have been used to build a mosque on the island.

## LOSSES TO SHIPWRECKS

Throughout the period of Portuguese dominance in the Indian Ocean and the Maldives, the losses of Portuguese shipwrecks were extremely high.

The Portuguese trading season lasted from September to April since all the harbours on the west coast of India were closed for the remaining south-west monsoon. They aimed to leave Lisbon after Easter to round the Cape of Good Hope and catch the tail-end of the south-west monsoon winds off the east coast of Africa, ending up in Goa in September or October. The return journey aimed at leaving Goa, or Cochin, with the north-east monsoon.

It was estimated that whereas only 31 ships had been wrecked between 1500 and 1579, no fewer than 35 were wrecked in the 30 years between 1580 and 1610. Losses for the century 1550 to 1650 were estimated to be between 112 and 130.

Some of these vessels were lost by enemy action or other causes, but the majority were either wrecked on the coast of East Africa or else foundered in the Indian Ocean with all hands.

The wreck of the *Prazer e Allegria* in 1844 was the last occasion on which the Portuguese and Maldivians came into contact at the islands.

## DUTCH INTEREST IN THE MALDIVES

It wasn't long after Cornelis de Houtman – the pioneer Dutch explorer to the east – rounded the Cape in 1595, that the Dutch touched at the Maldives, ushering in a new period of prosperity to the region.

It was Cornelis de Houtman, in command of the *Lion* and his brother Fredrick, in command of the *Lioness*, who fell among the Maldives on June 1, 1599. They came across a small island (Nilandhoo, in South Nilandhoo Atoll) with many ruins of artfully built temples and altars *"so closely bound together by means of hewn grooves that the point of a knife could not be put between them, while at each corner a keystone held the entire work together."*

The chief pilot on board was Englishman, John Davis, who wrote extensively about trade and shipping routes:

> They report that there be 11,000 of these islands. They used a pilot who spoke some Portuguese to guide them through the "channel named Maldivia", in latitude 4° 15' N. The trade of shipping through this channel is very great of divers nations, from most places of India.

In 1602, it was noted that business could be done in the Maldives, and with the formation of the Dutch East India Company, profitable trade growth began in India and the Far East. The Dutch sent numerous vessels to the East in the early 17th century but it wasn't until 1640 that a vessel laden with rice was sent to the Maldives to ascertain the nature and prospects of trade at the islands. In 1662 a ship was sent to the Maldives to trade in cowries which the Dutch exported most profitably throughout the latter part of the 17th and 18th centuries.

It soon became apparent to the Dutch that an accurate survey of the Laccadives and Maldives groups was needed to protect the company's ships and valuable cargos. In 1671, instructions were issued by the Dutch government in Ceylon to carry out a survey, but it wasn't until 1834 that a detailed and accurate survey of the Maldives was carried out by the English.

## EARLY BRITISH INVOLVEMENT IN THE MALDIVES

England became influential and active in the Indian Ocean through the activities of their East India Company with its ships plying between the ports of this region and Europe from the late 17th century.

The wreck of the *Persia Merchant* in August 1658, was the first recorded direct contact between the people of Britain and the Maldives, although other Englishmen had, in the past, been aboard foreign ships in the Maldives. One of these was the pilot of the *Corbin*, wrecked on July 2, 1602, who was beheaded after attempting to escape captivity.

William Hedges was among the first Englishmen to sail in among the islands in the *Recovery* in 1685, but judged it to be unsafe to be known to be English as *"our nation having lately gott an ill name by abusing ye inhabitants of these islands".*

Further contact with the islanders occurred with the wreck of the H.M.S. *Cato* in 1783, followed by the *Hayston* in 1819. The crew of the *Hayston* were well treated but nothing was ever heard from those aboard the *Cato*, wrecked with all hands, it was believed, near Malé. She was a new ship of 50 guns and on board was Vice-Admiral, Sir Hyde Parker on his way to take up his new appointment as commander-in-chief of the East Indies Station.

Reports of the disaster filtered back many years later from Captain A.I Dickson of the *Fancy*, giving gruesome accounts of the reported massacre of the ship's company, who had been saved from the wreck only to meet their deaths, it was stated, *"by being tied together, two by two, and cast into a hole which was then filled up by the natives with stone and earth. This was stated to have been in retaliation for the rape of a 'Moor girl' ".*

## ISLAND SURVEY 1834-36

By 1832, the reefs of the Maldives had already claimed several English ships and it appeared strange to James Horsburgh, Hydrographer to the East India Company, that an exploration of the Maldives had never been undertaken when *"this extensive and remarkable barrier of isles and dangers is situated directly in the route of ships coming from Europe, and destined for the island of Ceylon".*

Several English ships had in the past recorded having passed through channels of the Maldives. These included: the *Rooke Frigate*, in February 1700, the *Albemarle* in October 1707 and the *Rochester* in 1715; but their reported positions left confusion of the true channel locations.

Early navigators were liable to errors of a most dangerous degree. One company vessel, the *Darby*, in 1715 was carried by currents to near the coast of Sumatra, but was perceived by the captain to be among the Maldives.

By the 1830s, company ships could be navigated with "such precision" that an error of 20 or 25 miles in longitude should be considered inadmissible. Captain Owen, a navigator of the Royal Navy said it was a shame that the Maldives should continue to be an "absolute scarecrow" to nineteenth century navigators, when it had been familiarly visited by those of the 16th and 17th centuries.

The Maldives were duly surveyed by Commander Moresby of the Indian Navy between 1834 – 36 in the *Benares*, with the *Royal Tiger* and *Maldiva* as tenders. During the course of the survey, two ships, the *Adonis* and *Vicissitude*, were wrecked in the islands. Commander Moresby praised the kindness and hospitality of the islanders in their treatment of the officers and crew of the two vessels, which were wrecked at night on Thaa Atoll in 1835, and Ihavandhippolhu in 1836. Moresby wrote:

During the two years we were employed surveying among these islands, and in constant intercourse with them, they always treated us with kindness and respect, yet with shyness and suspicion, supposing our motives for making a minute survey of their islands had other ends than to guide shipping in their navigating to India.

The new charts of the islands clearly highlighted the safe navigable channels and geographic boundaries of the islands and opened up the 'Middle Passage' to India, passing eastward of Madagascar and between the Seychelles and the Chagos Archipelago, and through the One-and-a-half-degree channel in the Maldives.

Despite this newfound wealth of information, no fewer than 16 European ships, mostly of British origin were wrecked on the islands between 1850 and 1880 and to this day, the reefs of the Maldives remain a formidable barrier to shipping in the Indian Ocean.

Old style dhoanis are still used by most diving centres.

A more recent design is finding favour with many operators.

The original Maldivian mas dhoani was designed and modified by the fishermen and built for simple and efficient sailing. The primitive form of fishing mas dhoani was constructed by sewing the plank strakes together – a method used throughout the Indian and Arabic region and still practised in parts of the region today. Later wooden dowels and copper nails were used.

The mas dhoani is an open boat, sturdy with a shallow draft, which can be sailed at 6 – 7 knots and has the ability to face moderate to rough seas. It has a long projecting prow that is purely decorative, and a tapered stern ending in a sternpost that contributes to the good sailing qualities as well as serving as a rudder post.

Timber from the coconut palm is used below the water line as it is more durable and plentiful than other timbers. It is also heavier and provides greater stability. Imported hardwoods are used elsewhere with two light timbers on top to provide buoyancy and to keep the craft upright if she capsizes. Water can then be bailed out. The hull of a dhoani is covered in fish oil to preserve the timber and aid its passage through the water.

These resilient craft are built by master craftsmen using few tools and no plans, their skills being passed down from generation to generation as an oral tradition. Boat carpenters are known as kissaru vadin – carpenters who can provide shapely things – and command high wages and a respected position in the community. Completing a 13-metre dhoani can take two months using simple hand tools – chisels, mallets, axe, saws and cord powered drill.

The diving dhoani has been adapted from the mas dhoani with few modifications. In the late 1960's engine power was introduced to the Maldives and the open powered dhoani was provided with a deck and sunshade to provide a means of transporting divers to sites.

The prow, which is removable, remains on the bow of many diving dhoanis, but in 1985 a dhoani was built with a flat and extended bow to make loading and unloading more easy. At the time many Maldivians laughed at the sight, but it was more efficient and today many dhoanis have adopted this design.

# Famous Shipwrecks of the Maldives

There have been hundreds of shipwrecks in the Maldives throughout the centuries but of all the recorded wrecks, six stand out above all others.

## THE *CORBIN*

The *Corbin* was a French ship of 400 tons which set sail from St Malo with the *Croissant* on May 18, 1601, in search of trade with the east. Plagued by misfortune and ill discipline, the *Corbin* was destined for disaster and met its end on Goidhoo, or Horsburgh Atoll, on July 2, 1602. It was carrying a cargo of silver and attempted salvage at the time of loss was unsuccessful.

At the start of the journey, a bad omen occurred when the mast broke and the crew threatened to jump ship. Sickness, and desertions threatened the expedition before the ship had even begun to cross the Indian Ocean. The stifling heat had destroyed many provisions, the water was putrid, fish and meat had gone bad and were full of big worms, butter had turned to oil, and scurvy was rampant. A short stay of 15 days at Malailli, one of the Comoros islands, vastly improved the health of the crew before they crossed the Indian Ocean.

On July 1, some reefs and islands were sighted which were correctly recognised as the Maldives by the English pilot. The night was supposed to be spent beating about, but the *Corbin* was virtually left to herself. During the night the captain was ill and in his bunk, the mate and second mate were drunk and the watch was asleep. In the early hours of the morning of July 2, the ship struck the reef.

Of the 40 or so survivors, one band of 12 men stole a boat and made it to India. Only four of the remainder survived the five-year captivity. One of them was Francois Pyrard, who wrote about his adventures when he returned to Europe. It wasn't until February 1607, when an expedition from Chittagong invaded the capital, that Pyrard and his three remaining companions were taken to India and eventually returned to France. Ironically, it was the excellent cannon on board the *Corbin* that the raiding party was after, which eventually freed the captives.

The treatment of Pyrard and his companions by the Maldivians was uncharacteristically cruel but their fate was largely determined by their conduct in the days following the wreck of the *Corbin*. All the silver and the most precious merchandise were stowed at the bottom of the ship which, after running onto the reef was under water and irretrievable. What remained of the silver was hidden in their waistbands.

During their first night on Fulhadhoo, they hid their waistbands for fear they should be searched by the islanders. At length, the sailors obtained little to eat and were dying of hunger, so they unearthed the coins and offered money for food, which they received. In turn, the natives would give nothing except for money and before long the coins started to run out. In The *Voyages* of Francois Pyrard of Laval to the East Indies. (Hakluyt Society, 1890), Pyrard wrote:

> Those who had money, and who by this means could obtain food, filled their bellies without discretion; and being in a country where the air is very unhealthy for all strangers, even for those of a similar climate, they fell ill, and died one after another, nay more, in place of receiving aid and consolation from their fellows, those who were without money and in great need came and stripped them, and took their money before they were dead, the healthy who survived fought with one another who should have it, and banded themselves two against two, and finally messmate against messmate, with so little charity, that they would see their comrades and fellow countrymen die before their eyes without giving them any assistance or succour. I have never seen a sight so pitiable and deplorable.

Pyrard was taken with two other crew members to another island, Fehendhoo. Unlike the others, they had no belts of money and although this caused some trouble at first, they found they were better off with nothing, as little by little, the natives gave them some food.

News of the wreck and the money reached Malé and commissioners were sent to Fulhadhoo to secure the wreck on behalf of the sultan. All merchandise and money from shipwrecks automatically became the property of the sultan and Maldivians were prohibited from selling anything to the shipwreck victims. When the commissioner arrived at Fulhadhoo, he demanded to know who had the money from the vessel. To get hold of it, he arrested all the inhabitants, even the women, and had their thumbs put into cleftsticks and squeezed and bound with iron clasps, to see if they would confess. The villagers on the island of Pyrard's captivity were in no trouble when it was proved they had taken nothing, for which they were grateful.

Pyrard took great pains to learn their language and by doing so was able to largely determine his own destiny and obtain an insight into Maldivian society never before seen by a westerner, on which he wrote extensively.

I have remarked that nothing served me so much, or so conciliated the goodwill of the people, the lords, and even the king, as to have a knowledge of their language, and that was the reason why I was always preferred to my companions, and more esteemed than they.

The wreck of the Corbin may have passed unnoticed through history were it not for the historical accounts left by Francois Pyrard. His account of the wreck and ensuing captivity makes compelling reading and his description of life in the islands and the customs of the people make his book a valuable source of reference for historians and students of Maldivian history and culture.

## THE *HAYSTON*

The *Hayston*, a three-masted English vessel commanded by Captain Sartorius, set out from Isle-de-France (nowadays Mauritius) for Calcutta on July 1, 1819. For several days bad weather had prevented them from taking any observations and on July 20 at 8pm, some reefs were noticed in the gloomy darkness. There was little time to tack and the ship struck the reef on Maamakunudhoo Atoll on the north west of the Maldives. Within a quarter of an hour, there was seven feet of water in the hold and the ship's crew were at the mercy of the elements.

Next morning the sailors discovered they had run on to an enormous reef, as far as the eye could see, that turned out to be covered with water on the high tide. A small islet was seen by telescope 25 km away which they called the "Isle of Hope". On the 22nd, three sailors tried to reach this isle by raft but were never seen again.

On the 24th, every sailor was employed in building a raft large enough to carry them all but when it was nearly completed the Lascar sailors, from the west coast of India, cut the rope and sailed away. One man who tried to reach them, was threatened with an axe.

The long boat was taken out from the ship but was damaged on the reef and went adrift with a woman and her two daughters and three men, who were never heard of again. Then the barge was launched and it was not long before she capsized and split on the reef.

A Maldivian sailing boat was seen and appeared to be heading in their direction, so an officer, Schultz, and some crew gave chase in a dinghy. After several hours rowing, they found they were separated from the boat by a big reef and it passed by without noticing the castaways.

Two more sailors, Serang and his brother, were separated from the remaining survivors when a raft on which they were paddling between the reef and the shipwreck, was caught in the current and drifted away to the south east. In another accident, a rope was stretched between the reef and the ship and a young boy died trying to return to the ship.

Finally, on the 26th some sailors embarked on the small dingy and sailed for the Isle of Hope. They were discovered by fishermen from the island of Makunudhoo and the remaining passengers were rescued. The survivors arrived in Malé on August 4 and were treated with much hospitality.

On August 10, Serang and his brother arrived in Malé. After drifting away on their raft, they spent three nights and four days out at sea and passed eleven islands before they landed on an uninhabited island. They were both very weak and survived on coconuts before being rescued by a passing fishing boat. They were conducted to the island where the fishermen lived and were treated with much kindness.

On August 14, the six Lascars who stole the large raft, arrived at Malé. They resorted to lies to explain the infamy of their behaviour, claiming the raft had been broken, had gone adrift and the current had carried them away. Despite their treachery, they were treated equally by the sultan.

The wreck of the *Hayston* is noted for the humanity of the Maldivians and generosity of the sultan. In all cases, the castaways were well provided for and the sultan would not allow them to pay for anything in his country. Officer Schultz wrote:

> Let the Christians blush thinking that, though they profess a religion that enjoin the most tender charity, you turned out, in our minds, to be, as it were, superiors to them in the practice of virtue and humanity.

## THE *RAVESTEIN*

The 800 ton Dutch East Indiaman *Ravestein* was sailing to Jakarta from the Netherlands with a valuable cargo of gold and silver when it ran aground near Mathiveri Island in Ari Atoll on May 9, 1726.

At the time of loss, nine chests of silver and one chest of gold were recovered.

The captain, Antony Klink, sent the rest of the crew to Malé, while he remained for one month at the island near where the vessel was lost. The arrogant conduct of Klink tested the patience of the Maldivians, in particular, Sultan Ibrahim Iskandar II (1720 – 50 AD). In a letter sent to the Dutch Governor of Ceylon, the sultan said Klink did nothing but complain bitterly of the inhabitants of the islands.

> He [the captain] expected them to work like European sailors, not taking into consideration the fact that they are only wretched creatures who look upon the smallest service extracted from them as a grevious oppression. You are well aware gentlemen, of the nature of the islanders.

When the captain arrived in Malé on June 13, he demanded from the sultan 50 men and four large boats to save the property of the company. The sultan was outraged by this extraordinary demand and gave no answer and, in any case, was not prepared to send boats to the site as the vessel was cast away on a place to which a small boat can approach only with difficulty, as the seas were rough and the surf dangerous.

The Dutch were invited to return in the calmer months to attempt further recovery and the crew of the shipwrecked *Ravestein* were returned to Ceylon with the gold and silver chests and other goods recovered from the wreck.

## PERSIA MERCHANT

One night in August 1658, five months after her departure from England, the *Persia Merchant* was wrecked on Maamakunudhoo Atoll, while en route to Bengal. On board were eight chests of silver and probably gold from West Africa. Salvage was attempted at the time of loss but was unsuccessful.

Many were drowned, but the 50 survivors were well treated by the islanders and after one month they were given a good boat in which they sailed to Sri Lanka. Among the survivors was Captain Roger Williams and the mariner-captain Roger Middleton, who wrote an account of his adventures to his family after reaching India.

Middleton said the ship filled with water quickly, leaving the survivors with nothing and within four hours she had broken into pieces. One of the boats sunk under the ship, leaving just one other to rescue the victims. The survivors found their way by boat and broken pieces of the ship to an uninhabited island south of Makunudhoo, but without food, drink or arms. Middleton wrote:

> Being without food, wee ranged about the island. Wee found a well of watter, of which wee dranke like pigeons, lifting head and harts for soe greate a mercy. Thus drinking watter, by good providence wee found coker nutt trees, which is both food and rayment, soe we went by the sea side and found little shell fish and the like, but wanting fire wee tooke sticks and rubbed them together untill they kindled, thus wee lived heare ten or twelve dayes, not knowing wheather it was better for us to be seen by the Neighbouring Islanders, for the ancient seamen sayd they would cutt our throats. Att last there arived three of their boats full of men, which wee dreaded but could not resist.

The stricken castaways were taken to the island of Kuburudhoo (South Thiladhunmathee) *"where wee had fish and other good things, as hony and rice, on which wee fedd like farmers"*. For the price of a gold chain and a 100 dollars from one of the merchants, they obtained a vessel and sailed to Ceylon.

## PRAZER E ALLEGRIA

The *Prazer e Allegria* left Lisbon, Portugal, on November 8, 1843 with 84 convicts and relief officers and others, bound for Goa, India. She reached the Cape of Good Hope with the loss of 29 convicts from scurvy and on March 16, 1844, the crew sighted several islands which the captain declared were the Maldives. With the current running at three miles an hour towards land, the captain continued on the same course.

Major de Quinhones, who was in charge of the convicts, said in a report of the disaster:

> At about 4 o'clock in the evening the ship was so near land that we could see the people distinctly; and it was then that a little boat manned by blacks, and with an English Jack fixed at the poop, came off from one of the islands. Approaching the ship one of the Moors pointed towards a channel which lies between three or four islands. The Captain hailed the Moors, and told them to come on board; but seeing the convicts they immediately departed through fear, lowering the Jack. Thus we were committed to the current, which every moment drove us much nearer land, and upon a reef of coral which lies opposite the second island. The night was dark, and there was lightning; the breakers dashed incessantly on the sides of the ship, forcing her more on to the reef; at length the rudder broke, and the ship rested; but a large leak was sprung. All of us worked the pumps, but it was impossible to reduce the water.

The ship had struck the reef off Muli Island in Mulaku Atoll and on the morning of the 18th, the passengers and crew were transported to Muli Island without loss of life. On the following day the cock-boat, the long boat, and a hired boat from the villagers were despatched in order to procure more provisions but all three boats were sunk by waves. Eleven lives were lost, mostly convicts.

The 104 survivors remained on the island of Muli for five days before being transported to the "King's Island". It took seven days sailing by day only and stopping the night at islands to reach Malé. The captain hired two Katamarans to transport the survivors to Ceylon, among whom were two ladies and three children.

## GURAIDHOO WRECK

In the 16th century, a Chinese ship with a cargo of porcelain and Chinese merchandise was wrecked near the island of Guraidhoo in South Malé Atoll. The story is best told by Pyrard, who visited the island in 1605.

> I was at that island one day, and saw the mast and rudder of the ship that was lost there. I was told it was the richest ship conceivable. It had on board some 500 persons, men, women, and children, for the Indians take the greater part of their household to sea with them. These 500 persons were nigh all drowned, and there remained but a hundred saved. This ship came from Sunda (Indonesia), laden with all kinds of spices and other merchandise of China and Sunda. Judging merely from the mast of this vessel, I thought it the largest I had ever seen, for the mast was taller and thicker than those of the Portuguese carracks; and the king of the Maldives built a shed of the length of the mast to keep it as a curiosity. I saw also another mast and a top much larger than those of Portugal. Thus was I led to believe that in the Indies they build vessels larger and of better material than in Portugal or anywhere else in the world. The greatest ships come from the coast of Arabia, Persia, and Mogor, and some have as many as 2,000 persons on board.

Old folk on Guraidhoo still talk about a wooden ship believed to be wrecked on Medhu Faru near Guraidhoo centuries ago; however no visible remains are to be seen.

# Safaris: Away into the atolls

One of the best ways to experience the diving in the Maldives is on a safari dhoani. In the past ten years the number of boats operating has increased exponentially. Whether it's the appeal of diving those remote sites, sleeping under the stars, or getting lost for a few hours on a deserted island, there is nothing quite like the carefree existence that goes with the live-aboard.

Many diving safaris begin at the airport upon arrival, but most start and end at Hulhumalé harbour. It provides a secure anchorage and has relieved much of the pressure on Malé's new harbour. The Hulhumalé harbour accommodates more than 100 boats, mostly dhoanis that have been converted into live-aboard vessels. The traditional style dhoanis have beautifully decorated prows and fluted stern decking. Other more modern boats are being built specifically for diving and no longer have these features. A trip to Malé's new harbour is well worth the visit, where supplies are loaded onto smaller dhoanis. They jostle for space at the concrete wharf where diving compressors, tanks and supplies are loaded directly from pickup trucks to the boats and fuel and water arrive in drums to be pumped on board later.

At Malé's new harbour, strange and unfamiliar sights and sounds fill the air. A rudder is secured with coconut twine. An engine is lifted out of a dhoani, drawing a crowd. A large wooden vessel from India casts a shadow over the smaller ones in the early morning sun. Workmen are hammering, drilling and staining timber. Wooden masts puncture the skyline and

anchor lines from the boats create a jigsaw pattern on the waters surface like a gigantic spider web. Dhoanis slide effortlessly over them. Amid the activity is a pervasive calm, a peaceful, relaxed atmosphere so characteristic of the islands. On fishing dhoanis, men while away their time playing cards or drinking tea on the foredeck.

When all the supplies are loaded, safari dhoanis depart on their different routes. Ari Atoll and Felidhe are popular destinations, with stops at South Malé Atoll on the way. Or, going north with stops in North Malé Atoll, are the more remote destinations of Baa and Lhaviyani Atolls. For a completely isolated destination, divers are now heading for Haa Alifu, diving sites in the newly opened atolls on the way. Or they head to the far southern atolls, which are now also open for tourism.

A sense of complete and utter freedom engulfs divers as they see the last of Malé's concrete mirages disappear over the horizon behind them. They look ahead to another island just beginning to surface. Their Maldives diving safari has only just begun.

*Top to bottom:*

*A safari stop at Guraidhoo in South Malé Atoll*

*Unusual sights such as this tractor awaiting transport to one of the outer islands are part of every day life in Malé.*

*A traditional safari style dhoani used by Voyages Maldives.*

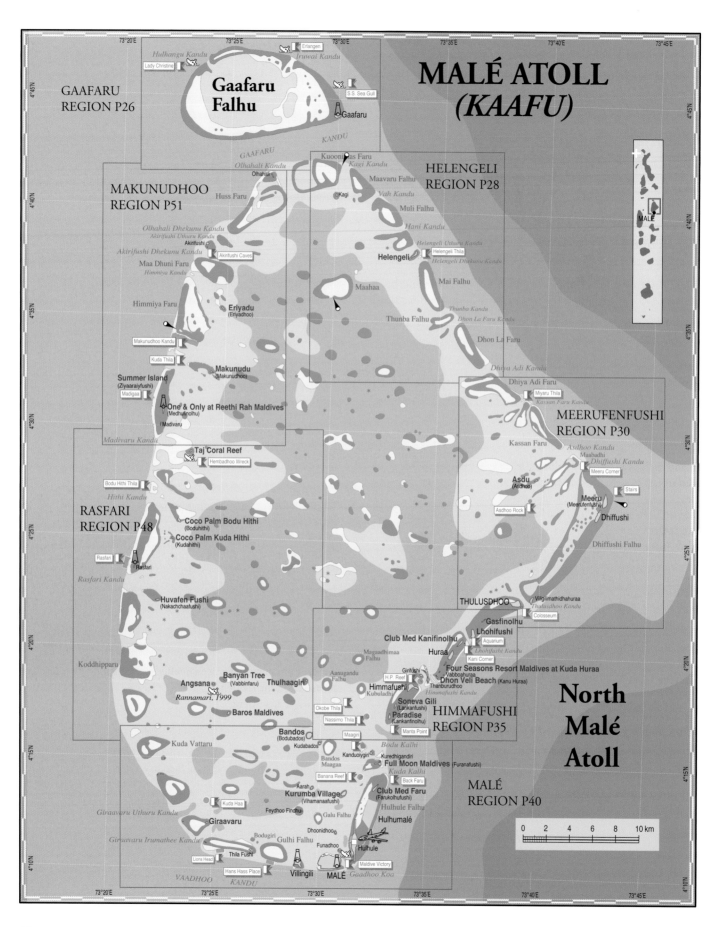

# MALÉ ATOLL
# *(KAAFU)*

GAAFARU
REGION P26

*Hulhangu Kandu*
Lady Christine
Erlangen
*Iruwai Kandu*

**Gaafaru
Falhu**

S.S. Sea Gull

Gaafaru

*GAAFARU*
*KANDU*

MALÉ

MAKUNUDHOO
REGION P51

*Olhahali Kandu*
Olhahali

Kuooni as Faru
*Kagi Kandu*
Maavaru Falhu
*Vah Kandu*

HELENGELI
REGION P28

Huss Faru

Kagi

Muli Falhu

*Olhahali Dhekunu Kandu*
*Akirifushi Uthuru Kandu*
Akirifushi
Akirifushi Caves

*Hani Kandu*

*Akirifushi Dhekunu Kandu*

Maa Dhuni Faru
*Himmiya Kandu*

Helengeli
Helengeli Thila
*Helengeli Uthuru Kandu*

*Helengeli Dhekunu Kandu*

Himmiya Faru
Eriyadu
(Eriyadhoo)

Maahaa

Mai Falhu

*Thunba Kandu*
*Dhon La Faru Kandu*

Makunudhoo Kandu

Thunba Falhu

Dhon La Faru

Kuda Thila

Makunudu
(Makunudhoo)

*Dhiya Adi Kandu*

Summer Island
(Ziyaaraiyfushi)

Dhiya Adi Faru
Miyaru Thila

Madigaa

One & Only at Reethi Rah Maldives
(Medhufinolhu)

*Kassan Faru Kandu*

MEERUFENFUSHI
REGION P30

Madivaru

*Madivaru Kandu*

Kassan Faru

*Asdhoo Kandu*
Maabadhi
*Dhiffushi Kandu*

Taj Coral Reef
Hembadhoo Wreck

Asdu
(Asdhoo)

Meeru Corner

Stairs

Bodu Hithi Thila

Asdhoo Rock

Meeru
(Meerufenfushi)

*Hithi Kandu*

Dhiffushi

RASFARI
REGION P48

Coco Palm Bodu Hithi
(Boduhithi)

*Dhiffushi Falhu*

Coco Palm Kuda Hithi
(Kudahithi)

Rasfari

Rasfari

*Rasfari Kandu*

Huvafen Fushi
(Nakachchaafushi)

Viligilimathidhahuraa
*Thulusdhoo Kandu*

THULUSDHOO

Colosseum

Gasfinolhu
Lhohifushi

Club Med Kanifinolhu

Koddhipparu

Aquarium

Huraa

*Lhohifushi Kandu*

Kani Corner

Banyan Tree
(Vabbinfaru)

*Magaadhimaa Falhu*

Girifushi

Four Seasons Resort Maldives at Kuda Huraa

Angsana
*Rannamari, 1999*

Thulhaagiri

*Aanugandu Falhu*

H.P. Reef
*Vabboohuraa*
*Thanburudhoo*

Dhon Veli Beach (Kanu Huraa)

Himmafushi

Baros Maldives

*Kubuladhi*

Okobe Thila

Soneva Gili
(Lankanfushi)

HIMMAFUSHI
REGION P35

Bandos
(Bodubados)

Nassimo Thila

Maagiri

Paradise
(Lankanfinolhu)

Manta Point

Kudabados

Kuda Vattaru

*Bodu Kalhi*

Kanduoiygiri
Kuredhigandiri

North
Malé
Atoll

Bandos
Maagaa

Full Moon Maldives (Furanafushi)

*Kuda Kalhi*

Banana Reef

Back Faru

Aarah

Kurumba Village
(Vihamanaafushi)

Club Med Faru
(Farukolhufushi)

MALÉ
REGION P40

Kuda Haa

Feydhoo Findhu

*Hulhule Falhu*

*Giraavaru Uthuru Kandu*

Giraavaru

Galu Falhu

Hulhumalé

Dhoonidhoo

0  2  4  6  8  10 km

Bodugiri
Gulhi Falhu

Funadhoo

Hulhule

*Giraavaru Irumathee Kandu*

Lions Head

Thila Fush

Hulhule

Maldive Victory

Hans Hass Place

Villingili

MALÉ
*Gaadhoo Koa*

*VAADHOO*
*KANDU*

# Chapter 2 - North Malé Atoll Islands *(Kaafu)*

*North Malé Atoll is the principal atoll of the Maldives and includes Malé, the island capital. The administrative capital is the island of Thulusdhoo. North Malé Atoll, which includes Gaafaru, is 69 km long and 39 km at its widest point. There are 50 islands in North Malé Atoll and several small islets. There are eight inhabited islands (counting the airport) and out of the 42 uninhabited islands, 27 are resorts and most of the remaining 15 are privately leased with some buildings on them. Many resort islands are close enough to the airport for transfers to be made by traditional dhoanis, but those more distant ones usually use speedboats and seaplanes to save time. Transfers to the more distant islands by engine dhoani can take just over four hours.*

**Malé** has grown to its physical limits of 192 hectares and has a registered population of 47,862, although the transient population may exceed 80,000. In 1922, the archaeologist H.C.P. Bell noted Malé's population was 5200. The word Malé has been shortened from the Sanskrit word *Maaliu*, which means big, or principal island. In later times Malé was called *Mahal*, meaning palace island, as it has traditionally been the seat of power for kings.

In *The Story of Sigiri*, historian Senarat Paranavitana says the founder of the first ruling royal family was Taya-malla. He was the leader of a breakaway group of the Kalabhra people, who made their way to the Maldives from Madagascar in the 12th century. Taya-malla wed a princess from an ancient Sinhalese royal family that was exercising sovereignty in the Maldives at the time. When the Sinhalese king died, Taya-malla received the sovereignty of the Maldives, and became the founder of the Kalabhra dynasty. In 1153 AD, his grandson, Dhunei Kalaminjaa (Dhovimi) converted to Islam after ruling for 22 years as a Buddhist king. He adopted the title Sultan Muhammad-ul-Adil, and ruled for a further 13 years before sailing to Mecca, never to return.

Old Malé, used to have an eight foot high wall with 10 forts around three sides of the island. Only one fort was located in the centre of the unwalled southern side, where water was too shallow for sailing craft.

The forts were constructed during the reign of Sultan Shuja'i Muhammad Imad-ud-din 1 (1620-48 AD) after an attack on Malé in April 1632 by an armada of 15 Portuguese ships. The armada, led by Domingos Ferreyra Belliago, aimed to capture Malé and insert Dom Felipe, the converted Christian Maldive prince in Goa, as the new king. The armada failed after the Sultan was notified in advance of its arrival. When the armada arrived, Malé was well fortified and the only entrance to the island was stopped up with ships filled with stones.

Each fort, or bastion, had its own cannon, many of which originated "by the grace of God" from early shipwrecks. A further 14 cannons were purchased at Achin (Sumatra). By the early 19th century many of the cannons were largely ineffective.

Satellite photo of Malé. Population pressures have forced all the available reef to be reclaimed for development .

In 1819 Captain Sartorius wrote:

> I was told [there were] one hundred cannon between the fortification walls and in the ten bastions. Some of the cannon are of cast iron, the biggest number 12. Most of the guns, if not all of them, originate from the Netherlands. They are not in good fittings, neither are they in good condition. The bastions are as well in a bad state.

The cannons may have been ineffectual but they were greatly esteemed for their ceremonial valve. In the 1867 *Indian Ocean Directory*, it is written:

> The sultan and headmen are much pleased if a ship on her arrival salutes with a few guns, which compliment they return.

The old fort and bastions, which were of much interest to early travellers, were demolished in the 1960s during the rule of former President, Mr Ibraheem Nassir. The remains, including cannons, were pushed into the sea and the land reclaimed for future development. Many cannons were covered forever, others were left along the waterfront and on the reef. For years, dhoanis utilised these heavy cannons for mooring their boats in the harbour, but they have been gradually recovered and repositioned at points of interest around Malé. Two cannons are

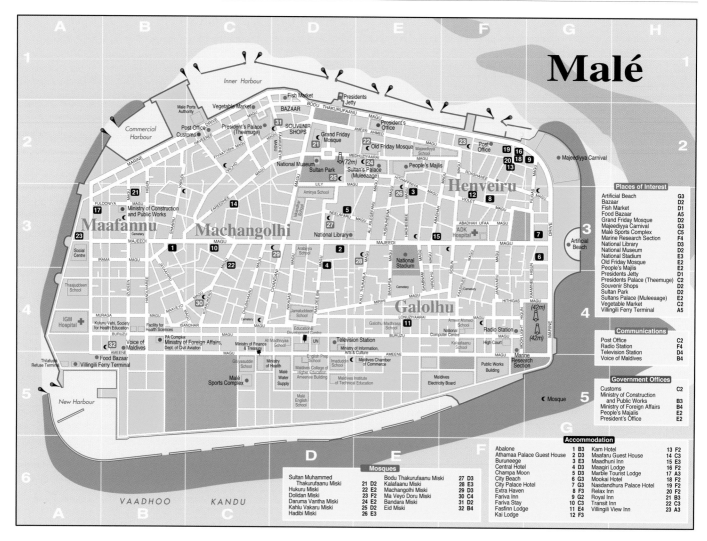

on display at the President's jetty. Nine cannons were recovered from the reef on the north east side of Malé early in 1995 before reclamation work began.

Malé used to be dominated by the old palace, which was partly demolished under President Nassir. The street now called Meduziyaraiy Magu was previously closed off at either end by large gates, and a fort protecting the palace, the A'Koattey Buruzu, was inside. The present day museum was once part of the old palace and in place of the demolished sections of the palace is 'Sultans Park'.

Malé also had more than 15 public bathing tanks located mostly near mosques. These were taken away to prevent the spread of malaria. One street on the eastern side, Henveru Kebu Ala Magu, now called Sosun Magu, was used for making anchor ropes. Twine made from coconut fibre was spun into a thick rope and laid out from one end of the street to the other.

**Funadhoo** is a strategic island close to Malé which has added its fair share of intrigue to the history of the Maldives.

Funa is a hardwood tree with white flowers (*Calophyllum inophyllum*) and *dhoo* means island. Ships anchor in Malé's outer harbour to the west of Funadhoo, and as far north as Dhoonidhoo and Galu Falhu. Many ships have come adrift in these waters and some remains of early ships can be found.

There are several graves here including, Captain J.C. Overend, who died in Malé in 1797 after his ship, *The Tranquebar*, was stranded on one of the islands.

The head of Utheemu Ali Thakurufaanu is also buried there. Utheemu Ali fought alongside his famous brothers, Muhammad and Hassan, during an eight year guerrilla war that finally ousted the Portuguese from Malé in 1573. Uthheemu Ali was slain by the Portuguese and his head delivered to the governor in Malé as a gift. The head was stolen by Maldivians and secretly buried at Funadhoo. His body was buried at Thakandhoo in Haa Alifu Atoll. The island has always been used for government purposes. It was a refinery for shark oil, had a coconut fibre mill to make ropes, a poultry farm and is now an oil storage island.

**Hulhule** was once two small islands joined together in 1968 in order to extend the airport's runway. The other island was Gaadhoo. Hulhule was once used by royalty as a holiday resort. The island was surveyed for an airport by the British in 1960 and the first aircraft landed on a temporary runway in 1960. On the south-west side of the reef is the remains of an old wreck. It lies 200 metres to the north of the *Maldive Victory* shipwreck and is sometimes referred to as the 'Portuguese wreck', however, it is more likely to be the remains of a Baggala from India which may have come adrift during a cyclone in 1820 that wrecked more than 30 vessels. The remains of the bow's copper sheeting and some partially exposed timbers lie near the reef on the bottom at 37 metres while copper rods, more timbers and coral encrusted pieces of metal lay scattered away from the reef over a distance of 30 metres.

**Hulhumalé** is the largest land reclamation project undertaken in the Maldives and will provide the future housing and commercial needs in the Malé region and will also help solve the over crowding problem in Malé. Ground level of Hulhumalé has been raised to 2 metres above mean sea level, making it the highest island in the Maldives and thereby reducing the possibility of wave inundation. Phase 1 of the project began in 1997 and was completed in 2002 with a land area of 195 hectares. Phase 2 will enclose Farukolhufushi and is expected to be 240 hectares. Phase 3 will be dedicated to the extention and further development of the airport and is expected to be 350 hectares.

**Dhoonidhoo** means bird island, and is nowadays used to house political prisoners. It has an old building on it which was the residence of the British governor until 1964.

**Feydhoo Finolhu** is the education island, where school children have holiday camps, school seminars, and scout camps. The island was completely washed away in 1960, partly as a result of the removal of sand for building purposes. The sand gradually replaced itself and with the aid of reclamation from the lagoon, the island was re-established.

**Aarah** is the president's holiday resort.

**Vihamanaafushi** is a very old island and was originally known as Viharanapura. *Viha* means poison and *manaa* means forbidden. It is believed a Buddhist monastery existed on the island in early times. The first president of the Republic of Maldives, Mohammed Amin, was buried there. He died in 1954. Vihamanaafushi opened as Kurumba Village in 1972 and was the first resort in the Maldives.

**Farukolhufushi** means island on the edge of the reef. It was uninhabited in early times although it was leased to a Maldivian family who holidayed there. Farukolufushi Tourist resort was established in 1973 and was later taken over by Club Mediterranee. The Club Med entertainment and dining complex burned down in 1994 resulting in extensive renovations. Farukolhufushi has a big lagoon which is a popular overnight anchorage for safari boats because of its close proximity to the airport. Between Farukolufushi and Furanafushi is Kuda Kalhi, a small channel through which much of the boat traffic between Malé and some islands to the north pass. *Kalhi*, is a word meaning pupil of the eye, warning locals to look sharply when passing through the channel. Currents can be treacherous here, especially during the north-east monsoon and there are also a couple of hidden, shallow reefs just inside the atoll. Banana Reef is one of them – a popular dive location. Large schools of dolphin use this channel when migrating through the atoll.

**Furanafushi** is another island with early Buddhist origins and was once called Puranna Pura. It began as Furana Tourist Resort in 1973 and has since been rebuilt as the luxurious Full Moon Maldives, complete with swimming pool, gymnasium and business centre. It has a good lagoon and harbour and has excellent coral and good snorkelling on the south side of the island. There are a couple of privately owned buildings perched on a small reef near the entrance to Furanafushi lagoon. These are used for a tropical reef fish export operation.

**Kuredhigadu** is a tiny island on the north side of Furanafushi reef. Whale sharks are sometimes seen cruising along the outside reef edge across Kuda Kalhi and Bodu Kalhi during the south-west monsoon. On December 25, 1923, a baggala with full cargo struck Furanafushi reef in a storm and sank. No visible evidence of the wreck remains but an anchor lies on the reef a considerable distance to the north of Furanafushi in 32 metres of water.

**Kanduoiygiri,** is also called chicken island because it had a poultry farm on it. The sea-cow, or dugong, known locally as *Kandu-geri* is on record as visiting this and nearby islands, mostly at night. The sea-cow is traditionally regarded by many as a *dhevi*, a kind of spirit, both visible and invisible. It may be malévolent or harmful and hinder good health; or it may be helpful. It may require sacrifice in the form of flowers or even as blood of birds or animals. The sea-cow is a malévolent dhevi and mainly observed on clear moonlit nights. When seen by Maldivians, the believers take fright, fearing for their lives or some misfortune to themselves or their family. The sea-cow has also been sighted in earlier times at Vihamanafushi, in North Malé Atoll and Fihalhohi and Gulhi in South Malé Atoll. One was seen at Vattaru in Felidhoo Atoll in 1986. The sea-cow in the Indian Ocean is now very rare and threatened with extinction.

**Bandos** was settled in ancient times and the original inhabitants were believed to be a tribal group of Tamils from India. In 1602, Pyrard noted that people were living there and that the water was favoured much above that of Malé. The island was made an orphanage in 1962 and in 1968 the orphanage was moved to Villingili. Bandos was the second resort island in the Maldives and commenced operating in 1972. It became well known for its diving, particularly shark feeding at Bandos and Banana Reef. It now has a permanently staffed medical clinic and de-compression chamber.

**Kuda Bandos** is an unspoilt island that has been made a public reserve. It is especially popular for day-trippers from Malé. On Fridays Malé residents flock to the island for picnics. In the past, the stretch of water between Bandos and Kuda Bandos was reserved for the traffic of ships carrying very important messages to the sultan's island, Malé. This was the rule and it effectively served early warning to the sultan that something was happening in the Northern Atolls, such as looting by pirates, a shipwreck, or a fleet of Malabar pirates heading towards Malé.

*Kuda Bandos has been reserved for public use as a picnic island. On Fridays Malé residents flock to Kuda Bandos for their weekly day off work.*

**Thulhaagiri** was an uninhabited island before opening as a resort in 1980. A *thulhaa* is a half coconut shell tied to a stick and used to retrieve water from water jars. The small, almost perfectly round island could well be imagined as being like a *thulhaa*.

**Lankanfinolhu,** eight km north of the airport, started as a tourist resort in 1979. It was rebuilt and the lagoon dredged to create more land in 1994 and renamed Paradise Island.

**Lankanfushi** opened as Hudhuveli Resort in 1980 and has since been rebuilt as Soneva Gili Resort. It is believed that Lankanfinolhu and Lankanfushi were once part of the same island but eroded away in the centre, dividing the islands and leaving small sandbanks in its place.

**Himmafushi** was a major fishing island but the people now earn their main income from tourism, selling handicrafts, souvenirs and boat building. Himmafushi was once two islands, since joined together. The other was Gaamaadhoo. A guest house used to be located on Himmafushi to cater for low-budget travellers but this was closed in 1984 because of the negative social impact of travellers on the island community. A prison is now located on Gaamaadhoo. The outside reef has one of the best right-hand surfing waves in Malé Atoll. Surfing was previously banned here for security reasons but is now open.

**Girifushi** is a military training camp.

**Thanburudhoo** is named after a plant *Tamburu, (Biloba pescaprae)*, which has a heart-shaped leaf and violet flower and spreads like a vine along the sand. This plant has a fruit the same shape as the leaf and is used for medicine. During the south west monsoon there are good, clean left-and right-hand waves breaking off the outer reef of this island.

*The island of Thanburudhoo with Girifushi in the background.*

**Kanu Huraa** opened as Leisure Island resort in 1981. Its name was later changed to Tari Village and has now been redeveloped as Dhon Veli Beach & Spa Resort. *Kanu* means corner and *Huraa* is an island with more coral than sand. Dhon Veli is a popular resort for surfers during the months of April until November when the winds are predominantly from the south west and conditions are ideal for surfing. Here, surfers paddle out from the island to the swells pumping onto the reef. The break is called 'Pasta Point', after the popular dish served up to Italian guests. When working, this wave creates hollow lefts which have the speed and power to attract some of the world's greatest names in surfing.

**Vabboahuraa** is a small privately leased island. It has a long jetty leading to the sandbank island of Rahgandu.

**Kuda Huraa** opened as Kuda Huraa Resort in 1977. It was rebuilt in 1996 and named Four Seasons Resort .

**Huraa** is an inhabited island which was once joined to Kuda Huraa but like so many islands, erosion eventually split them. On Huraa is a mangrove swamp that fills with water at high tide.

**Kanifinolhu** is 16 km from the airport. It opened as as resort in 1978 and was upgraded in 1992. It has a good anchorage and is now a Club Med resort.

**Lhohifushi** opened as a resort in 1979. Lhoss is a tall tree (*Morindaefolia*) which is prevalent on this island. Surfing is popular at this island.

**Gasfinolhu** started out as a camping resort in 1980. There is a small island near the edge of the reef with one coconut tree on it.

**Thulusdhoo** is an inhabited island surrounded by sandy beaches. It is the administrative capital for North Malé Atoll and visited by island traders who sell their salted fish *lonu mas* at the government warehouse. It has a good deep-water lagoon and large trading boats and safari dhoanis anchor here. It has a boatyard where new-era style dhoanis are constructed of fibreglass. Many resorts are upgrading their fleet of diving and transfer dhoanis with the faster and more practical Thulusdhoo made boats. This island has a Coca-Cola factory on it.

The locals here are well known for their *boduberus*, an island dance performed by men to the beat of a large drum. The drum is made from a hollowed coconut tree and traditionally covered with the skin of a stingray. The drum-beat of the boduberu – the *baburu* – came from Africa. It starts off slow, gets quicker, then finishes in a frenzy leaving dancers in a state of delirious exhaustion.

*The inhabited island of Thulusdhoo showing the outer barrier reef of Malé Atoll.*

**Viligili-mathidhahuraa** is uninhabited and was once two separate islands until they were joined by natural deposition of sand. There is also a good anchorage in the lagoon here for shallow draft vessels. Picnic boats take advantage of the island's seclusion.

**Dhiffushi** is an inhabited island and lies on the northern end of Dhiffushi Falhu. Fishing is the main industry of the island and dhoanis loaded with freshly caught tuna make their way down to the Malé fish market almost daily. Three baggalas were wrecked on the reef of this island: the *Dheen Ganja* in 1898, *Deylaa* in 1903, and the *Jandar* in 1911.

**Meerufenfushi** means sweetwater island. It was an uninhabited island until it opened as a resort in 1978. It is a large, heavily timbered island with lush vegetation. In the past it was a popular stopover for fisherman who refilled their water pots from the island's abundant reserves of rainwater. Meeru is the most eastern island in Malé Atoll.

**Asdhoo** is a resort inside the atoll, 37 km from the airport.

**Helengeli** is the most isolated resort in Malé Atoll. Helengeli Tourist Village started as a resort in 1979. It is 51 km from the airport and if travelling by dhoani, a trip from Malé takes about three and a half hours. *Helengeli* means shaking island reef, so-named because of its exposure to heavy seas during the north-east monsoon. In 1996, renovations to the resort were completed and the channel across the shallow house reef was deepened. Divers have the advantage of diving isolated and pristine locations. Non-guided housereef dives can be made at any time of the day.

At Dhon La Faru reef, just south of Helengeli, a wooden ship from the Laccadives was wrecked in February 1991 and on Helengeli reef the 1397 ton *Swiss* was wrecked on May 20, 1890. She was sailing from Pondicherry to Marseilles and was a total loss. No remains of this ship have ever been found. Another ship, the *Dharuma*, a sailing vessel owned by the government, ran aground on this reef on January 24, 1962. It was a total loss.

Five km inside the atoll is a large reef called Maahaa. A *haa* is a reef with a passage through it and boats travelling north can pass through this large reef at a passage marked by a light on the southern side. To the north of Helengeli is a long narrow reef extending into the atoll called Dhigu Dhuni Falhu. This is a long arrow shaped reef to be wary of when travelling north.

**Kagi** is a small picturesque island surrounded by a white sandy beach and a shallow lagoon. The island is privately leased and in 1997, a jetty and a gas storage depot was constructed. Boats arriving here for picnics or stopovers may be charged a small amount per visit.

*Large schools of herring (seen in this photograph) are attracted to Kagi's shallow lagoon.*

**Gaafaru** is an inhabited island that stands alone on one of the largest single reefs in the Maldives. Gaafaru Falhu is eight km long, 15 km wide and has two natural deep water openings to the north and a shallow entrance near Gaafaru island. For a small price, fisherman are happy to entertain visitors with a boduberu in a warm, friendly atmosphere. Gaafaru Falhu lies on the southern side of the Kaashidhoo Kuda Kandu which has since early times been one of the major shipping routes through the Maldives archipelago. This reef is virtually invisible during storms and many ships have come to grief. *Aracan*, a Glasgow registered ship of 1174 tons ran aground on August 12, 1873. It was sailing from Rangoon to London with a crew of 34. There were nine passengers and full cargo. *Clan Alpine*, a wooden barque of 363 tons was wrecked on this reef in 1879 while travelling from Mauritius to Bombay with a cargo of sugar. *SS Sea Gull*, a ship of 1012 tons with a crew of 32 and three passengers was wrecked in 1879 while travelling from Calcutta to London. *Erlangen*, was a 97 metre German ship of 3,500 tons that was wrecked on August 20 1894 while travelling from Colombo to Hamburg. *SS Crusader*, was sailing with a cargo of sugar when wrecked in 1905 and *Lady Christine*, a 863 ton ship was wrecked on April 16, 1974 about 200 metres west of Hulhangu Kandu. (see page 26 & 27)

**Olhahali** is an uninhabited island with a shallow channel on the north side. The island is small and vegetation here is sparse but it is a popular stopover with day-trippers making snorkelling and dive trips to the island. A secure overnight anchorage can be made inside Huss Faru.

**Akirifushi** means coral island. It is uninhabited and Maldivian fishing boats anchor here. There is good snorkelling and diving on this reef. Nearby is a reef called Himmiya Faru. *Himmiya* is the area between two reefs and this lagoon, with entrances at either end, is quite secure. It has a good anchorage in both the north-east and south-west monsoons.

**Eriyadhoo** is 38 km from the airport and takes about three hours if travelling by dhoani. Eriyadhu Island Resort opened in 1982. It has a good beach and lagoon and excellent snorkelling on the house reef which closely surrounds the island. There are many small reef fish and regular sightings of manta rays, eagle rays and tuna are made here. The resort is the most northerly on the western side of the atoll and gives divers the added advantage of being able to dive many sites without contacting any other divers.

**Makunudhoo** opened as Makunudu Island Resort in 1983 and recent renovations have given this resort a distinctive Maldivian character with the additional benefits of air conditioning and hot water. *Maku* is a kind of leech. In former times it was a convenient overnight anchorage for sailing dhoanis heading between the northern atolls and Malé. Francois Pyrard stopped here on his way to Malé after his ship, *The Corbin*, ran aground on Fulhadhoo reef in Goidhoo Atoll in 1602.

**Ziyaaraiyfushi** opened as a resort in 1983. *Ziyaaraiy* is the resting place, or grave, of a holy man. Tradition says that a man named Mathukkalaa, believed to be the grandson of the Maldivian Christian king Hassan IX (baptised in Cochin in 1552), is buried here. Mathukkalaa and his brother sailed from India to Malé during the reign of Ibrahim Iskandar I (1648 – 87 AD) with the intention of taking the crown. His brother was killed in Malé but Mathukkala was drowned and his body washed onto this island. The resort is now named Summer Island Village.

**Medhu Finolhu** opened as Medhufinolhu Tourist Resort in 1979, and later changed its name to Reethi Rah, which means beautiful island. It has a wide lagoon, popular with windsurfers.

**Madivaru** is a small privately leased island at the southern end of the reef.

**Hembadhoo** has a close-fringing housereef ideal for snorkelling, especially around the jetties. It opened as Hembadhoo Island Resort in 1982 and was renovated in 1997. It is now called Taj Coral Reef Resort.

**Boduhithi** was an inhabited island a long time ago and Boduhithi Coral Island resort was opened in 1979. *Hithi* means bitter. It is now called Coco Palm Bodu Hithi.

**Kudahithi,** is an exclusive retreat with only six cottages. Guests can visit Boduhithi if they require diving. Kudahithi was once a small sandy cay before coconut palms and bushes were planted here. It is now called Coco Palm Kuda Hithi.

**Rasfari** is an uninhabited island with little vegetation and is surrounded by a wide shallow reef. There are plans to make Rasfari Island and its entire associated reef a protected nature reserve.

**Nakatchchaafushi** opened as Nakatchafushi Tourist Resort in 1979. It was rebuilt and opened in 2004 as Huvafen Fushi. A

*The island of Rasfari showing the telecommunications tower.*

*Nakatchchaa* was an astrologer, often an important official in the sultan's court who was in charge of determining the auspicious times for various activities of state. He had considerable influence over many island affairs. The island is 20 km from the airport and has a good beach on the northern side and a long sand spit at either end.

**Baros** was inhabited in early times but became uninhabited in the late 1700s. Baros could have been named after the once rich Kingdom of Baros in north-west Sumatra with whom Maldivians used to trade but more likely it was an island to accommodate people with *baros-bali*, a skin disease often associated with leprosy. Baros is a semi circular shaped island and opened as a tourist resort in 1973.

**Ihuru** opened as a resort in 1979. It has been rebuilt as Angsana Resort & Spa. An *ihuru* is a Fanditha man; a conjurer or wizard and practitioner of religious science. He is also an astrologer and herbalist and when, for instance, a crop is sown, he must sow the first seeds. Later, when harvest approaches, he must read the 'signs' and cut the first crop. From those seeds he makes a pudding to eat as an offering. Ihuru island is a small, heavily wooded, almost perfectly circular-shaped island with a turquoise lagoon enclosed by a close fringing reef.

**Vabbinfaru** means round soil island. It has a wide beach and a large lagoon surrounding the island. It opened as a resort in 1977 and is now called Banyan Tree.

**Giraavaru** is a very old name by which the aboriginal people of the islands are known. *Gira* means island washing away and *varu* means a group of people or islands. The Giraavaru people living in Malé today have been swept from one island to another in recent years. The people moved from Giraavaru to Hulhule in 1968 and when the airport authorities took over the island, the people were moved to Malé. The Giraavaru people, who claim to be descendants of a South Indian Tamil tribe, were once the most powerful community in the Maldives. Today, the Giraavaru people are a small surviving community identified only by the older women wearing long dresses with distinctive neck embroidery. Giraavaru Tourist Resort opened in 1980.

**Thilafushi** is a new island which has emerged between Giraavaru and Viligili. It is without doubt the fastest growing island in the Maldives. Otherwise known as 'trash' island, Thilafushi is the solution to Malé's garbage disposal problem. The island began in 1992 and has grown considerably in size. A barge operates between the new harbour and the island.

**Villingili** was inhabited in ancient times and was burnt and looted a number of times, mostly by frustrated Malabar pirates unable to penetrate the defences of Malé Island. The people were moved to Hulhule in 1961. In 1962 a prison was established. In 1973, Villingili resort opened. It was closed again in 1990 to allow the overpopulated capital of Malé to expand. The island is now inhabited.

*The airport island of Hulhule was once two islands joined together to make the airport runway. Hulhumalé is a newly reclaimed island.*

# Diving North Malé Atoll

*The sea bed east of Malé Atoll shelves steeply to 2000 metres and to the west less steeply to over 300 metres. The presence of deep, clear waters all around the atoll means excellent visibility, especially with ingoing currents. Pelagics such as barracuda, trevally and tuna, and big schools of fusilier, snapper and sharks all congregate at the entrances to the channels, attracted by the movement of water and the food sources carried with them. Depths inside the atoll are generally 40 to 50 metres and the bottom is mostly sand. There are many shallow water reefs inside the atoll and those just below the surface are clearly defined by sharp contrasts in water colour. Most of the diving in North Malé Atoll is in the channels, or kandus, through the outer barrier reef of the atoll. There are around 20 channels on the eastern side and 16 on the west. Drift diving is the most common method of diving. The channels on the western side are generally wider, some with big thilas across the openings. The greatest concentration of diving is in the southern end of the atoll where many of the resorts are located. This was the first area to be dived when resorts began springing up in 1972. Some of the finest sites are to be found here and although many of them have been heavily dived, in general, the sites remain in good condition.*

*Most divers tend to steer away from the populated island of Malé because of the heavy boat traffic. The reefs in the north of North Malé Atoll are less frequently dived than those to the south and with an absence of any islands between Helengeli and Meerufenfushi – a distance of 20 km – a sense of isolation and freedom make the dives in this north east region even more memorable.*

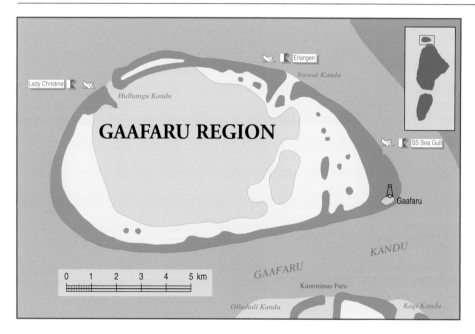

## Gaafaru wrecks

One of the main shipping routes through the Maldives is in the 10 km wide channel between Gaafaru Falhu and the small atoll of Kaashidhoo. A number of ships have drifted too far south in the channel, only to find themselves wrecked on Gaafaru Falhu. There are at least six wrecks recorded on Gaafaru Falhu (see Gaafaru p24). Some wrecks have been located and the most likely identity of three of them has been established. Some wreckage lies in deep water and more research is needed before their identity can be determined.

### SS Sea Gull ★★★

The *SS Sea Gull*, a ship of 1012 tonnes with a crew of 32 and three passengers was wrecked in 1879, 200 metres north of the shallow entrance to Gaafaru. The anchor of the *Sea Gull* is on the reef at one metre and is visible at low tide. H.C.P. Bell, archaeologist of the Maldives, first visited the Maldives in 1879 to investigate this wreck. Most of the ship is on the reef top at 45° to the reef edge. The remains are heavily encrusted in coral but certain parts can be distinguished. What looks like the engine and some rib sections lie just below the surface on the edge of the reef. At nine metres the reef starts to fall steeply away to more than 50 metres. There are many grouper around the wreckage and a surprising number of spider shells. There is one cave at 30 metres near the wreck but the wreck is the main feature of this dive.

### Erlangen ★★★

The wreck of the 3,500 tonne German ship *Erlangen* lies 1.5 km west of Iruvai Kandu. It was named after the German city of Erlangen and was travelling from Colombo to Hamburg with general cargo when it was wrecked in 1894. No lives were reported lost. Many of the remains are on the reef top above 15 metres. The remainder is over the edge to 50 metres.

**Diving:** The remains of the bow section, including anchors, anchor chain, anchor winch, davits and steel plates from the hull lie on the reef top and are heavily encrusted in coral. A section of ribbing protrudes from the reef between 15 and 20 metres and makes an interesting backdrop for photographs. The wreckage is about 30 metres wide. Over the years, the ship has broken in half at a depth of 30 to 35 metres and the stern section is resting on its starboard side. The propeller is at a depth of about 45 metres and among the stern are two boilers in about 35 metres.

Fish life is interesting with many juvenile wrasse in the shallows and nudibranchs feeding on the coral algae. There are black-saddled coral grouper, as well as emperor. Oriental and harlequin sweetlip are common and there are a couple of giant sweetlip roaming the mid sections. Black snapper swim freely around the wreck.

**Diving hints:** This is an excellent wreck dive but it is easy to be tempted to go to great depths. A safe plan is to dive first to where the ship is broken in half and view the remains from there, then return slowly back up the reef where a safety stop can be comfortably made while looking over the shallower parts of the wreck.

*The wreck of the Erlangen is broken into two sections with the stern section lying in deep water off the edge of Gaafaru Falhu reef. The bow section lies on top of the reef and is heavily encrusted in coral.*

### Lady Christine ★★★

| | |
|---|---|
| Location: | outside reef |
| Depth: | 5m – 30m |
| Fish life: | excellent |
| Coral growth: | average |
| Features: | wreck, reef fish, caves |

### History

The *Lady Christine* was engaged in survey work and laying communications cable when it ran onto the north west of Gaafaru Falhu at 11pm on April 16, 1974. A local tugboat tried unsuccessfully to pull the ship off the reef in rough weather and big waves. Another big tugboat was immediately called from Singapore to try and rescue the ship with its valuable cargo of cables and communications equipment.

The ship was holed and two days after running onto the reef the engine room and much of the inside was filled with water. One week later it was full of water and the Singapore tug boat was still on its way. Meanwhile local workers were paid a lot of money to save the cable and contents. When the ship's owners arrived by chartered aircraft, they were shown the rescued cable, all neatly coiled and proudly displayed by the workers. Desperate measures were employed to save the ship but even two days of blasting the

*The wreck of the Lady Christine.*

reef to make a channel was ineffectual. The ship was stripped of anything of value and abandoned. Divers can see the holes in the reef caused by blasting.

### Diving

The *Lady Christine* was driven high onto the reef 300 metres west of Hulhangu Kandu and part of the bow remains visible even at high tide. Most of the wreckage lies scattered on the upper reef slope to a depth of 10 metres. The wreckage and pitted reef provides a protected environment for a wide range of marine life such as surgeonfish, yellow-back fusilier, parrotfish, moray eels, pufferfish, grouper, head-band butterflyfish, crescent-tail bigeye and moorish idol. The variety of marine life is awesome; it's not uncommon to find hawksbill and green turtles, napoleon, eagle rays, barracuda and sting rays all in the one dive.

A vertical wall drops to more than 50 metres on the outside, visibility is usually excellent. There are interesting caves at 30 metres with seafans and sponges. One cave has a swim-through to the next and another has part of the wreckage inside. Nurse sharks are often seen inside. This dive offers a great combination of wreckage and marine life.

**Diving hints:** Once the wreck has been located it's a good idea to dive directly down to view the caves and look into the clear waters for large pelagics, then return to the shallows among the wreckage for the remainder of the dive.

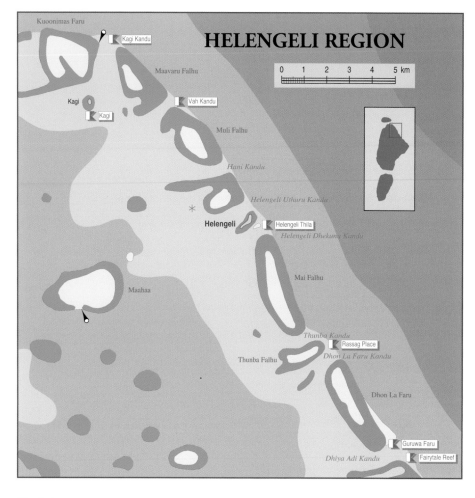

Map: HELENGELI REGION

0  1  2  3  4  5 km

Kuoonimas Faru
Kagi Kandu
Maavaru Falhu
Kagi
Kagi
Vah Kandu
Muli Falhu
Hani Kandu
Helengeli Uthuru Kandu
Helengeli
Helengeli Thila
Helengeli Dhekunu Kandu
Maahaa
Mai Falhu
Thunba Kandu
Rassag Place
Thunba Falhu
Dhon La Faru Kandu
Dhon La Faru
Guruwa Faru
Dhiya Adi Kandu
Fairytale Reef

There are three caves located 100 metres from the outside reef which are connected with swim-throughs. They start at 28 metres, rising to 15 metres. A further 100 metres inside the channel are two large caves close together, one at 28 metres the other at 25 metres. The 25 metre cave has a huge seafan inside. Near the caves at 15 metres are angelfish, pufferfish and filefish, and if divers look closely they may also find well camouflaged leaf fish.

### Guruwa Faru ★★

*Guruwa* means sweetlip in Dhivehi and this is the home of many oriental and harlequin sweetlip. The site lies on the north side of Dhiya Adi Kandu. Lobsters are in the shallow caves and turtles are regularly found grazing on this reef.

### Fairytale Reef ★★

On the south side of Dhiya Adi Kandu are long overhangs between 10 and 15 metres featuring delicate blue and yellow soft corals on the ceilings. During the southwest monsoon, when currents mainly flow out of the channel, large mantas, four and five metres across, are common in groups of four or more around coral rocks on the corner at five metres. They favour this location because of the currents which accelerate over the shallow reef on the corner, bringing a good supply of zoo plankton. If entering with a strong ingoing current on the corner, divers should descend quickly below the reef edge to avoid being swept over the reef top.

### Kagi ★

There is a narrow fringing housereef around Kagi and a shallow lagoon inside. On the south east side of the island is a jetty; a good starting point for a housereef dive. Fish life is prolific, especially in the morning and evening. More commonly seen fish include smaller-sized flower grouper, emperor, and pelagic snub-nose pompano. Also seen along the reef edge are schooling rabbitfish. On the sandy bottom of the island lagoon are white-barred sleeper goby and swirling about in the shallows are schools of tiny herring, often being chased by baby trevally.

### Vah Kandu ★★★

The channel is quite nice around the entrance and in the middle of the channel are caves at 30 metres. Fish life includes sharks, eagle rays and sting rays. The sandy bottom of the channel lies at 25 to 30 metres.

### Rassag Place ★★★

This is a channel dive on the south east point of Thunba Falhu with a steep dropoff from three to 25 metres, then sloping more gently into the channel.

*White-barred sleeper goby, Amblygobius semicinctus. White bars clearly identify this goby. It is mostly found in lagoons and on protected slopes and lives in a burrow which it digs with its mouth.*

*Giant grouper, Epinephelus lanceolatus, juvenile form. The juvenile and younger fish are white or yellow blotched. Adult fish appear grey.*

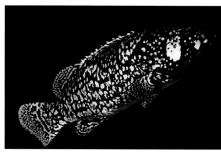

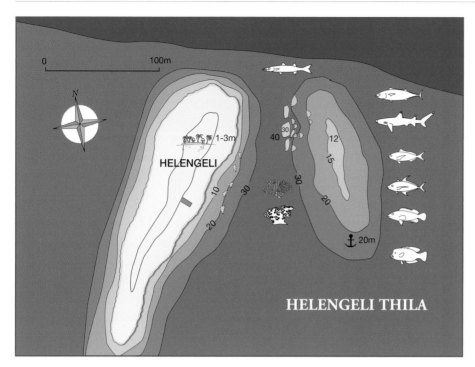

Black snapper, Macolor niger. Adults are all black but juveniles look very different being black and white.

Helengeli and surrounding reefs.

### Helengeli Thila ★★★★

| | |
|---|---|
| Location: | Helengeli Dhekunu Kandu |
| Depth: | 12m – 30m+ |
| Fish Life: | abundant |
| Coral growth: | excellent |
| Features: | reef fish, seafans, pelagics, sharks |

For the sheer abundance of marine life, Helengeli thila is hard to beat. The reef top is between 12 and 15 metres and currents through this channel can be treacherous. The thila is about 150 metres in length. The north west side of the thila has the most interesting reef formation, with steep cliffs and caves and outcrops of reef. It is

Giant grouper, Epinephelus lanceolatus. This grouper photographed at Helengeli Thila is immense. The giant grouper can grow up to two metres in length.

only about 50 metres to Helengeli housereef but in between is a deep channel at around 40 metres. The cliffs and caves are below 25 metres and bristling with seafans, both large and small. Four outcrops of reef rise from the depths of the channel, the most shallow being 30 metres. They are liberally sprinkled with soft coral.

Around from the caves on the south side at a depth of 20 metres is a big coral covered anchor. Its origins are unknown but there could be some connection with the 1397 tonne *Swiss*, which is reported to have struck the reef and sunk near Helengeli on May 29, 1890, while sailing from Pondicherry to Marseilles.

In the surrounding waters of the thila, divers can observe a school of white tip reef sharks, interspersed with great barracuda, tuna, trevally and schools of black snapper. Schools of fusilier can be so dense they block out the light. One big rare Giant grouper, *Epinephelus lanceolatus*, 1.6 metres in size, has made this reef a regular haunt. Large napoleon frequent the site and sharks are often seen in the channel.

**Diving hints:** To observe the beauty of the seafans and gorgonian bushes tucked away in deeper crevices and caves, it is a good idea to take a torch. If on a safari boat, as always, under no circumstances anchor on the dive site. If there is a strong current running, be prepared to abort the dive if it is too strong, especially with an outgoing current. If diving in a current, make sure safety balloons are carried and be prepared to use them when making an open water safety stop.

### Kagi Kandu ★★

There is a small bay on the north west side of Maavaru Falhu with overhangs between 10 and 15 metres with lots of lobster inside. The sand channel bottoms out at 25 metres.

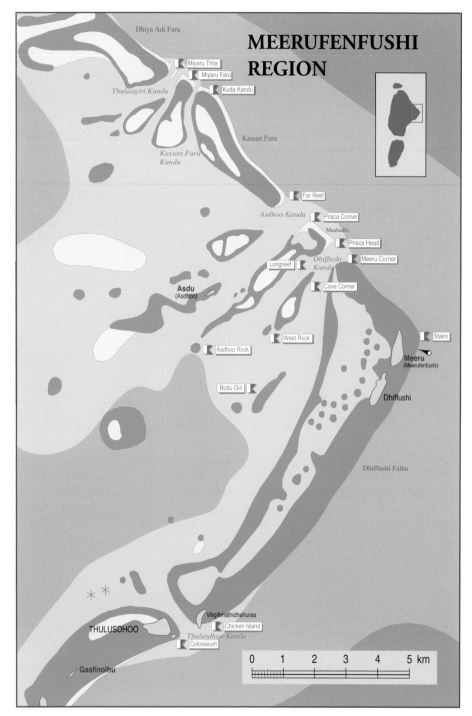

MEERUFENFUSHI REGION

*Black-saddled coral grouper,* Plectropomus laevis. *Like many grouper, this is pretty fish and brightly coloured. It is a reef dweller, often found living in caves. It can change colour dramatically. from that shown to dark all over.*

*Black pyramid butterflyfish,* Hemitaurichthys zoster. *Butterflyfish are generally characterised by the long snout and short snout species. Long snouts are for fossicking around the coral, while short snouts are generally for feeding on zoo plankton.*

attracted to the many small invertebrates on the steep walls. Schools of black pyramid butterflyfish swim off the reef edge feeding on zoo plankton. Large schools of barracuda, some tuna, the occasional grey reef shark and large napoleon are all to be seen here.

### Far Reef ★★

The best diving is at a large set of coral rocks between 10 and 15 metres where commonly observed reef fish include oriental and harlequin sweetlip, blue-striped snapper, trumpetfish, and grouper. At the approach to the rocks on the south side is a sandy gutter that lies between the reef proper and a finger of reef further out. The sand gutter, rises from 30 to 20 metres near the rocks. On the sand a few white-tip reef sharks and sting rays are usually seen.

### Kuda Kandu ★★★

On the north west side of Kassan Faru Kandu is a channel dive with a steep reef between one and 30 metres. Best diving is between 10 and 20 metres near the corner where there is a large rock rising to three metres. The caves on the corner between 10 and 25 metres and the abundance of fish life make this site a favourite with divers.

There are steep cliffs from five to 25 metres, overhangs and one big cave at 20 metres with a swim- through to 10 metres and seafans. Reef fish include grouper and squirrelfish in the caves, moorish idol and long-nosed butterflyfish, which are

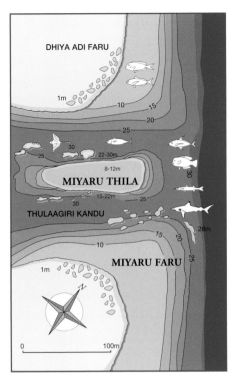

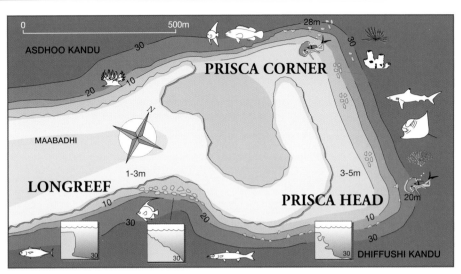

## Miyaru Faru ★★★

| | |
|---|---|
| Location: | north east side of Thulhaagiri Kandu |
| Depth: | 3m – 30m |
| Fish life: | above average |
| Coral growth: | very good |
| Features: | sharks |

*Miyaru* means shark in Dhivehi and this is a place to view the grey reef shark. A large overhang at 28 metres on the outside corner of Thulhaagiri Kandu is an ideal place to stop and view the sharks. They are mostly seen with an ingoing current. Visibility is usually good at these times and when holding on at the overhang great numbers of pelagics, such as barracuda, trevally, and tuna can be seen. Eagle rays are surprise visitors here and often grazing along the reef are powder-blue surgeon.

## Miyaru Thila ★★★

Nearby in the same channel is a long and narrow thila with many big coral rocks off the north west side. Big schools of fusilier cover this interesting thila, also napoleon, eagle rays and trevally. Often grazing along the reef are powder-blue surgeon. Best diving is with an ingoing current.

## Prisca Head ★★★

| | |
|---|---|
| Location: | Dhiffushi Kandu |
| Depth: | 5m – 25m |
| Fish life: | abundant |
| Coral growth: | good |
| Features: | caves, reef fish |

This is a classic channel dive, starting on the outside corner where there are many caves to 25 metres. There is one big cave at 20 metres with a swim-through to 10 metres and seafans. Colourful reef fish include moorish idol, bannerfish, and schools of black pyramid butterflyfish. Large schools of barracuda and tuna swim through the channel.

## Longreef ★★

Inside Dhiffushi Kandu is Longreef. In a strong current, it can be dived with Prisca Head. The total length of this reef is four km, so it is not surprising that this is a popular drift diving location. The reef slope changes from steep with many caves at the eastern end to a vertical wall further inside.

*Trumpetfish,* Aulostomus chinensis. *Often 'rides' on the back or in the shadow of a non-predatory fish such as a rabbitfish or parrotfish to get closer to prey.*

*Looking east along Maabadhi Faru with Dhiffushi Kandu on the right of picture and Asdhoo Kandu on the left. Longreef is a four km long drift dive along the south side of Maabadhi Faru. At the far end of the reef is Prisca Head.*

*Powder-blue surgeon,* Acanthurus leucosternon. *Surgeons have a scalpel-like blade on each side of their tail that can be venomous. The blades are for fighting and fish can sometimes be seen with cuts to their body. The powder-blue surgeon is an algae feeder found in large schools grazing on the reef.*

*Humpback snapper,* Lutjanus gibbus. *Large schools congregate over reefs during the day but at night they spread out over the bottom to feed on invertebrates and fish.*

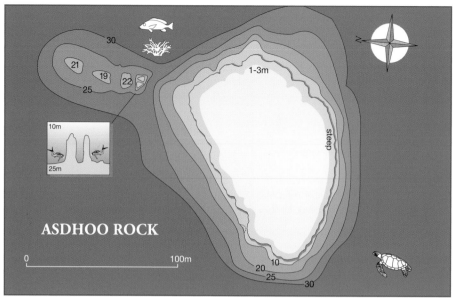

ASDHOO ROCK

**Prisca Corner ★★★**

| | |
|---|---|
| Location: | north point of Maabadhi reef |
| Depth: | 10m – 25m |
| Fish life: | above average |
| Coral growth: | very good |
| Features: | caves, mantas |

The outside reef offers deep, clear water with the chance of seeing shark and big schools of fish. On the corner are several caves – three very large ones – one of which starts at 28 metres and rises with a swim- through to 15 metres. Tall-fin batfish slice through the currents around the entrance to this cave. A conglomeration of coral rocks lie in shallow water at 10 metres on the outside reef and here mantas visit during the south-west monsoon. A large number of cleaner wrasse living among the rocks await their visit. There are plenty of sponges, seafans, and featherstars deeper on the corner and inside the caves are grouper, squirrelfish and bigeye. At least two species of anemonefish, Clark's anemonefish and the black-footed anemonefish, are common on the lower part of the reef at 20 metres just inside the channel.

**Cave Corner ★★**

There are big caves to a maximum depth of 28 metres. Inside are many seafans and soft coral while on the reef are large schools of snapper.

**Asdhoo Rock ★**

| | |
|---|---|
| Location: | south-west end of Maabadhi reef |
| Depth: | 3m – 25m |
| Fish life: | above average |
| Coral growth: | very good |
| Features: | coral pinnacles, snapper, coral |

Both experienced and novice divers will find this an exceptional dive. Best diving is on the north side where the reef drops steadily from three to 25 metres to a ridge that pushes northwards for 100 metres. On the ridge are isolated coral patches surrounded by large schools of humpback and blue-striped snapper. A pair of coral pinnacles on the ridge, five metres high, are one of the most unusual coral formations to be found in the area. Around the reef can be seen turtles and remora while on the reef top are healthy stands of hard coral.

*Blue-striped snapper,* Lutjanus kasmira. *They have four blue stripes on the body but another closely related species, the five-line snapper,* Lutjanus quinquelineatus, *has an extra stripe. Bluestripe snapper appear in schools by day and capture their prey by night.*

*Crescent-tail bigeye,* Priacanthus hamrur. *Big eyes are a small family with large eyes that usually hide in caves. They can change their colour rapidly from red to red stripes to silver to fit in with their surroundings.*

## Westrock ★

This is a small reef inside the atoll. It is a good beginners dive with the best diving on the south east side between five and 15 metres. The reef slopes to a sandy base at 15 metres where garden eels and sting rays are common. The reef top has good coral.

## Bodu Giri ★

A larger reef ideal for beginners with a maximum depth of 20 metres. Best diving is on the north west side where there is a steep wall with many blue triggerfish and masked bannerfish. High on the wall are lobsters, sea anemones and occasionally turtles.

## Meeru Corner ★★★

One of the most popular dives in the area is Meeru Corner. It is located on the outside corner at the north end of Dhiffushi Falhu. The reef drops vertically from five to 30 metres to a section called the 'wall'. This part of the reef offers a unique experience to divers found in few other locations.

*Yellow sweeper,* Parapriacanthus ransonneti, *are found swimming in large schools around bombies and in caves.*

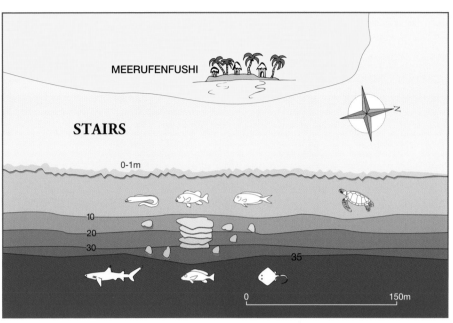

## Stairs ★★

| | |
|---|---|
| Location: | outside reef near Meerufenfushi |
| Depth: | 10m – 30m |
| Fish life: | above average |
| Coral growth: | good |
| Features: | large coral rocks, reef fish |

This unusual coral formation is like an apartment building with levels rising from 30 to 10 metres on the outside of the reef. It has many reef dwelling occupants and its nooks and crannies appear overcrowded with reef fish. On the reef at the base of the stairs are white-tip reef sharks and turtles while sting rays are regularly seen on the outlying sandy patches. Several species of grouper and giant morays prefer the ground floor apartments while oriental sweetlip, surgeon and pufferfish have staked a claim upstairs. Large schools of yellow sweeper seem to have no preference and occupy all levels.

**Diving hints:** Currents are not usually strong here and this dive is suitable for all experience levels. Having dived the deeper depths, divers can make their way back up the reef to spend the remainder of the dive on the reef top. If the surf is crashing on the reef, divers should swim away from the reef at the end of the dive and make an open water safety stop.

*Scribbled pufferfish,* Arothron mappa. *Juveniles have a more colourful pattern. Adults grow to 60 cm and lose much of the pattern. They have a flexible skin that can be inflated like a balloon by pumping water internally. This is a characteristic defensive mechanism for all puffers to prevent them being eaten.*

*The Rainbow runner,* Elagatis bipinnulata, *is a pelagic fish – an open water swimmer that swims freely between the atolls.*

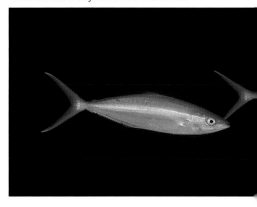

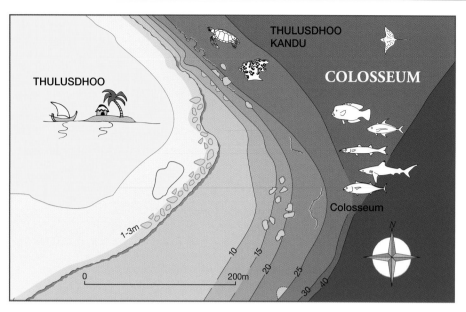

*The island of Thulusdhoo looking east towards the outside of the atoll. The 'Colosseum' lies on the corner.*

### Colosseum ★★★

| | |
|---|---|
| Location: | south side |
| | Thulusdhoo Kandu |
| Depth: | 3m – 25m |
| Fish life: | above average |
| Coral growth: | very good |
| Features: | pelagics, sharks |

On the outside corner is the 'colosseum', a semi-circular cliff 40 metres long and two metres high at a depth of 24 metres. With an ingoing current, this is a good place for divers to anchor themselves and watch pelagic fish in action. Barracuda, big-eye trevally, blue-fin jack, rainbow runner and dog-toothed tuna are persistent performers here while grey reef shark, napoleon, and eagle rays frequently drop by. Soft corals flourish on the reef slope leading into the channel and turtles graze here. Once inside the channel, the wall banks up steeply into layers of ledges with caves in the shallower depths at 15 metres. The long reef gives divers the opportunity to drift dive well inside the atoll.

### Chicken Island ★★★ (Kukulhu)

| | |
|---|---|
| Location: | Thulusdhoo Kandu |
| Depth: | 5m – 30m |
| Fish life: | above average |
| Coral growth: | good |
| Features: | reef fish |

On the outside reef are coral rocks around 10 metres where many reef fish are to be found, including black-spotted and scribbled puffers. A couple of caves at 20 metres are worth a look, then a long drift into the channel follows, until reaching a great overhang spiralling down from three to 25 metres. This is the start of a 100 metre section of cliffs, caves, coral rocks and swim-throughs – well worth exploring. Soft coral is a feature in a cave at 15 metres and morays are common among the overhangs.

**Diving hints:** The north side of Thulusdhoo Kandu extends into the atoll for almost two km so if the current is too strong on the corner, a less stressful and safer dive can be made anywhere along this channel wall.

*Black-spotted pufferfish,* Arothron nigropunctatus. *It has a strong beak and, like all puffers, stores poison in its liver and ovaries, making it dangerous to eat unless prepared by an expert.*

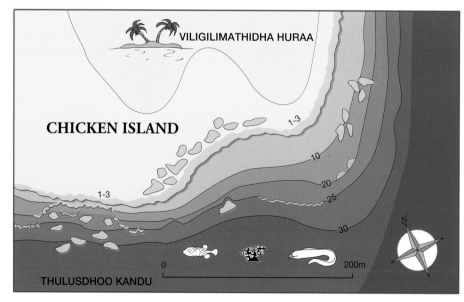

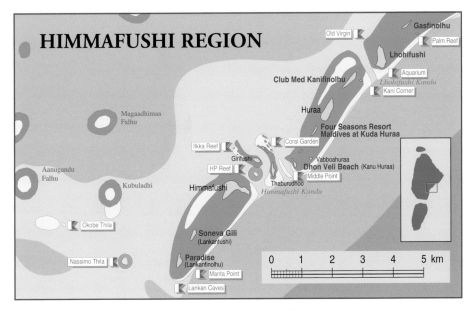

# HIMMAFUSHI REGION

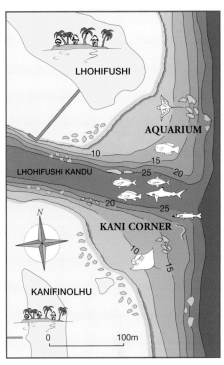

## Aquarium ★★

| Location: | north side Lhohifushi Kandu |
|---|---|
| Depth: | 10m – 25m |
| Fish life: | abundant |
| Coral growth: | very good |
| Features: | reef fish, sharks |

On the outside reef slightly to the north of the corner, is a conglomeration of coral rocks at 15 metres with masses of reef fish of every description, hence giving the site its name. There are also moray eels at the rocks and on the sand bottom at 25 metres are white-tip reef sharks and sting rays. A couple of caves at 25 metres are worth a look. The corner sweeps back more than 90° into Lhohifushi Kandu across a gradually sloping reef covered in soft coral to a steep cliff inside the channel. The reef inside is full of caves from 15 to 25 metres and a long drift is well worth the experience.

*Dog-toothed tuna,* Gymnosarda unicolor.

**Diving hints:** Like Kani Corner, currents can be fierce at the entrance and special care should be taken on the acute corner of Lhohifushi as currents can drag divers away from the reef.

## Kani Corner ★★★

| Location: | south side Lhohifushi Kandu |
|---|---|
| Depth: | 5m – 25m |
| Fish life: | above average |
| Coral growth: | very good |
| Features: | pelagics, sharks |

Kani Corner is one of the most exciting drift dives in the atoll. The outside reef bottoms onto a sandy slope at 30 to 35 metres where white-tip reef sharks and eagle rays can be seen. During the south-west monsoon, mantas return to coral rocks at 25 metres.

The corner to the channel is marked by a small ledge with a cave at 25 metres. Around this point are a variety of schooling fish like snapper and fusilier and pelagics such as great barracuda, blue-fin jack, and dog-toothed tuna. Napoleon meander about this area keeping a watchful eye on aquatic intruders. Soft coral is prevalent on the gentle slopes of the reef corner and higher up at 15 metres are coral rocks with aggregations of oriental sweetlip. Inside the channel the reef banks up to a sharp dropoff between five and 20 metres with

caves and overhangs down the face, continuing in this fashion through the long Lhohifushi Kandu.

Diving hints: Currents flow mainly into the channel during the north-east monsoon and mostly out during the south-west monsoon. They can be exceedingly swift in this narrow passage and divers may encounter plenty of turbulence here, as well as the prolific marine life. Care should be taken with a strong outgoing current. Divers are wise to start well inside the channel if diving at these times and to stay close to the reef and more shallow on the corner.

*Great barracuda,* Sphyraena barracuda.

**Palm Reef ★★** (One coconut tree reef).

Opposite Gasfinolhu on the outer reef edge is a small sand bank with one coconut tree growing on it. Alongside is Palm Reef. The best diving is around a series of coral rocks between 10 and 20 metres where reef fish including parrotfish, moorish idol, surgeon, angelfish and snapper all gather. Nurse sharks are often seen under the ledges. Around the base of the rocks, goatfish are found rummaging in the sand and rubble and on a sand plateau at 20 metres on the south west side of the rocks are several white-tip reef sharks.

**Old Virgin ★**

This is an easy beginners dive with a maximum depth of 20 metres to the sandy bottom. Old Virgin lies on the inside reef, slightly north of Lhohifushi. It is an arch in the reef at 10 metres through which divers can easily swim. The reef edge has many crevices and small inlets in the shallower depths where reef fish find protection and delicate hard coral grows.

**Coral Garden ★** (Blue Lagoon)

Thaburudhoo channel has a great deal to offer divers. The long reef on the south side of Thaburudhoo Kandu guarantees plenty of options for divers. On the outside are grey reef sharks while inside the channel, Coral Garden is an excellent dive suited to beginners with a maximum depth of 18 metres. The coral along this reef is stunning and a multitude of small reef fish live among it.

**Middle Point ★★★**

Located in the centre of Thaburudhoo Kandu is a reef that peaks at 17 metres. The bottom of the channel is 25 to 30 metres. The reef top has a good covering of soft coral and sea anemones and in the caves are seafans. Nurse sharks spend some of their daylight hours in these caves. It is a long swim of about 75 metres across the channel to the reef but well worth the exercise. Care should be taken with currents, especially outgoing ones.

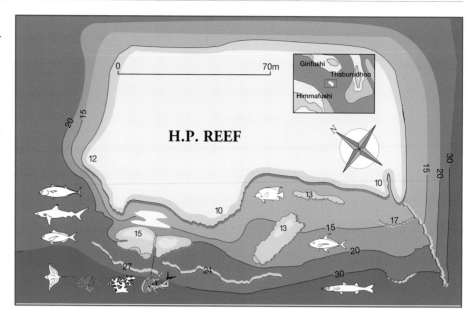

**HP Reef ★★★** (Rainbow Reef)

PROTECTED MARINE AREA

| | |
|---|---|
| Location: | thila south side of Girifushi Island |
| Depth: | 9m – 27m |
| Fish life: | abundant |
| Coral growth: | very good |
| Features: | soft coral, seafans, reef fish, pelagics |

HP Reef is another exceptional dive with a spectacular reef formation. The entire length of the reef on the south west side is filled with outcrops of reef, caves and crevices. At the north west side is a large outcrop of rock divided from the reef by a narrow sand channel. The outside of this rock drops steeply from 15 metres to a large cave at 24 metres. The ceiling of the cave is adorned with blue coral and at one end of the cave is a narrow swim-through called the 'chimney', leading to the top of the rock. The soft coral and seafans clutter the sides of the cliffs and overhangs and are nourished by the strong currents streaming through Himmafushi Kandu.

Large schools of big-eye trevally and blue-fin jack, rainbow runner, barracuda, and dog-toothed tuna make this reef a playground for pelagics. Grey reef sharks and eagle rays join in the action and yellow-back fusilier concentrate here in big schools. On the reef top are many species of angelfish such as the three-spot, emperor and regal angelfish. Masked bannerfish swim around the hard coral on the reef top, along with many other reef fish.

**Diving hints:** Currents can be strong and should be respected. A safety balloon is a necessity for making open water safety stops if there is current. Girifushi is under the control of the National Security Service. Diving is prohibited when the red flag is flying from the jetty.

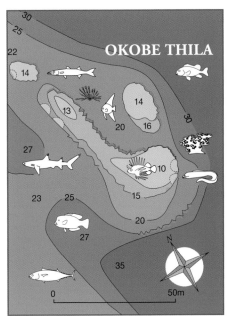

Above: *Regal angelfish,* Pygoplites diacanthus. *There are around 80 species of angelfish with various common names. The regal or empress angelfish, as it is also known, is among the most beautiful.*

Above top: *This regal angelfish photographed at HP Reef has a very unusual and rare colour form with variations never seen anywhere else.*

Below: *Three-spot angelfish,* Apolemichthys trimaculatus. *Angelfish can be distinguished from butterflyfish by a sturdy cheek spine like the one shown below.*

## Okobe Thila ★★★ (Barracuda Thila)

| | |
|---|---|
| Location: | south east of Thulhaagiri |
| Depth: | 10m – 25m |
| Fish life: | abundant |
| Coral growth: | very good |
| Features: | pelagics, reef fish |

This spectacular site has many different features and can be dived in a number of ways. It is one of those sites that seems to get better with every dive. There are three sections of reef to this thila, the smallest reef being no more than 10 metres in diameter, while the larger one is about 50 metres in length. A hole in the larger reef at 13 metres makes an ideal starting point from where dhoanis can secure a line. All three reefs are pitted with nooks and crannies, steep ledges, overhangs and caves providing a veritable feast of marine life for divers. Some features include several well-camouflaged scorpion fish on the reef top, common lionfish around the ledges, large moray eels in the caves and a thick covering of soft coral on the steep walls of the medium sized reef. Napoleon are well acquainted with divers. A school of tall-fin batfish are usually seen between the reefs but they have been known to disappear for long periods. Schools of barracuda and trevally, and the odd dog-toothed tuna are common around the reef, while in the

recesses of the small reef are featherstars, oriental sweetlip, triggerfish, bannerfish and squirrelfish.

A ridge extends northward from the thila at 22 metres, leading to a big reef that rises to eight metres. There are a couple of caves and ledges on the edge of the big reef. White-tip reef sharks are seen on either side of the ridge.

**Diving hints:** Divers should be careful when venturing away from the thila as it is easy to get lost in poor visibility and to run short on air. Sufficient air should be kept to return to the rope where any remaining air can be spent on top of the reef before making a slow ascent to five metres for a safety stop.

## Ilkka Reef ★★

At the north western end of Girifushi faru is Ilkka Reef. It is a thila 100 metres long and 30 metres wide and rises to within three metres of the surface. A smaller thila can be found 20 metres across the sand to the south. It rises to eight metres. The depth surrounding the thilas is no more than 20 metres. There are plenty of reef fish and peeking out of their burrows on the sand and rubble base are arrow dart goby and red fire dart goby.

Nearby at the northern end of Girifushi faru is **Potato Reef ★**. It is located in the middle of a narrow sand saddle. It is a big rock at 15 metres and is home to a number of grouper and a morays. On the sand flats around Potato reef are a number of sting rays.

*Smallscale scorpionfish,* Scorpaenopsis oxycephala. *Has venomous spines and is often mistaken for a stonefish.*

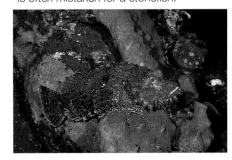

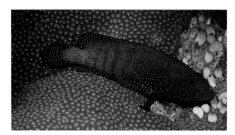

*Peacock rock-cod,* Cephalopholis argus. *Rock-cods are from the large grouper family and most species have rounded tails and pretty spots.*

*Flower grouper,* Epinephelus fuscoguttatus. *The flower grouper is shy and often found hiding in the back of caves.*

*Snub-nose pompano,* Trachinotus blochii.

*White-lined grouper,* Anyperodon leucogrammicus. *When it is a juvenile, this cunning fish mimics the Vrolik's wrasse,* Halichoeres vrolikii. *It preys on damselfish which mistake it for the harmless wrasse.*

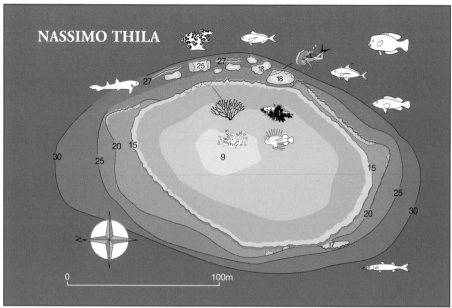

NASSIMO THILA

**Nassimo Thila** ★★★★

(Paradise Rock, Virgin Reef).

PROTECTED MARINE AREA

| | |
|---|---|
| Location: | 1.5 km west of Lankanfinolhu |
| Depth: | 10m – 30m |
| Fish life: | abundant |
| Coral growth: | excellent |
| Features: | pelagics, soft coral, seafans, pinnacles |

This reef is regarded by many as one of the best thilas in North Malé Atoll. The top of the thila is between 10 and 15 metres and oval in shape. The main attraction are several large pinnacles scattered randomly on the north east side of the thila. These are exposed to the full force of the currents and a spectacular display of soft coral is on all the rock faces and overhangs. The top of the pinnacles are at depths between 18 and 25 metres and most drop away steeply on the outside. Around them are napoleon, big-eye trevally, black snapper, red bass and a couple of great barracuda.

On the main reef, long overhangs and caves between 15 and 20 metres extend almost the entire length of the eastern side. At the northern end is a cave at 20 metres with delicate blue soft coral on the ceiling and a nurse shark is often inside.

At the southern end, the overhangs are full of seafans, both small and large. On the eastern side is a shallow cave and swim-through leading to a narrow gutter which cuts through to the reef top. Here scorpionfish and tiger cowrie shells may be found.

On the reef top are many species of grouper including the large flower grouper, white-lined grouper and peacock rock-cod. Near the reef edge at the north eastern end are several massive porite corals five metres in diameter, which is the highest point of the reef at nine metres. Small schools of snapper seem to converge at this point.

**Diving hints:** With a favourable current and good conservation of air, a leisurely dive can be made for the entire length of the reef, weaving in and out of the coral peaks and along the overhangs before rising to the top of the reef. However, to do this within no-decompression limits, depth should be limited to around 25 metres to maximise bottom time. Divers should spend plenty of time on the reef top, making their way, if the current permits, to the more shallow porite coral at the north eastern end before making a safety stop. A parachute, or safety balloon should be carried at this site.

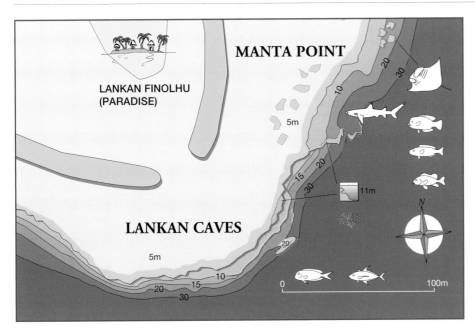

*Large manta,* Manta birostris.

## Manta Point ★★

## Lankan Caves ★★★

| | |
|---|---|
| Location: | outside reef of Lankanfinolhu |
| Depth: | 5m – 30m |
| Fish life: | above average |
| Coral growth: | very good |
| Features: | manta rays, caves |

Manta Point has a world-wide reputation as being one of the most consistent sites for attracting large numbers of manta ray.

In eight metres of water on the south east corner of Lankanfinolhu reef are several large coral rocks which mark the point where mantas converge during the south-west monsoon season. Mantas have been photographed here as early as April and as late as December. These rocks are one giant cleaner station for the mantas. Blue-streak cleaner wrasse, *Labroides dimidiatus*, often working in pairs, can be observed swimming out to the hovering mantas to remove old skin and parasites. The mantas circle the rocks awaiting their turn to be cleaned and when finished they swim gracefully up and down the reef feeding on zooplankton in the shallow water.

On a sandy section at 20 metres are a number of white-tip reef sharks and near the southern tip of Lankanfinolhu reef is Lankan Caves. A steep cliff and a long cave between 10 and 30 metres marks the start. In the cave at 11 metres is a huge seafan. A long section of overhangs and caves between five and 15 metres characterizes the southern point of the reef. There are many parrotfish, surgeon, trevally and emperor along this reef. On the reef top are large, well formed table corals with schools of sergeant major damselfish, oriental sweetlip, napoleon and sometimes snub-nose pompano swimming among them.

**Diving hints:** A good dive plan for this reef is to dive shallow on the outside reef hopefully to see some mantas at the coral rocks, swim down to the sand where the white-tips are, then meet the cave at 30 metres, come up to 10 metres with the cave and finish at the southern end.

Divers are asked not to chase or harass mantas (the same applies to turtles) as they are easily frightened and less inclined to return in the future. Do not hold the top of the coral rocks or the mantas may think the cleaning station is occupied. Try to stay all together at a discreet distance away. Do not swim around, stay quiet on the bottom and hold only dead coral.

There are two species of manta commonly seen in the Maldives: the Large manta and the smaller Schooling manta. Mantas tend to be observed hovering over the cleaner stations more often when there is a current. If there is no current, they have to flap their 'wings' and cannot remain stationary. Mantas have no venomous spine on their tail. Male mantas have two small tube-like projections called claspers at the base of their tail. Sometimes you can observe swelling on the underbelly of the female, indicating she is pregnant. The young are born with their 'wings' folded. Mantas have their own unique fins which extend forward to scoop up the zoo plankton into their wide gaping mouths.

*Sergeant major,* Abudefduf vaigiensis.

39

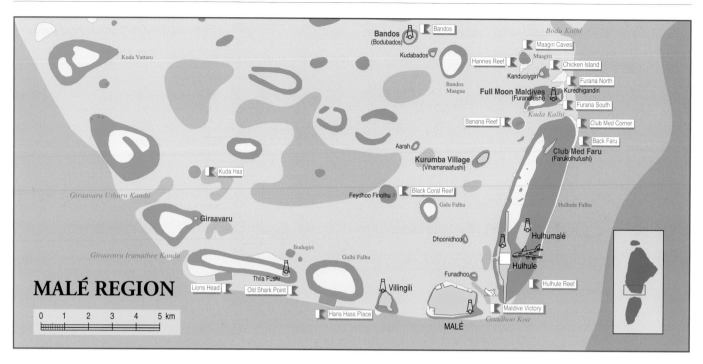

MALÉ REGION

0  1  2  3  4  5 km

*Banded shrimp are often seen around the mouths of fish, like moray eels and grouper. They serve their hosts by removing external parasites and waste food. They have long antennae to seek out fish for their cleaning station.*

*Spotted garden eel, Heteroconger hassi. Garden eels are common on sand flats in lagoons and between reefs. They feed on zooplankton floating over them and grow to about 40 cm.*

## Hannes Reef ★★★

| | |
|---|---|
| Location: | west side of Maagiri reef |
| Depth: | 20m – 30m |
| Fish life: | abundant |
| Coral growth: | very good |
| Features: | abundant fish |

Maagiri reef is a popular dive destination with a number of diving points. Hannes Reef is a small outcrop of rock lying near Maagiri reef at a depth of 20 metres. When visibility is good it can be seen from the main reef across a sand saddle at 23 metres. The reef is no more than 30 metres in diameter and at the top is a large hole where diving dhoanis sometimes tie their lines. Dense schools of blue-striped snapper congregate around this reef and on the deeper side at 32 metres are a couple of caves with big, shy grouper and as many as 12 lionfish. Invertebrates thrive here, including banded shrimp and small crabs co-existing with sea anemones. Pipefish are common and on the sand between the thila and the reef is a field of garden eels.

**Diving hints:** This dive is spoilt if too many divers visit it at once and care should be taken not to damage the top of the coral reef with fins.

## Maagiri Caves ★★★

On the north side of Maagiri reef a big rock at 20 metres appears to have broken away from the reef creating a semi-circular cliff with a canyon. There is also a big overhang here. Nearby are many small caves between five and 30 metres. Snapper, big-nose unicornfish, triggerfish, angelfish, fusilier and eagle rays can be seen around the rock. On the reef top is a beautiful display of coral.

## Maagiri Thila ★

This is a series of rocks rising from around 20 metres on the eastern side of Maagiri reef. Healthy stands of hard coral lie above 15 metres. It is a good site for beginners.

*Common lionfish, Pterois volitans.*

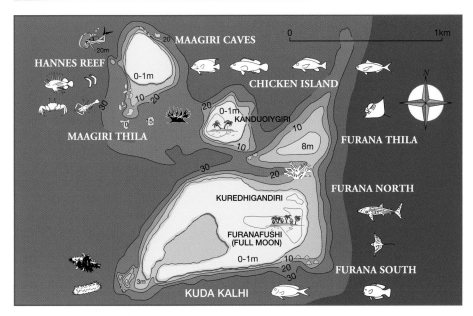

### Furana North ★★   Furana Thila ★★★

| Location: | north side of Furanafushi |
|---|---|
| Depth: | 5m – 25m |
| Fish life: | average |
| Coral growth: | good |
| Features: | sharks, reef fish |

Divers usually start their dive on the eastern side of the island where it is well protected during the south-west monsoon season. The reef top is gnarled and stunted down to 10 metres because of wave action but there is plenty of fish life. The reef drops steeply on the outside.

There are a number of diving options. With an ingoing current, divers usually drift into the atoll on the north side of the island where many triggerfish are to be found.

With a gentle ingoing current divers can venture out to Furana Thila rising to eight metres on the north side of Furanafushi. There are many surprises here including nurse sharks, eagle rays mantas and even whale sharks during the south-west monsoon. Divers can visit caves at 26 and 20 metres on the south and west sides of the thila, then drift across to the south side of Kanduoiygiri.

Near the main entrance to Furanafushi Lagoon, is a small thila with nice caves. Boat traffic can be heavy so divers are advised to make sure they display a divers flag.

### Furana South ★★ (Kuda Kalhi)

| Location: | south side of Furanafushi |
|---|---|
| Depth: | 3m – 30m |
| Fish life: | above average |
| Coral growth: | very good |
| Features: | pelagic fish, reef fish, coral |

With an ingoing current, divers begin on the eastern side of Furanafushi on a reef plateau at 10 metres that drops away steeply to more than 70 metres. The reef top has been battered by wave action and hard massive coral dominates the reef top but it has created an ideal environment for small reef fish such as damselfish and butterflyfish.

Best diving is above 20 metres and on the south corner are a couple of small caves at 10 and 15 metres. In the open ocean are shark, eagle rays, dog-toothed tuna, snapper, and napoleon. This can be a long drift dive and well inside Kuda Kalhi channel at five metres is excellent table coral.

When visibility is good watch closely into the channel for big fish. Whale sharks are occasionally sighted along this reef during the south-west monsoon season and on the surface, large schools of dolphin are sometimes seen making their way through the atoll.

### Chicken Island ★★ (Kukulhu Island)

The island's correct name is Kanduoiygiri. It has good reef on the north, north east and south sides and these can be dived separately.

### Back Faru ★★

Farukolufushi outside reef is a long, easy drift dive popular with most resorts in the area because it offers good protection from strong winds during the south-west monsoon and is not greatly affected by currents. Visibility is usually good and many surprise encounters with big fish occur here. These include hammerhead sharks, eagle rays, great barracuda and turtles.

### Club Med Corner ★★★

Located on the same reef as Back Faru at the entrance to Kuda Kalhi channel, is an interesting cave with big coral rocks at 24 metres. With an ingoing current divers will always see schools of surgeon, humpback snapper, large sweetlip and soft coral. Just around the corner inside the channel at 10 metres are coral rocks sometimes with schools of powder-blue surgeon around them and many species of boxfish and pufferfish. Turtles favour this reef and have been seen sleeping in caves at night.

**Diving hints:** strong inflowing currents at the corner drag divers down and away from the reef.

*Yellow box fish, Ostracion cubicus. Box fish have a tough shell made of bony plates with spaces for fins, eyes, mouth and gills. They have strong jaws for eating molluscs and breaking open the holes of tube worms. They release a toxin from the skin which can kill other fish – and itself – if collected and placed in a confined area.*

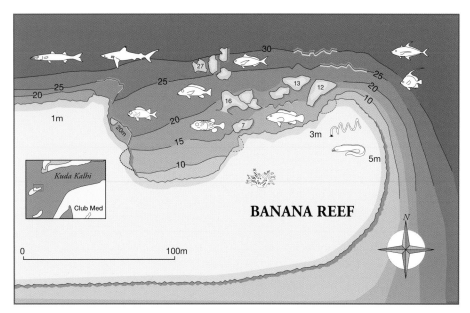

**BANANA REEF**

*Kuda Kalhi*

*Club Med*

0                 100m

*Shadowfin soldierfish,* Myripristis adusta. *Soldierfish are of the same family as the squirrelfish. They come out from caves and overhangs to feed at night.*

Below: *The island of Farukolhufushi showing Club Med Corner and Back Faru. Banana Reef is the small reef at the top in the middle of the channel.*

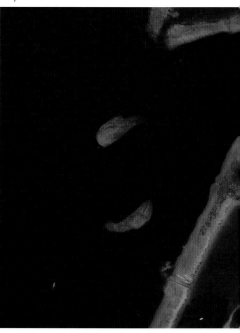

## Banana Reef ★★

PROTECTED MARINE AREA

| | |
|---|---|
| Location: | inside Kuda Kalhi |
| Depth: | 3m – 30m |
| Fish life: | abundant |
| Coral growth: | excellent |
| Features: | coral, reef fish |

Banana Reef, named after its shape when viewed from the air, was one of the first dive sites to be discovered in the Maldives. It is the most northern of the two reefs west of Club Med. The best diving is at the north eastern end where there are big spectacular rocks, caves, deep gutters and precipitous overhangs. The scenery is amazing and around these big rocks, predatory fish like shark, barracuda, trevally and black snapper converge.

*Immaculate soldierfish,* Myripristis vittata, *are found in caves or ledges and often swim upside down. All have big eyes which are adapted to the dark caves. Most species feed on zooplankton.*

On the eastern fringe of the reef in 15 metres is a school of up to 1000 schooling bannerfish. These distinctive fish have long dorsal fins and vertical black and white bands and always inhabit the same area. At times they are so thick that divers can barely see through them. Here also are large morays that entwine themselves in green coral trees.

The caves have several species of grouper and some, like the snout-spot grouper, have become quite tame, mainly through fish-feeding. There are some pufferfish and many smaller species of wrasse. Cleaner wrasse are common, often swimming well out from the reef and into schools of blue-dash fusilier. Big schools of fusilier are everywhere, most noticeably the smaller striped fusilier and the moon fusilier.

At the western end a semi-circular wall drops steeply to 25 metres. There is a big cave here between 10 and 15 metres with a multitude of squirrelfish, including sabre squirrelfish, immaculate soldierfish, and shadowfin soldierfish. Many swim upside down and all have big eyes to see in the dark. A little deeper is a small cave at 20 metres often with a moray and grouper inside. During strong currents this concave wall, known as the 'Washing Machine', generates swirling down currents. The Maldivian grubfish thrives on the rubbly bottom near the 'washing machine' at around 20 metres. Grey reef sharks are regularly seen.

On the reef top is some of the best table coral seen in North Malé Atoll and on cliffs and ledges between three and 10 metres are colourful sponges and coral.

**Diving hints:** During the north-east monsoon, spring tides combine with north easterly winds creating extremely strong currents from the east. Be wary if diving at these times and if caught in the 'Washing Machine', don't fight it but stay close to the reef and ride it out.

*Striped fusilier, Pterocaesio trilineata. A common fish in the Maldives mostly around 12 cm in length and seen in large schools feeding on zoo plankton. They are fast swimmers and are mostly seen in the lagoons and sandy areas. At night they shelter within the reef to sleep.*

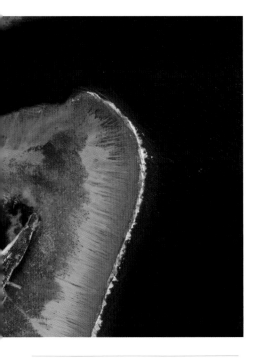

*Maldivian grubfish, Parapercis signata. A common fish endemic to the Maldives. Likes sandy lagoons, rubble and protected reefs. While the grubfish looks similiar to lizardfish, they move around more and feed mostly on the bottom, whereas lizardfish feed off the bottom.*

## Bandos ★★

On the north east side of Bandos is a short section of reef, about 75 metres long, with a big overhang dropping from five metres to 12 metres. At either end is a cave. Snout-spot grouper and morays are quite tame here. The overhangs are covered in sponge and attract moorish idol and butterflyfish. Close to the overhang at the eastern end is a big coral rock rising from 20 to 12 metres where tall-fin batfish, trevally, and snapper are seen. One of the great attractions of this reef are the black-tip reef sharks seen at 25 metres.

## Black Coral Reef ★★

On the east side of Feydhu Finolhu is a vertical wall 300 metres long with small caves, shallow overhangs and some swim-throughs. The wall drops to 30 metres before levelling out to a sandy bottom but the best diving is above 15 metres. Black coral trees some laden with mother-of-pearl oyster shells are common and give the reef its name.

The branches of this coral appear greyish on the outside, but underneath the thin coating is the semi precious black coral used in making jewellery and ornaments. On the bushes are black, yellow and green featherstars, some curled up, others with their arms outstretched to filter-feed on drifting zooplankton.

Along the reef edge are colourful emperor angelfish, delicate flame basslet, the distinctive clown trigger fish and long-nosed butterflyfish. The wall is rich in invertebrates: tiny cleaner shrimp occupy little holes, cucumbers and starfish cling precariously to the wall and encrusting sponges of all colours: yellow, blue, green and tubed white ones, compete for space.

## Funadhoo ★

There is an interesting reef to the south-east of the island with caves and ledges but diving is not encouraged here because boat traffic can be heavy.

*Black-tip reef shark, Carcharhinus melanopterus. These sharks are common in shallow water, often in the lagoons of islands. They grow to around 1.5 metres and are identified by their brownish colour and black-tip dorsal fin.*

## Hulhule Reef ★

On the outside of Hulhule Island is a long reef, well protected from storms from the south west. It is quiet and unspectacular but visibility is usually good. When combined with the southern end of the reef, with its sharp corner and steep dropoffs, this dive – with the current going into Gaadhoo Koa – has a lot to offer.

To the east of Feydhu Finolhu is **Galhu Falhu reef**. This reef has been heavily mined for coral in the past and is now part of an ongoing project to monitor coral growth in mined reef areas. Artificial reef structures were placed on the reef in 1990 in areas where coral mining 20 years ago have shown no signs of recovery. According to a report by Dr Susan Clark, who initiated the project, coral recruitment to the artificial areas has been rapid, depending on the type of structure employed. Continued testing of artificial structures may lead to a viable method of encouraging widespread coral growth on denuded reefs.

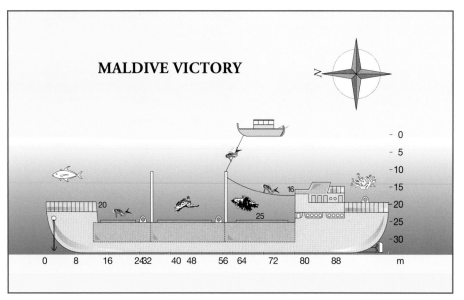

*Big-eye trevally,* Caranx sexfasciatus.

## Maldive Victory ★★★

| Location: | south-west of Hulhule reef |
|---|---|
| Depth: | 15m – 35m |
| Fish life: | average |
| Coral: | good |
| Features: | wreck |

### History

It started out as a dramatic disaster in the early hours of Friday February 13, 1981, but the wreck of the *Maldive Victory* quickly became a focal point for divers and was soon being hailed as a boon for the local diving industry. The wreck lies upright, tilted slightly to port in 35 metres of water on the sandy bottom just off Hulhule reef. The 3500 tonne, 83 metre freighter struck the reef at almost full speed after the captain lost his way in the buoy-marked channel. Its hull was badly gashed and it sank within minutes. All passengers and crew survived. The 10- year-old freighter was sailing to Malé from Singapore with a full cargo of supplies, mainly for the resort islands. On the day of the disaster, diving instructors were quickly on the scene but were detained by the National Security Service before being released to officially dive on the wreck and report their findings.

According to Maldivian divers, the salvage operation lasted nine months with teams of up to 20 divers a day retrieving the goods. Today, the wreck is stripped bare of anything of value. There are, however, a few cassette players remaining on deck. They are passed from one diver to the next and held playfully up to ears, as though they were still transmitting music played on that fearful night of Black Friday 13th, in February 1981.

### Diving

A buoy has been fixed to the mast at 12 metres making descents easier in strong currents. The currents can be treacherous here but once on the deck, there is plenty of protection. The entire ship can be comfortably seen in one dive. A good plan is firstly to swim from the mast along the superstructure to the bow. On the way along the deck are three large holds that are wide open and easy to penetrate. Take your torch! At the bow is an anchor that swings in the current. A large school of trevally gather here. From the bow return to the stern of the ship and finish at the bridge. A rope has been tied from the bridge at 16 metres to the mast to make ascents easier.

*An eerie silence envelops divers as they descend towards the bow of the Maldive Victory*

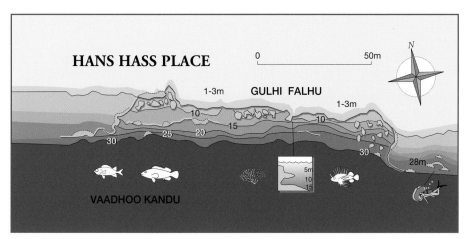

*Looking west. Viligili followed by Gulhi Falhu and Thilafushi Falhu. Hans Hass Place is half way along Gulhi Falhu. Old Shark Point is in the channel between Gulhi Falhu and Thilafushi Falhu.*

## Hans Hass Place ★★★ (Kikki Reef)
### PROTECTED MARINE AREA

| | |
|---|---|
| Location: | middle of Gulhi Falhu, south side |
| Depth: | 3m – 30m |
| Fish life: | abundant |
| Coral growth: | excellent |
| Features: | hard coral, caves, |

Kikki Reef is a spectacular wall dive 100 metres long overlooking the depths of the Vaadhoo Kandu. It is set back into a large cavity in the reef and starts at either end with jagged overhangs cutting through the reef between five and 30 metres. A long swim-through in the wall at 28 metres is a good starting point if the current is flowing to the west. The best diving is between five and 15 metres where there are many caves and ledges. Small delicate purple seafans cover the ceilings of the overhangs and in the caves are many species of grouper. The caves are also full of immaculate soldierfish and shadow-fin soldierfish. Commonly seen on this reef are the scribbled filefish, trumpetfish and the freckled hawkfish.

If divers look carefully on the reef they may see well camouflaged leaf fish, and in the caves are white-banded possum wrasse and cheeked pipefish. This reef is covered in invertebrates and is a marvel for the variety of reef fish it houses.

**Diving hints:** Divers are advised at this site to take their time and look for the little things on offer. While closely studying the fauna be particularly careful with buoyancy control as many of the overhangs are shallow. Stay out from the overhangs if not in full control.

*White-banded possum wrasse, Wetmorella albofasciata. A secretive little fish seen in the back of caves. Quite common, but usually only seen with a torch.*

*Cheeked pipefish, Corythoichthys insularis. Is found mostly on the floor in caves and on sand flats. It has a long tube-like mouth to feed. Pipefish make up the same family as seahorses and seadragons.*

*Freckled hawkfish, Paracirrhites forsteri. Also called blackside hawkfish and usually seen on the more shallow sections of reef. It perches on its ventral fins at high points of coral waiting for potential prey.*

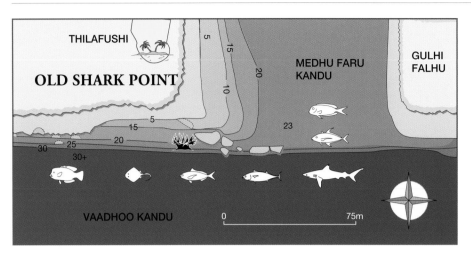

## Old Shark Point ★★★

| | |
|---|---|
| Location: | south side of Thilafushi |
| Depth: | 5m – 30m |
| Fish life: | above average |
| Coral growth: | very good |
| Features: | grey reef sharks |

Old Shark Point is easily located on the outside corner of Thilafushi or 'Trash Island', the site of the Malé refuse dump. The western corner of the channel is a great dive because of the rocky outcrops peeling away into the deep blue waters of the Vaadhoo Kandu. There are pelagics like blue-fin jack, dog-toothed tuna, and mackerel scad. Grey reef sharks are regularly seen here in 30 metres of water.

There is a long spiralling gully between a shallow cave starting at 10 metres and the rocks at 30 metres. Among the overhangs and gullies, are many fish and invertebrates. There are numerous anemonefish in the shallower depths with as many as 40 being counted in one sea anemone.

Everywhere along the reef are napoleon, fusilier, surgeon and some titan triggerfish, while in the caves to the west are sting rays.

**Diving hints:** Currents can be turbulent at this site. Currents can flow south through Medhu Faru Kandu into the Vaadhoo Kandu, where it often meets another current flowing east through the Vaadhoo Kandu. This intersection of currents, while usually resulting in a

thrilling dive, also pushes divers away from the reef, sometimes up, other times down. Care should be taken during these times to stay close to the reef.

## Lions Head ★★

PROTECTED MARINE AREA

| | |
|---|---|
| Location: | Vaadhoo Kandu |
| Depth: | 3m – 25m |
| Fish life: | above average |
| Coral growth: | very good |
| Features: | grey reef shark |

This protrusion of rock juts ominously towards the 4.5 km wide Vaadhoo Kandu. The site is flushed with clear water from the 500 metre deep channel making it ideal for viewing the territorial grey reef sharks that patrol the area. A gently sloping ledge on the east side of the rock at 10 metres is a suitable place to sit and wait for the show to begin. When shark

feeding was practised in the Maldives, this was the theatre, nowadays, shark feeding is not encouraged and sharks can usually be found in their natural state without being harassed into a feeding frenzy.

To the east of Lions Head is a long straight section of reef with caves and overhangs at five metres. Many invertebrates, such as lobsters, octopus, sea anemones, sponges and pin-cushions are found on this section of reef and blotched porcupine fish are familiar inhabitants. More caves and overhangs are found at 20 and 25 metres but the best diving is in the shallow water between five and 10 metres.

**Diving hints:** There is no need to fear grey reef sharks in the Maldives. They are curious and often come within a few metres of divers. If, however, a shark puts on an aggressive display by lowering its head, pointing its pectoral fin downwards and swimming rapidly back and forth, then calmly back-up against the reef and retreat from the water.

*Mackerel scad,* Decapterus macarellus. *These are tasty fish often served at the tea shops in Malé.*

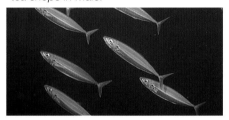

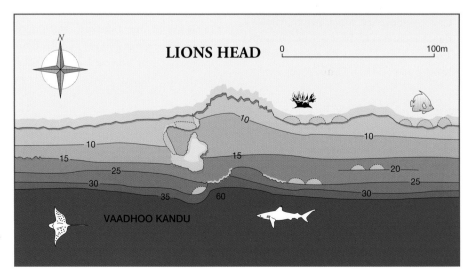

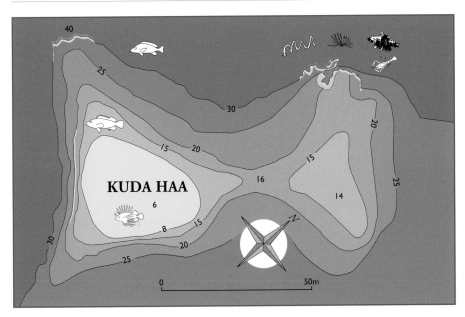

Featherstars anchor themselves with legs or 'cirri', although some species grasp the substrate with their arms.

Large-eye emperor, Monotaxis grandoculus. This species is usually seen in pairs or small schools. Young juveniles appear with a dark band along their sides and older fish have three vertical white stripes. Mature fish can grow to 50 cm and loose their stripes.

**Kuda Haa ★★★**

PROTECTED MARINE AREA

| | |
|---|---|
| Location: | thila north of Giraavaru |
| Depth: | 6m – 30m |
| Fish life: | abundant |
| Coral growth: | very good |
| Features: | coral, reef fish |

There are two peaks over a length of about 100 metres and although the thila does not have as many spectacular rock features as many others, the fish life here is as prolific and diverse as any reef in the Maldives. The twin peaks rise from the atoll floor to 14 metres and 6 metres and among the delicate coral on the reef top are numerous species of damselfish. Circling above the reef are large schools of flame basslet and blue-striped snapper. There are also many freckled hawkfish, long-nose filefish, and scorpionfish,

Grey reef shark, Carcharhinus amblyrhynchos.

including the common lionfish on the reef top. Featherstars have also found this a good site to spread their arms and catch the zooplankton that flows freely through the atoll.

One of the features of the reef is a cave between 25 and 30 metres at the end of a ridge on the north side. Inside is a big bushy black coral tree with oyster shells. On the sandy, rubbly area east of the cave at 25 metres are many species of shrimp goby. Careful and patient observation of these shy fish may reward divers with a glimpse of their near-blind commensal shrimp.

There is a steep ledge at 35 metres at the end of a ridge on the western side. On the slopes of this ridge are big grouper including the giant grouper and the flower grouper. Also of interest on this ridge are two commonly seen species of emperor, the large-eye emperor, usually seen in pairs or small aggregations and the gold-spot emperor, often in schools and clearly distinguished by the glowing gold spot on its tail.

**Diving hints:** There is not a lot of protection from strong currents at this site. Divers should take special care not to knock the brittle green coral trees on the reef slopes.

Gold-spot emperor, Gnathodentex aurolineatus. These schooling fish have a bright gold spot which stands out against dark backgrounds helping the fish orientate in schools.

Long-nose filefish, Oxymonacanthus longirostris. A long-snouted fish growing to 8 cm that hides in corals.

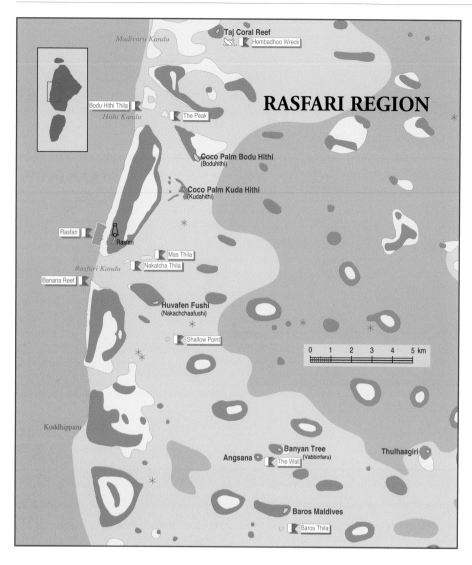

RASFARI REGION

### Nakatcha Thila ★★★

This thila lies inside Rasfari Kandu. It is a medium sized thila with a maximum depth of 26 metres. It has big bright caves and magnificent overhangs starting at 10 metres.

### Mas Thila ★★★

In Dhivehi, *Mas* means fish and the lack of coral on this reef is made up for by the quantity of fish life. It has a maximum depth of 30 metres and is about 150 metres long. Vast schools of plankton eaters like schooling bannerfish and fusilier congregate on the northern end of the thila. Sometimes cruising along the reef edge are schools of barracuda, rainbow runner and a number of big tuna, often alone and other times in twos and threes. On the reef slopes are green coral trees and sting rays.

### Banana Reef ★★ (west)

On the south side of Rasfari Kandu a wide reef plateau sloping to 10 metres extends into the channel. On the outside corner are inlets dropping to a sandy bottom at 25 metres. On the sandy bottom are garden eels and goatfish, while on the reef slope are big schools of blue triggerfish. They can be seen everywhere on the reef with their tails sticking out from small holes. There are also large schools of smaller fish like flame basslet, black pyramid butterflyfish and surgeon. Lionfish are fairly common. One ridge extends seaward near the corner and has a sharp dropoff from about 30 metres with seafans. The channel is shallow and sandy at 17 metres. On the upper reef are morays, lobsters, snapper and fusilier. Manta rays are seen here during the north-east monsoon.

*Looking west. Rasfari and the outer reef.*

### Baros Thila ★★★

To the south of Baros is a thila with the top at eight metres. On the north side are a couple of caves and overhangs at 27 metres. On the west side is sand at 23 metres then another ridge of reef continues at 22 metres. Baros thila is well known for its grey reef and white-tip reef sharks. Also feeding here are barracuda and big dog-toothed tuna. During the north-east monsoon sharks and pelagics are mostly found on the eastern side while during the south-west monsoon they are usually on the western side. The best time for diving here is usually February, March and April.

### Wall ★

At Ihuru there is good snorkelling and diving on the housereef. The wall is a popular shore dive where about half a dozen sting rays are regularly fed and as a result are quite tame.

### Shallow Point ★★

To the south of Nakatchchaafushi is a small thila with the reef top at eight metres. The reef slopes gently to around 20 metres. Coral growth is lacking but there are plenty of blue-striped snapper, surgeon and batfish. One of the main features of this reef are the hundreds of sea anemones with black-footed anemonefish. This fish is only found in the Maldives and they thrive on this reef. The small saddled pufferfish is common and on the sand and coral rubble are many lizardfish.

## Rasfari ★★★

### PROTECTED MARINE AREA

| | |
|---|---|
| Location: | outside Rasfari |
| Depth: | 10m – 30m+ |
| Fish life: | above average |
| Coral growth: | very good |
| Features: | sharks, under water scenery, eagle rays |

There is plenty of variation of topography with sandy inlets and ridges cutting across a wide outside reef. Resting on the sandy slopes are white-tip and black-tip reef sharks. The visibility is usually very good and an offshore reef, circular in shape with the top at a depth of 28 metres, can be seen from the main reef. This reef is more like a thila and on the inside the depth is 30 metres while on the outside it drops off to well over 40 metres. The top of the thila provides an excellent viewing location for deep water pelagics. Close encounters with grey reef sharks, schools of big-eye trevally, great barracuda and schools of eagle ray very often take place here. Oceanic white-tip sharks have been reported here.

Also of interest to fish watchers is the oceanic triggerfish that comes in around the full moon for nesting on the deeper sandy slopes.

On the main reef is an interesting terrain of coral ridges and patches of sand where there are large schools of green-face parrotfish, and many different types of reef fish.

**Diving hints:** The thila is some distance from the reef edge and divers should allow sufficient air to return to the reef to carry on the drift dive. Beware of running low on air for the return if diving deeper on the outside of the thila. Currents can increase rapidly in strength on the corner of Rasfari Kandu and divers should be careful of outgoing currents pushing them away from the reef. Safety balloons should always be carried here.

The parrotfish family are called *Landaa* in Dhivehi. The soft, white, tasty flesh is a favourite among Maldivians. Sultan Mohamed Shamsudeen III (1904–1934) was famous for this fish diet. Every day the head man from Hulhule, then inhabited, had to bring 2-3 fish to Malé for the Sultan.

*Green-face parrotfish,* Scarus prasiognathus. *Parrotfish have strong beak-like jaws to scrape algae and weed off coral. They consume great quantities of coral and deposit the remains all over the reef. The green-face parrotfish occurs mostly on the outside reef in great schools of say 100 and adds significantly to the build-up of coral sand.*

*Oceanic triggerfish,* Canthidermis maculatus. *The females lay eggs once a month about one week before the full moon in a nest prepared by the male. Eggs hatch three to four days later and the young drift off with the stronger currents away from predatory reef fish.*

*Females are dark with white spotting as shown in the photograph.*

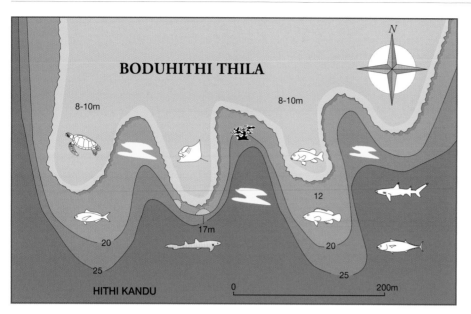

## Bodu Hithi Thila ★★★

| | |
|---|---|
| Location: | thila inside Hithi Kandu |
| Depth: | 8m – 25m |
| Fish life: | average |
| Coral growth: | poor |
| Features: | mantas, reef fish |

This is a long drift dive with the best diving on the southern end. The reef top is at eight to 10 metres and there are three bays in the reef with sandy bottoms between 15 and 25 metres. On one point is a cave at 17 metres that divers can see through. There are sometimes four to six nurse sharks inside. Hard coral cover is poor but there is plenty of healthy light blue and yellow soft coral. Along the reef slopes are big schools of fusilier, some tuna, grouper and sweetlip. On the sand bottom are white-tip reef sharks. Manta rays are seen here between December and April and turtles frequent the reef top all year round. If currents are quite strong then this thila is favoured above others because of its size.

## Hembadhoo Wreck ★★

| | |
|---|---|
| Location: | near the jetty at Hembadhoo |
| Depth: | 15m – 22m |
| Fish life: | above average |
| Coral growth: | good |
| Features: | wreck, reef fish |

The wreck is a former tug-boat, sunk by the dive school in 1988. It is marked by a buoy and the wreck is an easy shore dive. The wreck is 16 metres long with the top at 15 metres and the bottom at 22 metres. The boat is a focal point for marine life and is a fish-watcher's delight. In the waters surrounding the wreck are blue-fin jack, black snapper and midnight snapper. Around the rocks and in the wreck are schools of tiger cardinal fish, sabre squirrelfish and tame snout-spot grouper. Bushy black coral trees are already well-established on the wreck.

Divers return to shore along the reef edge to the jetty. It is worth spending some time at the jetty as it has its own unique variety of marine life. Often seen here is a cow-tailed sting ray, with its distinctive long tail, and schools of snub-nose pompano, from the trevally family. There are a lot of juvenile wrasse as well as surgeon and schools of rabbitfish, that are mainly herbivores feeding on algae growth under the jetty.

## Peak ★★★

Another big thila inside Hithi Kandu. The best diving on the Peak is on the southern side. The top of the reef is at eight to ten metres and is about 300 metres long. On the reef slopes are plenty of small caves and one larger one that divers can swim through lies at the south east end. Around the cave entrances are tallfin batfish and lionfish, while grazing on the slopes are numerous species of parrotfish. Other reef fish include bannerfish, snapper, napoleon, and fusilier. Eagle rays are often seen swimming through the channel. The reef bottoms out onto sand beds at 30 metres or less where sting rays are found at regular intervals. Hard coral cover is poor but in the caves are seawhips and sturdy seafans. Mantas are seen between December and April.

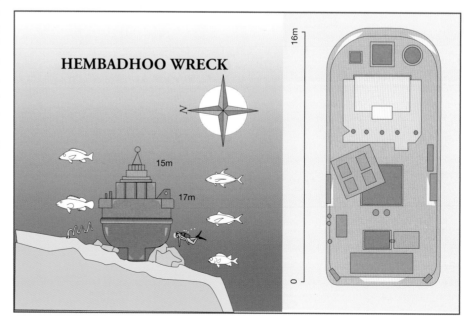

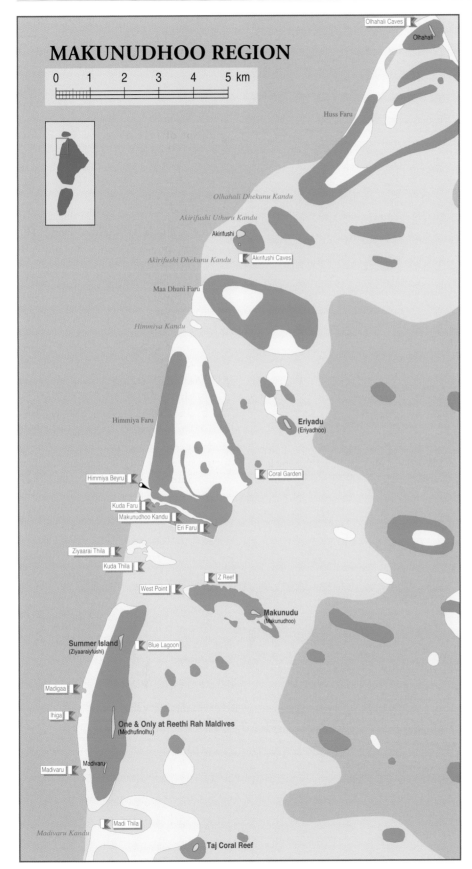

# MAKUNUDHOO REGION

0  1  2  3  4  5 km

*Tiger cardinal,* Cheilodipterus macrodon. *Also called the wolf cardinal, this small fish is often seen in large schools in caves and along steep walls. Cardinalfish have two dorsal fins and usually have distinct markings of spots and horizontal stripes along the body. Cardinalfish have large eyes and leave their caves at night to feed on the mass of night time zooplankton. The large mouth is used by the male to incubate eggs.*

## Madi thila ★★★

In Madivaru kandu is a huge underwater thila, the biggest in North Malé Atoll, which is four km wide and rises in parts to three metres. The north west side is called Madi thila and often during the north-east monsoon, mantas feed along this part of the reef.

*Schooling rabbitfish,* Siganus argenteus. *Schools can be seen grazing on weeds and algaes around resort jetties. The spines of rabbit-fish are venomous and painful. In Australia they are called 'happy moments' and said to cause fishermen to dance around the deck, hence the common name.*

Dolphins are a welcome sight when travelling through the atolls.

*Black-spot worm goby,* Gunnelichthys monostigma. *These are very shy fish found in sandy areas. Although fairly common they are not often seen as they are quick to dart into their sand burrows if frightened by divers.*

*Long-rayed sand diver,* Trichonotus elegans. *The males of this species have long filaments for display purposes. They are found in sandy areas, like lagoons, and have attractive black patterns which stand out against the white sand. They grow to 12 cm and feed on zoo plankton, and are in large numbers at Blue Lagoon.*

## Madigaa ★, Ihiga ★ and Madivaru ★

On the outside reef off Medhu Finolhu (Reethi Rah Resort) are three similar dives. All are good for beginners. Each dive starts at a small inlet in the reef at 10 metres and all of them slope to a sandy bottom that continues to 30 metres.

At Ihiga and Madigaa, isolated coral rocks are scattered around the sand and attract a wide variety of marine life, including grouper, sweetlip, snapper and moray eels. At Ihiga is one big rock with a small cave at 16 metres. Sting rays and white-tip reef sharks are common on the sand at all sites. Sometimes there are six or seven sharks close together. Garden eels are thickly spread across the sand and look like a field of corn wavering in the breeze. At Madivaru, leaf fish can be found at a rock at 15 metres and at all sites there is a good chance of seeing eagle rays at any time and manta rays between December and April. The reef top is between five and 10 metres. Generally the quality of the coral growth on the reef top is poor. This is partly due to rough seas crushing coral on the outside of the atoll.

## Blue Lagoon ★

Keen divers often make interesting discoveries in the lagoons of their resort island. At Ziyaaraiyfushi, Blue Lagoon is the housereef dive and is marked by a buoy near the end of the jetty. This dive has a sandy bottom and sloping sandy edge from around four to 20 metres. It has varied invertebrate and fish life and with clear water conditions and good light, excellent photos can be obtained. Pufferfish, banded trevally and triggerfish make good subjects and on the sand are four or five different species of lizardfish. Goby like the sandy environment and the white-barred sleeper goby and timid black-spot worm goby can be observed here when diving carefully and with patience.

Another uncommon fish occurs about 100 metres to the south of the diving buoy. It is the long-rayed sand diver. It is a shy fish, not more than 10 centimetres long, and here big schools of them occur. At this point the sand bed is rich with dollar urchins. These urchins are visible one moment, then 30 seconds later can bury themselves in the sand.

## West Point ★★

The western end of Makunudhoo reef is known as West Point. It is good for beginners with reef topography being a main feature.

*Indian Lizardfish,* Synodus indicus. *Mostly found preying on the sand of lagoons.*

## Z Reef ★

This dive is at the north west end of Makunudhoo reef. It has some interesting terrain with sand corridors running roughly parallel to the reef at depths around 15 metres. The sand is spread in a zig-zag fashion between a second coral reef barrier that rises to three metres before dropping to a sandy bottom at 25 metres on the outside. Coral growth is generally poor, but the reef features some nudibranchs and flatworms as well as bigeye and butterflyfish, while on the sand are garden eels, goatfish and white-tip reef sharks.

## Ziyaarai Thila ★★★

In the middle of the wide channel between Himmiya Faru and Ziyaaraiyfushi is a long thila running roughly east-west at about nine metres below the surface. At the western end, nearer the outside of the atoll, manta rays are seen during the north-east monsoon.

## Kuda Thila ★★★★

This is a spectacular 100 metre long thila located on the south side of the larger Ziyaari Thila. The top of Kuda Thila is at 16 to 18 metres and off the southern side are a line of large rocky outcrops beginning at depths ranging from 22 to 25 metres. Between the rocks and Kuda thila is a canyon with a depth of around 28 metres. There are plenty of overhangs on this thila and soft coral is on all the cliff faces. Shark and napoleon are regulars while on the reef top are big schools of blue-striped snapper and small schools of surgeon.

**Diving hints:** Divers should be aware that extremely strong currents occur in Makunudhoo Kandu and can be dangerous, especially outgoing ones. Divers can see most of the features of the reef if they limit their depth to 25 metres to maximize bottom time before ascending to make an open water safety stop. A safety balloon should always be carried here.

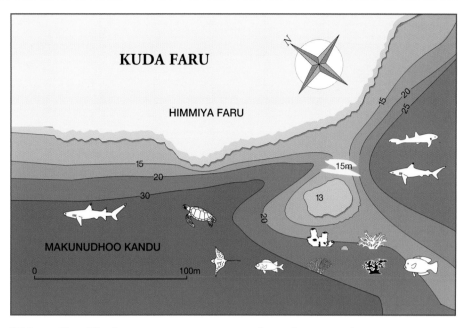

## Makunudhoo Kandu

The entire north side of Makunudhoo Kandu has been declared a PROTECTED MARINE AREA. It is just over two kilometres in length and has several popular dive points.

## Kuda Faru ★★★ (Saddle, Shark Point)

| | |
|---|---|
| Location: | Makunudhoo Kandu |
| Depth: | 13m – 25m |
| Fish life: | abundant |
| Coral growth: | very good |
| Features: | sharks, reef fish, coral |

Kuda Faru is one of the diving highlights of the north west. It is a finger of reef extending into the channel about 500 metres from the outside corner of Makunudhoo Kandu. The reef is like a thila. The top is at 13 metres, slightly oval in shape and about 50 metres long. It is separated from the main reef by a sand saddle at 15 metres. The thila extends into Makunudhoo Kandu for some distance on the southern side. The northern side of the thila is the best place to view both white-tip and grey reef sharks. With a strong ingoing current divers can hang on to dead coral at this point and look over the deep sand valley leading to the saddle where as many as 20 sharks, many juvenile, can be seen at one time. The reef top has a good range of hard and soft coral

and on the outer slopes are sponges, seawhips and seafans. Eagle rays can be seen here between November and May.

There is a large overhang at 27 metres with squirrelfish roaming the dark interior and nurse sharks are sometimes found inside. Turtles and napoleon are usually seen.

Diving hints: Currents are funnelled through the saddle at an accelerated rate. Even slight currents become swift torrents here. Strong ingoing currents may make the swim back to the main reef difficult so a safety balloon should always be carried here in case an open water safety stop has to be made.

*Banded trevally, Carangoides ferdau, and dollar urchins in Blue Lagoon.*

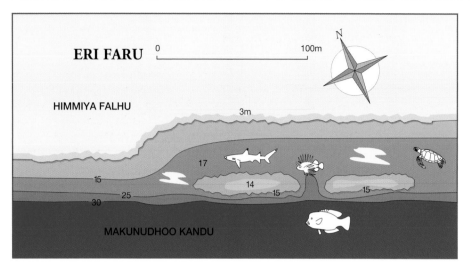

ERI FARU

0          100m

N

HIMMIYA FALHU

3m

17

14          15          15

15

25

30

MAKUNUDHOO KANDU

### Eri faru ★★

| | |
|---|---|
| Location: | Mukunudhoo Kandu |
| Depth: | 5m – 25m |
| Fish life: | above average |
| Coral growth: | very good |
| Features: | white-tip reef sharks, reef fish |

This is a good beginner's dive. Experienced divers will relish the great diversity of marine life here too. A recess in the reef has created a long sheltered inlet with a sand bottom about 17 metres deep. White-tip reef sharks are seen resting on the sand bottom.

On the outside of this 20 metre wide sand street is a long reef with the top at 14 metres, descending to more than 30 metres on the outside into Makunudhoo Kandu. On the reef are a range of invertebrates: featherstars of all colours, spider shells, sponges, lobster and seastars. Healthy hard coral covers the reef and seafans are patchy. Lionfish and napoleon are everywhere. Turtles are frequently seen along the entire reef of Makunudhoo Kandu. This dive is a refreshing change and full of fascinating features.

### Coral Garden ★

Located on the eastern side of Himmiya Faru, this is an excellent dive for beginners. It has a small thila two metres from the surface just out from the main reef. As the name suggests it has plenty of quality hard coral, mostly young and

delicate. A multitude of reef fish live among the coral and it is easy to spend the entire dive here. The current can go both ways along the reef and the best way to dive here is to start well upcurrent and drift along the reef onto the garden.

### Himmiya Beyru ★★

On the outside of Himmiya Faru is a small indentation in the reef, 500 metres to the north of Makunudhoo Kandu corner. It is a good beginners dive with a reef sloping gently from five to 25 metres. Just out from the main reef is a small thila

at 25 metres, making the site a good dive for more experienced divers as well.

### Akirifushi Caves ★★

The caves lie on the southern side of Akirifushi. They are about 150 metres west of an exposed rock on the reef edge. This entire reef is alive with coral growth and a healthy range of reef fish and well worth a dive. The reef bows in and out and the dropoff is characterised by steep walls between three and 25 metres. At one point is a range of caves and ledges all the way down the reef-face. Inside the caves are yellow soft coral, sponges and seafans with featherstars attached. There are also patches of stinging hydroids. The reef is a haven for morays, sting rays, turtles and pufferfish.

### Olhahali Caves ★★

These caves are on the northern side of Olhahali. There are a couple of small caves at 15 and 20 metres but the main attraction is a big cave 40 metres long at a depth of 25 metres. On the ceiling is blue and white soft coral, also some seafans and sponges on the walls. At its base is a mixture of sand and coral on which seawhips grow.

*White-tip reef shark,* Triaenodon obesus. *White-tip reef sharks are easily distinguished by their white-tip dorsal fin and are often seen resting on sand flats. They grow to around 1.5 m and usually return to the same area. Small schools are known to occupy the same cave.*

# Sea turtles

"Turtles were of such a size that the shell of one would suffice to roof a little hut or cot, and to cover ten or more persons sitting. There were vast numbers of them at the Maldives and some little islands you may see inhabited by no other animals than these great turtles, but covered with them."

*Francois Pyrard, Voyages,*
*1602 – 1607.*

Turtle shell has always been a major export of the Maldives. It was traded with Arabia, India and China and greatly sought after by kings, lords and rich people. It was made into boxes and caskets garnished with gold and silver and into bracelets, hair combs and other ornaments. Turtle products are still snapped up by buyers everywhere and with the advent of the tourism industry in the Maldives, the wholesale slaughter of turtles for their precious shell has led to a serious decline in their numbers. Turtle flesh and eggs are also sought after foods and as habitats become invaded by humans, so too does the survival of the species become threatened. The abundant turtles Pyrard saw – "of such a size to roof a little hut" – were most probably the loggerhead or leatherback turtle. Where are these great turtles today? Divers rarely see a leatherback. Tourists are now being made aware that their purchase of jewellery or gifts made from turtle shell is a threat to the turtle population.

Five of the seven known species of turtle in the world are seen in the Maldives. All turtles have a strong horny beak, none have true teeth. They use paddle-shaped flippers to propel themselves to speeds up to 35 km per hour. During the nesting season females return to land to lay their eggs in a nest dug into the sandy beach. After around two months the hatchlings go back to the sea. Turtles live long lives – thought to be up to 50 years and can survive long periods without food.

**Hawksbill sea turtle** *Eretmochelys imbricata.* The most commonly seen turtle along the reefs of the Maldives.

It has a beautifully coloured shell which serves as an effective camouflage in coral reefs. They measure up to 91 cm and weigh between 113 – 182 kg, and are easily identified by a 'beak-like' upper jaw that resembles a hawk's bill. They feed on algae, sea-grasses, barnacles, fish, and sponges.

**Green sea turtle** *Chelonia mydas.* They are predominantly vegetarian, feeding mostly on algae and sea grasses. Attain 100 cm and weigh between 113 – 182 kg.

**Loggerhead sea turtle** *Caretta caretta.* Loggerheads have powerful jaws and are mostly carnivorous feeding on shellfish,

sponges and jellyfish. Attain 114 cm and weigh between 113 – 182 kg.

**Olive ridley sea turtles** *Lepidochelys olivacea.* Olive ridleys are omnivorous, eating shrimp, snails, fish, crabs, jellyfish, sea grasses and algae. Attains 66 cm and weighs between 36 – 41 kg.

**Leatherback sea turtle** *Dermochelys coriacea.* The leathery covering has five ridges that run the length of the shell. They are dark brown and feed mostly on jellyfish. Attains 178 cms and weighs between 320 – 590 kg.

*Hawksbill sea turtle,* Eretmochelys imbricata.

*A close-up of a Green turtle. It has a shorter beak than the Hawksbill.*

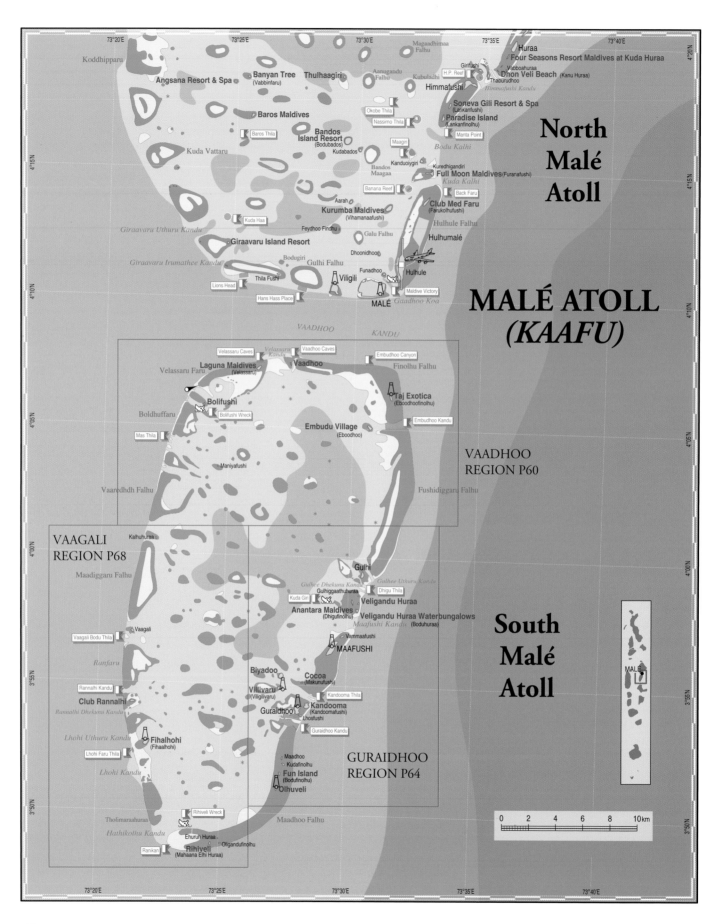

# Chapter 3 - South Malé Atoll Islands *(Kaafu)*

*South Malé Atoll is 36 km long and 19 km wide. There are 30 islands of which three are inhabited, 10 are uninhabited and 17 are resorts. The capital of the atoll is Maafushi. The atoll is separated from North Malé Atoll by the 4.5 km wide Vaadhoo Kandu. Transfers from the airport to the resorts are mostly by speedboat but some of the closer ones still use engine dhoanis. Rough seas can sometimes be experienced in the Vaadhoo Kandu.*

**Eboodhoofinolhu** is a long narrow island eight km from the airport. It opened as Embudhu Finolhu Island Resort in 1979. It is now called Taj Exotica Resort. An *Eboo* is a tasty berry found on many islands. It ripens all year on a prickly bush that grows to two metres. Eboodhoofinolhu has a big sandy lagoon ideal for watersports and a boat was sunk in the lagoon for divers.

*Embudu Village Resort and Embudhoo Kandu.*

**Eboodhoo** is a pear shaped island with a narrow lagoon and close-hugging reef that drops away to 20 metres or more onto the floor of the inner atoll. The reef is ideal for snorkelling with good coral cover and abundant reef fish. Embudhu Village started as a tourist resort in 1979.

**Fushidhiggaru Falhu** is a long reef that lies between Eboodhoo and Gulhi. It is the most eastern point of the atoll. During the rough seas of the north-east monsoon, the reef becomes virtually invisible and many unrecorded Maldivian ships and dhoanis have been wrecked here.

**Gulhi** is a very old, inhabited island renowned for its fishing. A *gulhu* is an earth pot used to carry three or four litres of water. It is the traditional means of carrying water on a dhoani. A mosque was built here during the reign of Sultan Mohammed Shamshuddeen III (1904 – 1934 AD). The island has a good entrance suitable for deep drafted boats and a shipyard and slipway has operated here since 1984. The island is, however,

surrounded by dangerous reefs which throw up unexpected waves during storms in the south-west monsoon. Boats coming to Gulhi or passing through Gulhee Dhekunu Kandu have been wrecked here. Several years ago a boat with a family of six went down here with many of them killed.

**Gulhiggaathuhuraa** is a small island that houses the machinery, boats and dive school for the resorts of Dhigufinolhu, Veligandu Huraa and Boduhuraa. It is connected by a long walkway to these islands.

**Dhigufinolhu** means long sandbar. The island is about 400 metres long and 60 metres wide and started as a tourist resort in 1981. It lies well inside the reef and is surrounded by a sandy beach and a big shallow lagoon, ideal for windsurfing. The resort is now called Anantara Maldives.

**Veligandu Huraa** means sand hill. In 1984 the island was transformed into a picturesque resort called Palm Tree Island. There is good diving and snorkelling on the outside reef.

*The islands of Dhigufinolhu (right foreground), Veligandu Huraa (left) and Boduhuraa .*

**Boduhuraa** opened as a resort in 1998 and is now called Veligandu Huraa Waterbungalows. It is the fourth island on the reef and is connected by walkway to Veligandu Huraa.

**Vammaafushi** is an uninhabited island.

**Maafushi** has been inhabited for a long time. It is a well known fishing island and the State Trading Organisation (STO) has a centre here. They buy dried tuna from the fishermen. *Lonumas* is tuna and reef fish that has been salted, then washed in salt water and dried in the sun. *Hikimas*, is tuna cut into four pieces and prepared firstly by boiling it for two to three hours in salt and fresh water. It is then smoked for a day before being dried hard in the sun. The island also has a prison on it.

**Makunufushi** is a long narrow island with a sand bar four times the length of the island extending from the eastern side. It has a shallow, clear lagoon on the southern side and deep water ideal for snorkelling on the northern side. This reclusive resort caters for up-market tourists and opened as Cocoa Island resort in 1981.

**Biyaadhoo** opened as Biyadoo Island Resort in 1982. It has an area of about 10 hectares and is so heavily treed that the bungalows, set in from the beach, can hardly be seen. It has a close fringing reef allowing convenient diving off the island. The island was previously inhabited, then deserted around 1830.

**Viligilivaru** opened as Villivaru Island Resort in 1981. It is the twin island of Biyaadhoo; similarly, heavily treed with a small lagoon. It has a long reef extending out to the south of the island. It was formerly inhabited but became uninhabited around 1830. Later, Biyaadhoo and Viligilivaru accomodated the sick and needy of the Maldives with the men being housed on Biyaadhoo and the women on Viligilivaru.

**Kandoomaafushi** means mangrove tree island. A *Kandoo* is a mangrove tree and *Maa* is a general term for flower (*finnifen maa* is the flower that produces rosewater.) *Maa* can also mean big. Kandooma Tourist Resort opened in 1985 and shares some exciting dive locations with its resort neighbours.

*Looking south at islands in South Malé Atoll.*

**Guraidhoo** is a very old island with a rich history. Guraa is a parrot. There are many isolated reefs in this area and a good knowledge of the intricate reef systems is required to navigate here. Guraidhoo lagoon offers dhoanis excellent protection from the north-east monsoon. It is a popular anchoring location for safari dhoanis because they can tie off at the beach allowing easy

access to the island. In the past, Guraidhoo was a popular resting place for sultans and during rebellion or outside invasion, sultans fled to the protection of this island. The 65th sultan, Hussain Faamuladeyri Kilagefannu (1609 – 1620 AD) was buried here. In 1971 a guest house catering for up to 35 people was opened on Guraidhoo but, like Himmafushi in North Malé Atoll, it was closed in 1984 because of the undesirable western influence on the local population. Today, more than 25 shops cater for the influx of tourists visiting the island from nearby resorts.

**Lhosfushi** is a small uninhabited island connected to Guraidhoo by a narrow landbridge which can be reached at low tide. Chickens run wild on the island. *Lhoss* is a lettuce tree (*Morindaefolia*).

**Maadhoo** lies at the north end of a big reef formation known as Maadhoo Falhu. This was once the biggest and most populated island in South Malé Atoll but has since been largely washed away and is now uninhabited.

**Kudafinolhu** is an uninhabited small sandbank.

**Bodufinolhu** is a larger island that opened as Fun Island Resort in 1980.

**Olhuveli** opened as a resort island in 1979. It was once inhabited and the second most populated island in South Malé Atoll. *Olhu* is a word used to describe a deeper place in the reef where boats can go in and out. *Veli* means sand so this could have referred to the sandy entrance allowing boats entry to the inner lagoon.

**Ehuruh Huraa** is an uninhabited island on the outside of the reef. It is appropriately called bird island because of the large number of herons and terns nesting there.

**Oligandufinolhu** is another uninhabited island called rising sun island. There was a fourth island nearby with coconut trees but it was washed away in 1983.

**Mahaana Elhi Huraa** means island of the grave. It opened as Rihiveli resort in 1983. It was at this island passing fishermen made a shrine at a site believed to have been the grave of another fisherman.

**Tholhimaraahuraa** is a reef that was once a small island, since washed away. It is renowned for fishing. *Tholhi* means long fish, such as trumpetfish, cornetfish, and barracuda and *maraa* means to be dead.

**Fihalhohi** was previously uninhabited and started as a resort in 1982. *Fiha* means to bake and being the last island in the south west of the atoll, the name is believed to have originated from fishermen cooking on the island before setting out on their westward journey to Ari Atoll.

**Rannalhi** opened as a resort in 1978. *Ran* means gold and *nalhi* means measure. In old times goods such as rice were measured by a nalhi, which was a rounded object, sometimes made of gold, weighing about 1kg. *Rah* also means island and it could be that the shape of this island resembled the shape of a nalhi.

Many of the islands in South Malé Atoll did not have coconut trees until the reign of Sultan Mohammed Shamshuddeen III (1903 – 1934 AD). At this time a powerful minister, Sayyidh Kilegefanu, who had a lease on North and South Malé Atolls, started planting coconut trees on many of the sandy islands, including Rannalhi. The trees were imported from Addu Atoll, which was renowned for the size and quality of its coconuts and the trees from Rannalhi are said to grow some of the biggest coconuts in the northern atolls.

**Vaagali** is an uninhabited island. *Vaa* means jungle and *gali* is branching coral and here the thickets of coral gave the island its name. It has a good anchorage in the shallow lagoon.

**Kalhuhuraa** was an uninhabited island now washed away. One old Maldivian said his father used to collect coconuts from the island 100 years ago. *Kalhu* means black and from this reef black coral is found.

**Maniyafushi** is classed as an uninhabited island but is now being used as a base for grouper exports.

**Bolifushi** opened as a resort in 1982. *Boli* means shell and it is believed that the money cowrie, for which the Maldives were famous, were harvested from here.

**Velassaru** was an uninhabited island before opening as a resort in 1974. It is now called Laguna Maldives.

**Vaadhoo** opened as a resort in 1978. This island has a rich history and was once much larger and inhabited by the original people of the Maldives. A temple and statues uncovered from the island ten years ago during building prove the people were Buddhist. The channel between Velassaru and Vaadhoo is the route by which many sailing boats coming from the south pass. In the past, ships passing through here lowered their foresail, or *thummathi*, as a signal of respect for the sultan. If the ship had square sails it lowered its top sail, or *tafaru*.

*Vaadhoo Kandu with depths to 25 metres*

## The Blessed Mahogany Log

One day a large mahogany log was washed onto the beach of a deserted island. The valuable log was found by fishermen who devised a plan to return at a later date and claim what was legally the sultan's property. The fishermen made an oath of secrecy and agreed to divide the log equally among themselves. A young boy looked on but was not included in the agreement.

They buried the log high on the beach and marked the place with a few stones. They left, vowing to return one day to collect the log and take it back to their island.

As the months passed, other fishermen, who stopped regularly at the island, noticed the stone markings high on the beach. Thinking the stones indicated the site of a grave, they placed little flags of decorated coconut palms on the grave to protect the owner on his long passage into the next world. Over time the grave became a shrine of sticks and flowers regularly tended by the passing fishermen.

Several years passed before the fishermen finally decided to return and collect the log. The young boy had since grown, but despite his protestations for a share in the bounty, he was overlooked and told that since he was only a boy when the log was found, he was not entitled to a share.

When the fishermen returned, they found the site carefully tended and covered in fresh flowers. They dug a deep hole and retrieved the log, then replaced the decorations as they were. The log was taken back to the fishermen's island where it was distributed.

In the meantime, the boy grew resentful and told the atoll chief of the mahogany log and, being a serious crime to cheat the sultan of his rightful possessions, the fishermen were rounded up and taken to Malé to answer the charges.

Representatives from the justice department were sent to the gravesite which they reluctantly dug up. No body was found, only a small branch of the mahogany log that was buried there. The fishermen were found guilty of their crime and the deserted island became known as Mahaana Elhi Huraa – the island of the grave – later to open as Rihiveli resort.

# Diving South Malé Atoll

*North and South Malé Atolls are separated by the Vaadhoo Kandu with a depth of 500 metres through which current streams can be very strong, attaining a rate of four knots or more. There are many popular dive sites with spectacular dropoffs and caves along both sides of this channel. South Malé Atoll has six channels on the eastern side, most of which provide excellent long drift dives, and 12 channels on the western side. There is one main channel – Velassaru Kandu – in the north and another – Hathikolhu Kandu – in the south. The eastern side of the atoll is characterised by two long reefs, the 14.5 km long Maadhoo Falhu and the 10.5 km long Fushidiggaru Falhu, which is the most easterly point of the atoll. Depths inside the atoll are mostly between 35 and 45 metres.*

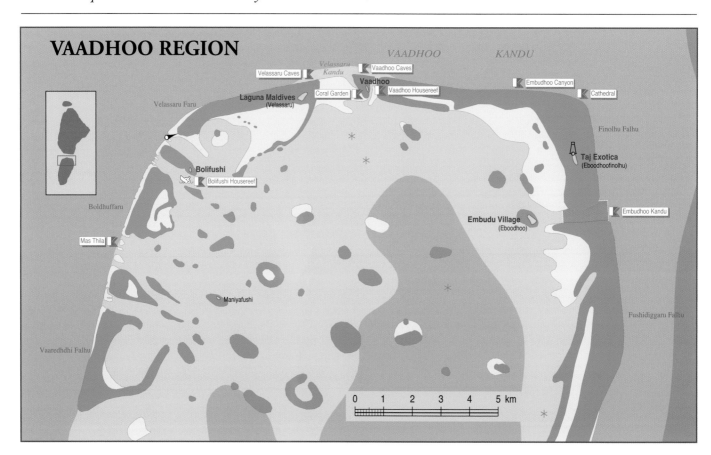

### Velassaru Caves ★★★

| | |
|---|---|
| Location: | north side of Velassaru |
| Depth: | 5m – 30m |
| Fish Life: | average |
| Coral Growth: | very good |
| Features: | caves, coral |

The caves are found directly to the north of Velassaru (Laguna Maldives) and range in depth from 15 to 32 metres. The caves cut into the vertical wall of the reef causing a jagged appearance, like the edge of a serrated knife. Some of the caves have sandy bottoms and make ideal resting places for sting rays, turtles and nurse sharks. A pleasant safety stop can be made on top of the reef in five metres where there is plenty of healthy hard coral.

### Vaadhoo Housereef ★★

The channel on the east side of Vaadhoo island is a popular dive with resort guests. The north east corner of Vaadhoo reef pushes out into the channel like the point of an arrow. At the channel entrance are many caves, with sharks and trevally outside, while inside the channel, is a more gently sloping reef to 20 metres with many morays, snapper and grouper.

There is a sandy bay 250 metres from the corner with coral rocks and stands of delicate branching acropora coral teeming with colourful fish life, including butterflyfish, moorish idol, blue-face angelfish and flame basslet. The reef alongside the resort is steep to 25 metres and is an ideal starting point for shore dives.

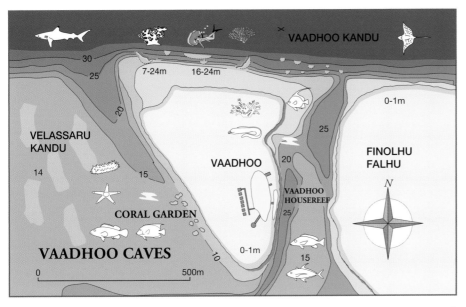

VAADHOO KANDU

30
25
7-24m    16-24m

20

VELASSARU
KANDU

14                    15

VAADHOO            20            0-1m

25

CORAL GARDEN

FINOLHU
FALHU

N

VAADHOO
HOUSEREEF

25

VAADHOO CAVES

10            0-1m

0            500m

15

*Yellow-margin triggerfish,* Pseudobalistes flavimarginatus. *Unlike the titan triggerfish, it is not aggressive.*

## Vaadhoo Caves ★★

| | |
|---|---|
| Location: | north side of Vaadhoo |
| Depth: | 3m – 30m+ |
| Fish life: | very good |
| Coral growth: | excellent |
| Features: | caves, eagle rays, gorgonians, coral |

The Vaadhoo Caves are similar to the Velassaru Caves, and are one of the most spectacular cave dive sites in South Malé Atoll. There is a string of caves along the steep wall of the Vaadhoo Kandu beginning with one big cave from seven to 25 metres

on the north west side of Vaadhoo reef. There is a long overhang at 30 metres and a narrow cave with a swim-through from 16 to 24 metres. There are more caves on the north east side of Vaadhoo reef.

## Coral Garden ★

The bungalows on the west side of Vaadhoo island overlook Coral Garden. It is an ideal site for novice divers or those seeking a more shallow and leisurely repetitive afternoon dive. The reef is covered in a dense layer of coral down to 12 metres before levelling off to the sandy

base of the channel. The fine display of hard coral attracts numerous reef fish that dart in and out of the branching coral. On the sandy base are many yellow-margin triggerfish. They nest during the full moon period and when nesting they are spaced about 15 metres apart. On the reef slopes are titan triggerfish. They have their own territory which they guard ferociously during the breeding period.

**Diving hints:** If a titan triggerfish approaches too close, flick your fin at it.

*Titan triggerfish,* Balistoides viridescens. *Also called the dotty triggerfish, the titan is easily identified by its strong teeth and distinctive white 'glass eye' that stealthily examines divers in its territory. The titan usually nests along the reef slope and will not hesitate to attack divers. When aggressive it displays a dorsal spine which can be locked in the upright position. The titan is often seen crunching its powerful teeth into coral heads, breaking off pieces to get to tasty tube worms. The titan is considered good eating by Maldivians and is seen in the fish market skinned with its disquieting fang-like teeth still exposed. It is widely used in 'fandita' charms because when it is taken from the water it takes a long time to die and has an aura of immortality about it.*

*Octopus can instantly change colour to simulate the reef environment.*

*Spiky soft coral and gorgonian sea fans live on drop-offs and slopes.*

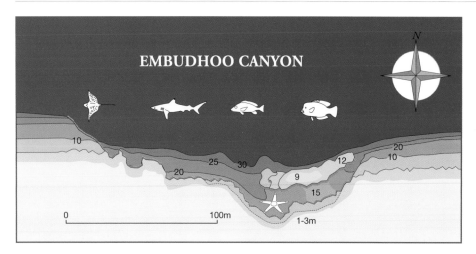

EMBUDHOO CANYON

*Two-colour parrotfish, Cetoscarus bicolor. Parrotfish begin life as females and are mostly dull coloured before turning into males and adopting a brighter colour. The juveniles of this species are mostly white with a red stripe. Adults graze the reef in small groups of say ten mixing with other species in the shallows at high tide. At night they sleep in a mucous cocoon among the coral.*

## Embudhoo Canyon ★★

| | |
|---|---|
| Location: | north side of Embudhu Finolhu |
| Depth: | 10m – 30m |
| Fish life: | above average |
| Coral growth: | very good |
| Features: | canyon, sharks, eagle rays |

A large chunk of rock looks to have fallen out of the reef leaving a vast canyon 50 metres long with caves and overhangs. Divers can begin upcurrent from the canyon and drift in the deep blue waters of the Vaadhoo Kandu – sometimes among eagle rays, napoleon and sharks – before gliding into the narrow canyon at 20 metres. The top of the rock is at nine metres while the main reef rises to five metres. The bottom of the canyon peaks at 15 metres in the middle. On the main reef is a long cave protected from the currents and full of marine life. There are more caves and overhangs on the outside at 30 metres. Black snapper and black jack are seen here. If the current is not too strong it is worth circling the rock at different depths to explore all its features. This is an unforgettable dive and one of the highlights of South Malé Atoll.

## Cathedral ★★★

Located in the Vaadhoo Kandu near the Embudhu Finolhu channel marker is a section of reef 150 metres long that undercuts itself creating a dome-like structure from which its name is derived. The reef looks more like a wave, with the lip at 10 metres and the base at between 25 and 33 metres, before dropping away into the deep Vaadhoo Kandu. The long, hollow cavern is awe-inspiring and divers can 'surf' the cathedral when the current is running. Tuna, eagle rays, morays and turtles share this reef with divers.

*Juvenile two-colour parrotfish, Cetoscarus bicolor.*

*Black jack, Caranx lugubris.*

*Right: Giant moray eel, Gymnothorax javanicus. Maintains a territory among the coral, living in holes and crevices that it will defend if provoked. Morays are seen continuously opening and closing their mouths to force water over their gills. This is also an invitation for cleaner shrimp, Stenopus hispidus, and blue-streak cleaner wrasse, Labroides dimidiatus, to come inside to clean out waste and parasites. Morays have large central teeth useful for tearing the flesh of its prey. They feed mostly at night but have poor eyesight, relying more on smell to guide them to fish and invertebrates.*

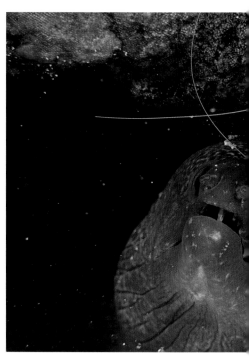

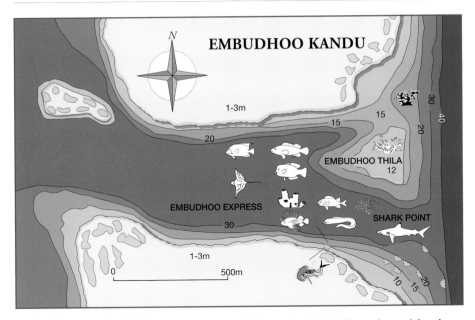

EMBUDHOO KANDU

soft coral decorates the reef plateau. A ledge and small cave lie on the south side of the thila. Reef fish abound in large numbers and this site is suitable for beginners if the current is favourable. Sharks are also present on the outside of the thila.

Most of the channels in north west South Malé Atoll are relatively shallow with one or more thilas at the entrances. At **Mas Thila** ★★ there are many small caves and sharks and trevally and at **Bolifushi Housereef** ★★ is the wreck of a nine metre fibreglass yacht which attracts white-tip reef sharks, napoleon, triggerfish, remoras and eagle rays.

*Snout-spot grouper,* Epinephelus polyphekadion. *The juvenile of this species has two distinct black spots under the eyes. It is found around caves and wrecks and can become very tame.*

*Embudhoo Kandu Cave*

### Embudhoo Kandu ★★★
PROTECTED MARINE AREA

| | |
|---|---|
| Location: | first channel south of Embudhu Finolhu resort |
| Depth: | 5m – 30m |
| Fish life: | above average |
| Coral growth: | very good |
| Features: | coral, reef fish, sharks, caves |

The entire Embudhoo channel has been declared a protected marine area. The south side of the channel is an exhilarating two km long drift dive known as **Embudhoo Express**. With an ingoing current, the express steams ahead at full throttle, giving divers the ride of a lifetime. Predictably, currents at the channel entrance attract a range of pelagics, large napoleon and eagle rays. The south corner is sometimes called **Shark Point** after the grey reef sharks seen here. There are many small caves on the corner and a couple of long shallow overhangs between 14 and 30 metres. Under the overhangs are numerous snout-spot grouper. These fish are also called smalltooth grouper and brown-marbled grouper. They are well camouflaged and lie in wait for prey swimming in too close to the ledges. Inside the channel is one huge cave between five and 25 metres with a swim-through at 11 metres. Many dives start on the outside reef and finish around this cave. It is worth checking out the marine life inside. It is rich in seafans and sponges and attracts large morays, angelfish, octopus, lionfish and squirrelfish.

### Embudhoo Thila ★★ (Coral Garden)
Embudhoo thila is a beautiful underwater reef on the north corner of Embudhoo Kandu. The reef top is between 12 and 15 metres and a splendid display of hard and

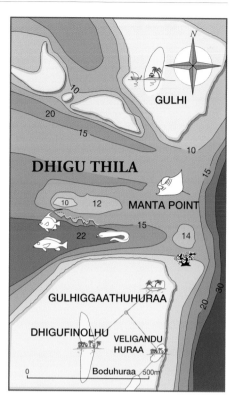

the channel. On the north and south sides of the thila there is sand on the bottom that levels out at 20 to 25 metres. On the south side is a wall with overhangs and caves between 15 and 20 metres. There is a rich display of soft coral on the reef and seafans in the caves. Fish life on the thila is prolific with large schools of basslet and snapper and aggregations of bannerfish and sweetlip.

The trough between the thila and Dhigufinolhu reef rises from 25 metres on the inside to 14 metres near the corner. In outgoing currents, this creates a funnelling effect that sweeps up nutrients and zooplankton making favourable feeding conditions for mantas. Divers often refer to this place as **Manta Point**.

**Diving hints:** There are many ways to dive this channel depending on the current. If the current is not too strong, divers can venture across the entire entrance and because the channel is not deep they can finish their dive midway if running low on air. The thila can be dived separately or with Manta Point. If the mantas are about then this channel provides plenty of entertainment.

### Dhigu Thila ★★★ (Bushy Thila)

| | |
|---|---|
| Location: | Gulhee Dhekunu Kandu |
| Depth: | 10m – 25m |
| Fish life: | above average |
| Coral growth: | very good |
| Features: | mantas |

This long thila lies in the middle of Gulhee Dhekunu Kandu. The entrance across the face of the channel is flat and shallow with depths around 15 metres or less. The thila runs east – west, rising to around 10 metres at the western end. The eastern end joins the shallow entrance to

## Miyaru Faru ★★

The southern end of Fushidhiggaru Falhu is known for its sharks, which gives the reef its name. On the corner are overhangs at 17 metres and a sand bottom at 20 metres. With an ingoing current white-tip and grey reef sharks, eagle rays, napoleon and sometimes hammerhead sharks can be seen on the corner.

## Kuda Giri Wreck ★★

This steel wreck is located on the south west side of a small reef west of Dhigufinolhu. It lies upright between 20 and 35 metres. It is an excellent reef for beginners and night divers.

## Maafushi Caves ★★

There is one spectacular cave on the north side of a small reef between Maafushi and Dhigufinolhu. Its opening is on the reef top at five metres and the cave drops through the reef to an opening at 20 metres. Eagle rays are often seen here. Great photos.

## Cocoa Corner ★★

The north side of Biyaadhoo Kandu has many caves and overhangs near the corner between five to 20 metres. The channel wall is steep – at one point it is undercut from five to 20 metres – whereas the outside reef corner slopes more gently. The channel is quite deep, descending to 40 metres. Inside the channel 200 metres from the corner, is a large outcrop of reef 20 metres long at a depth of 30 metres. Turtles frequent the reef, as well as surgeon and black snapper.

*Kuda Giri wreck.*

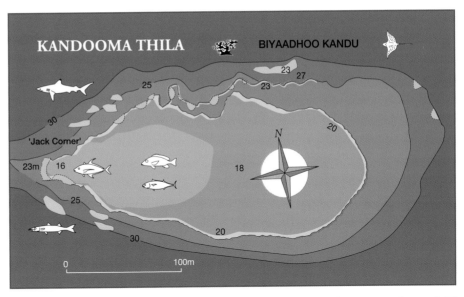

KANDOOMA THILA — BIYAADHOO KANDU

'Jack Corner'

100m

## Kandooma Thila ★★★★ (Ran Thila)

| | |
|---|---|
| Location: | Biyaadhoo Kandu |
| Depth: | 16m – 30m |
| Fish life: | abundant |
| Coral growth: | very good |
| Features: | pelagics, reef formation, soft coral, sharks |

Shaped like a teardrop, this 300 metre long thila is nothing to cry about. It is one of the most exciting dives in South Malé Atoll and boasts great scenery as well as prolific fish life. The west and north sides are the most spectacular, with the top at 16 metres. The reef top at the east end drops away to 20 metres, making it a challenging dive for experienced divers only.

At 'Jack Corner', there is a cave at 23 metres with soft coral but the main feature here are the dense schools of big-eye trevally and snapper. Sometimes there are dog-toothed tuna and barracuda.

There are several large outcrops of rock near the west corner on the north side covered in bright soft corals. These are a focal point for black snapper, blue-fin jack, eagle rays, and sharks. On the reef edge there are caves at 23 metres and overhangs full of interesting marine life.

**Diving hints:** If the current is flowing out of the atoll then timing is critical if divers want to begin at Jack Corner. Divers may have to begin their dive well upcurrent

making a quick descent to the reef. If depth is limited to 25 metres, then sufficient bottom time can be obtained to explore all the major features of the reef. The further east along the thila divers go, the deeper the reef edge and caves become. Currents can be very strong so it is essential a safety balloon is carried for making open water safety stops.

## Kandooma Caves ★★

One of the underwater marvels of the Maldives are the huge caves on the reef corner near Kandooma island. They are among the largest caverns to be found in the tourist atolls. Just 50 metres from the corner are two huge caves close to one another; one is at 20 metres with a hole in the roof at 10 metres; the other is at a depth of 16 metres. The 16 metre cave is about 70 metres long and has a curly overhang blocking out much of the light inside. Take a torch! Inside are yellow sponges, seafans and small tube corals and very often giant morays.

Further inside the channel are overhangs and another two caves, one of which starts at 10 metres and has a hole in the top at three metres. There are many grouper and squirrelfish to be found in the caves and along the reef are clown triggerfish, napoleon, sweetlip and angelfish.

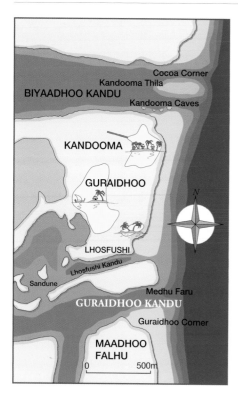

### Guraidhoo Kandu
#### PROTECTED MARINE AREA

The entire Guraidhoo channel, between Guraidhoo Faru and Maadhoo Falhu has been declared a Protected Marine Area. There are in fact two channels, Lhosfushi Kandu and Guraidhoo Kandu, separated in the middle by a reef known as Medhu Faru. The channel has an intricate reef system with many diving alternatives. It is one of the premier diving locations in the Maldives and the focus of plenty of diving activity in South Malé Atoll.

### Lhosfushi Kandu ★★

The channel on the north side of Medhu Faru has a very shallow, narrow sandy entrance 10 metres wide at a depth of five metres such that if you blink, you miss it. The channel deepens inside to a sandy bottom to 30 metres. There is plenty of fish life inside including gobies, butterflyfish, schools of snapper, fusilier, tuna, napoleon and white-tip reef sharks. There are also large morays, and during the south-west monsoon there are manta rays. Another regular visitor is a guitar shark.

### Sandune ★

This is an adjoining reef one kilometre inside Lhohifushi Kandu with an undulating sandy bottom around 15 metres on the north side. Mantas are also known to frequent this reef.

### Medhu Faru ★★★

The south side of Medhu Faru has many impressive features making it one of the most scenic drift dives in the atoll. With an ingoing current, divers can start on the outside reef where a long ledge at 30 metres sweeps round the corner into Guraidhoo Kandu. Visibility is usually very good with an ingoing current and with wavering seafans springing out from the ledge, soft coral in abundance and big fish – sharks, barracuda and napoleon – in the open ocean, this is a sensational start to an exhilarating dive.

Near the corner, the wall of the channel becomes more steep and the current accelerates through the pass. A large rock draped in soft coral lies near the corner forming a small canyon at 18 metres. Sharks, trevally, tuna and fusilier congregate here.

*Red bass*, Lutjanus bohar. *From the snapper family. The juvenile in this photo shows two light spots which become visible in dull light. Feeds on fish and crustaceans and grows to 50 cm.*

The channel floor is at 35 metres and at 10 to 15 metres, there are caves and ledges well worth a visit. One big overhang cuts through the reef from three to 30 metres. A sandy bay 250 metres inside the channel is a good starting point for a dive with an outgoing current.

**Diving hints:** Strong outgoing currents can be dangerous at Medhu Faru because of currents sweeping through both Guraidhoo and Lhosfushi Kandu, pushing divers away from the outside reef. Stay shallow on the outside corner at these times.

*Spotted eagle ray*, Aetobatus narinari. *The well defined shape of the beak gives the eagle ray its name. It has a longer and more whip-like tail than the sting ray, but still has a serrated, venomous spine on the upper side at the base of the tail. It has sharply pointed wings that can grow up to 130 cm across. The spotted eagle ray is a strong graceful swimmer that feeds on molluscs and crustaceans.*

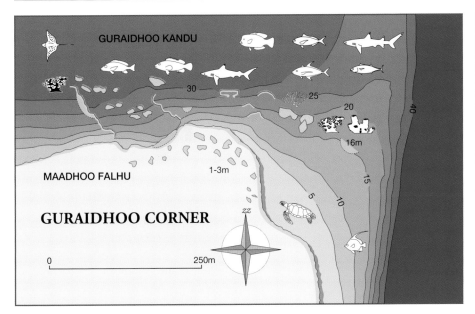

GURAIDHOO KANDU

30

25

20

16m

1-3m

MAADHOO FALHU

**GURAIDHOO CORNER**

40

15

5

10

0                    250m

*Dog-toothed tuna,* Gymnosarda unicolor.

**Guraidhoo Corner ★★★**

| | |
|---|---|
| Location: | south side of Guraidhoo Kandu |
| Depth: | 3m – 30m |
| Fish life: | abundant |
| Coral growth: | very good |
| Features: | sharks, eagle rays, napoleon, reef fish |

With either an outgoing or ingoing current, Guraidhoo Corner promises a unique diving opportunity for viewing a wide range of fish life. The outside reef has many reef fish including schooling bannerfish, which always inhabit the same area, as well as turtles and many species of grouper.

Near the corner, big schools of fusilier, rainbow runner, tuna and trevally congregate, while on the corner at 25 metres, grey reef sharks and snapper prey on fish. A large tame napoleon has become an identity on both sides of the channel and is quick to track down divers. A long cave with fans, sponges and soft coral at 16 metres on the corner is a quiet refuge, not only for cave-dwelling fish, but for divers seeking a break from the currents.

Inside the channel, a series of caves and overhangs occur at 10 metres while below are numerous outcrops of reef. At one point inside the channel is a huge overhang descending from the reef top at five metres

to over 30 metres. With an outgoing current, a school of eagle rays often hover around the overhang at 20 metres. Along the bottom of the channel at 35 metres are white-tip reef sharks. Divers never get bored at this site and each dive is full of new discoveries and surprises.

**Diving hints:** Currents can be troublesome through this channel and dives may

have to be aborted during spring tides. With a strong ingoing current divers may find themselves being pushed onto the reef top at the corner in which case it is better to stay below 15 metres. A whirlpool effect dragging divers up and down occurs near the big overhang. Stay close to the reef at these times. With strong outgoing currents start well inside the channel and take care not to dive too deep, especially on the corner, as currents will drag divers outside making it difficult to return to the reef.

*Napoleonfish,* Cheilinus undulatus. *Also called the giant maori wrasse because of the scribbled line patterns on its head reminiscent of Moari warriors. The juvenile has no hump on its head but develops one as it gets older. A large fish that can protrude its mouth.*

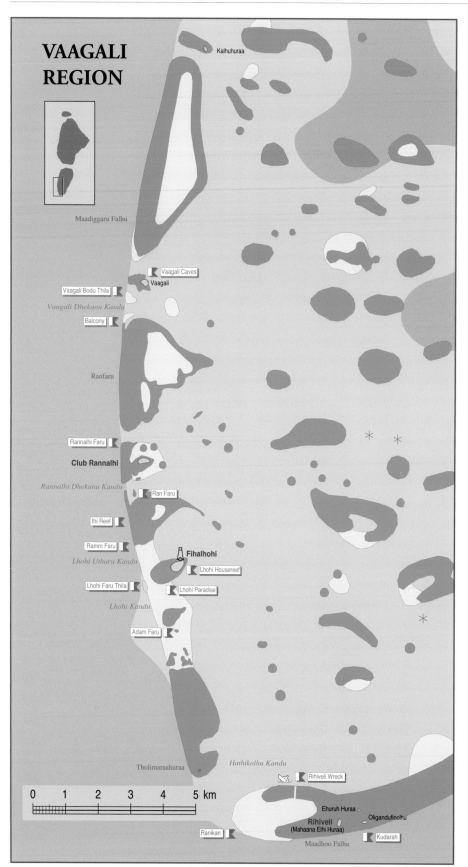

# VAAGALI REGION

Kalhuhuraa

Maadiggaru Falhu

Vaagali Caves
Vaagali

Vaagali Bodu Thila
*Vaagali Dhekunu Kandu*

Balcony

Ranfaru

Rannalhi Faru

**Club Rannalhi**

*Rannalhi Dhekunu Kandu*

Ran Faru

Ihi Reef

Ramm Faru
*Lhohi Uthuru Kandu*

**Fihalhohi**

Lhohi Housereef

Lhohi Faru Thila

Lhohi Paradise

*Lhohi Kandu*

Adam Faru

Tholimaraahuraa          *Hathikolhu Kandu*

Rihiveli Wreck

Ehuruh Huraa
Oligandufinolhu

**Rihiveli**
(Mahaana Elhi Huraa)

Ranikan                                         Kudarah

Maadhoo Falhu

| 0 | 1 | 2 | 3 | 4 | 5 km |

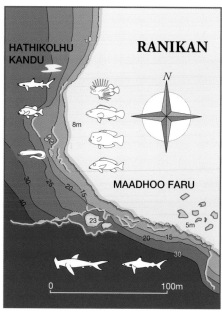

HATHIKOLHU KANDU          **RANIKAN**

N

8m

30
26
20
15
40

23
20                      5m
15
30

MAADHOO FARU

| 0 | | | 100m |

### Ranikan ★★★

| | |
|---|---|
| Location: | western point of Maadhoo Falhu |
| Depth: | 5m – 30m |
| Fish life: | above average |
| Coral growth: | very good |
| Features: | sharks, napoleon, sweetlip, over-hangs |

The eastern side of the 2.5 km wide Hathikolhu Kandu is marked by a large rock at 23 metres with caves peeling across the channel entrance to over 40 metres. Hammerhead sharks have been seen here along with grey reef sharks. There are a number of black cheek morays on the top of this rock so take care if holding the rock to view the sharks! To the north of this rock are superb ledges and small caves at around 10 metres with delicate coral and many species of grouper and lionfish. Inside the channel is a barren patch of reef 50 metres long. However, past this patch, the coral and ledges return and there is a small cave at 15 metres that is a den for white-tip reef sharks. Outside the cave on the sandy bottom at 20 to 25 metres are numerous white-tips and a school of oriental sweetlip. A family of napoleon, with as many as five juveniles, swim close to divers. At ledges around 15 metres are angelfish, snapper and leaf fish. This site has great variety in marine life and is a delightful dive with the right conditions.

**Diving hints:** Currents usually flow south out of the atoll and currents can become quite swift, so a quick descent to the protection of the reef edge is desirable.

**Rihiveli Wreck:** The entire eastern side of Hathikolhu Kandu is a popular destination for Rihiveli divers. On the south side of the Rihiveli entrance in 15 metres, is a small steel wreck sunk by the resort.

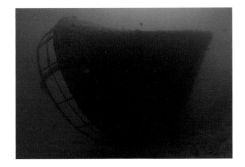

### Kudarah ★★

On the outside reef near the small island of Oligandufinolhu is an ocean dive with the reef wall sloping from three to 30 metres. Another reef further out runs parallel to the wall and in between is a sand bottom at 30 metres. The top of this long outer reef is 25 metres and on the outside is a steep dropoff. Big fish and sharks are seen here.

### Lhohi Faru Thila ★★★

There are a number of thilas near Fihalhohi on the outer rim of the atoll. Lhohi Faru Thila is a long thila with the top at 10 metres and caves at 30 metres on the outside. Large napoleon are a feature at this reef.

### Adam Faru ★

A popular reef for beginners with depths between five and 20 metres. It comprises several large flat patches of reef surrounded by sand channels. There are many sweetlip here.

### Lhohi Housereef ★

An easy shallow, sand dive for beginners with a reef slope from one to 15 metres. Two female sting rays, Dumbo and Carmen, have been trained to accept food from divers. They are a major attraction at the resort.

Oriental sweetlip, Plectorhynchus orientalis, *and blue-streak cleaner wrasse. Oriental sweetlip favour reef habitats usually where caves are available but are seen in small aggregations on the reef slope. Sweetlip are also called grunts because of clearly audible sounds which are amplified by their air-filled bladder.*

### Lhohi Paradise ★

On the south side of Fihalhohi is an easy beginner's dive with a maximum depth of 20 metres. Small patches of reef occur on the sandy bottom and they are inundated with smaller fish like cardinalfish, basslet, damselfish and bullseye. Fish like humpback snapper, pufferfish, clown triggerfish and trevally make this dive a worthy location.

### Ramm Faru ★★

On the north side of Lhohi Uthuru Kandu is Ramm Faru, which has coral rocks rising to 15 metres. Morays and lionfish are found here.

### Ihi Reef ★★

This location lies further north on the outside reef. In Dhivehi ihi means lobster. There are several caves at 15 metres.

### Ran Faru ★★

In the channel south of Rannalhi is a reef with the best diving between 10 and 25 metres. Fish life is diverse and includes eagle rays, mantas in the north-east monsoon season, white-tip reef sharks, nurse sharks, and tuna.

*Black cheek moray,* Gymnothorax breedeni. *A smaller more aggressive moray which lives in holes sometimes emerging to bite the hand of divers who get too close. The moray's bite is not poisonous but the wound can become easily infected since the teeth are inevitably contaminated with decayed food particles. The greatest damage is done if the hand is pulled out of the mouth. If left still, the moray usually opens its mouth and departs, leaving a few punctures. Divers should take care before grasping coral to check for morays. Young morays in particular often withdraw into their holes and emerge to bite when threatened.*

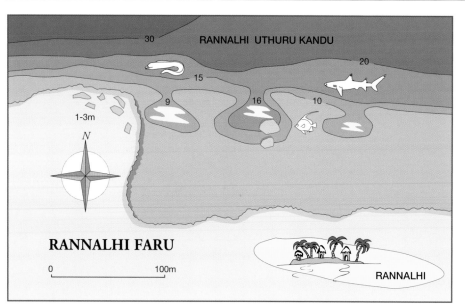

**RANNALHI FARU**

0       100m

RANNALHI

The thila is 250 metres wide with the best diving on the northern end, where there are many caves and overhangs between 15 and 30 metres. One big cave at 26 metres is full of soft coral, seawhips and black coral bushes and is a refuge for squirrelfish, snapper and sweetlip. There are turtles, schools of fusilier, large napoleon and massive coral at 15 metres teeming with bannerfish and featherstars. The western wall is long and steep while the eastern wall slopes gently with some caves and good fish life.

## Vaagali Caves ★★

On the north side of Vaagali divers can start with an outgoing current at the anchorage and drift around the cave-studded reef. Most caves are between 10 and 18 metres and many are rich in sponges and black coral bushes with oyster clams. Two caves have swim-throughs and there is very good coral on the reef.

## Rannalhi Faru ★★

| | |
|---|---|
| Location: | north side of Rannalhi |
| Depth: | 3m – 25m |
| Fish life: | above average |
| Coral growth: | very good |
| Features: | underwater landscape |

On the north side of Rannalhi Faru, the reef juts into Rannalhi Uthuru Kandu and drops steadily from one to 30 metres with good coral, many triggerfish, sharks and morays. Inside the channel, the top reef turns south leaving behind some interesting terrain between 10 and 15 metres with a series of sandy bays scattered among the reef.

## Balcony ★★

On the north side of Ranfaru is a viewing platform at about 24 metres that features sharks, eagle rays, barracuda and a school of napoleon. Balcony is an extension of the reef into Vaagali Dhekunu Kandu and drops in steps from three to 24 metres.

The entire reef around the island of Vaagali has very good diving. There is a secure bay for anchoring on the north east side and night diving here is excellent, with many coral rocks on the sand at 20 metres near the sheltered entrance to the bay.

## Vaagali Bodu Thila ★★

| | |
|---|---|
| Location: | south side of Vaagali |
| Depth: | 5m – 30m |
| Fish life: | above average |
| Coral growth: | very good |
| Features: | caves, reef fish |

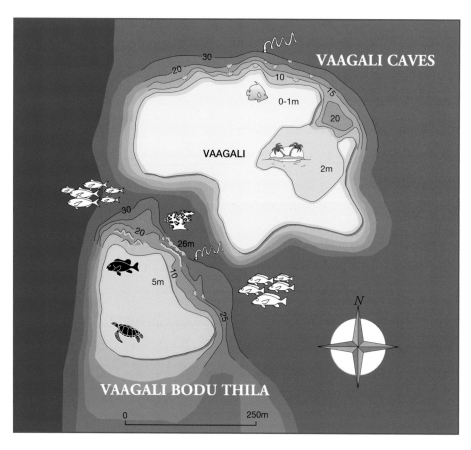

VAAGALI CAVES

VAAGALI

**VAAGALI BODU THILA**

0       250m

# Freedivers of the Maldives

Long before the introduction of diving equipment to the Maldives, fishermen were free-diving to well in excess of 30 metres to retrieve lost anchors, cargo from wrecked vessels, baitfish and pearl shell.

Young men learning to dive discovered that the deeper they went, the greater the pain in their forehead and ears became. The valsalva method of equalising was not practised by Maldivians. Instead, when pain was felt in their air spaces while descending, they clenched a fist and banged their forehead to relieve the pressure. The term *kamalhifalhun* was used to descibe this method.

Divers were often unable to equalise and sometimes surfaced with blood streaming from their noses. Bleeding was regarded as a rite of passage into the adult world of deep diving. The occasion was carried throughout their lives, much like today's divers carry a certification card.

The depth that a diver could go was most important to the diving dhoani captain. He wanted only those who could go deep. To determine which divers went deepest, each diver was given a white cloth to wear around his waist. Since there were no depth metres, depth was determined by visibility. The deeper the diver went, the less of the white cloth could be seen. Those judged by the captain as going the deepest were selected to join the next diving expedition.

Black coral and pearl shell diving was carried out by four or five divers in an eight metre dhoani. This was steadily rowed along the reef edge until they could see coral trees below in the clear, calm seas. If the sea became choppy, then coconut oil was spilled into the water to improve visibility at the surface. Mostly divers worked in the calmer months, not June or July.

When a large piece of black coral eight to ten centimetres thick was found, the first diver carried a rope from the surface and tied it to the stem of the bush before surfacing. A second diver then used the rope to descend quickly to the bush and begin cutting. Sometimes a third or fourth diver would repeat the procedure until the coral tree was cut free and pulled to the surface. Divers continued with this method, staying under the water for long periods.

Pearl shell grows on black coral trees, and some trees have as many as 15 or 20 shells growing on them. It takes on average 50 or 60 shells to produce one pearl and the pearl is found by carefully sifting through the meat of the shell. Before bringing the tree and pearl shell to the surface, divers used to place the tree in a hessian bag. If the tree was too big then hessian was wrapped around the base of the tree.

Divers believed that if they did not use the hessian on the trees then the shells would spit out their valuable pearl. Pearls are used not only for decorating rings and broaches but for medicinal purposes. When used as medicine, pearls are put in a container and melted over a fire. The grey residue remaining is used as a herbal medicine for heart patients and people with mental illness.

Diving for baitfish without the aid of masks or fins, was sometimes dangerous work. The baitfish most sought after by fishermen is called *boadhi* and is used to catch tuna and bonito. To catch this baitfish, fishermen lay a square carpet of coconut fibre much like a cricket pitch, called a *madhuri*, onto the ocean floor near a reef. A diver then swam down with a handful of smelly fish, known as *filimas* and placed it on the carpet to attract the baitfish. The diver was also required to check if the baitfish were feeding and to instruct the fishermen when to pull up the carpet.

Divers handling smelly fish are vulnerable to attack from sharks lurking near the reef and stories of encounters with sharks are legendary. When diving in areas where sharks were found, divers carried palm leaves into the water to wave at sharks if threatened. Often, because the diver was not wearing a mask, he would not see the shark coming.

Diving for anchors has always been an important task for the divers. When the Indians from Bombay were busy trading in the Maldives in the 1940s, they came in their baggalas laden with cargo, anchoring in the waters of Malé's outer harbour. Occasionally an anchor became stuck on the reef or an anchor rope broke in a storm and the anchor was lost. Water in the outer harbour is up to 50 metres deep. If a good diver was not to be found in Malé then a message was despatched to Faadhippolhu Atoll – an atoll renowned for its divers – for the services of a diver to recover the anchor.

Today, scuba gear is used by many islanders to collect products of the sea, but it is refreshing to see traditional baitfish collecting methods still employed in the outer atolls with the skill of bait divers remaining an integral part of the fishing process.

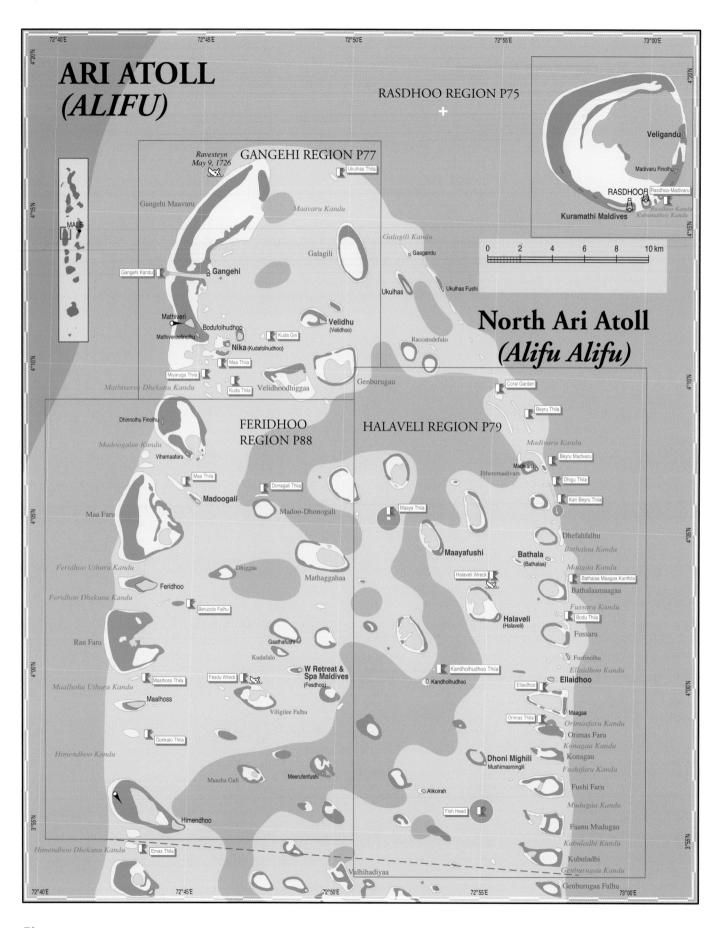

# ARI ATOLL
## *(ALIFU)*

RASDHOO REGION P75

MALE

GANGEHI REGION P77

*Ravesteyn*
*May 9, 1726*

Ukulhas Thila

Veligandu

Madivaru Finolhu

RASDHOO   Rasdhoo-Madivaru

Kuramathi Maldives   Rasdhoo Kandu
                     *Kuramathee Kandu*

Gangehi Maavaru

*Maavaru Kandu*

Galagili

*Galagili Kandu*

Gaagandu

Ukulhas

Ukulhas Fushi

Gangehi Kandu

**Gangehi**

Mathiveri

Bodufolhudhoo

Mathivereefinolhu

Kuda Giri

**Velidhu**
(Velidhoo)

Raccatudefalo

0   2   4   6   8   10 km

# North Ari Atoll
## *(Alifu Alifu)*

**Nika** (Kudafolhudhoo)

Maa Thila

Miyaruga Thila

Kuda Thila

Velidhoodhiggaa

Genburugau

Coral Garden

Beyru Thila

*Mathiveree Dhekunu Kandu*

Dhinnolhu Finolhu

FERIDHOO
REGION P88

HALAVELI REGION P79

*Madivaru Kandu*

*Madoogalee Kandu*

Vihamaafaru

Madivaru

Beyru Madivaru

Etheremadivaru

Dhigu Thila

Maa Thila

Donagali Thila

Kari Beyru Thila

**Madoogali**

Madoo-Dhonogali

Maaya Thila

Dhefahfalhu

*Bathalaa Kandu*

Maa Faru

*Maagaa Kandu*

**Maayafushi**

**Bathala**
(Bathalaa)

Bathalaa Maagaa Kanthila

*Feridhoo Uthuru Kandu*

Dhiggaa

Mathaggahaa

Halaveli Wreck

Bathalaamaagaa

*Fussaru Kandu*

Bodu Thila

**Feridhoo**

*Feridhoo Dhekunu Kandu*

**Halaveli**
(Halaveli)

Fussaru

Fustinolhu

Berucolo Falhu

Ran Faru

Gaathafushi

Kudafalo

*Ellaidhoo Kandu*

Kandholhudhoo Thila

**Ellaidhoo**

Maalhoss Thila

Fesdu Wreck

**W Retreat &
Spa Maldives**
(Fesdhoo)

Kandholhudhoo

Ellaidhoo

Maagaa

*Orimasfaru Kandu*

**Maalhoss**

Viligilee Falhu

Orimas Thila

Orimas Faru

*Maalhohu Uthuru Kandu*

*Konagaa Kandu*

Donkalo Thila

**Dhoni Mighili**
Mushimasmingili

Konagau

*Fushifaru Kandu*

Fushi Faru

*Himendhoo Kandu*

Maasha Gali

Meerufenfushi

Alikoirah

*Mudugaa Kandu*

Fish Head

Faanu Mudugau

*Kubuladhi Kandu*

**Himendhoo**

Kubuladhi

*Genburugau Kandu*

*Himendhoo Dhekunu Kandu*

Emas Thila

Valhihadiyaa

Genburugaa Falhu

# Chapter 4 - North Ari Atoll Islands *(Alifu Alifu)*

*For administrative purposes, Ari Atoll is divided into North Ari Atoll (Alifu Alifu) which includes Rasdhoo Atoll and the tiny atoll of Thoddoo, and South Ari Atoll (Alifu Dhaalu). The capital of North Ari Atoll is Rasdhoo and South Ari Atoll is Mahibadhoo. There are a total of 70 islands in Ari Atoll and many sand banks, some of which are becoming islands while others are being washed away. Rasdhoo Atoll is nine km in diameter while Ari is 96 km long by 33 km wide. There are a total of 18 inhabited islands in Ari Atoll. There are a further 52 uninhabited islands of which 26 are resorts. The principal occupation of Ari Atoll islanders used to be catching turtles, weaving sails, coral collecting and coral carving but they are good fishermen and are traditionally renowned for their shark catching to produce oil for the timbers of dhoanis. Their shark catching traditions are still strong and often at odds with divers who wish to keep the sharks in the water. Coconut production of the atoll is also high. Many islanders now turn to the resorts for employment. Resort development escalated in the early 1990s and has now peaked. No more resorts are expected to be constructed in the atoll.*

**Thoddoo** is a remote island 11 km north of Rasdhoo Atoll. It lies on a tiny atoll two km in diameter and is surrounded by water over 200 metres deep. *Thoddoo* is a Sinhalese word meaning island on the big reef. It is famous for its watermelon and vegetable growing as well as betel leaf and chillies. The people are regarded as well educated, many of them holding government positions. Traditional entertainment and dancing are popular pastimes. The remains of a Buddhist Dhagaba was excavated in 1958 and a statue of a Buddha was found. The Buddha's head is now in the museum in Malé. Several other mounds exist and are yet to be excavated.

**Veligandu** began as a resort in 1984.

**Madivaru Finolhu** is a small sandbank now almost gone.

**Rasdhoo-Madivaru** is uninhabited but was once quite big until most of the island was washed away. *Rasdhoo* means the first or beginning island and *Madi* means ray. Rasdhoo Kandu is well known for its manta rays but better known for its scalloped hammerhead sharks. From as far back as the local islanders remember, Rasdhoo Madivaru has been famous for its 'headsharks'. The fishermen occasionally caught the shark on their lines but the headshark was difficult to catch. The fishermen believe there is a big cave deep down where the sharks live. The water outside the atoll is deep and no one has disproved the story.

**Rasdhoo** is a very old inhabited island with Buddhist origins. It is the administrative island for North Ari Atoll but was formerly the administrative centre for the whole of the atoll.

**Kuramathi** is two km long and 500 metres wide. It became uninhabited in 1970 when the population of 124 settled on Rasdhoo. Kuramathi Tourist Resort started in 1977. It was the first resort in Ari Atoll and began as a diving camp with 12 bungalows. It now has over 250 rooms divided into three parts of the island. There is Kuramathi Village at the south east corner, the Blue Lagoon, and the Kuramathi Cottage Club. The resort is now called Kuramathi Maldives. The island has a rich history and excavations carried out in 1988 revealed a large area was formerly occupied as a Buddhist monastery. Relics were uncovered and many graves found.

On May 29, 1868, the 965 tonne iron ship *Reindeer* with a crew of 26 and sailing from Mauritius to Galle, was wrecked on the reef of Kuramathi. No remains of the wreck have been found but this is not surprising as the reef drops almost vertically to more than 200 metres around Rasdhoo Atoll. The ship could easily have found a deep resting place.

**Gangehi** is a small uninhabited island lying near the 2.5 km long Gangehi Kandu. It opened as a resort in 1987.

**Mathiveri** is an inhabited island which, like Kuda Folhudhoo (Nika Hotel) and Bodufolhudhoo, has a big Nika tree on the island. *Mathiveri* means upper portion and refers to the island's position at the north of the atoll. The old mosque on this island was built during the reign of Sultan Ibrahim Iskandar I (1648 – 1687 AD).

**Mathivereefinolhu** is a small, secluded uninhabited island which Nika Hotel guests regularly visit for picnics.

**Bodufolhudhoo.** Fishing is the main occupation of the islanders.

**Kudafolhudhoo** opened as Nika Hotel in 1983. It has a large Nika, or banyan tree *(Ficus benghalenses)* over 130 years old. The branches of the Nika tree are strong and flexible and used for supporting the sails of dhoanis. The island is well vegetated, partly because of tonnes of soil imported for growing plant and fruit. Nika is noted for its splendidly designed hand-crafted bungalows which are circular in shape, like a shell, with high thatched ceilings, and curved slated windows.

**Velidhoo** means sandy island and opened as a resort in 1989. It is now called Velidhu Island Resort. It has a protected lagoon with a good anchorage for dhoanis.

*Rasdhoo in foreground and Kuramathi.*

**Ukulhas** is an inhabited island with fishing being the main occupation. East of Ukulhass on the outer rim of the atoll are the remains of two small islands, Ukulhas Fushi, which is a sandbank with three bushes and Gaagandu, which was an island with a stone foundation washed away a long time ago. *Gaagandu* means big stone.

**Madivaru** is another uninhabited island and as the name suggests *madi*, or manta rays, are common in the waters around this island.

**Bathala** is an oval-shaped island which opened as Bathala Island Resort in 1983. A *battala* is a sweet potato. The island has a house reef close to the island with surrounding waters dropping to around 30 metres – ideal for snorkelling and diving from the island.

**Ellaidhoo** is the twin island of Bathala – similar in shape and well vegetated. It started as a resort in 1985. It has no lagoon but the island is surrounded by deep water to around 30 metres and is easily accessible to snorkellers and divers from the island.

**Maayafushi** is a half-moon shaped resort island with a big lagoon that offers good anchorage. It opened as a resort in 1983.

**Halaveli** is similar in shape to Maayafushi and has a big reef and lagoon. Both islands have good sailing and windsurfing. Halaveli opened as a resort in 1983. *Hala* is a tree *(Suriana maritima)* with hard wood and small leaves.

**Maagaa** is a small uninhabited island on the outside of the atoll.

**Kandholhudhoo** is an uninhabited island. *Kandholhu* is a type of wild lily that grows on the islands.

**Mushimasmingili** is a small island designated as a marina. It has tourist accommodation and is called Dhoni Mighili.

**Alikoirah** is a small uninhabited island.

**Himendhoo** is a big inhabited island at the eastern end of Himendhoo Faru. The islanders mostly engage in fishing. The island has a long history and Buddhist relics are found from time to time.

**Maalhoss** is another inhabited island with an ancient history. *Lhoss* is a lettuce tree *(Morindaefolia)* and this island is very fertile with big trees.

**Fesdhoo** lies nine km east of Maalhoss and opened as Fesdu Fun Island resort in 1982. It has a very good house reef for snorkellers and divers. *Fesko* is a small bush with blue or white flowers *(Tephrosia tenuis)*. It is often used in local medicine, especially for urinary complications. The resort is now called W Retreat & Spa Maldives.

**Gaathafushi** is an uninhabited island, popular with day trippers from Fesdhoo.

**Feridhoo** is a big fertile inhabited island also with Buddhist origins. Many of the islanders are descendants of slaves brought to the Maldives by sultans. Sultan Hassan III (1442 – 1467 AD) returned from Mecca with 70 slaves and later Sultan Hassan Nooradhdheen (1779 – 1799 AD) brought back slaves from his trip to Mecca. Later the slaves were freed and sent to Kudafari in Noonu Atoll and Feridhoo. The slaves mixed with the local people and today many of the islanders are big and dark with curly hair.

**Madoogali** was an inhabited island until 1943 when the 43 remaining people were taken to Mandhoo. The island became a resort in 1989. *Madoogali* means island formed by portions of coral stones. It has many trees and excellent snorkelling, especially at the south western end where nurse sharks are sometimes found under the coral boulders.

**Vihamaafaru** is an uninhabited island three km to the north across Madoogali Kandu. It has some palm trees and bushes and good snorkelling on the reef. The island name means big poison reef. A small sandbank lies to the north on the same reef.

*Mushimasmingili is a small island called Dhoni Mighili.*

# Diving North Ari Atoll

*Ari Atoll has depths of around 300 metres on the eastern side, while on the west depths drop quickly to over 2000 metres. Rasdhoo is connected to the northeast part of Ari by a submarine plateau with depths from 183 metres to 274 metres. Depths within Rasdhoo Atoll are to 35 metres while in Ari depths are mostly between 35 metres and 55 metres but reaching up to 80 metres in one part. Ari Atoll has no long stretch of barrier reef and all faces of the encircling reef have many passages into the atoll, except the south face which has one break. The inside of the atoll is much encumbered with coral reefs, many of them dry at low tide, but the atoll has many thilas, for which the atoll is famous. Most of the thilas have interesting coral formations and are host to a profusion of marine life. All the reefs on the western side are big, hard coral reefs that appear naturally designed to protect the atoll from the fierce seas that prevail during the south-west monsoon. Heavy waves have pounded the west side breaking off chunks of coral rock and in some places long channels more than a metre deep have been cut into the reefs. On the eastern side the reefs are smaller with many more entrances, and as they do not get the heavy ocean swell of the western side, the corals tend to be more fragile.*

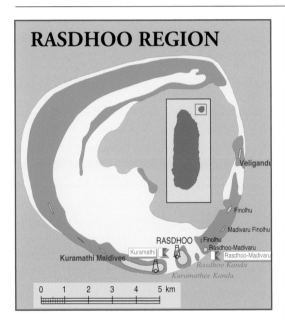

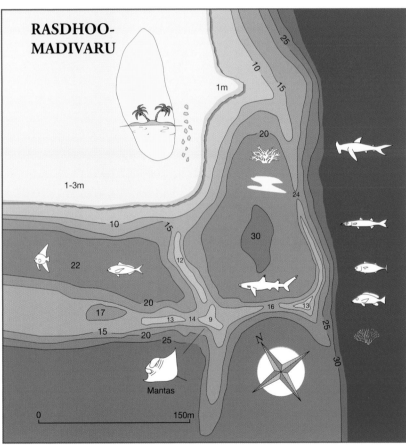

### Rasdhoo-Madivaru ★★★

Location:         outside corner of
                  Rasdhoo-Madivaru island
Depth:            9m – 30m+
Fish Life:        abundant
Coral growth:     very good
Features:         hammerhead sharks, mantas,
                  reef fish

It is from the deep waters on the outside wall of Rasdhoo-Madivaru that scalloped hammerhead sharks, *Sphyrna lewini*, rise in the early hours of the morning to accessible viewing depths. These residential sharks prefer to swim in large schools and are timid, but in the clear waters divers can get a good look at their peculiar head shape. They are easily recognised by the laterally extended snout with eyes at the tips of their T-shaped heads.

Rashoo-Madivaru has one of the most spectacular – and confusing – reef formations to be found in Ari Atoll.

A narrow spur, like a suspension bridge, extends out from the reef of Rasdhoo-Madivaru part of the way across the channel rising to a peak at 13 metres. On the seaward side of the spur, the reef descends almost vertically to around 200 metres.

The deep blue waters on the outside of the spur contrast with the turquoise blue reflecting from the sand floor at 30 metres on the inside of the channel. Along the spur is a profusion of fish life ranging from pelagics like schooling barracuda, trevally, and little tuna – which are rarely seen underwater although very common – to reef fish like blue-striped snapper, fusilier and schools of flame basslet.

On the outside wall are many seafans while on the spur is healthy hard coral. A school of tallfin batfish and often white-tip reef sharks are seen. At the end of the suspension bridge, a deeper, less interesting ridge continues across the channel, but another ridge turns at right

*On the outside reef of Gangehi Maavaru is an old anchor, three metres long, believed to be from the Dutch East Indiaman Ravestein, wrecked on May 9, 1726 (see p15).To date, no detailed archaeological assessment of the site has been undertaken. It is hoped that some limited excavation will eventually provide material to be developed for museum displays and education.*

angles leading into the channel. It dips and rises to another peak at nine metres. At this high point, four ridges converge like a mountain peak and it is a favourite haunt of manta rays where they are cleaned by cleaner wrasse. There are less pelagics inside the channel but a greater abundance of small fish like damselfish, butterflyfish, blue triggerfish and schools of striped fusilier.

**Diving hints:** Depths in the clear waters on the outside of the atoll can be deceptive and it is easy to go too deep, so care should be taken, especially while engrossed in viewing the hammerhead sharks. It's a good idea to take a compass on this dive if planning to explore the inner formations of the channel as orientation can be confusing.

### Kuramathi Housereef ★

At Kuramathi there are two wrecks close by the island, sunk by the dive school. The first was a local dhoani called Tomton sunk 20 metres from the jetty in 1976. It is not deep and is ideal for beginner divers. The other wreck sunk on

*Schooling barracuda,* Sphyraena flavicauda.

the housereef in 1987 was a 30 metre steel cargo ship. It rests on the bottom at 18 metres with the top at 10 metres.

The house reef dive begins at the outside corner of the island and Kuramathee Kandu. At this point a ridge at 20 metres cuts across the channel. The channel wall slopes gently from 10 metres to the sandy bottom at 27 metres. Inside the channel, another small ridge at about 10 metres cuts across the channel near the jetty, leaving a well protected and interesting dive location with good coral growth and fish life.

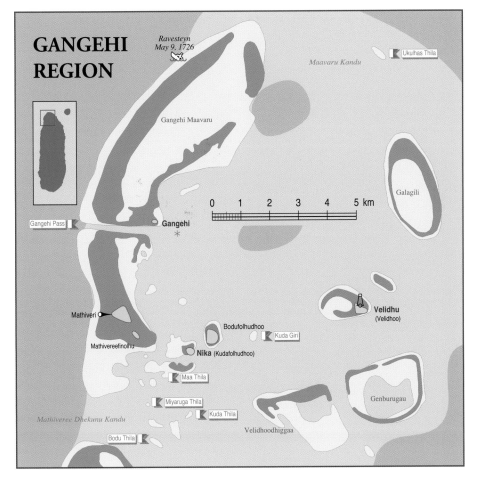

**GANGEHI REGION**

Ravesteyn
May 9, 1726

Ukulhas Thila

Maavaru Kandu

Gangehi Maavaru

Galagili

0  1  2  3  4  5 km

Gangehi Pass

**Gangehi**

Velidhu
(Velidhoo)

Mathiveri

Bodufolhudhoo

Kuda Giri

Mathivereefinolhu

**Nika** (Kudafolhudhoo)

Maa Thila

Genburugau

Miyaruga Thila

Kuda Thila

Mathiveree Dhekunu Kandu

Bodu Thila

Velidhoodhiggaa

### Ukulhas Thila ★★★★

| | |
|---|---|
| Location: | Maavaru Kandu |
| Depth: | 13m – 30m |
| Fish life: | above average |
| Coral growth: | very good |
| Features: | manta rays |

Along the outer north eastern rim of Ari Atoll is a long chain of underwater reefs which pop up from the 30 metre bottom at regular intervals. Ukulhas Thila is one such long, narrow pinnacle. The 300 metre long thila has a relatively flat top at around 15 metres with a slope that steps down to 25 metres and 30 metres. There are three sets of large coral rocks along the reef top at 13 metres that are cleaning stations for manta rays, which are found here between the months of December and April. The mantas feed around the reef top, scooping up zooplankton as it drifts with the current up the side of the thila. Schools of fusilier, are also busy feeding around the reef top. There are many other fish types attracted to this isolated outcrop of reef including grouper, tuna, morays, turtles and sharks. Blue-striped snapper are always in abundance and eagle rays are regularly seen gliding gracefully past the reef.

**Diving hints:** Current can be strong and the seas turbulent here as there is little protection. Divers may have to begin their dive up-current from the thila and drift quickly down to the protection of the reef. Ukulhas Thila has an established reputation for manta rays and as it is regularly visited by divers, it is important not to frighten the mantas by chasing them. Mantas are naturally curious and if divers hold onto a piece of dead coral at a discreet distance from the cleaning stations, then the mantas will continually circle and hover above them. Since this reef is in the open ocean, a safety balloon is an essential accessory for this dive.

### Maa Thila ★★

South west of Kudafolhudhoo is a large reef called Maa Thila. The south side is a long drift dive with an undulating terrain that rises from the sandy bottom at 25 metres to the reef edge at 10 metres. There are two sand ridges leading away from the reef; one at 18 metres, the other at 20 metres. Around these ridges are white-tip reef sharks. There are plenty of coral boulders around the base of the reef that are surrounded by reef fish. On the slopes are many snapper, bannerfish and yellow-back fusilier. This reef has an interesting shape that leads divers around corners, over ridges and into a bay before finishing the dive on the reef top around coral patches at six to eight metres.

### Bodu Thila ★★

*Bodu* means large and this is a big 500 metre long thila starting at a depth of eight to 10 metres. There are many coral rocks between 10 and 20 metres and in the middle of the reef is a saddle that dips to 14 metres. Surrounding depths are to 25 metres.

### Kuda Giri ★

One km to the east of Bodufolhudhoo is a shallow protected reef ideal for beginners. It is an oval-shaped reef with very good coral above 10 metres. It has a gentle slope to a sandy bottom at 25 metres. There are many sea anemones at shallow depths and plenty of small reef fish, especially wrasse. One attraction is a burrowing crab at 23 metres.

### Gangehi Pass ★★

One of the longest channels in Ari Atoll is Gangehi Pass. There is good diving on both sides of the 2.5 km long channel with the better diving just inside the channel. On the north side are large coral rocks around 20 metres and a 200 metre long cave between the depths of 15 and 20 metres. There are many groupers in the cave and also sting rays. Napoleon are common during the months of June, July and August.

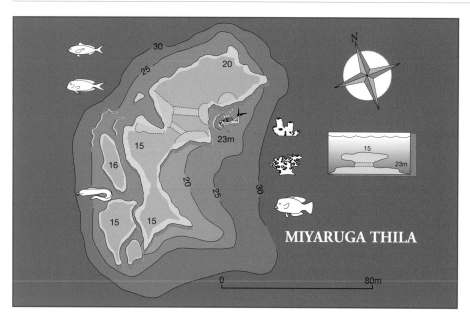

MIYARUGA THILA

0          80m

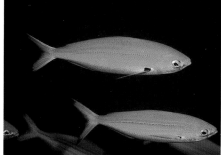

*Thin-lined fusilier,* Caesio varilineata. *A common species seen in schools along the dropoffs of reefs.*

### Miyaruga Thila ★★★★

| | |
|---|---|
| Location: | south west of Kudafolhudhoo |
| Depth: | 15m – 25m |
| Fish life: | abundant |
| Coral growth: | excellent |
| Features: | tunnels, canyon, caves, reef fish |

This thila is about 80 metres long and quite deep with the top at 15 metres. The landscape is stunning and divers can easily circle the reef in one dive if current permits. On the south west side is a canyon between two large coral outcrops and the main thila. In the middle of the reef are two tunnels about one metre wide, one at 21 metres, the other at 23 metres that pass right through the reef. A steady stream of fish, noticeably schools of blue-dash fusilier and thin-lined fusilier, pass through the holes like sheep through a gateway. Much of the thila is undercut with caves and the surface is coated in soft coral and colourful sponges. Clown triggerfish, morays and surgeon are prevalent in the caves and napoleon are a welcoming sight to divers.

**Diving hints:** Currents can be strong and a quick descent to the protection of the reef may be necessary. This site is an excellent location for photographers and divers will appreciate the irregular reef formation.

### Kuda Thila ★★

| | |
|---|---|
| Location: | Mathiveree Dhekunu Kandu |
| Depth: | 6m – 25m |
| Fish life: | above average |
| Coral growth: | very good |
| Features: | reef fish, coral |

Kuda Thila has two main reef bodies, one longer than the other. The larger portion peaks at six metres, the smaller one at 12 metres. A saddle at 18 metres divides the two reefs which bend in a 'V' shape at the junction. Overall, the thila is not as small as the name suggests, being at least 100 metres in length. Between the two peaks are big schools of surgeon and blue triggerfish and also small aggregations of bannerfish and some angelfish. Green coral trees grow on the slopes on the north side. At the eastern end is a small flat reef plateau at 20 metres with a half-moon shaped cave on the end. The cave has pretty soft blue coral on the ceiling and a sand bottom at 25 metres. Two ridges continue off to the east to deeper depths. On the south side near a cave at 24 metres is a cliff with four big black coral trees. Game fish, like banded trevally and bluefin jack, dart around the cliff edge while white-tip reef sharks are frequently seen at deeper depths. On the reef top is healthy soft and hard coral, featherstars and many smaller fish. Several napoleon swim around this reef.

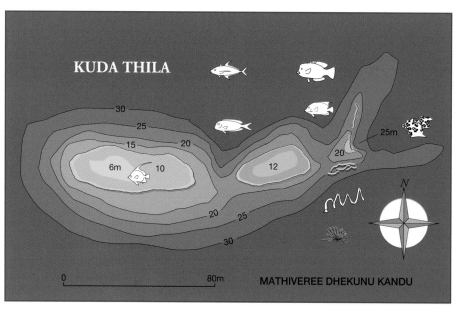

KUDA THILA

MATHIVEREE DHEKUNU KANDU

0          80m

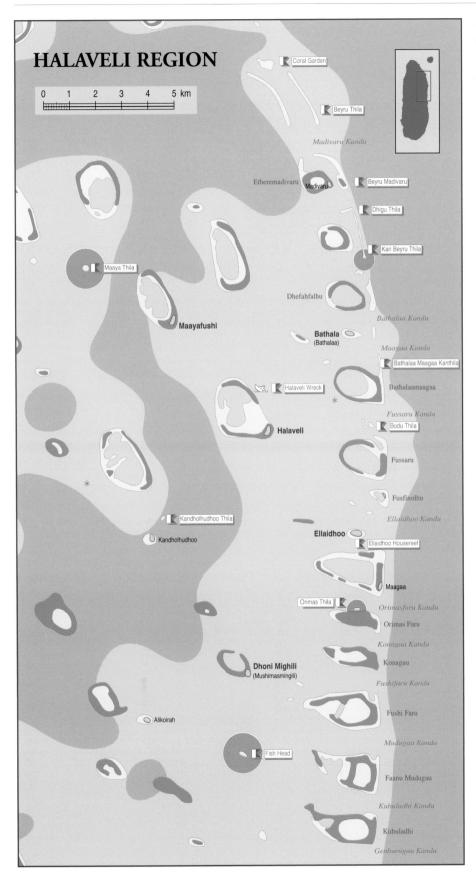

HALAVELI REGION

0 1 2 3 4 5 km

Coral Garden

Beyru Thila

Madivaru Kandu

Etheremadivaru  Madivaru  Beyru Madivaru

Dhigu Thila

Kari Beyru Thila

Maaya Thila

Dhefahfalhu

Maayafushi

Bathala
(Bathalaa)

Bathalaa Kandu

Maagau Kandu

Bathalaa Maagaa Kanthila

Halaveli Wreck

Bathalaamaagaa

Fussaru Kandu

Bodu Thila

Halaveli

Fussaru

Fusfinolhu

Ellaidhoo Kandu

Kandholhudhoo Thila

Kandholhudhoo

Ellaidhoo

Ellaidhoo Housereef

Maagaa

Orimas Thila

Orimasfaru Kandu

Orimas Faru

Konagaa Kandu

Dhoni Mighili
(Mushimasmingili)

Konagau

Fushifaru Kandu

Alikoirah

Fushi Faru

Mudugaa Kandu

Fish Head

Faanu Mudugau

Kubuladhi Kandu

Kubuladhi

Genburugau Kandu

## Coral Garden ★★

This site has small clusters of reef with beautiful coral and many blue-striped and yellow-back fusilier dashing around the coral. Turtles and barracuda are sighted here and sometimes nurse sharks and mantas. Generally, white-tip reef sharks are prowling around on the sandy bottom at 20 to 30 metres.

## Beyru Thila ★★★

This thila is a long reef lying north to south on the outer edge of the atoll to the north east of Madivaru. The sea tends to get choppy out here when there is wind and currents.

Divers can dive the length of the thila on either the east or west side. Both are interesting with caves and overhangs at 25 to 30 metres. Scattered around the thila are large tuna, napoleon and plenty of snapper. Eagle rays, barracuda and grey reef sharks are regularly seen. On the reef top, large coral rocks offer a change of scenery and sometimes nurse sharks are seen among them.

On the outside of Madivaru is a big reef known as **Beyru Madivaru**. The reef becomes more shallow at the southern end and on the outside of this reef hammerhead sharks are known to frequent the deeper waters.

## Dhigu Thila ★★

In the channel to the south of Madivaru lies this narrow, 400 metre long thila running east to west. It is also called Toroka Thila. The reef top is about three to five metres in the centre and 10 to 12 metres on the west side. The reef to the east is deeper and finishes off on an 18 metre plateau that turns towards the south. On the southern side are caves and overhangs at 22 to 26 metres. There are three points jutting off the main reef to the south. At the last point on the deep south east corner are caves at 30 metres. Barracuda, white-tip and grey reef sharks, eagle rays and sometimes mantas and napoleon can be found here.

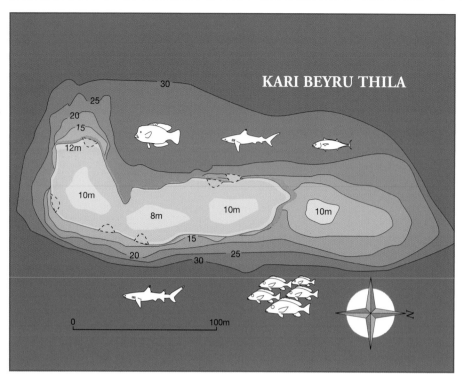

KARI BEYRU THILA

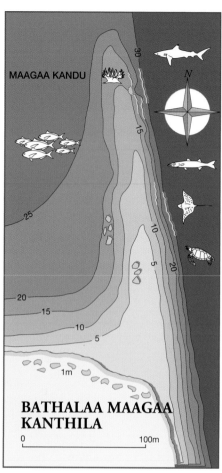

MAAGAA KANDU

BATHALAA MAAGAA KANTHILA

0                    100m

**Kari Beyru Thila** ★★★

PROTECTED MARINE AREA

Location:       3 km north of
                Bathalaa
Depth:          8m – 30m
Fish life:      abundant
Coral growth:   very good
Features:       sharks, napoleon,
                tuna, stone fish

This is a long, narrow thila, stretching north to south down the eastern edge of the atoll. There are many interesting caves rich in corals. The east side slopes to 35 metres and the west to 25 metres. The northern end slopes steadily down to 30 metres with many large coral blocks on the top. Fish life is varied with tuna, snapper, white-tip and grey reef sharks and napoleon. Also stone fish, sting rays and sometimes mantas.

**Bathalaa Maagaa Kanthila** ★★

Location:       north side of
                Bathalaa Maagaa
Depth:          5m – 30m
Fish life:      above average
Coral growth:   very good
Features:       reef fish, tuna,
                barracuda, sharks

A long, narrow spur, about 20 metres wide starts at Bathalaa Maagaa and extends for 500 metres northwards into Maagaa Kandu. The top gradually becomes deeper until reaching the bottom at 30 metres. The eastern side of the spur is the outside of the atoll and drops steeply from 20 metres. There are one or two small caves at the northern end on the outside. Visibility is usually better on the outside and barracuda, tuna, turtles, sharks and sometimes eagle rays are quite likely to be seen here. The reef top is covered in a variety of coral. There are sponge balls with ascidians and hydroids at the deeper end while closer to the main reef are sea anemones and big porite corals– home for aggregations of sweetlip and bannerfish. Blue-dash, yellow-back and striped fusilier are all over the reef and there are small schools of big-nose unicornfish and snapper.

**Diving hints:** This is a good dive for beginner and intermediate divers but care should be taken to allow sufficient air to return to the shallower end of the reef, especially in strong outgoing currents.

*Blue-dash fusilier,* Pterocaesio tile. *When seen below about 10 metres, a blue dash clearly shows along the fish's side. They usually occur in big schools and the flashing blue streaks are designed to deceive its predators.*

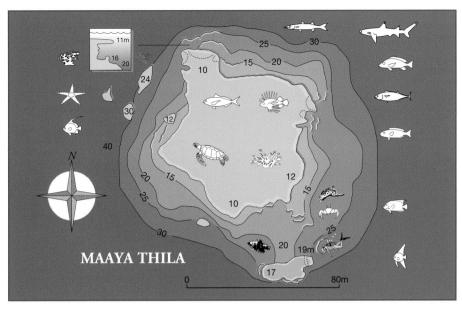

MAAYA THILA

*Clown triggerfish,* Balistoides conspicillum. *A brightly coloured fish popular with aquarists. Inhabits outer reef slopes and dropoffs and feeds on small bottom living animals.*

## Maaya Thila ★★★

PROTECTED MARINE AREA

| | |
|---|---|
| Location: | 4 km north west of Maayafushi |
| Transit: | The right side of Halaveli should be aligned with the left side of Ellaidhoo |
| Depth: | 6m – 30m |
| Fish life: | abundant |
| Coral growth: | very good |
| Features: | grey reef sharks, white-tip reef sharks, reef fish |

If Fish Head is the grey reef shark capital of the Maldives, then Maaya Thila is the white-tip reef shark capital. Although grey reef sharks are common here, the smaller white-tips are the centre of attention, with dozens of them circling the reef. Maaya Thila is about 80 metres in diameter and can easily be circumnavigated in one dive – if the current is favourable – although it is not uncommon for divers to spend the entire dive in one area to digest the incredible diversity of marine life. The top starts at six metres and the reef edge drops from 12 metres to depths of 30 metres and more. Several coral outcrops occur on the north west and south sides. There are many caves and overhangs all around the thila. At a big cave on the north side are a feast of fish ranging from the white-tips

(which usually frequent the side of the reef where the current is strongest), dog-toothed tuna and great barracuda to blue-face angelfish, moorish idol, tallfin batfish, parrotfish, butterflyfish, clown triggerfish and lionfish. There are also other delights for the careful observer like stonefish and anglerfish. A big rock on the south side has a one metre wide swim-through at 19 metres. On the reef top are many fusilier and blue-striped snapper and a large turtle is a regular around the reef. This dive is a

fish-watcher's delight and the beautiful soft coral and gorgonians on the reef faces are a great attraction.

**Diving hints:** Diving boats usually tie a rope to the reef on the upcurrent side or at a permanent mooring on the reef top so a controlled descent during strong currents is possible. Divers should aim to return to their rope with plenty of air where the remaining time can be spent nearby on the reef top. Diving boats come and go so don't forget which rope belongs to your boat.

*White-tip reef shark,* Triaenodon obesus *at Maaya Thila.*

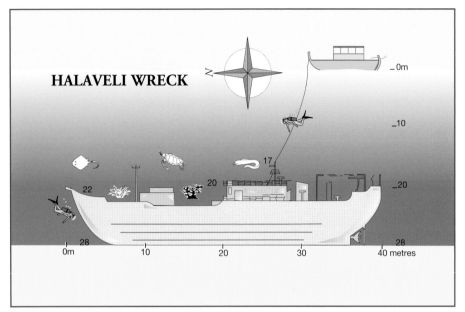

HALAVELI WRECK

*Exploring the Halaveli wreck.*

### Halaveli Wreck ★★★

| | |
|---|---|
| Location: | 1.5 km NNW of Halaveli |
| Depth: | 20m – 28m |
| Fish life: | average |
| Coral growth: | poor |
| Features: | wreck, sting rays |

The Halaveli wreck, also known as the Razza wreck, is a 38 metre cargo vessel sunk by the Halaveli diving centre in 1991. It sits upright with the bow facing north, 40 metres from the reef. The deck

*Black-spotted sting ray. The sting rays at Halaveli wreck are fearless and although they brush up against divers, they are harmless unless provoked.*

is at 20 metres and the bottom is on sand at 28 metres. Apart from the wreck itself, the main attraction are four large sting rays that have been trained to take food. It took instructors from Halaveli six months to train them and now they are quick to surround divers in anticipation of a free feed. Three of the rays are female black-spotted sting rays up to 1.5 metres in size. The fourth is a brown female ray of similar size. Sting rays naturally feed by smothering and crushing their prey, and sucking the contents into their mouths on the underside of their belly, so the rays tend to swim over divers, often brushing against them. A small turtle has made a home for itself on the wreck and a couple of large morays have also taken up residence. Some coral has already taken hold, most noticeably some pretty soft coral on the telegraph mast.

**Diving hints:** The rays are most active in the afternoon and can sometimes become quite aggressive in their attempt to obtain food. Divers should keep their hands away from the rays' mouths as they suck so hard as to draw fingers inside. Divers should not attempt to ride or chase the rays as at least one diver has been injured while grabbing hold. They should only be fed by instructors with knowledge of their habits.

### Sting Rays

"There is a little fish about a foot long, or thereabouts in length, square at the four corners, and covered with a shell of one piece, with only the point of its tail turned back to serve it for a helm. It is the most delicate eating imaginable; the flesh is white, firm and without any bones. You would say it was chicken, so good is it. The larger rays, however, they skin, and with the dried skin, after it is well stretched, they make their drums, using none other."

*Francois Pyrard, Voyages,*
1602-1607.

The winglike fins of the sting ray extend forward to encompass the head. A pair of large openings behind the eyes enable them to draw in water which they pump out through their mouth. This disperses the sand allowing them to feed. Sting rays eat shells and crabs but also fish. They have a serrated spine on the upper side at the base of the tail. The sting ray can swing its tail sideways and upward and forward over its head, driving the spine into the limb or body of the victim. When the skin covering over the serrated spine is ruptured, venom escapes along grooves into the perforated wound.

The skin of the sting ray is still used on the *boduberu*, the drum used in traditional dance music, and for the *tari*, which is like a tamborine.

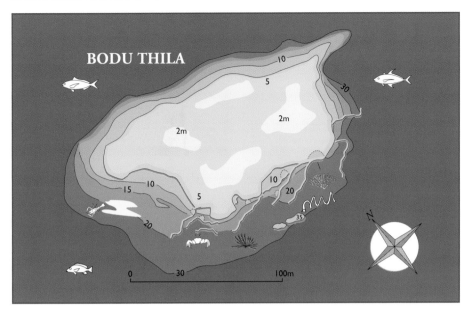

*Pink-bar shrimp goby,* Amblyeleotris aurora. *There are a number of species of shrimp goby which live in burrows in the sand and coral rubble in association with shrimps. The nearly-blind shrimp digs and maintains the burrow while the shy and protective goby guards the entrance, signaling with its tail if it is safe or not for the shrimp to come out. In some habitats, numerous pairs can be found within close range of one another.*

### Bodu Thila (East) ★★★

| | |
|---|---|
| Location: | midway between Bathalaa Maagaa and Fussaru |
| Depth: | 5m – 30m |
| Fish life: | abundant |
| Coral growth: | excellent |
| Features: | cliffs, seafans, coral, reef fish |

To the east of Halaveli in Fussaru Kandu, are three thilas within a small area of 500 metres. Sometimes referred to as Tin Thila, the largest is Bodu Thila and is 250 metres long. The others are Medhu Thila and Kuda Thila. Bodu Thila is the closest to the outside rim of the atoll, and has an amazing variety of marine life with spectacular cliffs and overhangs on the south side. With an outgoing current, divers usually start at a large sandy bay at the western end of the thila beginning at five metres. On this sand slope is a big colony of shrimp goby which appear more tame than at most other locations. If divers approach the goby very carefully, they are quite likely to see the shrimp at the mouth of the goby's burrow. Along the cliff walls and overhangs are thick coverings of large seafans and black coral bushes. On the lower slopes are green coral trees. At the south east end is a big cave dropping from the top of the reef to 25 metres where there are seafans with featherstars, large schools of big-eye

trevally, humpback snapper, blue-dash fusilier and many other fish swimming out from the wall. Many of the ledges start deep at 25 metres or 30 metres and spiral upwards into the cliff wall. On the reef top is a lumpy landscape of porite coral full of christmas tree worms.

### Medhu Thila ★★ & Kuda Thila ★★

are much smaller and divers can easily swim around the 30 metre wide Kuda Thila. Depths are between five and 25 metres. There are small caves and some steep walls on both thilas and heavy concentrations of marine life, including big-eye trevally, sharks and sting rays. On the reef tops are many species of damselfish, like the three-spot humbug, also butterflyfish, and angelfish.

*Threadfin butterflyfish,* Chaetodon auriga. *Butterflyfish have distinct colour patterns and are easily recognised. The threadfin butterflyfish is often seen in pairs on the upper reef slope feeding on small invertebrates.*

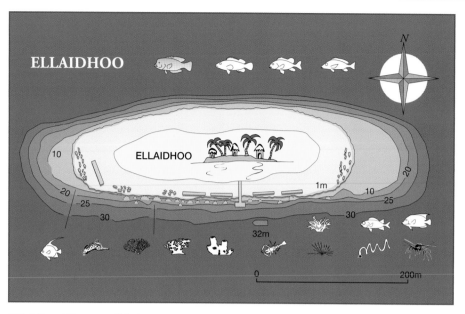

ELLAIDHOO

ELLAIDHOO

*Ellaidhoo boasts a great housereef dive.*

### Ellaidhoo Housereef ★★

| | |
|---|---|
| Location: | south side of Ellaidhoo |
| Depth: | 1m – 25m |
| Fish life: | very good |
| Coral growth: | excellent |
| Features: | caves, seafans, reef fish |

Of all the resorts in the Maldives, Ellaidhoo has one of the best and most convenient housereef dives. Divers can literally step off the jetty or swim from the beach to a 750 metre long wall dive studded with caves full of seafans, hard coral, sponges, featherstars and soft coral. For most of the reef, the wall is undercut below 20 metres to the sand bottom at 25 to 30 metres. Most of the caves are between 10 and 15 metres, some being just big enough to swim into without damaging the coral. Near the jetty is a 15 metre long wreck lying upside down with the bow facing west in 32 metres of water. A big grouper is usually found here. To the west of the jetty are no fewer than 15 caves between 11 and 14 metres, two of which are 20 metres long. One has a great number of large seafans and whips. Many of the caves are full of soldierfish and squirrelfish, also masked bannerfish, long-nosed butterflyfish, moorish idol, triggerfish, oriental sweetlip, midnight snapper, and blue-face angelfish, to name a few. At both the west and east ends of the reef are excellent acropora and porite coral on the reef top. At the western end in four to five metres are schooling bannerfish. Divers can also see lobsters, napoleon, sting rays, morays and nudibranchs. Ellaidhoo divers can dive the housereef whenever they like and rarely complain of being bored.

**Kandholhudhoo Thila** lies to the north of the island of Kandholhudhoo and eagle rays, turtles, and sometimes manta rays, can be seen here.

*Nudibranch,* Jorunna funebris, *found in the caves of Ellaidhoo.*

*Long-nosed butterflyfish,* Forcipiger flavissimus. *There are two species of butterflyfish with a long snout that look similiar: the long-nose butterflyfish and the very-long-nose butterflyfish. The long snout enables the fish to extract small crustaceans and worms from tiny cracks in the coral.*

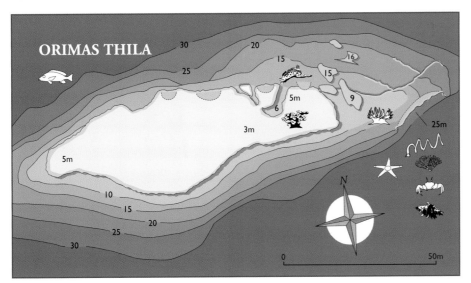

ORIMAS THILA

Phyllidiella, Phyllidia varicosa, at Orimas thila.

**Orimas Thila ★★★** (Maagaa Thila)
PROTECTED MARINE AREA

| | |
|---|---|
| Location: | north side of Orimas faru |
| Depth: | 3m – 30m |
| Fish life: | abundant |
| Coral growth: | excellent |
| Features: | coral, caves, reef fish |

Orimas Thila is sometimes called Maagaa Thila after the island to the north. The northern side of this 100 metre long reef has a superb landscape with a number of distinctive features that make it stand out from many other sites. It has a long, narrow crack in the reef top at six metres which is overloaded with smaller marine life. The reef face is steep and jagged and has a long cave that meanders along the reef between the depths of 15 to 18 metres. The cave is covered in fine weed-like soft coral, seafans and black coral bushes. At the eastern end are large coral rocks with crevices and canyons. Further to the east, the reef descends gradually to 30 metres. Sea anemones are prevalent all over the reef but a big patch is concentrated on the eastern side at around 15 metres. On the south east side is another cave at 25 metres with black coral bushes and nudibranchs.

The southern side of the thila slopes gradually to 30 metres in a uniform fashion. Schools of blue triggerfish and blue-striped snapper are found at the western end. On the reef top are stands of fire coral, staghorn coral and large table coral. There are fish of every description and most noticeably flutemouth.

**Diving hints:** This is an excellent site for divers who are prepared to take their time and concentrate on the smaller fish and interesting features of the reef. Because it is a small reef, extra care should be taken not to disturb the marine life or damage the fragile coral with fins.

*Below: Black-footed anemonefish, Amphiprion nigripes. This anemonefish is one of the few fish species indigenous to the Maldives. It finds protection among the tentacles of sea anemones. The tentacles contain poison and tiny harpoons at the tip, called nematocysts which can pierce the skin of small animals and inject a fatal poison. The anemonefish is coated with a layer of mucus that protects it against the nematocysts. In return for the protection it receives, the aggressive actions of the anemonefish warn its host if a predator such as a butterflyfish – which feeds on the tentacle tips – is nearby. The sea anemone can then withdraw its tentacles.*

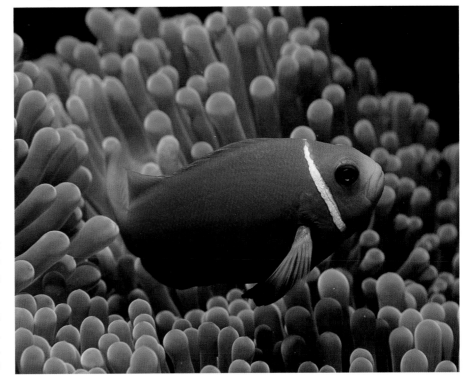

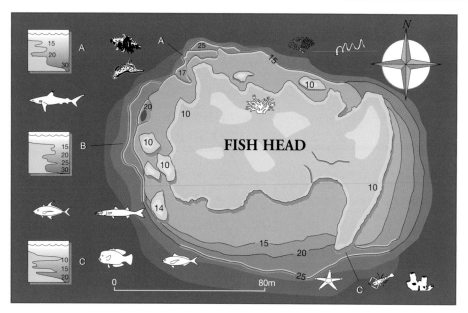

## Fish Head ★★★

(Mushimasmingili Thila)

PROTECTED MARINE AREA

| | |
|---|---|
| Location: | 3 km south of Mushimasgali |
| Depth: | 10m – 30m+ |
| Fish life: | abundant |
| Coral growth: | very good |
| Features: | sharks, reef fish, underwater scenery |

Fish Head fits the classic definition of a thila, being a large isolated flat-top reef rising sharply from the inner atoll floor at 40 to 50 metres to around 10 metres from the surface. The presence of a large school of grey reef sharks, combined with the favourable underwater scenery and the wide variety of marine life, have given this reef the reputation of being among the ten best dive sites in the world.

**History:** Ari Atoll fishermen have traditionally fished for sharks at Fish Head and divers were first drawn here by the regular appearance of fishing dhoanis at this site. Sharks were taken mainly for their oil but with shark fins commanding high prices on the Asian market, sharks are in big demand. Ari Atoll fishermen have been reluctant to give up one of their most productive fishing grounds for the sake of diving tourists. With this backdrop of conflicting interests, the government stepped in in 1995 to declare Fish Head a Protected Marine Area to ensure that it continues to cater for the expectations of divers.

**Diving:** The square-shaped reef is about 80 metres wide and can be circled in one dive if divers wish, providing the current is not too strong. There are ledges and caves at different depths around much of the reef and for the most part, there is a big undercut from about 25 to 30 metres before the reef tapers to the bottom slopes. The north and north west sides have a particularly interesting landscape at reasonably shallow depths, making it ideal for the less experienced diver, while at depth, are caves with all the usual features including seafans and black coral bushes.

Divers tend to stay more shallow at Fish Head, hovering around the reef edge at about 15 metres as this gives the best all round view of a family of about 20 resident grey reef sharks.

**Sharks:** The sharks are usually seen on the up-current side of the reef. The advantage that Fish Head has over other shark watching sites is that the habits of the sharks can be observed at close range from a secure position on any part of the reef. On occasions, sharks can even be seen at cleaner stations where they expose their glistening teeth to the fastidious cleaner wrasse. Photographers will get few better opportunities to photograph these graceful predators than at Fish Head.

**Marine life:** The abundant fish life begins at the surface, where the water boils with the silver flashing of fusilier. Below, divers are greeted by a family of napoleon, one of them more than 150 cm long. There are many pelagics here including giant trevally and schooling barracuda, which circle like a pack of wolves anticipating a kill. The reef has contrasting features and one favourable impression in deeper water is the straight wall on the northern side where a field of large seafans sprout from the reef edge.

**Diving hints:** At times there may be several boats tied to the thila and many divers. Take note of which boat is yours and return with enough air to make a safety stop on the way up. Take care not to kick or break coral.

*Great barracuda,* Sphyraena barracuda.

# Sharks

### Shark legend

One of the earliest records of sharks in the Maldives comes from Francois Pyrard, at the beginning of the 17th century, who sets the tone of legend by describing a certain fish that "eat and devour men which God sends to punish them for their sins".

Pyrard wrote: "The Maldivians have assured me that these fish go in troops, and have many a time attacked little boats and fishers wherries, and capsizing these, have devoured men. You see there many of the people that have lost a leg or an arm, or a hand, or have been wounded elsewhere in their bodies by the bites of these fish. I have seen many at the Maldives thus maimed; indeed, I have seen some of these fish caught with whole limbs of men in their bellies." In Pyrard's day, those most at risk may have been divers collecting bait fish without masks, but Pyrard's observations are surprising when we consider that reports of shark attacks on swimmers or divers today are extremely rare and limited to people feeding, or provoking sharks.

### Shark fishing

The greatest threat to sharks in the Maldives today is human. Demand for shark-fin in the Asian market has reduced the number of sharks in many areas to a fraction of what they once were. Maldivian fishermen can earn a sizable income from the shark fins, yet the long term cost to the environment of losing these high order predators cannot be calculated. Shark fishing inside the atolls is forbidden by Maldivian law, but shark fishing outside the atolls is allowed. These laws are abused and there is little control over what fins are obtained 'legitimately' on fishing lines outside the atolls. Shark jaws and shark teeth are also popular tourist items, but little thought is often given to the consequences of purchasing these items from the tourist souvenir shops. Seeing sharks in the water is much more desirable from a diver's point of view. With new resorts proposed for the outer atolls and safari boats expanding their range of operations, a total ban on shark fishing would appear to be the only way to ensure the Maldives diving tourism market can be maintained and strengthened. Providing financial incentives and alternative job opportunities for displaced fisherman may be one of the requirements of such a ban, but the benefits would be international recognition and a thriving diving tourist market.

*Grey reef shark,* Carcharhinus amblyrhynchos.

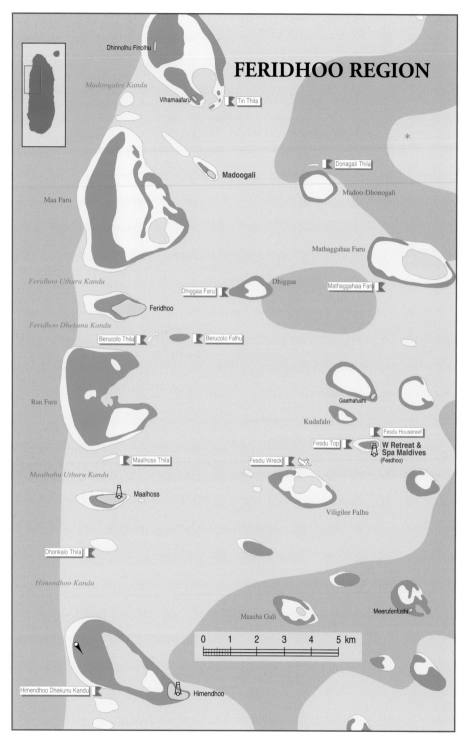

## FERIDHOO REGION

again to the shadowy depths below. The visibility is usually very good and hammerhead sharks have been seen here. A large coral encrusted anchor, was lifted from the outside reef at 25 metres by Moofushi dive school in 1994. No other remains were found in the vicinity of the anchor. The anchor is on display at the resort. About 150 metres inside the channel is the best place to start with an ingoing current. There is a long overhang starting at 20 metres and rising to five metres here. Beautiful seafans and whips cling to the bottom and walls of the overhang and inside are emperor angelfish, sweetlip and squirrelfish while outside hover black snapper and midnight snapper. Further inside the channel, the reef again exposes its interiors with more crevices plunging from five metres back down to 20 metres. Further across the channel in 35 metres are several large outcrops of reef where white-tips and grey reef sharks are found. There are also barracuda and big dog-toothed tuna.

In the four km wide Himendhoo Kandu is a large thila called **Donkalo Thila**. The best diving here is on the south side, which has an excellent wall with overhangs and plenty of fish life. Mantas are regularly seen here during the north-east monsoon season and whale sharks have often been sighted in Himendhoo Kandu.

### Fesdu Housereef ★★

Divers are fortunate to have a housereef with an excellent wall dive virtually on their bungalow doorstep. The reef drops to 20 metres and has plenty of hard coral, large morays, octopus, stonefish and lionfish. There are also sting rays on the bottom and occasionally eagle rays.

Close by, only three minutes by dhoani from the resort, is **Fesdu Top ★**, an exciting reef with the best diving at depths from 15 to 20 metres. There are many caves, some with lobsters. Fish life includes turtles, blue-striped snapper and lionfish.

### Himendhoo Dhekunu Kandu ★★

| | |
|---|---|
| Location: | south side of Himendhoo Faru |
| Depth: | 3m – 30m |
| Fish life: | above average |
| Coral growth: | very good |
| Features: | reef fish, sharks |

There is four km of reef to drift dive in this channel and for convenience it can be divided into three parts: the outside corner, the channel and inside. On the outside corner, the reef slopes slowly to 15 metres before falling away steeply to 30 metres. It then steps out and drops

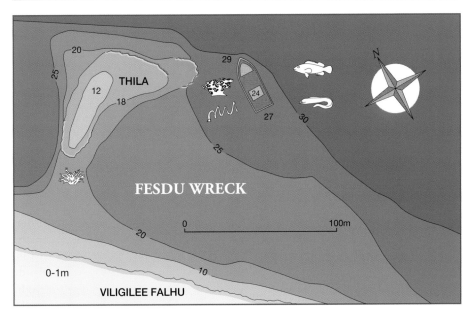

Around the island of Feridhoo are many reefs and thilas well worth exploring. A good start is at **Berucolo Falhu** where there is reasonable diving on the west side. Nearby on the west side is **Berucolo Thila**, starting at about four metres.

### Dhiggaa Faru ★

Three km east of Feridhoo is a reef with the best diving on the western corner. It has steep walls to 20 metres with some crevices and caves between 10 and 20 metres. There is one big cave with a swim-through on the corner at 10 metres. Sting rays are seen on the sandy floors of the caves and some small morays are on the slopes. There are many butterflyfish, including the teardrop butterflyfish.

### Mathaggahaa Faru ★

Eight km east of Feridhoo is a long, effortless drift dive suited to beginner divers. There are some large deep caves with sandy floors between 10 and 20 metres allowing easy and controlled access. Inside are some small black coral bushes with oyster shells. On the reef are large sea anemones with Clark's anemonefish. There are also juvenile sweetlip, common lionfish, pufferfish and blue triggerfish. There is plenty of invertebrate life including large sea-squirts in the shallower waters and banded shrimp.

### Donagali Thila ★★

On the north side of Madoo-Dhonogali is a 150 metre long thila with the top at nine metres. There is a sandy bottom at 25 metres between the main reef and the thila and on the outside the depth drops to 30 metres.

### Tin Thila ★★

There are three peaks to this 150 metre long thila that rise to six metres. The saddles between them are at depths around 12 metres. The east side drops to sand at 30 metres while the west side is more shallow to 20 metres. There are caves at the south end sometimes with nurse sharks. There is fine coral, large lionfish and mantas in March.

## Fesdu Wreck ★★★

| | |
|---|---|
| Location: | north side of Viligilee Falhu |
| Depth: | 24m – 29m |
| Fish life: | above average |
| Coral growth: | good |
| Features: | wreck, reef fish |

The wreck of this 30 metre coastal fishing trawler lies upright on the bottom at 29 metres with the bow facing almost north. The top of the wheelhouse is at 24 metres and the propeller is at 27 metres. Coral is already well established and a couple of good sized black coral bushes are growing off the stern. Among the superstructure are moray eels and in the engine room are big grouper.

The wreck lies at the end of a small thila that is about 50 metres out from Viligilee Falhu. The top of the thila is at 12 metres and is usually visible from the surface. There is extensive soft and hard coral growth all over the thila and plenty of fish life but there are few caves or interesting rock formations.

*The Fesdu wreck lies in 28 metres of water.*

## Maalhoss Thila ★★★ (Bluecaves)

On the northern side of Maalhoss in Maalhohu Uthuru Kandu is Maalhoss Thila, otherwise known as Bluecaves. The top of the thila is at about six metres and on the south side is a line of caves starting at around seven metres. The caves are more shallow on the east side and descend one after the other down to about 27 metres on the western side. The ceilings are covered in soft coral in a mixture of colours, mostly white but also blue and violet. The snowy coloured soft coral is among the finest to be seen in Ari Atoll and the decorated caves make a surreal backdrop for underwater photographers.

*Marine life at Maalhoss Thila.*

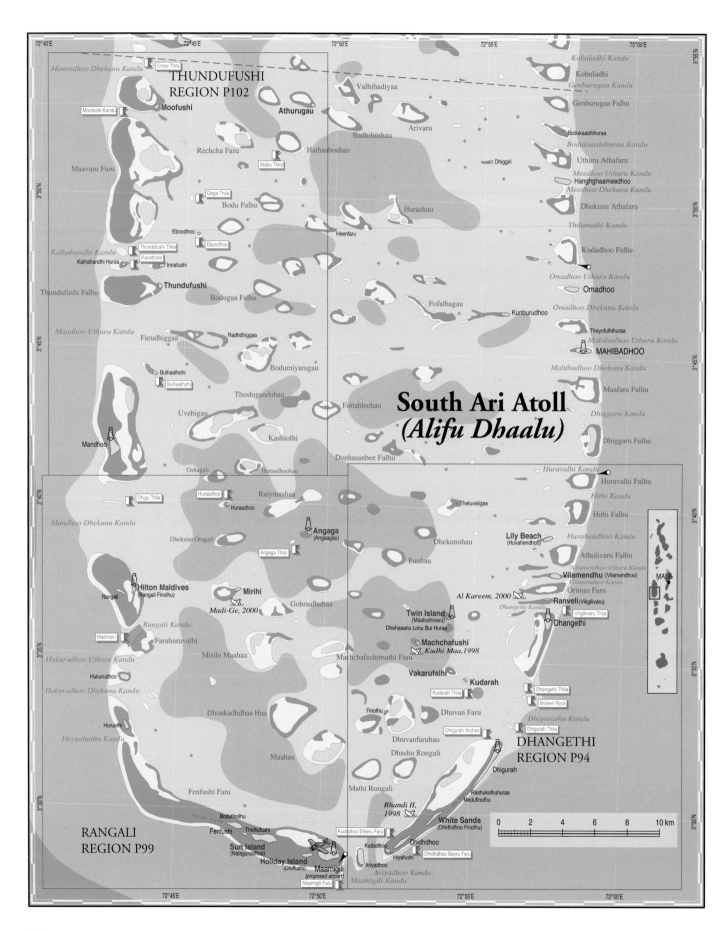

72°40'E  72°45'E  72°50'E  72°55'E  73°00'E

*Himendhoo Dhekunu Kandu*

Emas Thila

**THUNDUFUSHI
REGION P102**

*Kubuladhi Kandu*

3°55'N

Kubuladhi
*Genburugau Kandu*

Moofushi Kandu

**Moofushi**      **Athurugau**

Genburugaa Falhu

Valhihadiyaa

Bodukaashihuraa
*Bodukaashihuraa Kandu*

Rechcha Faru      Hathaaboahau      Badhibinhau      Arivaru

Uthuru Athafaru

Atabu Thila

*Meedhoo Uthuru Kandu*
**Hanghghaameedhoo**
*Meedhoo Dhekunu Kandu*

3°50'N

Dhiggiri

*Maavaru Faru*

Dega Thila

**Bodu Falhu**

Heenfaru      Hurashau

Dhekunu Athafaru

*Thilanathi Kandu*

Eboodhoo

Eboodhoo

Kudadhoo Falhu

Thundufushi Thila
Panettone

*Kalhahandhi Kandu*

Kalhahandhi Huraa      Innafushi

*Omadhoo Uthuru Kandu*
**Omadhoo**

**Thundufushi**

*Bodugaa Falhu*

Fofalhagau

*Omadhoo Dhekunu Kandu*
Kunburudhoo

3°45'N

*Mandhoo Uthuru Kandu*

Farudhiggaa      Radhdhiggaa

Theyofulhihuraa
*Mahibadhoo Uthuru Kandu*
**MAHIBADHOO**

Bodumiyarugau

**South Ari Atoll**
*(Alifu Dhaalu)*

Maafaru Falhu

Bulhaalhohi

Bulhaalhohi

Thoshiganduhau

*Mahibadhoo Dhekunu Kandu*

*Dhiggaru Kandu*

Uvehigau

Fottahleehau

Dhiggaru Falhu

Kashiolhi

**Mandhoo**

Donhasanbee Falhu

Oshagali      Hurasdhoohau

*Huravalhi Kandu*

Huravalhi Falhu

3°40'N

Dhigu Thila

Hurasdhoo      Raiymashaa

*Hithi Kandu*

Theluveligaa

Hithi Falhu

*Mandhoo Dhekunu Kandu*

Hurasdhoo

Dhekunuhau

**Lily Beach**
*(Huvahendhoo)*

*Huvahendhoo Kandu*

Athulivaru Falhu

Dhekunu Orugali      **Angaga**
*(Angaagau)*

Funhau

*Vilamendhoo Uthuru Kandu*
**Vilamendhu** *(Vilamendhoo)*
*Vilamendhoo Dhekunu Kandu*

Angaga Thila

Orimas Faru

**Ranveli** *(Viligilivaru)*

Al Kareem, 2000

*Dhangethi Kandu*

**Hilton Maldives**
*(Rangali Finolhu)*

**Mirihi**

*Madi-Ge, 2000*

Gohraalhuhaa

**Twin Island**
*(Maafushivaru)*

Dhehasanu Lonu Bui Huraa

Viligilivaru Thila

**Dhangethi**

3°35'N

Rangali

*Rangali Kandu*

Madivaru

Faruhuruvalhi

Mirihi Maahaa

**Machchafushi**
*Kudhi Maa, 1998*

Dhangethi Thila

Broken Rock

*Hukurudhoo Uthuru Kandu*

**Vakarufalhi**      **Kudarah**

Hukurudhoo

*Hukurudhoo Dhekunu Kandu*

Machchafushimathi Faru

Kudarah Thila

Finolhu      Dhuvan Faru

Dhigurah Thila

Huruelhi

Dhonkadhdhaa Hau

Dhigurah Arches

*Dhigurashu Kandu*

**DHANGETHI
REGION P94**

*Heygahathu Kandu*

Maahaa

Dhuvanfaruhau

Dhashu Rongali

Dhigurah

Fenfushi Faru      Bodufinolhu

Mathi Rongali

Rashukolhuhuraa
Medufinolhu

3°30'N

Fenfushi      Tholhufushi

**RANGALI
REGION P99**

**Sun Island**
*(Nalaguraidhoo)*

**Holiday Island**
*(Dhiffushi)*

**Maamigili**
*(proposed airport)*

Maamigili Faru

Kudadhoo Etheru Faru

*Rhandi II,
1998*

**White Sands**
*(Dhidhdhoo Finolhu)*

Kudadhoo      **Dhidhdhoo**

Hiyafushi      Dhidhdhoo Beyru Faru

Ariyadhoo

*Ariyadhoo Kandu*

*Maamigili Kandu*

0      2      4      6      8      10 km

MALÉ

72°45'E  72°50'E  72°55'E  73°00'E

# Chapter 5 - South Ari Atoll Islands (*Alifu Dhaalu*)

**Bodukaashihuraa** means big coconut island and is an uninhabited island on the eastern rim of the atoll.

**Hanghghaameedhoo** is a mouthful in anyone's language! A feature is the tomb of Sultan Ibrahim III (1585 – 1609 AD). Sultan Ibrahim was murdered by Malabar invaders who sacked the capital in 1609 and overtook the fleeing sultan's vessel. Maldivian historian, Hassan Ahmed Maniku says: "It is stated in legend that Sultan Ibrahim III was the first king in the Maldives to have used the parasol [sunshade] and therefore until very recent times every king or prince who had the privilege of using it officially, remembered Sultan Ibrahim and presented one to his shrine. In 1978 when I visited this tomb I saw the remnants of several parasols there." (Vanavaru No 3, 1989.)

**Dhiggiri** is a small uninhabited island with a long reef.

**Omadhoo** is a very old inhabited island with fishing being the main occupation of the islanders.

**Kunburudhoo** is an uninhabited island with a long reef on the western side. *Kunburu* is a type of creeper that grows on the sand.

**Mahibadhoo** is the capital of South Ari Atoll. It has an atoll office and a fish processing centre and cold storage.

**Huvahendhoo** opened as Lily Beach resort in 1994. The house reef borders the island and is ideal for snorkelling and diving.

**Vilamendhoo** opened as a resort in 1994. It is a larger, more heavily timbered island and used to be a regular stopover island for fishing boats where they obtained fresh water. The north and south side of the island are a short step away from deep water and a healthy coral reef.

*The island of Hanghghaameedhoo and Uthuru Athafaru reef.*

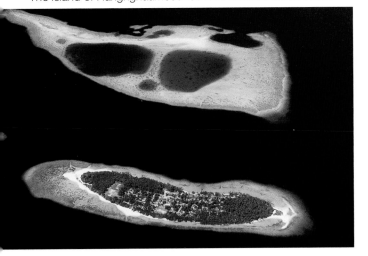

**Viligilivaru** is a small island that opened as Ranveli Beach Resort in 1991. The island is situated on a narrow two km long reef. In the past, safari dhoanis used to pull into the beach on the north side of this island, attracted by the excellent snorkelling and diving.

**Dhangethi** is an inhabited island clearly distinguished from others by a large *Nika*, or Banyan tree in the middle, which can be seen from afar. Nobody knows how old the tree is, some say more than 200 years. Its roots, spread over a large area, seem to confirm this. The main occupation of the islanders is fishing but work at neighbouring resorts has increased in previous years.

Story telling is a favourite pastime among the islanders. The Dhangethi Islanders have a keen sense of humour and are the source of some popular folk stories. A favourite story told in the tea shops of Malé is about a fisherman from Dhangethi who was sailing to Malé one clear night with a full moon. On board was a large clay pot full of drinking water. When the fisherman became thirsty and bent to dip his ladle in the pot he saw the reflection of the moon inside. He quickly slammed down the lid thinking he'd captured the moon. When he arrived in Malé he excitedly carried the pot of water to the palace and presented the sultan with the moon. The sultan, who was a learned man, laughed uncontrollably and dropped the pot of water, breaking it on the ground. The fisherman was horrified. "Now look what's happened", he said, "the moon's escaped."

*The Banyan tree on the island of Dangethi is a likely source of many island stories.*

**Maafushivaru** opened as Twin Island resort in 1991.

**Dhehasanu Lonu Bui Huraa** has very little vegetation. The name is believed to have come from two men (named Hassan) drinking salt water on the island.

**Machchafushi** means island coming up. It opened as Machchafushi Island Resort in 1992.

**Vakarufalhi** opened as a resort in 1994. *Vakaru* is a part of a coconut tree.

**Kudarah** started as a resort in 1991.

**Dhigurah** lies on the south east rim of the atoll. *Dhigurah* means long island and at three km, it is indeed the longest island in the atoll. It is also one of the most picturesque with its long beach, protected lagoon and thatched huts mingling with heavy foliage down to the water's edge. The lagoon also offers good anchorage to safari boats during the north-east monsoon. The island is continually growing, or being washed away. There are sandbanks at the southern end.

**Dhidhdhoo Finolhu** started as Ari Beach Resort in 1987. It was the first resort in the south of Ari Atoll and was at that time one of the most isolated resorts in the Maldives. Other resorts were soon developed in the area. Nowadays, the number of bungalows has been increased and the island redeveloped. It has been renamed White Sands Resort.

**Dhidhdhoo** islanders have a reputation as being strong and fair skinned people. Legend has it that in the past a French vessel was wrecked on the reef of this island and that from the sailors who stayed on, new blood was introduced to the island.

**Kudadhoo** is a small uninhabited island near the edge of the reef next to Dhidhdhoo.

**Hiyafushi** is another uninhabited island. *Hiya* means 69 so perhaps this island was the 69th island to be counted in the atoll.

**Ariyadhoo** is an uninhabited island at the very south of Ari Atoll. It is privately leased as an agricultural island with fruit trees and coconut trees planted in neat rows. It was once an island of importance and Ari Atoll is derived from the name of this island. In 1959 sites on the island were excavated and part of an old Buddhist monastery was uncovered. Various artifacts were found including a phallus measuring 38 cm in length and 30 cm in circumference at the base. Further excavations on two Havittas in 1988 uncovered both Hindu and Buddhist relics.

**Maamigili** lies on the 15 km long Fenfushi Faru, which is the longest reef in the atoll. Islanders are well known for making limestone for building blocks and for coral and sand mining. There is an old mosque on the island built at the end of the 17th century. A new harbour and airport are being constructed and they are expected to service the south of Ari Atoll.

**Dhiffushi** opened as Holiday Island resort in 1994.

**Nalaguraidhoo** is a larger island that opened as Sun Island resort in 1996. *Nala* means pretty and *guraa* is a parrot.

**Nalaguridhoo** is an island where shear-water birds dig their burrows.

**Tholhufushi** is a small uninhabited island.

**Fenfushi** means good water island. It is an old inhabited island and the islanders are well known for their coral carvings and tombstones and for building mosques from stone. The Fenfushi Friday Mosque is the same design as Malé's Friday Mosque and is a fine example of their craftsmanship. It was built during the reign of Sultan Mohammed Ibn Al Haj Ali (1692 – 1701 AD). Restoration of the mosque is now being carried out. Sadly, the artists are old and few carry on the carving tradition. Tombstones are now mostly made with cement and stone carving is a dying art. Several sandbars have formed alongside Fenfushi and one day they may form another island.

**Huruelhi** is a small uninhabited island with low vegetation and lies on the north side of Heygahathu Kandu.

**Hukurudhoo** is an uninhabited island with lush vegetation. It was once an inhabited island named Hukuruelhi. On the south west side of the island is a large pile of rocks. *Hukuru* means Friday and islanders tell a story of how the pile of rocks originated and the island became uninhabited. It is said that on one Friday, when the fishing season was very good, the islanders went fishing instead of going to prayers, which invoked the fury of Allah. A whale was seen following the boats out to sea and when the fishermen failed to return, the remaining islanders built a tower of rocks from where they could look out for the lost boats. After the fishermen disappeared, the remaining people moved to another island. It is possible the rocks built up as a result of a cyclone, as the long reef extends to the south west in the direction from which a cyclone would blow.

Sperm whales are occasionally sighted in deeper waters around the Maldives. They hold a special place in Maldivian folklore and Maldivians call them *Odi Kaan Bodu Mas*, or 'boat eating big fish'. Early Arab mariners used to fire arrows at *Al-baba* as encounters with boats were not uncommon. Smaller whales were hunted then boiled in cooking pots to obtain oil, which was used for stopping up the seams of boats after they were sewn together.

**Rangali Finolhu** first opened as Rangali Island Resort in 1992, then the Maldives Hilton in 1997. *Ran* means gold and *gaa* is coral stone. The name may have originated from the bright coloured coral stones glittering in the sun on the reef.

**Rangali** is an uninhabited island on the outside of the same reef.

**Mirihi** lies 6.5 km east of Rangali resort. It opened as Mirihi Marina in 1989. The south side of the island borders the edge of the reef and offers good snorkelling. Mirihi is a bushy creeper with small yellow flowers (*Wedelia calendulacea, biflora*) and is often used in local medicine. It is a potent medicine and a measure of its strength is its reputation for driving away snakes. It is said that if an island has Mirihi bushes, then there will be no snakes on that island. There is only one variety of snake found in the Maldives. It is a 60 cm poisonous one called *nannugathi*, and if it is beaten with a branch of Mirihi then, it is said, the snake will die.

**Angaagau** lies in the middle of the atoll and opened as Angaaga Island Resort in 1989.

**Hurasdhoo** is an uninhabited island called Pineapple Island by nearby resorts. The island is more fertile than many others and at one time someone started growing pineapples there. They now grow wildly and the sweet smell of ripened pineapples attracts many crabs, as well as tourists, to the island. The island is easily recognised by a single coconut tree in the centre. Picnics and snorkelling are regularly made here as there is good access to the beach. Hurasdhoo is one island where frigate birds come to rest.

**Mandhoo** is a larger inhabited island with big trees and lush vegetation. It is very fertile and vegetables are grown here. The islanders are good fishermen. Mandhoo has been inhabited for many centuries and Buddhist relics have been found on the island.

**Bulhaa Lhohi** is uninhabited and lies four km north east of Mandhoo. It has few coconut trees and bushes, but a good sandy beach with access to the island and a good anchorage. Picnics are popular here and there is excellent snorkelling and diving on the south west side of the island. Bulhaa means cat but there are no cats to be seen on this island.

**Rahdhdhiggaa** is a small, uninhabited, low-vegetation island 4.5 km to the north east of Bulhaa Lhohi. It has a good anchorage inside the lagoon and a sand entrance to the beach.

**Thundufushi** opened as a resort in 1990. *Thundu* means the edge or point and this island lays on the eastern point of Thundufushi Falhu. There is good snorkelling on the house reef and beside the long jetty.

**Innafushi** is uninhabited with low vegetation.

**Kalhahandi Huraa** is a sandbank island.

**Eboodhoo** is another uninhabited island three km north east of Innafushi. It has a good cover of trees, nice beach and excellent snorkelling and diving, especially on the south side. It is often visited by day-trippers and the island has a long jetty. *Emboo* is a small, wild fruit that grows on bushes (*Glochidion littorale*).

**Heenfaru** lies eight km to the east of Eboodhoo and is a small sandbank island with no trees and little scrub.

On the outside of the atoll is a big reef **Maavaru Falhu**. It has no island but offers good anchorage in all seasons.

**Moofushi** opened as a resort in 1990. The island has many trees and *moo* is the root of a tree.

**Athurugaa** lies nine km east of Moofushi. It started as Athurugau Island Resort in 1990. *Athurugaa* means stones without any arrangement. It has a good snorkelling reef on the south eastern side of the island.

*Islands in the south of Ari Atoll with Maamigili in the foreground followed by Ariyadhoo.*

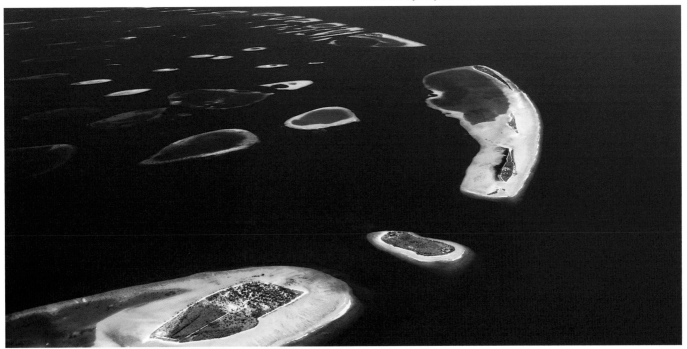

# Diving South Ari Atoll

*South Ari Atoll has many excellent thilas, both within the atoll and in the channels. There are also four wreck dives. One of the feature areas is the Dhigurashu Kandu, where the thilas spring up from the outer rim of the atoll like 10 pins in a bowling alley. There are around 12 thilas in the 4.5 km wide channel of which only a handful are frequently dived. Some are quite deep and hard to find and the frequent swift currents and choppy seas can make diving conditions hazardous. Only experienced divers with knowledgeable boatmen should attempt the diving here at these times. The southern outside reef in the vicinity of Ariyadu Kandu, has become famous for the regular all-year-round appearance of whale sharks. Mantas and sharks are also prevalent at many locations, with Madivaru being the most documented site for mantas.*

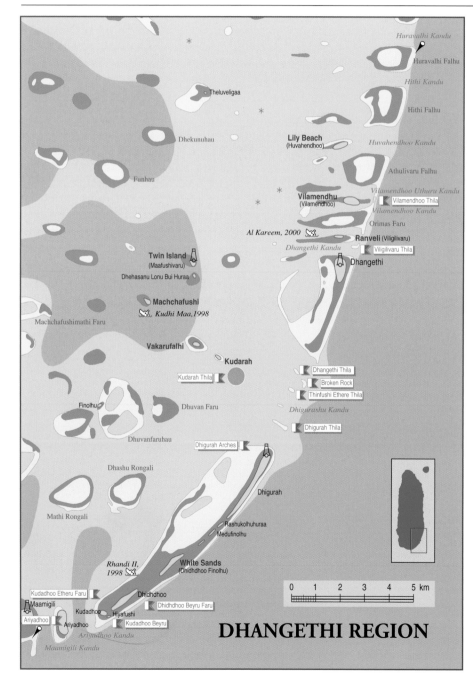

### Vilamendhoo Thila ★★★

On the outside of Vilamendhoo is a narrow thila that rises from 25 metres at either end to six metres in the centre. On the west side is a steep drop-off with caves from 10 to 25 metres. There are many large seafans here, good hard and soft corals and plenty of fish life. The outside slopes more gradually to 25 metres. At the northern end is a big rock and cave at 25 metres. There is good coral on the reef top and mantas are often seen in this area.

### Viligilivaru Thila ★★★

Is a 500 metre long thila lying east to west in Dhangethi Kandu. It then swings north for another 250 metres outside Viligilivaru. The thila rises to six metres from the sandy channel floor at 20 metres.

*Scribbled filefish, Aluterus scriptus. A larger species of filefish growing to one metre and sometimes referred to as the scribbled leatherjacket because of its tough leathery skin. Its first dorsal fin has a strong spine which can be locked in the upright position.*

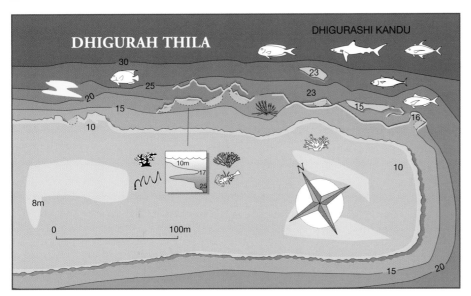

### Dhigurah Thila ★★★

| | |
|---|---|
| Location: | southern end of Dhigurashu Kandu |
| Depth: | 10m – 30m |
| Fish life: | abundant |
| Coral growth: | very good |
| Features: | reef fish, over hangs, caves |

Dhigurah Thila is the biggest thila in the channel. It is also the most visible thila from the surface. The long sausage-shaped thila is about 500 metres long with the best diving on the north eastern side. The reef edge is at 10 metres and for most of the reef there are overhangs beginning at 15 metres that step down in tiers to the bottom at about 30 metres. There are at least three caves, one at a depth of 18 metres with a deep cut 50 metres in length. Inside, on the cave floor is a forest of long seawhips, seafans and black coral bushes with bright yellow featherstars. There are many smaller species of wrasse, cardinalfish and tiny shrimp.

At the eastern end of the reef is a big rocky outcrop. It looks to have once been a cave that has now collapsed. At this end are greater concentrations of pelagic fish with many tuna and shark and jacks. Emperor angelfish, both juvenile and adult, are commonly seen all along the reef slope. There are also large numbers of big-nose unicornfish, and scribbled filefish as well as massive schools of blue-dash and yellow-back fusilier. There is healthy coral on the reef top and soft coral hanging off the ledges. Because of its large size, this thila is given preference over the other thilas in the channel when weather or current conditions are marginal.

### Broken Rock ★★★

| | |
|---|---|
| Location: | Dhigurashu Kandu |
| Depth: | 12m – 28m |
| Fish life: | abundant |
| Coral growth: | very good |
| Features: | canyon, reef fish, soft coral |

Broken Rock is the most eastern thila of those commonly dived in Dhigurashu Kandu. It is around 80 metres long and what clearly distinguishes this thila from the others in the channel, is a canyon, about one to three metres wide and up to 10 metres deep. It slices through the reef from the south east to the north west. The top of the reef is 12 metres and the canyon reaches a maximum depth of 24 metres. Another large rock exists on the eastern side of the reef. There are many different ways to dive this thila but swimming carefully through the 50 metre long canyon is one of the highlights. The strong currents and protected pockets on the reef have made an ideal environment for an amazing variation in marine life from strong branching seafans and soft coral to schools of barracuda, fusilier, tallfin batfish and turtles.

**Diving hints:** Photographers will have numerous surprise photo opportunities here, however extreme care should be taken against damaging the coral. When the current is running it is not advised to take cameras as sharp corners, jutting outcrops and narrow squeezes make this site especially vulnerable to diver damage.

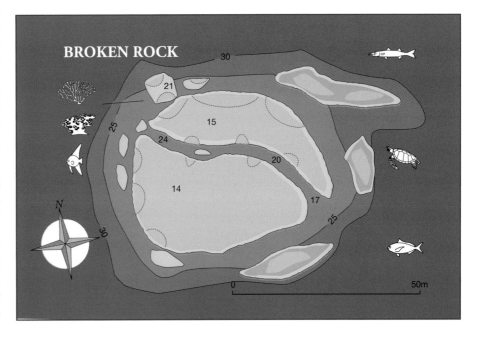

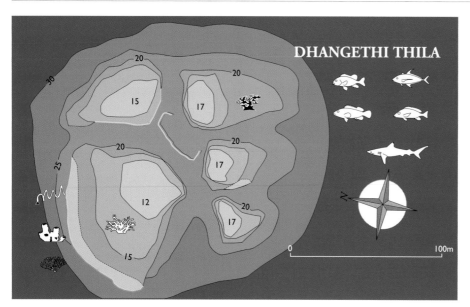

DHANGETHI THILA

*The Al Kareem was scuttled on the north side of Ranveli Village in 2000.*

### Dhangethi Thila ★★★

| | |
|---|---|
| Location: | Dhigurashu Kandu |
| Depth: | 12m – 25m |
| Fish life: | abundant |
| Coral growth: | excellent |
| Features: | canyon, seafans, caves |

This is a small, deep, flower-shaped thila located 50 metres from a larger reef that rises to six metres. Diving usually begins and finishes on the larger reef, where there are caves and overhangs at more shallow depths. An open water safety stop is often required with a strong current. The walls of the canyons and floors of the deep overhanging caves are covered with seafans and seawhips. This is a challenging dive and delightfully memorable thila; one of the jewels in the chain of thilas scattered across the channel.

### Thinfushi Ethere Thila ★★★

In Dhigurashu Kandu is a stunning thila between eight and 25 metres featuring caves with seafans and soft corals. Fish life is abundant and coral growth is excellent. The thila has one of the most spectacular displays of seafans to be found anywhere in the atoll. Along the walls and inside the caves are large, healthy seafans – an indication of the strength of the currents flowing in and out of this channel. The 100 metre oval-shaped thila begins at eight metres and drops to over 30. Much of it is a continuous line of ledges, caves and overhangs, mostly at

depths from 14 to 20 metres. In the caves are many surprises including an occasional electric ray and nurse sharks. To the south east are some interesting reef outcrops with overhangs and caves.

### Dhigura Arches ★★

This is a drift dive covering about 300 metres of reef edge to the west of Dhigurah on the inside of Dhigurashu Kandu. The top of the reef is between three and five metres and drops away steeply to 24 metres. The reef edge is clearly seen on the surface by the change in iridescent blues. The arches have an interesting reef formation that is full of surprises. Along the reef edge are numerous small inlets, some five metres wide, others 10 metres or 15 metres in width, all occurring one after the other with depths to 15 metres. One never knows what to expect in the next inlet. Coral growth is good and among many of the inlets are coral outcrops with plenty of small reef fish. There are a few small caves, some with seafans. During the south-west monsoon season, schooling mantas and whale sharks are frequently seen.

*Seafans and large schools of fish are a feature of the caves at Dhangethi Thila.*

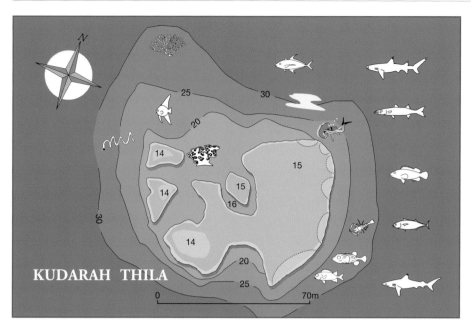

*Blue-fin jack* Caranx melampygus.

**Kudarah Thila ★★★★**

PROTECTED MARINE AREA

| Location: | 1 km south east of Kudarah |
|---|---|
| Depth: | 14m – 25m |
| Fish life: | abundant |
| Coral growth: | very good |
| Features: | reef fish, sharks, seafans |

One of the most exciting dives in South Ari Atoll is Kudarah Thila. The reef top is at 14 metres with sharp dropoffs to 20 and 25 metres on most sides. There are isolated outcrops of rock on the west side, a small canyon on the north side and a big, long cave at 20 metres on the eastern side. When the current is not too strong, divers can swim around this 80 metre long thila without too much difficulty. On the deeper more gentle slopes on the northern side are great expanses of large seafans. Such fields of fans are rarely seen and when the current is flowing they all sway as one. Swimming around the fan slopes are a number of grey and white-tip reef sharks. Pelagics like rainbow runner, great barracuda, blue-fin jack and tuna are drawn from the surrounding waters and seen in abundance. The reef outcrops on the western side are coated in soft coral and swimming around them are tallfin batfish. On the sand and rubble flats between the reefs at 15 metres are many species of goby, like the red fire dart goby and other small burrowers. At the big cave on the eastern side are many squirrelfish, some pufferfish, grouper and small fans and black coral bushes. At the northern end of the cave is a swim-through to the top of the reef. On the south side are many squirrelfish, some pufferfish, grouper and small fans and black coral bushes. There is also a small canyon on the top with many smaller fish.

**Diving hints:** This is strictly a dive for experienced divers. Strong currents are frequent and divers will usually start up-current and be required to descend quickly to the thila in these conditions. Unfortunately the reef top, which is rich in coral, bears many scars from boats that have in the past anchored on the reef top.

*Red fire dart goby,* Nemateleotris magnifica. *A strikingly beautiful fish usually found in pairs near their burrows. They come out to feed on zoo plankton when there is current.*

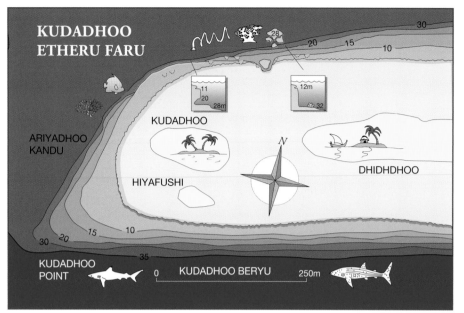

*Ring-eye hawkfish, Paracirrhites arcuatus.
Its distinctive eye pattern makes this little
fish unmistakable. Often found wedged in
coral heads waiting for prey.*

### Kudadhoo Etheru Faru ★★★

| | |
|---|---|
| Location: | inside reef corner near Kudadhoo |
| Depth: | 3m – 30m+ |
| Fish life: | abundant |
| Coral growth: | very good |
| Features: | steep wall, coral, reef fish |

There are few wall dives in Ari Atoll that can match this one. It has several features worth noting as they will ultimately determine the type of dive made here. Near the northern end of Kudadhoo island is a small 'bite' in the reef perhaps 15 metres wide which starts on the reeftop at three metres and drops to 12 metres. In the middle of the bite is a large coral rock that gives a canyon effect. In this small canyon are blackcoral bushes, tallfin batfish, masked bannerfish and soft coral. Over the reef edge directly below the bite, the wall drops sharply to sand at 30 metres. Near the base of this wall are four large boulders which look like they have broken away from the bite above. Fish life, coral and canyons are exceptional here. The steep wall continues to the corner of Ariyadhoo Kandu and is undercut at the base at 28 metres. At the undercut are black coral bushes with oyster shells, seawhips, seafans and large flower grouper. This sheer wall is coated in a layer of invertebrates that attract moorish idol and long-nosed butterflyfish

as well as big-nose unicornfish, blue-face angelfish, and clown triggerfish. Divers can continue their drift around the corner into Ariyadhoo Kandu where the wall becomes less steep. One good option though, is to spend the remainder of the dive on the corner above the wall at 12 metres where there is a profusion of hard coral and reef fish. The variety of fish life here is stunning, with many smaller species like the distinctive bird wrasse, the ring-eye hawkfish and the long-nosed butterflyfish being prevalent. There are also large morays and napoleon to ensure all types and sizes are well represented.

**Diving hints:** If diving with an outgoing current, it is a good idea to start before the bite and stay at 12 metres or above where there are some caves and overhangs. Once at the bite, then descend to the boulders at 30 metres. It is a good idea to limit the time spent around the boulders to about five minutes so that plenty of bottom time remains for the undercut in the wall at 28 metres.

### Kudadhoo Beyru ★★

Kudadhoo Point and Kudadhoo Beyru is a leisurely drift dive where the reef slopes gently from five to 20 metres. The reef then drops steeply to greater depths. Whale sharks are regularly seen along this reef as well as grouper and napoleon.

### Dhidhdhoo Beyru Faru ★★

About 1.5 km east of Kudadhoo Beyru, the outside reef has very good fish life but is better known for its whale sharks, which visit here more often than any other site in the atoll. Between the months of May and November the whale sharks and mantas continually return to this outside reef to feed and can often be seen on a daily basis. A mother and calf have been regularly sighted here as well as whale sharks travelling alone.

### Ariyadhoo ★★★

The western side of the island has a good, long reef sloping to 30 metres with caves at either end. The eastern side wall is more steep.

*Bird wrasse, Gomphosus caeruleus.
The long nose allows the bird wrasse to
pick out tiny invertebrates from the
cracks and crevices of reefs.
Gomphosus caeruleus is an Indian
Ocean species.*

The whale shark, Rhincodon typus is the largest of all fish, reaching 15 metres in length. It is a plankton eater and harmless to humans. They feed by siphoning water into their wide-open mouth and through the gill slits to filter out plankton. Whale sharks are usually seen cruising along in shallow water outside the atoll and divers fortunate enough to see one will find them curious and fearless. They sometimes allow divers to swim very close but care and consideration should be shown in the way divers approach them. Diving boats should remain well out of their migratory path and divers should not attempt to block their path or touch or ride them. If they are frightened, they will quickly depart and may not return. In early times, boat captains were very wary of whale sharks. If a captain saw one close to his boat, he would slap the water and the back of the shark with a stick for fear it would capsize his dhoani. Whale shark liver oil was used to waterproof dhoanis, and also for medicinal and black magic purposes.

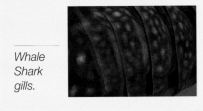

*Whale Shark gills.*

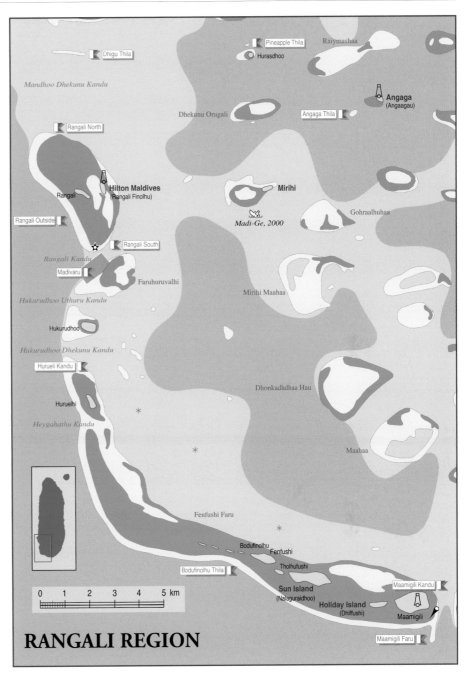

**RANGALI REGION**

### Maamigili Faru ★★★

The reef on the outside corner of Maamigili is a shallow platform that extends from the corner to the outer atoll rim. Sharks, grouper, pelagics, sting rays and turtles are common here.

### Maamigili Kandu ★★

On the inside of the channel are small caves, white-tip reef sharks, napoleon, sting rays and turtles.

Divers should be wary of strong outgoing currents through the channels on both sides of Ariyadhoo. One look at a map will show the funnelling effect the

reefs have in directing currents through these passages.

The big reef west of Ariyadhoo is Fenfushi Faru – the longest reef in Ari Atoll at 15 km in length. The inside of the reef has little to offer in the way of diving but the outside reef offers excellent visibility, long and easy drift dives, and many surprises including sharks, big tuna, turtles and good sized grouper as well as smaller reef fish.

### Bodufinolhu Thila ★★★

On the outside of Bodufinolhu is a 30 metre deep thila that comes up from the ocean depths 50 metres from the outside reef. Big fish and sharks tend to be attracted to this site.

On the north side of Huruelhi faru is Hukurudhoo Dhekunu Kandu, often called **Huruelhi Kandu ★★** a 30 metre deep channel where there are sharks and pelagic fish.

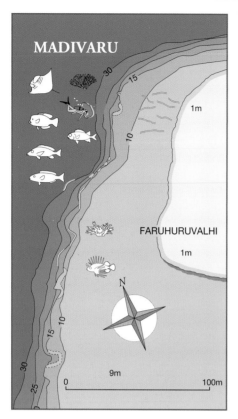

*Midnight snapper,* Macolor macularis. *Adults may form small aggregations, while juveniles usually swim alone. Juveniles are black and white, similiar to the juvenile black snapper,* Macolor niger.

*Doublebar goatfish,* Parupeneus bifasciatus. *Goatfish have two barbels on the chin which are used to detect food, such as crustaceans and worms. The doublebar goatfish swims along the edges of reef in sand and rubble. Other unrelated species can sometimes be seen trailing along picking up the leftovers.*

**Madivaru ★★★** (Manta Reef)

PROTECTED MARINE AREA

| | |
|---|---|
| Location: | south side of Rangali Kandu |
| Depth: | 5m – 25m |
| Fish life: | above average |
| Coral growth: | excellent |
| Features: | mantas |

Both sides of Rangali Kandu make exciting drift dives. The reefs here act like a funnel, forcing the water at accelerated speed both in and out of the atoll. During the north-east monsoon manta rays feed on the plankton-rich waters that generally flow with the currents out of the atoll. At the northern end of Faruhuruvalhi where many of the dives begin, there are erosion gutters on the reef top between five and 10 metres. They are one metre wide and just as deep and have been formed by heavy seas and strong currents. Here the reef slopes to 15 metres then drops quite sharply to 25 metres. There are many cavities in the reef, some overhangs, caves and two swim-throughs all with seafans. All along the reef are blue-striped snapper,

napoleon, parrotfish, basslet and juvenile and adult midnight snapper. In the caves are numerous squirrelfish and the occasional lionfish and on the reef top are excellent table corals.

**Diving hints:** The reef is subject to strong currents – which is one reason why the mantas are here – and at the southern end, the top reef drops down to a 10 metre plateau extending well out into the open ocean. Be prepared to abort the dive if currents are too strong or the seas too rough. Safety balloons should be carried.

**Rangali South ★★**

| | |
|---|---|
| Location: | north side of Rangali Kandu |
| Depth: | 3m – 25m |
| Fish life: | above average |
| Coral growth: | good |
| Features: | reef fish |

Rangali South is a classic long, drift dive with steep walls to 25 metres and many ledges and overhangs undercutting the reef. There are several big caves with seawhips and some small seafans and a number of isolated coral rocks on the edge of the wall. A wide sand-floored inlet with coral rocks on the bottom at 25 metres, divides the reef in two halves. Good sized morays are well established on the reef and large grouper move cautiously around the back of caves. Electric sting rays can be seen on the sand and in the channel sharks and eagle rays are sometimes sighted. On the reef top is a wide range of marine life including hawkfish and damselfish. Doublebar goatfish, yellow box fish, coral hogfish and aggregations of arrow dart goby are all vying for space.

*Manta Ray at Madivaru*

### Rangali Outside ★★

Most of the reefs on the west side of Ari Atoll are wave affected and the corals are gnarled and stunted. This reef is no exception. It is an easy outer reef dive with the reef top at 10 metres. If divers look carefully, they may find leaf fish in shallow water and nurse sharks among the coral bombies. There are many surgeon, including the big-nose unicornfish. Also large-eye emperor, parrotfish, and aggregations of tallfin batfish. Molluscs such as leopard cowries and spider shells can also be seen.

### Rangali North ★★

On the north side of Rangali Faru is a finger of reef protruding into Mandhoo Dhekunu Kandu. The reef slopes from three to 25 metres and has caves on both sides. The bottom at about 30 metres is mostly sand.

### Dhigu Thila ★★★

A long, narrow thila lying east – west, about one km on the south side of Mandhoo Faru. It is 12 metres to the top and has caves at 22 to 25 metres on much of the north side. Turtles are often seen.

### Pineapple Thila ★★★

Lies 100 metres to the north of Hurasdhoo. It is popular with day trippers who combine this dive with island picnics and snorkelling.

*Slender suckerfish, Echeneis naucrates. The remora is commonly seen swimming freely with, or clinging to sharks, turtles and rays by means of a suction disc on top of its head. This disc evolved from the dorsal spine. The remora feeds on the scraps of food left over from its host. It also removes parasites from the gills and skin of its carrier.*

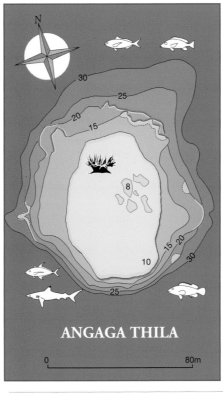

ANGAGA THILA

0                              80m

### Angaga Thila ★★★

| Location: | 1.5 km south west of Angaagau |
| --- | --- |
| Depth: | 8m – 30m |
| Fish life: | above average |
| Coral growth: | good |
| Features: | sharks, reef fish |

The thila is round and small and about 80 metres in diameter. There is one big cave on the northern side that has a good variety of marine life. This thila is one of the more interesting sites inside the atoll for grey reef sharks. There are many species of fish including grouper, basslet, and anemonefish, freckled hawkfish, suckerfish, and flutemouth as well as snapper, fusilier and trevally, but the main attraction is the grey reef sharks.

*Arrow dart goby, Ptereleotris evides. Sometimes called scissortail dartfish. They are common in the Maldives and often seen in pairs hovering above a burrow.*

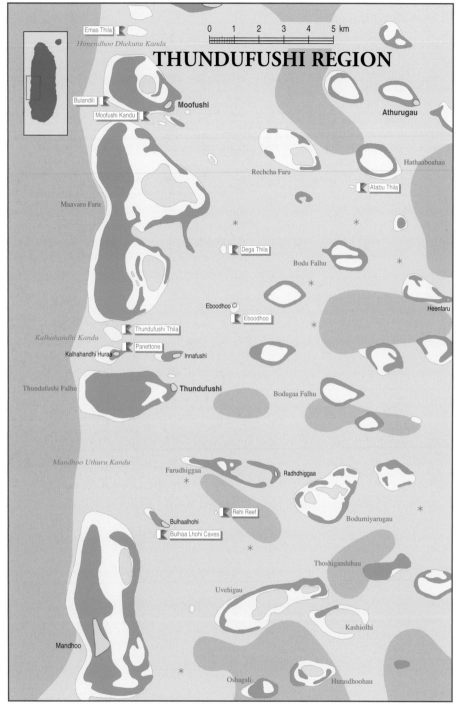

**THUNDUFUSHI REGION**

*Emas Thila*
*Himendhoo Dhekunu Kandu*
*Bulandili*
**Moofushi**
*Moofushi Kandu*
**Athurugau**
*Rechcha Faru*
*Hathaaboahau*
*Maavaru Faru*
*Atabu Thila*
*Dega Thila*
*Bodu Falhu*
*Eboodhoo*
*Eboodhoo*
*Heenfaru*
*Kalhahandhi Kandu*
*Thundufushi Thila*
*Panettone*
*Kalhahandhi Huraa*
*Innafushi*
*Thundufushi Falhu*
**Thundufushi**
*Bodugaa Falhu*
*Mandhoo Uthuru Kandu*
*Farudhiggaa*
*Radhdhiggaa*
*Rehi Reef*
*Bodumiyarugau*
*Bulhaalhohi*
*Bulhaa Lhohi Caves*
*Thoshiganduhau*
*Uvehigau*
*Kashiolhi*
*Mandhoo*
*Oshagali*
*Hurasdhoohau*

*Reindeer wrasse,* Novaculichthys taeniourus. *The beautiful juvenile loses its filamentous fins as it gets older. Adults grow to 24 cm and are known as rock-lifters because they are capable of lifting large pieces of coral with their teeth.*

## Rehi reef ★

Rehi reef is a giri 1.5 km east of Bulhaa Lhohi. The top of the reef is at three metres and the north and western sides are the most interesting. The rest appears rather dull, without many features or good coral growth. There is a big cave and ledges stepping from five to 15 metres on the north west side where there are black coral bushes and seafans, also harlequin sweetlip and snapper. Close by at 15 metres is an arch in the reef. Blue triggerfish and the less common boomerang triggerfish, gold-spot emperor, large-eye emperor, blue-dash fusilier and yellow-back fusilier are among the more commonly sighted fish on the reef. The barren part of the reef also has its unique marine life among the coral rubble and sand, especially the goby and juvenile reindeer wrasse at the southern end.

*Starry rabbitfish,* Siganus stellatus. *Often seen swimming along the shallow reef in pairs feeding on weeds and algaes.*

## Bulhaa Lhohi Caves ★★

On the south western side of Bulhaa Lhohi is an excellent reef suitable for both snorkellers and divers. The uninhabited island is ideal for picnics and safari boats take advantage of the island's good anchorage. Coral growth is very good and there is above average fish life. Night dives are popular here. The reef has many caves between seven and 20 metres. One cave at 16 metres is like a huge window and has a swim-through to another cave where seafans with featherstars dominate. It is an excellent location for photographers. Above this cave at 12 metres is another similar cave just as exciting.

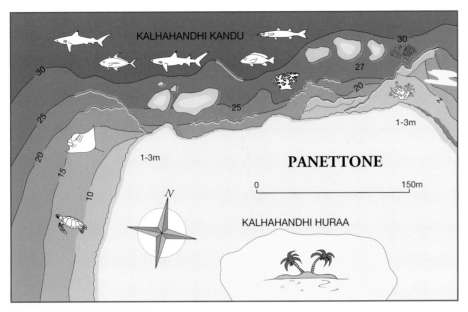

*Oriental Sweetlips at Thundufushi Thila.*

### Panettone ★★★

| | |
|---|---|
| Location: | north side of Kalhahandhi Huraa |
| Depth: | 5m – 30m |
| Fish life: | abundant |
| Coral growth: | excellent |
| Features: | reef formation, pelagics, soft and hard coral |

Panettone is an exceptional dive. *Kalhahandhi* is the Maldivian name for the giant trevally and this fish is common along the reef. There are many features of interest including reef outcrops at 27 metres where white-tips and grey reef sharks, barracuda and giant trevally gather. There are numerous overhangs down to 20 metres and one big cave between 10 and 20 metres with a brilliant display of soft coral and seafans. All the reef is covered in soft coral – no wonder as the current really streams through this channel. Turtles are frequently seen and during the north-east monsoon, mantas make a regular appearance. There are many reef fish especially snapper and a surprising number of starry rabbitfish.

**Diving hints:** With a strong outgoing current, divers can start from a protected sandy inlet on the inside near the big cave. Divers may find themselves being swept towards the top of the reef in which case they should swim down to the protection of the reef in deeper water. Extreme care should be taken with strong outgoing currents and divers should stay shallow on the outside reef at these times. Be prepared to make an open water safety stop if required.

### Thundufushi Thila ★★★

| | |
|---|---|
| Location: | Kalhahandhi Kandu |
| Depth: | 10 – 30m |
| Fish life: | above average |
| Coral growth: | very good |
| Features: | mantas |

A remarkably long and spectacular thila with many exciting features. It is a large and rounded thila, nearly one km in diameter with its best diving on the northern side. The thila drops in steps to deeper depths on the western side near the outside of the atoll. The channel bottoms out to a maximum of 35 metres inside Kalhahandhi Kandu. There are shallow caves with sabre squirrelfish and steep ledges for most of the dive between 10 and 25 metres. Several reef outcrops at 25 metres or deeper are well worth a closer look. Around them are schools of masked bannerfish and surgeon, moorish idol, striped fusilier and gold-spot emperor. In the channel are grey reef sharks, eagle rays, dog-toothed tuna, and mantas in the north-east monsoon season.

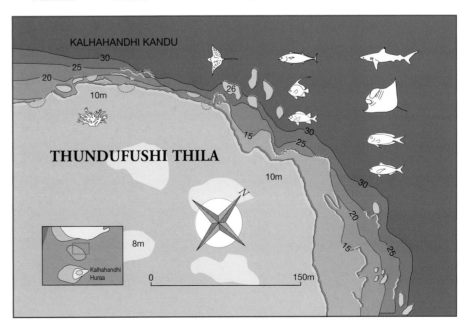

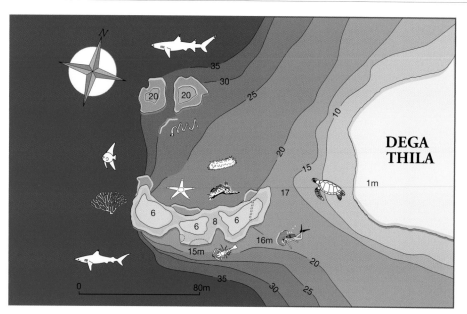

### Dega Thila ★★ (Gondoli Thila)

| | |
|---|---|
| Location: | 2 km north of Eboodhoo |
| Depth: | 6m – 30m+ |
| Fish life: | above average |
| Coral growth: | very good |
| Features: | pinnacles, tunnel, sharks |

A towering peak rising from more than 40 metres to six metres forms a narrow ridge extending westwards off the main reef. It is one of the most dramatic reef formations to be seen in the Maldives. A wall of seafans lies on the outside of the peak at 35 metres while around the reef are turtles, tallfin batfish, white-tip reef sharks and a school of grey reef sharks. The top of the peak at six metres is covered in small anemones and hard coral. A tunnel which divers can swim through cuts through the reef at 16 metres. Schools of yellow sweeper inhabit two large arches in the reef on the south side at 15 metres.

Another two rock pinnacles on the north side rise to 20 metres and can be included in this dive. There is a narrow canyon between these two pinnacles and black coral bushes sprout from the walls. The reef top features many species of damselfish, snapper, cardinalfish and wrasse. Big stands of branching coral occur on the main reef.

**Diving hints:** This dive is an ideal site for deep water speciality dives. Currents are normally very slight.

*Tall-fin batfish,* Platax teira. *Inhabits deep water and dropoffs either alone or in small schools. Juveniles have exaggerated tall fins and will migrate long distances with floating weed before settling on a reef. Batfish are one of the few species that eat jellyfish.*

*Tall-fin batfish,* Platax teira. *Juvenile form.*

### Eboodhoo ★

This is an uninhabited island. It has good diving with many caves and a couple of swim-throughs with seafans on the south side near the jetty between 15 and 20 metres. Marine life includes morays, sweetlip, pufferfish and porcupinefish, black snapper and turtles.

### Atabu Thila ★★★★

Is located 3.5 km south west of Athurugaa. It is a small thila not more than 70 metres long with the top at 17 metres. One big cave on the north side has a colony of tiny yellow wrasse and there are a few interesting ledges with big seafans on the east side. There is also a school of tallfin batfish, red snapper and on the reef top are many damselfish. However, the main attraction at Atabu Thila are 10 or more large dog-toothed tuna and grey reef sharks.

### Bulandili ★★

Named after the napoleonfish, Bulandili is a 1.5 km drift dive which covers the northern outside corner of Moofushi Kandu. Like the rest of the channel, there are many caves and ledges. Some caves and overhangs have collapsed leaving the shattered remains on the reef. Invertebrates are in abundance all over the reef. These include shrimp, sea stars, flat worms, pin cushions and sea cucumbers. Sea anemones cling to the reef top and soft coral thrives on the cliff faces. Napoleon, eagle rays and sharks stand out among the diverse marine life. Powerful seas and currents have eroded a trail of gutters on the outside reef top at 10 metres.

*Napoleonfish,* Cheilinus undulatus.

## Moofushi Kandu ★★

Five minutes by boat from Moofushi resort is a 1.5 km drift dive on the north side of Moofushi channel. A feature of this dive is at least three big cuttings in the reef forming overhangs and caves between 10 and 25 metres. The caves are full of marine life: seafans, whips, squirrelfish, grouper, emperor, and sweetlip. Many sharks, eagle rays and napoleon can be seen cruising the length of the channel.

## Emas Thila ★★★

| | |
|---|---|
| Location: | Himendhoo Dhekunu Kandu |
| Depth: | 10m – 30m |
| Fish life: | abundant |
| Coral growth: | very good |
| Features: | mantas, caves, reef fish |

Emas Thila is about one km long and is a gathering point for mantas during the north-east monsoon season. It is also an excellent drift dive on both the north and south sides of the thila. The reef top is 15 metres on the western or outside of the thila but rises to around 10 metres on the inside section. Mantas mostly focus on some coral rocks on the reef top on the outside of the thila. Along the reef edge is a shallow ledge at 15 metres. The outside reef slopes gently to 30 metres before dropping more steeply on the outside wall. Most of the thila is undercut by ledges and

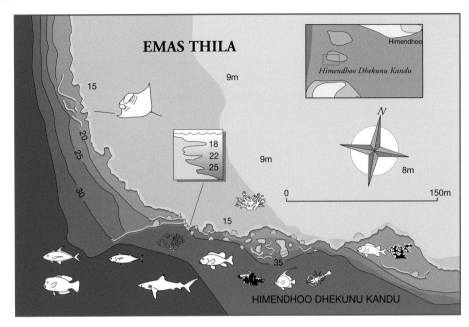

EMAS THILA

caves below 15 metres and all are filled with a vast number of fish. On the southern side, the channel cuts into the thila and here the ledges mingle, creating a spectacular series of caves directly below one another to a depth of more than 30 metres. This wall of caves continues for most of the thila. There are many seafans, seawhips, soft coral and squirrelfish in the caves and in the channel are big dog-toothed tuna, napoleon, and sharks. There is one terrace at about 30 metres on the southern side where coral rocks are grouped together forming small gullies and arches. Around the rocks are great schools of fish, most notably the masked bannerfish, but also harlequin sweetlip, oriental sweetlip, trevally, red bass and emperor.

**Diving hints:** Currents can be strong but because the thila is so big, experienced divers can make a comfortable drift dive in moderately strong currents. Safety balloons are essential.

*Masked bannerfish,* Heniochus monoceros.

*Harlequin sweetlip,* Plectorhinchus chaetodonoides. *Juveniles are distinctly marked with large spots and are known as clown sweetlip. They are nocturnal feeders mainly of bottom-living invertebrates. This large juvenile is undergoing pattern changes as it nears the adult stage.*

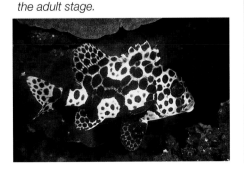

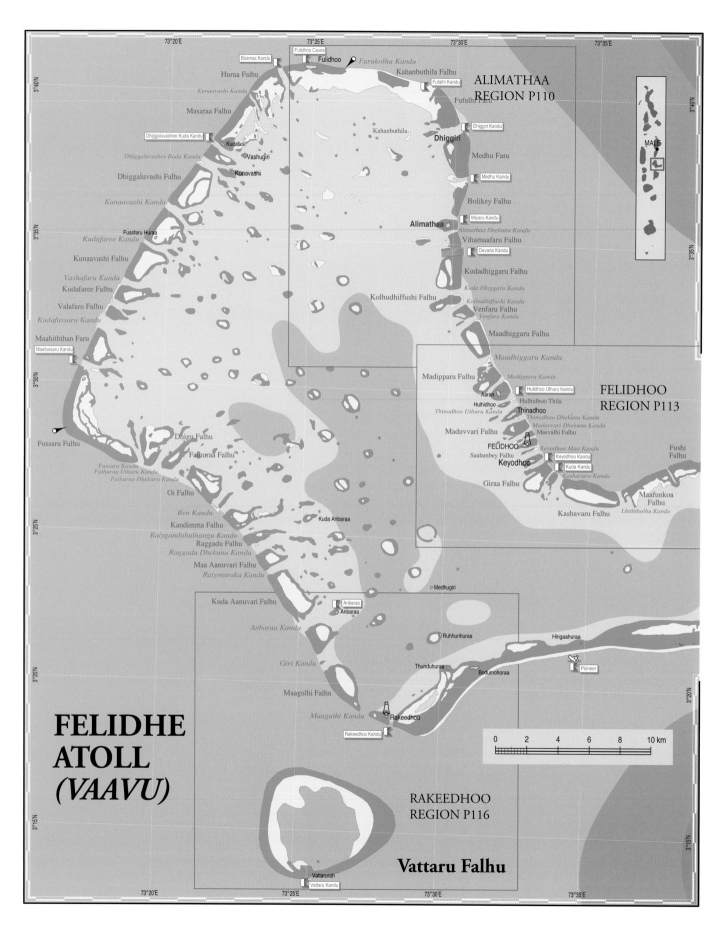

Boamas Kandu
Fulidhoo Caves
Fulidhoo
*Farukolhu Kandu*
Huraa Falhu
Kahanbuthila Falhu

ALIMATHAA
REGION P110

*Kunaavashi Kandu*
Fufalhi Kandu
Fufalhi Faru
Masaraa Falhu

Dhiggaluvashee Kuda Kandu
Kahanbuthila
Dhiggiri Kandu
Kudaboli
*Dhiggaluvashee Bodu Kandu*
Dhiggiri
Vashugiri
Medhu Faru
Dhiggaluvashi Falhu
Kunavashi
Medhu Kandu

*Kunaavashi Kandu*
Bolikey Falhu

MALE

Fussfaru Huraa
Miyaru Kandu
Alimathaa
*Kudafaree Kandu*
*Alimathaa Dhekunu Kandu*
Kunaavashi Falhu
Vihamaafaru Falhu
Devana Kandu
*Vashafaru Kandu*
Kudafaree Falhu
Kudadhiggaru Falhu
Valafaru Falhu
*Kuda Dhiggaru Kandu*
*Kudafussaru Kandu*
Kolhudhiffushi Falhu
*Kolhudhiffushi Kandu*
Maahiththan Faru
Venfaru Falhu
*Venfaru Kandu*
Maafussaru Kandu
Maadhiggaru Falhu

*Maadhiggaru Kandu*
Madipparu Falhu
*Madipparu Kandu*

FELIDHOO
REGION P113

Aaran
Hulidhoo Uthuru Kandu
Hulhidhoo
*Thinadhoo Uthuru Kandu*
Thinadhoo
*Thinadhoo Dhekunu Kandu*
Fussaru Falhu
Maduvvari Falhu
*Maduvvari Dhekunu Kandu*
Masvalhi Falhu
Dhigu Falhu
FELIDHOO
Fushi
Falhu
Faihuraa Falhu
*Keyodhoo Maa Kandu*
Saalambey Falhu
Keyodhoo
*Fussaru Kandu*
Keyodhoo Kandu
*Faihuraa Uthuru Kandu*
Kuda Kandu
*Faihuraa Dhekunu Kandu*
Giraa Falhu
*Kashavaru Kandu*
Oi Falhu
Maafunkoa
Falhu
*Ben Kandu*
Kuda Anbaraa
Kashavaru Falhu
*Lhiththolhu Kandu*
Kandimma Falhu
*Raiygandhuhulhangu Kandu*
Raggadu Falhu
*Raggadu Dhekunu Kandu*
Maa Aanuvari Falhu
*Raiymuraka Kandu*

Medhugiri
Kuda Aanuvari Falhu
Anbaraa
Anbaraa
*Anbaraa Kandu*
Ruhhurihuraa
Hingaahuraa
*Giri Kandu*
Pioneer
Thunduhuraa
Bodumohoraa
Maagulhi Falhu
*Maagulhi Kandu*
Rakeedhoo
Rakeedhoo Kandu

# FELIDHE
# ATOLL
# *(VAAVU)*

| 0 | 2 | 4 | 6 | 8 | 10 km |

RAKEEDHOO
REGION P116

**Vattaru Falhu**

Vattarurah
Vattaru Kandu

# Chapter 6 - Felidhe Atoll Islands *(Vaavu)*

*Felidhe Atoll is located on the eastern range of the Maldive archipelago and is separated from South Malé Atoll by the 14 km wide Fulidhoo Kandu. Felidhe Atoll is 42 km long and 55 km wide and shaped like a boot with the toe being Fotteyo Muli, which is a reef protruding from the northern tip of Fotteyo Falhu. Fotteyo Falhu is one long unbroken reef extending from Hurahu Kandu in the east to Rakeedhoo Dhekunu Kandu in the south. It is the longest reef in the Maldives being 55 km in length. The island of Fotteyo-bodufushi lies within the falhu and is the most eastern island in the archipelago. Felidhe Atoll has five inhabited islands, Fulidhoo, Thinadhoo, Felidhoo, Keyodhoo, and Rakeedhoo. There are 10 uninhabited islands of which two, Dhiggiri and Alimathaa, are resorts and there are several small sand islands with bushes. Vattaru Atoll is a small round shaped atoll 9 km wide that lies 4.5 km to the south of Felidhe Atoll. It has only one small uninhabited island, Vattarurah, and one kandu, Vattaru Kandu on the southern side of the atoll. This channel is now a Protected Marine Area and is a popular diving location. Safari boats often include this location on their Felidhe diving itinerary as well as a picnic at the island. A further 4.5 km south is Mulaku Atoll.*

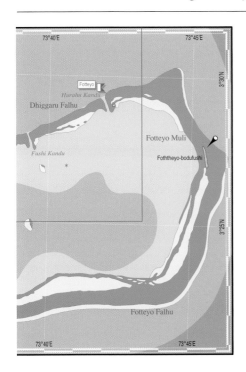

*Right: Looking south at a chain of islands and reefs in Felidhe Atoll. Aarah (foreground) followed by Hulidhoo, Thinadhoo, Felidhoo and Keyodhoo.*

**Fulidhoo** is a picturesque inhabited island with neat coral houses lining the streets and thatched roofed fishing huts spread among the palm trees along the shores. The island has a good harbour and is a popular stopover for safari boats. The island has always been used by fishermen travelling between Malé and the southern atolls. The islanders are famous for their *bandiyaa*, or 'pot dance', performed by the womenfolk. *Boduberus* are also popular pastimes with the menfolk and the regular flow of visitors gives the islanders an excuse to celebrate. The island is easily identified by a tall light on the eastern side of the island to mark the beginning of the atoll. There is a story related to the island of Fulidhoo which says that when the people were in the mosque attending Friday prayers, the Redhin (who were a group of mythical people who worshiped both idols and fire), came and set the mosque on fire. All the people, except for one, were burnt to death. The tomb of the survivor is still to be seen. (In *Islands Of The Maldives*, by Hassan Maniku).

**Dhiggiri** means long coral patch and opened as a tourist resort in 1982. It is a small round island set slightly back in the atoll with a good snorkelling reef.

**Alimathaa** opened as a resort in 1975 and was among the first resorts to open. It now has 70 rooms. *Ali* means light. The resort offers good snorkelling and diving along the housereef on the south side of the island. There used to be islands on the nearby reefs of Kudadhiggaru Falhu and Kolhudhiffushi Falhu but these were washed away.

**Aarah** is the fourth island in the atoll and is uninhabited. It is a new island with a few bushes. The island has a wide, shallow fringing reef preventing easy access.

**Hulhidhoo** is a small heavily treed uninhabited island with narrow fringing reefs on the north and south sides, which are excellent for snorkelling. *Hulhi* means a coconut, or fruit, with nothing to eat inside. If visiting the island be prepared for a little man appearing from the trees waving a sign reading: "Deserted island – $2.00".

**Thinadhoo** is the sixth island in the atoll and is sometimes called Mas Thinadhoo, or fish island. In the southern atolls, *Thina* is the breast of a woman.

**Felidhoo** is an inhabited island and the capital of the atoll. The island has a high radio mast. The islanders are mostly fishermen and are well known for their boduberus.

**Keyodhoo** is an inhabited island with a good anchorage in the lagoon. Safari boats often stop here to top-up water supplies and after dinner, crew members often desert ship to enjoy the local hospitality.

**Foththeyo-bodufushi** lies on the eastern fringe of the atoll. It is uninhabited and used to be two separate islands, Foththeyo and Bodufushi, before being naturally joined. It is a large island with a radio mast on it.

**Hingaahuraa** means moving island and is a small uninhabited island on Fotteyo Falhu.

**Bodumohoraa** is a further seven km west on the same falhu. It is a large uninhabited island with plenty of trees, a nice beach on the south side and a shallow water lagoon.

**Thunduhuraa** is a small sandbank island with no trees, only a few bushes.

**Ruhhurihuraa** is one and a half km to the north of Thunduhuraa. It is a small uninhabited island with coconut trees. *Ruh* means coconut tree and *huri* means there are.

**Rakeedhoo** is an inhabited island that lies at the southern tip of the atoll. Safari dhoanis sometimes anchor overnight on the north side of the island to make an early morning dive in Rakeedhoo Kandu.

**Anbaraa** is a medium sized deserted island with about 30 coconut trees and is 15 minutes by dhoani from Rakeedhoo. It has a good anchorage and is a pleasant island to visit for a barbecue on the beach. *Anbaraa* comes from the word ambergris, the valuable secretion from sperm whales sometimes found washed up on beaches.

**Kuda Anbaraa** is a small uninhabited island with some palm trees six km to the north of Anbaraa.

On the western corner of the atoll is a large reef called **Fussaru Falhu**. *Fussfaru* means invisible reef, so named because boats approaching the atoll from the west have no clearly visible islands to tell them where the atoll starts. On the next reef north – **Maahiththan Faru** – is another small nameless island with no trees. It has a radio mast on it.

**Fussfaru Huraa** is a small uninhabited island.

**Kudaboli** is an uninhabited island on Masaraa Falhu. *Kudaboli* means small shell island.

*Returning back to the resort after another magnificent trip in the Maldives..*

# Ambergris

The sea gives life to many myths and legends but few stories can match those that are born from the valuable nuggets of ambergris that can be found floating in the sea or washed on the beaches of islands.

Ambergris is a waxy substance produced in the intestines of sperm whales. Sperm whales eat deep sea squid and it is believed the undigested beaks of the squid cause irritation to the internal organs of the whale. In response, the whale produces a secretion which coats these beaks. It is this highly prized secretion, that is passed out at either end, that is of such value. When heated it gives out a particularly agreeable perfume. It is used for medicinal purposes and perfumes.

The Chinese of the 10th and 11th century called ambergris 'dragon spittle' and they collected most of it from the Liu Mountains (Maldives). Sheng-tseng wrote: "There are a great many coiled up dragons among the rocks of these islets. In spring they vomit spittle, which flocks of birds collect and swarms of fish suck up. The yellow kind is like fish glue, the black like the dung of bats, the white resembles pai-yao-chien."

The Arabs thought differently. Suleiman, wrote in the ninth century: "The sea throws up on the shore of these islands big lumps of amber: some of these pieces have the form of a plant, or nearly so. Amber grows at the bottom of the sea like the plants; when the sea is much disturbed, it throws up the amber in pieces like pumpkins or truffles."

The Portuguese soldier Barbosa, in the east between 1501 and 1517 was intrigued by it and wrote: "I have oft times asked these Moors what thing this ambergris was, and whence it sprang. Among themselves they hold it to be the dung of birds, and they say that in this archipelago among the uninhabited islands there are certain great fowls which alight on the cliffs and rocks of the sea, and there drop this ambergris, where it is tanned and softened by the wind, the sun, and the rain, and pieces both great and small are torn by the storms and tempests and fall into the sea until they are found or washed up on the strands or swallowed by whales."

An anonymous Portuguese writer writing prior to 1505, found out the true source of ambergris. He wrote: "On the shores of the Dyve islands, dead whales are to be found. They are often thrown ashore by the waves and the inhabitants cut them and make oil of their meat. Some of these whales have pieces of ambra like pinecones, big and

*Finding pieces of ambergris is like finding nuggets of gold.*

small ones, 20 to 40 or even 100 and sometimes up to 200 pieces joined in a big sticky bunch. This ambra they must deliver to the sultan, if they do not they are sentenced to death. Nobody tries to steal it as it is under penalty of death."

The value of ambergris is such that when one becomes suddenly rich it is commonly said that he has found ambergris, as though it were treasure. It was only the rich or royal, however, who kept it. In 1599, the English pilot John Davies reported being greeted near Malé by a "gentleman and his wife", and mentions that in the woman's casket were jewels and ambergris. The man, who was dressed "in the Turkish manner" and had rings with rich stones, is believed to have been Sultan Ibrahim III.

The freedom of the people has been bought with ambergris. In 1754 a piece weighing 152.8 kgs was presented to the French in return for their services in defeating a fleet of Malabar vessels that had been plundering the islands.

Ambergris found today is worth around US$20/gm and if exported is taxed 100% by the government. In March of 1995 a piece weighing 187 kgs, the second largest piece found this century, was found by fishermen off the island of Kelaa, in North Thiladhunmathee Atoll. The largest piece of 214 kgs was found in the early 1980s. Needless to say, finding a piece of ambergris is like unearthing a nugget of gold. However, the fortunate discoverer must grab hold of it first try – once touched it sinks to the bottom and takes days to surface!

# Diving Felidhe Atoll

*Felidhe Atoll is more isolated and less developed than the other tourist atolls. It has excellent scuba diving and snorkelling, remote uninhabited islands, sandbanks and the islanders are friendly and hospitable. For these reasons Felidhe Atoll is a popular destination for safari dhoanis and memorable trips and excellent diving is guaranteed. There are not many thila dives in this atoll, with most of the diving being in the 26 channels on the eastern side. These channels are mostly long and deep and suitable for advanced divers. Many have narrow entrances and when travelling down the eastern side of the atoll they can easily be passed unnoticed. On the outside of most of the channels, the reef plunges sharply to very deep depths, usually from the outside rim at around 35 metres. During the peak diving season of the north-east monsoon, the current flows inside the channels on the eastern side more often than it flows out, resulting in exhilarating, clear water diving, ideal for viewing sharks and pelagic fish. The channels on the western side are generally not as exciting as those on the east; however, with the current mainly flowing out of the atoll during the north-east monsoon, these locations have the advantage of attracting manta rays to feed on the zooplankton-rich waters. At the south end of the atoll near the island of Hingaahurra is the remains of the Pioneer, which was wrecked on this reef on May 13, 1958. The ship was on her way from Colombo to Malé when she ran aground.*

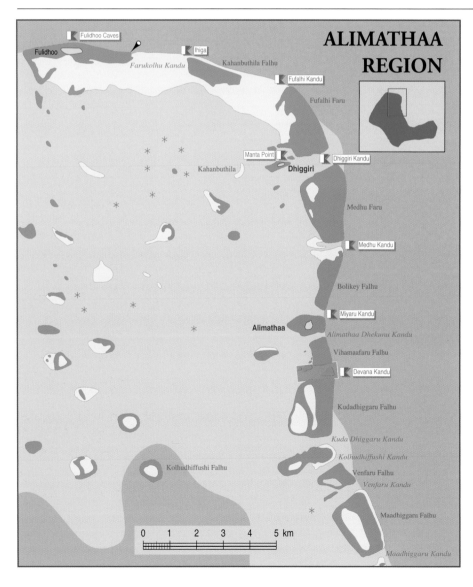

**Fulidhoo Caves ★★★**

Directly outside the island of Fulidhoo in line with the street that cuts through the island is Fulidhoo Caves. The reef slopes from three to 50 metres with caves and overhangs ranging in depth between 25 and 40 metres. The most interesting feature of this dive are the nurse sharks sleeping in the caves. Also seen are napoleon, eagle rays, morays and turtles.

**Ihiga ★★** lies on the eastern side of Farukolhu Kandu. The channel is shallow and on the corner are big barracuda, sharks and tuna. There are also caves on either side of the channel.

**Fufalhi Kandu ★★** is also called Reethi Kandu (*reethi* means beautiful) and is a shallow channel with caves and overhangs on the outside. At deeper depths there are a few overhangs with holes to swim through.

**Dhiggiri Kandu ★★★** is a deep channel with the dropoff on the outside edge around 45 metres. Caves and cliffs are found on the outside and on both sides of the channel.

**Manta Point ★** lies not more than 200 metres to the east of Dhiggiri resort. It is a small reef where mantas are seen during the south-west monsoon.

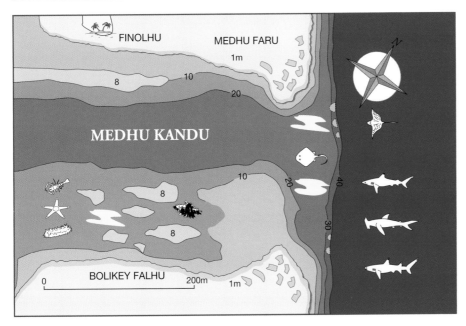

*Moon fusilier,* Caesio lunaris. *Feeds in schools on zooplankton and favours steep dropoffs and areas with current.*

*Head-band butterflyfish,* Chaetodon collare. *Many butterflyfish change their colourings by day and night. During the day while feeding, the head-band butterflyfish is brightly coloured but at night it appears more dull for camouflage against nocturnal predators such as moray eels.*

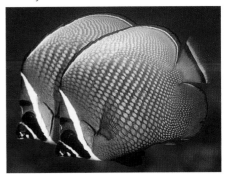

### Medhu Kandu ★★★ (Mas Kandu)

| | |
|---|---|
| Location: | channel south of Dhiggiri Kandu |
| Depth: | 10m – 30m |
| Fish Life: | abundant |
| Coral: | very good |
| Features: | corals, white-tips, reef fish |

The north side of the channel is the deepest part. The entrance starts with sand at 30 to 35 metres. Out from the sand are caves deeper than 35 metres. On the sand bed are white-tip reef sharks and sting rays. Inside the channel, the reef slopes between five and 20 metres.

The south side of Medhu Kandu, is an excellent location for photographers. The outside of the reef slopes from 30 metres to the depths below and on the corner of the channel is a small sand bed at 25 metres. The sand is surrounded by reef and white-tip reef sharks, eagle rays, sting rays and occasionally hammerhead sharks are found here. Over the shallow reef at around eight metres is more sand and patches of reef where there is an abundance of reef fish. Photographers can happily spend hours in this area where there is good protection from the currents.

### Miyaru Kandu ★★★

| | |
|---|---|
| Location: | Alimathaa Uthuru Kandu |
| Depth: | 5m – 30m |
| Fish life: | above average |
| Coral growth: | good |
| Features: | sharks |

*Miyaru* is the Dhivehi name for shark. On the north corner is a cave at 33 metres which is an excellent place for spotting grey reef sharks. There are more caves deeper on the outside reef. White-tip and black-tip reef sharks are seen inside the channel.

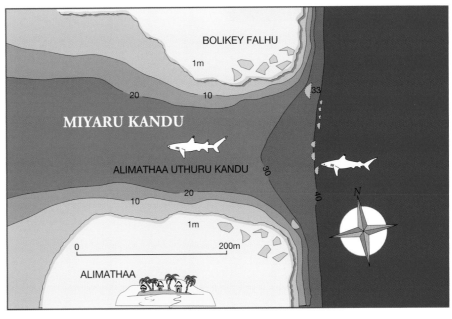

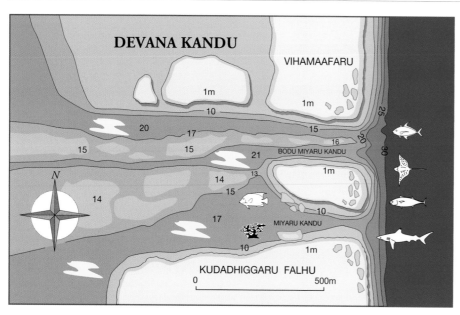

DEVANA KANDU

VIHAMAAFARU

1m

1m

10

25

20

30

20

17

15

16

15

15

21

BODU MIYARU KANDU

1m

N

13

14

15

14

17

MIYARU KANDU

10

10

1m

KUDADHIGGARU FALHU

0                                                500m

*Variegated lizardfish,* Synodus variegatus. *These are well camouflaged predators which position themselves, often in pairs, on coral heads waiting for prey. They have big mouths with sharp teeth and swallow their prey whole.*

## Devana Kandu ★★

### PROTECTED MARINE AREA

| | |
|---|---|
| Location: | second channel south of Alimathaa |
| Depth: | 5m – 25m |
| Fish life: | above average |
| Coral growth: | excellent |
| Features: | pelagic fish, sharks, coral |

The channel between Vihamaafaru Falhu and Kudadhiggaru Falhu is divided in the middle by a 250 metre long reef. The passage on the south side of the reef is called Miyaru Kandu by Maldivian fishermen. It is more narrow than Bodu Miyaru Kandu, which is the passage on the north side. The entire channel, both north and south passage, has been declared a protected marine area.

*Saddled pufferfish,* Canthigaster valentini *is from the smaller group of pufferfish growing to 12 cm. It is a shallow reef dweller and is omnivorous.*

With an ingoing current, divers can experience one of the most exhilarating drift dives in Felidhe Atoll. On the outside reef are caves and overhangs that drop vertically from 30 metres to the depths below. Grey reef sharks, eagle rays and pelagics are seen around the entrance to both passages, mostly during the north-east monsoon. The south passage has large coral rocks blanketed in soft coral with one rising to nine metres. Many reef fish have colonised these rocks and it is not uncommon to see blue-face angelfish, saddled pufferfish and variegated lizardfish.

In the middle of the north passage is a long narrow reef that rises slightly to 15 metres from the sandy floor at around 18 metres. As divers drift into the one km long channel, the north and south passages join. Coral is spread across the bottom of the 500 metre wide channel at a depth of around 15 metres.

**Diving hints:** The best diving is with an ingoing current and because of the size of this channel and the possibilities for diving both the north and south sides of the channel, boatmen should be carefully advised of the dive-plan. As always, drift diving over coral requires good control of buoyancy to avoid damaging the coral.

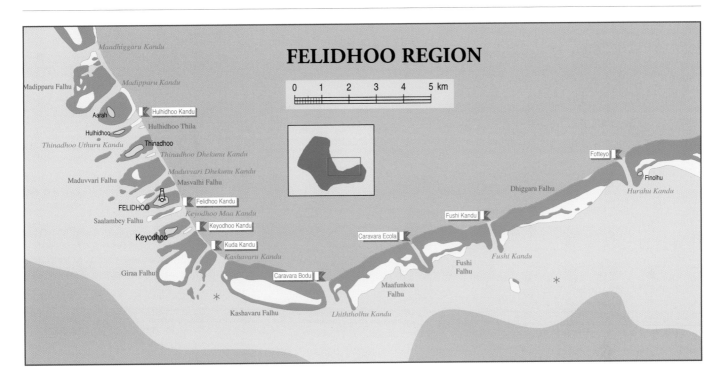

## Hulhidhoo Kandu ★★★

This is the channel between the two deserted islands of Aarah and Hulhidhoo. The best diving is on the outside reef of Hulhidhoo, which is pointed and shaped like a terraced rice-field with small overhangs between 20 and 35 metres. There are more caves from 35 metres to the sandy bottom at about 55 metres. The reef corner is marked by a cave at about 25 metres alongside a sand plateau with white-tips and sting rays. This corner is a good viewing point for pelagics including barracuda, trevally and tuna. Inside the channel are more caves, beginning with one at 18 metres followed by many more at shallower depths towards the end of the dive. This is a good place to find moray eels, turtles, snapper, napoleon and reef fish.

_Left: Blue-face angelfish,_ Pomacanthus xanthometopon. _This fish is among the most exquisitely coloured fish on the reef slope but is usually shy and found darting into coral heads and crevices. The blue-face angelfish, like other species of the same family, undergo dramatic changes in colour between the juvenile and adult stages._

## Felidhoo Kandu ★★

| | |
|---|---|
| Location: | channel on south side of Felidhoo |
| Depth: | 5m – 25m |
| Fish life: | above average |
| Coral growth: | very good |
| Features: | coral, reef fish |

This is a narrow channel about 50 metres wide between Felidhoo reef and Saalambey Falhu. The entrance to the channel is quite shallow at 16 metres but the channel gets deeper further inside. In the middle of the channel is a long, narrow reef surrounded by sand and rising to 15 metres. At the entrance is a patch of fire coral and on the north corner are impressive massive and staghorn corals and a colourful range of soft coral. Sharks are found around the entrance and inside are sweetlip and turtles. The quality of the reef deteriorates inside the channel but the entrance area is well worth a dive.

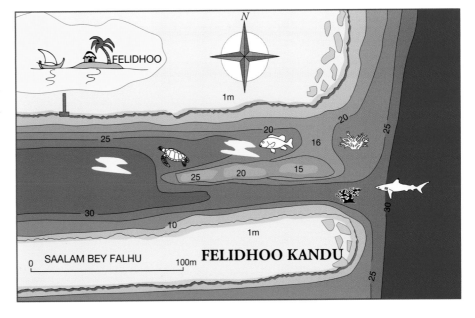

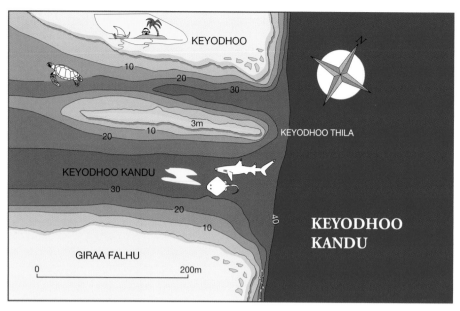

### Keyodhoo Kandu ★★★

Location:        channel on south
                 side of Keyodhoo
Depth:           5m – 30m
Fish life:       average
Coral growth:    good
Features:        reef fish

The entrance to the channel is at 35 to 40 metres. There are two possibilities to dive here. One is Keyodhoo Thila, the other is the south side of the channel on the corner of Giraa Falhu. The top of the thila lies at about three metres and descends smoothly to about 30 metres to the sand

bottom of the kandu. It is a narrow, long thila that begins at the entrance of the kandu and continues for 200 metres inside. On the outside, the thila falls away gradually before a sharp decline to the depths below.

On the south side at Giraa Falhu corner are a few caves on the outside and on the corner is a sand bed at 30 to 35 metres with white-tip reef sharks and sting rays. The channel wall slopes gently, like the thila, to 30 metres. Turtles are a familiar sight in this channel.

### Kuda Kandu ★★

Location:        second channel
                 south of Keyodhoo
Depth:           3m – 30m
Fish life:       above average
Coral growth:    very good
Features:        hard coral

The channel has a narrow entrance and in the middle is a mound of coral rising to 25 metres from the sandy bottom at 30 metres. This can be a long drift dive with an ingoing current but divers may prefer to begin their dive 200 metres inside the channel on the northern side where there are calm conditions and a variety of hard corals. A ridge continues to bend into the channel at 15 metres. At this bend coral covers the reef from 20 metres to the surface.

**Diving hints:** The area inside the channel is more protected from the stronger currents and makes an excellent location for snorkellers and photographers.

On the east side of Kashavaru Falhu is Lhittolhu Kandu. Divers often call this site **Caravara Bodu**. It is a wide channel and the entrance is around 40 metres. It has pretty coral slopes with plenty of reef fish.

Between Maafunkoa Falhu and Fushi Falhu is a site called **Caravara Ecola**. It is more narrow than Caravara Bodu and has an entrance at 40 metres with caves in the middle of the entrance. The channel also has pretty coral slopes.

**Fushi Kandu** is the next channel between Fushi Falhu and Dhiggaru Falhu. It is similar to many kandus in Felidhe Atoll with a sandbed on the corner about 30 to 35 metres, a few caves on the outside with sharks and pretty coral and reef fish inside.

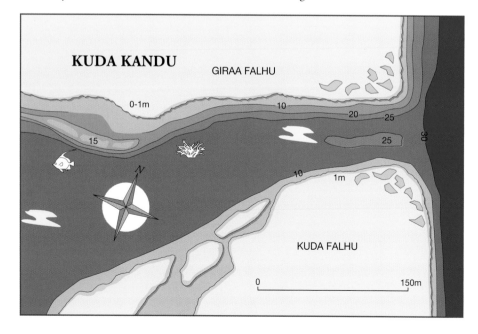

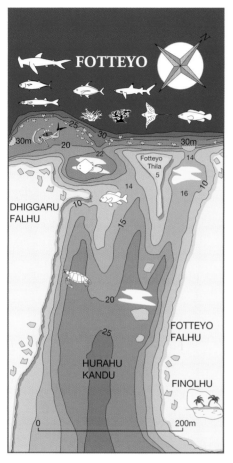

**Fotteyo ***

| | |
|---|---|
| Location: | Hurahu Kandu |
| Depth: | 3m – 30m |
| Fish life: | abundant |
| Coral growth: | excellent |
| Features: | caves, soft coral, seafans, sharks, reef fish |

An excellent dive regarded by many divers as the best dive site in the Maldives. It is a photographer's paradise and a mecca for marine biologists. This is a dive with many possibilities. The best diving is on the outside corner of Dhiggaru Falhu. Divers can start at a bend in the outside reef where there is a big cave at about 30 metres with holes you can swim through. Around the bend near the entrance to the channel is a special place with many caves and overhangs. These caves have a thick covering of wavering soft coral in all colours. They look like blooming cherry-blossoms in springtime. Most of the cherry caves are found between 25 and 40 metres and there are a few arches covered in soft coral, one of which divers can swim through.

The outside entrance to the channel at 22 metres is marked by a split in the reef. From here divers can proceed into the channel across a bed of sand with resting white-tip reef sharks. On the eastern side of this sand plateau is the inside entrance to the channel at 14 metres. It is characterised by a bed of beautiful hard coral and big schools of sweetlip. Just inside the channel is 'trigger valley'. Titan triggerfish are numerous here and when nesting around the full moon they become more aggressive.

On the outside of Fotteyo thila are more caves where big grouper can be found. At this point it is also possible to

*A small school of trevally move into the frame to add a touch of movement to this brilliantly coloured portrait of life forms at Fotteyo.*

spot eagle rays soaring in the currents. At the entrance to the second channel is a large cave at 18 metres. The channel rises to 14 metres at the pass and inside is a small sand bed at about 16 metres. On the inside of Fotteyo Thila is a mushroom-shaped coral rock at 15 metres. From here the channel opens up to a sand and coral studded bed between 20 and 25 metres.

In the course of this dive it is always possible to see schools of trevally, tuna, barracuda and grey reef sharks on the outside reef; white-tips and sting rays on the sand-beds of the channel; and turtles along the channel walls. For sunrise divers, there is the opportunity to see hammerhead sharks.

**Diving hints:** If current permits, it is a good idea to finish your dive around the beautiful, more shallow sections just inside the entrance at 14 metres. If current is strong, divers may cross back to the west wall of the channel over a finger of reef at about 10 metres then drift into 'trigger valley' and finish the dive along the western wall. Another diving option is to start on the reef corner near the cherry caves then swim across the entrance on the outside of the reef to the thila and into the second channel.

*Left and above: The remarkable landscape at Fotteyo is made all the more attractive by the delicate soft coral that covers the caves and grottos along the outside reef.*

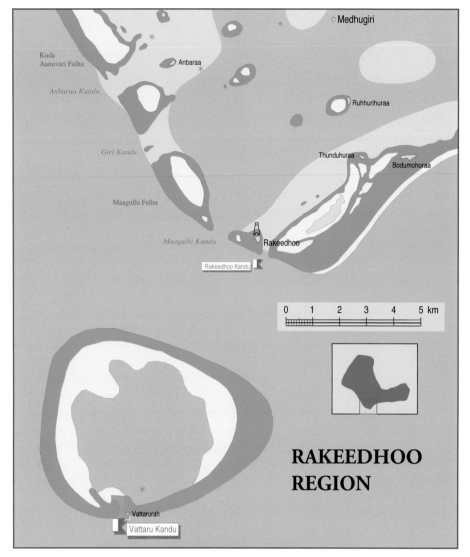

**RAKEEDHOO
REGION**

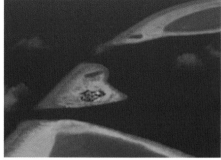

*Rakeedhoo Kandu*

### Rakeedhoo Kandu ★★★

| Location: | channel between Rakeedhoo and Fotteyo Falhu |
|---|---|
| Depth: | 3m – 30m+ |
| Fish life: | abundant |
| Coral growth: | excellent |
| Features: | coral, sharks, reef fish |

Rakeedhoo is one of five inhabited islands in the atoll and is the most southern island of the atoll. There are channels either side of Rakeedhoo but Rakeedhoo Kandu is the most popular channel for diving and is on the eastern side of the island. It is a deep channel with an entrance around 50 metres. On both sides of the channel, the corners are magnificent with coral caves and overhangs at different depths.

The corner on the Rakeedhoo side is better known for its terraces. The first step starts around 20 metres and steps descend to around 45 metres. Under each plateau, or coral step, are overhangs and caves covered in soft coral. At the deeper depths of terrace corner are big beautiful seafans and black coral trees. Terrace corner is a good location for spotting all kinds pelagics including a big school of big-eye trevally and sharks, even hammerhead sharks in the dim light of early morning. At shallower depths are turtles, napoleons, and sweetlips.

**Diving hints:** When there is a strong ingoing current it splits on the eastern side of Rakeedhoo reef sending divers either into the channel or along the outside reef of Rakeedhoo. The better choice is to dive the inside of the channel.

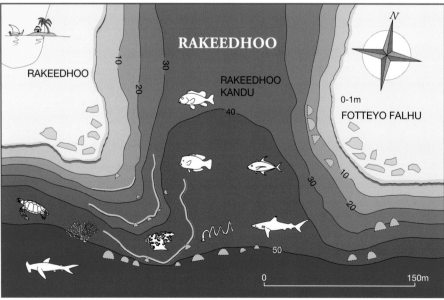

## Vattaru Kandu ★★

### PROTECTED MARINE AREA

Location: channel in south of Vattaru Atoll
Depth: 5m – 30m
Fish life: abundant
Coral growth: excellent
Features: sharks, coral

Vattaru is a small rounded atoll south of Felidhe Atoll about 45 minutes by dhoani from Rakeedhoo. There is only one kandu. It is on the south side near the small uninhabited island of Vattarurah. The island corner gives the best opportunity for an excellent dive. The corner drops steeply on the outside to about 45 metres, then slopes to a deep sandy bottom where there are big seafans and occasionally leopard sharks.

The entrance of the channel is around 32 metres. There are a few caves and overhangs near the entrance and many more on the outside of the reef. Near the corner, most caves occur between 10 and 20 metres. Fish life here is prolific with tuna, barracuda, trevally, schools of fusilier and white-tip reef sharks. Also seen are turtles and manta rays. There are more beautiful caves from about 30 metres outside the channel entrance. All the caves are covered with soft coral and in many are black coral trees and seafans.

**Diving hints:** For night divers, Vattaru Kandu is a brilliant location. With an

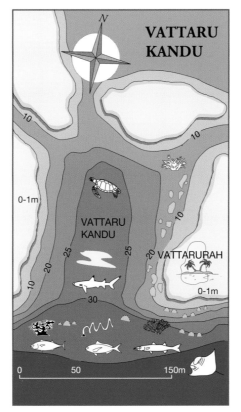

ingoing current, the island corner is the best place to start and then drift into the channel. Spread across the sandy bottom and on the reef slope are various shaped coral rocks which provide a sound refuge for sleeping napoleon and parrotfish.

## Anbaraa ★★

There is easy diving on the north side of Anbaraa with walls from five to 25 metres

*Strong currents in Rakeedhoo Kandu provide the nutrients for a colouful range of soft coral.*

and a few small caves with plenty of fire coral. It is a good location for an easy afternoon dive.

## Anbaraa Thila ★★

This is a small thila five minutes to the east of Anbaraa with the top at two metres. It is so small, divers can swim around it a couple of times at different depths. There is little current here. On the top is plenty of hard coral, excellent for snorkelling. White-tip reef sharks are found here.

There are some channels along the western side with good diving features. On the western point of Felidhe Atoll is **Maafussaru Kandu**. It is the channel between Fussaru Falhu and Maahiththan Faru. On the northern side of the channel is an interesting, gently sloping reef with a shallow entrance at 20 metres.

To the north is Dhiggaluvashee Kuda Kandu, also known as **Kudaboli Kandu**. The outside reef is at 35 metres and the southern corner has caves at about 25 metres. Near the entrance a finger of reef extends into the channel attracting plenty of grey reef and white-tip reef sharks.

There are two kandus in the north, **Kunaavashi Kandu** and **Boamas Kandu**. Both are suitable for experienced divers.

*Left: Sabre squirrelfish,* Sargocentron spiniferum. *Is named after a spiny bone protruding from the corner of its gill-cover. It is often found in small numbers hovering around the caves and overhangs. It is the largest species of the family growing to 40 cm.*

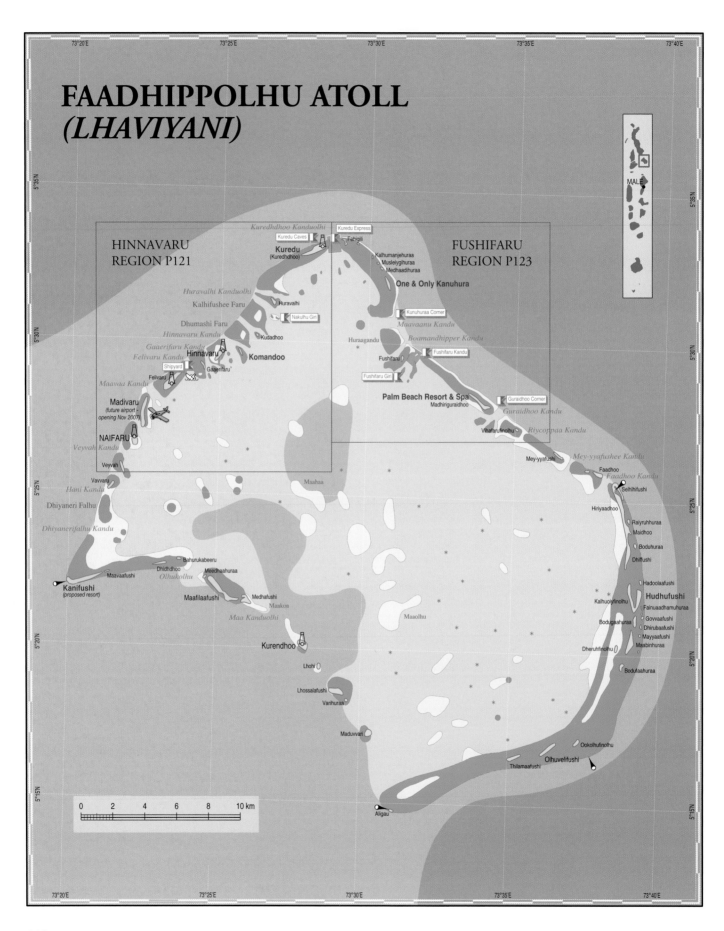

# FAADHIPPOLHU ATOLL
## *(LHAVIYANI)*

MALE

HINNAVARU
REGION P121

FUSHIFARU
REGION P123

Kuredhdhoo Kanduolhi

Kuredu Express
Kuredu Caves
Kuredu
(Kuredhdhoo)
Fahgili

Kalhumanjehuraa
Musleiygihuraa
Medhaadihuraa

One & Only Kanuhura

Huravalhi Kanduolhi
Kalhifushee Faru

Huravalhi

Nakulhu Giri

Kunuhuraa Corner
Maavaanu Kandu

Dhumashi Faru

Kudadhoo

Huraagandu
Boamandhipper Kandu

Hinnavaru Kandu

Gaaerifaru Kandu
Felivaru Kandu

Hinnavaru

Komandoo

Fushifaru
Fushifaru Kandu

Shipyard
Felivaru
Gaaerifaru

Fushifaru Giri

Maavaa Kandu

Palm Beach Resort & Spa
Madhiriguraidhoo

Guraidhoo Corner

Madivaru
*(future airport -
opening Nov 2007)*

Guraidhoo Kandu

NAIFARU

Vihafarufinolhu

Riycorpaa Kandu

Veyvah Kandu

Veyvah

Mey-yyafushi

Mey-yyafushee Kandu

Vavvaru

Faadhoo
Faadhoo Kandu

Hani Kanda

Maahaa

Selhlhifushi

Dhiyaneri Falhu

Hiriyaadhoo

Dhiyanerifalhu Kandu

Raiyruhhuraa
Maidhoo
Boduhuraa
Dhiffushi

Bahurukabeeru

Dhidhdhoo
Meedhaahuraa

Maavaafushi
Olhukollu

Hadoolaafushi

Kanifushi
*(proposed resort)*

Maafilaafushi
Medhafushi
Maakoa

Kalhuoiyfinolhu

Hudhufushi
Fainuaadhamuhuraa
Govvaafushi
Dhirubaafushi
Mayyaafushi
Maabinhuraa

Maa Kanduolhi

Maaolhu

Bodugaahuraa

Dheruhfinolhu

Kurendhoo

Bodufaahuraa

Lhohi

Lhossalafushi

Varihuraa

Maduvvari

Ookolhufinolhu
Olhuvelifushi
Thilamaafushi

0  2  4  6  8  10 km

Aligau

# Chapter 7 - Faadhippolhu Atoll Islands (Lhaviyani)

*Faadhippolhu Atoll is 37 km wide and 35 km long and lies 120 km north of Malé. It takes about eight hours sailing time from Malé to reach the atoll. There are four inhabited islands and 54 uninhabited islands, of which four are resorts. Another island, Hudhufushi resort and is under construction and Kanifushi is a proposed resort. The principal occupation of the islands is fishing. Felivaru has a fish canning factory that provides employment for workers from the nearby islands of Naifaru and Hinnavaru. Naifaru is a very populated island and reclammation works are planned to provide more space for housing. Previously, sail weaving and coir making were the major occupations of the islanders. The main entrance at the north of the atoll is the 500 metre-wide Kuredhdhoo Kanduolhi. The western side of the atoll is characterised by many small islands, reefs and narrow channels with the island of Kanifushi projecting sharply to form the west point of the atoll. The main entrance to the atoll is between the southernmost island of Aligau and Maduvvari. The eastern side of the atoll has longer reefs with fewer openings, culminating in the 30 km long barrier reef between Selhlhifushiand Aligau.*

**Naifaru** is a densely crowded island on the western rim of the atoll. It is the capital island of the atoll. Fishing is the main occupation of the islanders and the island is noted for its indigenous medicine. It is also famous for its handicraft, especially work with mother of pearl shell and black coral.

**Madivaru** houses the National Security Service for the northern atolls.

**Felivaru** is the location for the MIFCO fish canning factory, the major industry in the atoll. Lhaviyani is one of the best fishing atolls in the Maldives. Most of the fishermen live on Naifaru and Hinnavaru and unload their catch at the factory.

**Hinnavaru** is another densely populated island with fishing being the major occupation of the islanders. Employment at the neighbouring resort of Komandhoo and other newly developed resorts on the eastern side of the atoll has also created opportunities for employment.

**Komandhoo** is a small island with a 90 bed resort. It has a good covering of coconut trees and is a quieter version of its much larger sister island, Kuredu. It lies close by "The Shipyard", where there is excellent diving.

**Kuredhdhoo** was the first resort in the atoll and was established as Kuredu Camping Resort in 1978. It has since been redeveloped as a major 300-room resort. It is 150 kms from the airport and transfers are by seaplane or the resort's speed ferry.

**Kanuhuraa** is an island with many coconut trees and a good beach all around. It opened as a 200 bed resort called One & Only Kanuhura Resort in 2002. It is located in a large, but shallow lagoon.

**Madiriguraidhoo** is now a resort called Palm Beach Resort & Spa. It is located at the outer reef of the atoll, in a narrow, but long lagoon. A good beach surrounds the island. It is a relatively long island 1.25 km in length. The northern end is very narrow with little vegetation whereas the southern end has a width of about 250 metres. The shallow inner lagoon is 1.5 to three metres deep and many large sting rays can be found here.

**Dhiffushi** was once inhabited. It is also called Dhiffushimaadhoo. The remains of a mosque and a well are still visible. The *City of Victoria*, a ship from Colombo, ran aground on the reef of this island in 1966 but was refloated and renamed *Diffushimaadhoo*.

**Hudhufushi** is a very large and unique V-shaped uninhabited island with a very shallow lagoon in the middle. There are some mangroves inside the lagoon and the island is well vegetated by large shrubs and trees. There are a few coconut trees, but not many. Originally there were two islands, Hudhufushi and Kalhuoiyfinolhu, that joined together long ago. The island has beautiful beaches and has been selected for a 400 bed resort. It is still under construction. Access to the lagoon is currently limited to shallow drafted vessels. Many sting rays and baby sharks are found within the lagoon area of this tranquil hide-away.

*Kudadhoo in Faadhippolhu Atoll is an attractive uninhabited island ideal for picnics and excursions.*

**Olhuvelifushi** is an inhabited island.

**Kurendhoo** is an inhabited island also called Loakurendhoo.

**Maafilaafushi** was inhabited during the rein of Sultan Mohammed Imaaduddeen I (1620 – 1648 AD) and later the people shifted to Naifaru. Ruins of a old mosque and a cemetery with tomb stones can be found at the center of the island. A few years ago the Selected Island Development Unit in Malé' selected this large and thickly vegetated island as an extension for the over-populated islands of Naifaru and Hinnavaru. Large areas of jungle were cleared, a mosque and a school built and an administration complex established, however, only a few families shifted there, as people hesitate to leave their home islands. The island is now classed as being uninhabited. A channel cut across the reef when it was being inhabited, allows access to the island for small and large boats.

**Dhidhdhoo** is an uninhabited island also called Olhukolhu Dhidhdhoo. It is a narrow but long island with many coconut trees and during low tide a couple of sand banks stretch toward Olhukolhu, the channel to the east. An island called Olhugiri is said to have existed to the north but there is now little evidence of it.

**Kanifushi** is a proposed island resort.

*The 'Shipyard' in Felivaru Kandu is one of the main diving attractions in Lhaviyani Atoll. Coral growth on the wreck is extensive and many fish, including this tall fin batfish, have adopted the wreck as home.*

*The inner lagoon of Hudhufushi is a nursery for baby sharks.*

*An inner lake on the island of Faadhoo is unique to the atoll.*

# Diving Faadhippolhu Atoll

*Most of the diving in Lhaviyani Atoll is in the northern half of the atoll where the four resorts are located. They all share the pristine dive sites in the region and have many quality dive sites to choose from. The atoll has very few thilas, but many excellent channel dives. There are 13 channels on the western side, seven on the east and six wide ones in the south. In the north, the channels are generally quite narrow, with excellent coral and plenty of fish around the entrances. When conditions are favourable, divers can cross the channel openings where many chance encounters with sharks, eagle rays and other large fish occur. Suprisingly, there are not many coral reefs inside the atoll, but some occur near the channel entrances. These reefs are shallow and well protected and generally have interesting reef features. On the outside of the atoll are a few sites with steep walls and beautiful caves, providing good alternatives, especially when currents are strong. There are also two wrecks at the 'shipyard', giving divers an excellent variety of dives all within a relatively small area.*

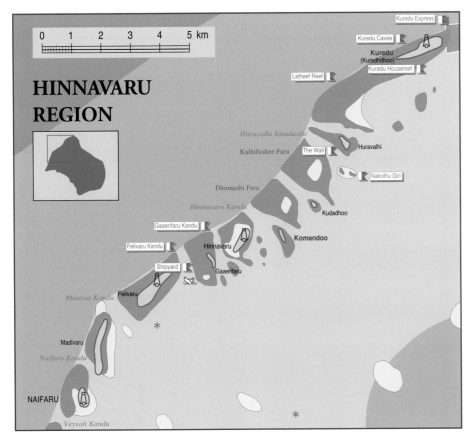

### Latheef Reef ★★

The steep outside reef of Kuredhdhoo features some beautiful caverns and reef formations. At this dive site, there are two sets of very large caverns with ceilings covered in brightly colored soft corals. There are swim-throughs and many nice angles creating perfect opportunities for photographers. The first set of caverns are found at 25 to 32 metres while the second set is shallower at eight to 16 metres.

### The Wall ★★

On the south side of Huravahli, the reef has a completely vertical wall, ending on the channel bottom at 33 metres. The dive site is relatively long and makes for a perfect drift dive. Divers can choose their own depth and see large overhangs from 25 to 30 metres, ledges at 20 metres and smaller caves between 15 metres and the surface. Divers will be impressed by the variety of marine life at the wall with many smaller fish occupying the vertical spaces.

### Gaaerifaru Kandu ★★★

Another exhilarating channel crossing between the outside reefs of Gaaerifaru and Hinnavaru. Like Felivaru Kandu, it offers a wide range of schooling fish, white-tip and grey reef sharks, turtles and eagle rays.

### Kuredu Caves ★★

Between three and 25 metres are a series of caves with sandy bottoms. They are filled with bright yellow soft coral and seafans. Squirrelfish inhabit the caves while outside are big schools of fusilier, snapper and reef fish of every description.

### Kuredu Housereef ★

The housereef dive is opposite the jetty and marked by three buoys. Divers start at the buoys, then cross the lagoon at the end of the dive. The reef has table coral and ledges with soft coral. There are white-tip reef sharks, eagle rays, turtles and schools of fusilier.

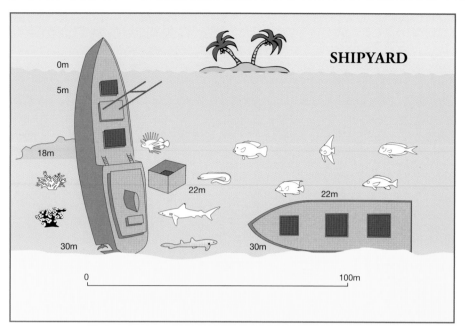

SHIPYARD

*Above water, the* Skipjack II *is an unsightly rusting hulk, but below, it is a pretty sight.*

## Shipyard ★★★

| | |
|---|---|
| Location: | east side of Felivaru Kandu |
| Depth: | 1m – 30m |
| Fish life: | abundant |
| Coral growth: | excellent |
| Features: | wrecks, soft coral, reef fish |

### History

There are two wrecks in the channel that separate the islands of Felivaru and Gaaerifaru. The site is easy to find as one of the wrecks, *Skipjack II*, has the bow protruding five metres out of the water. This ship was the mother ship for the Felivaru fish factory and spent some years permanently moored to the jetty at Felivaru. In 1985 it was decided the old Japanese ship was of no further use so it was stripped of anything of value and towed out to sea where it was to be scuttled.

Kuredu Island Resort tried to purchase the ship for a new dive site, but the authorities decided against it. In the end, they got their shipwreck for no charge. While it was being towed out to sea, workers began cutting holes in the ship's hull in preparation for the sinking. However the ship caught fire and because of the danger from chemicals and the fear of an explosion, it was cut loose. Diver, Hameed Ahmed, of Male recalls:

The fire spread quickly and the blazing ship was carried with the current back into the channel. Water started coming into the back and it went down on the reef stern first. The bow continued to burn for 20 days.

The shipwreck is now one of the main diving features in Faadhippolhu Atoll. The second wreck was also in use at the fish factory and was scuttled at the same location. It too was in a vertical position until 1992 when a storm caused it to settle on the sea floor.

### Diving

The stern of the upright ship lies on the bottom at 29 metres. The second wreck lies 40 metres away on its port side in 28 metres of water. In a remarkably short time the wrecks have been inundated in soft and hard coral, no doubt because of the strong currents streaming through the channel. There are caves at 18 metres with scorpion fish. In the wrecks are many morays, which glance inquisitively at divers from the protection of their metallic refuge, and in every recess are thick schools of yellow sweeper that glisten blindingly in torchlight. The wrecks have become home to a multitude of reef fish including boxfish, pufferfish, porcupinefish, napoleon, emperor angelfish, surgeon and red bass. A school

of tallfin batfish allow divers to come close and lying on the bottom of the wreckage it is often possible to see a nurse shark. In the channel, pelagics and grey reef sharks are regularly sighted.

**Diving hints:** Strong currents in the channel can make diving at the wrecks difficult. Some protection can be found on the lee side of the upright wreck but beware of strong current suction between the wreck and the reef. When conditions are favourable, the site is perfect for both beginners and advanced divers as the wreck is standing upright with the bow breaking the surface.

### Felivaru Kandu ★★★

On the north side of Felivaru by the fish factory, is an outside reef and channel dive, where the sloping outer reef offers some extraordinary cave diving. The main reason for going here, however, is to cross the channel between Felivaru and Gaaerifaru, where divers are likely to see schools of eagle rays, turtles, white-tip reef sharks and many smaller grey sharks, when the conditions are right.

### Nakolhu Giri ★★

A quite small but interesting inner reef about 25 minutes away from Kuredhdhoo. Steep slopes, overhangs and coral outcrops standing separately on the sandy bottom together with a nice, intact and colourful reef top makes this an ideal dive, especially for photographers. Gorgonians, sea anemones, moray eels, lionfish and many of the usual reef fish cover this reef from start to end. A very exciting inner reef dive.

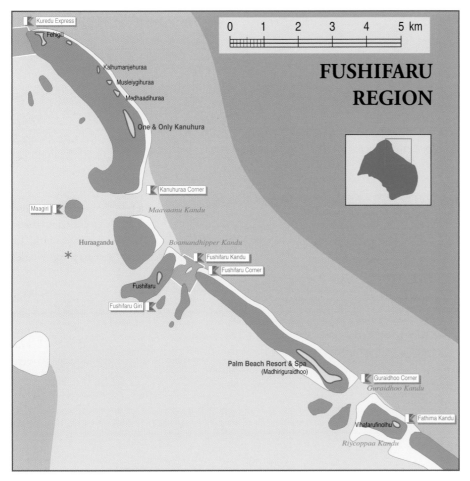

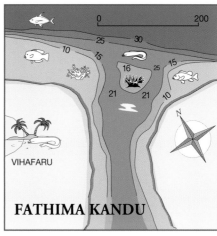

**FATHIMA KANDU**

### Fathima Kandu ★★★ (Riycoppaa Kandu)

Lying in the middle of Riycoppaa Kandu near the entrance is a thila with the top at 16 metres. It is richly covered in coral including excellent table coral, also sea anemones, giant morays, napoleon and a multitude of reef fish. Surrounding the thila are sand flats with depths between 20 and 25 metres. Across the sand is a beautiful top reef with big coral rocks and abundant fish life, such as trevally, snapper, fusilier, and sweetlip. The outside channel ledge drops off steeply from 40 to 50 metres with overhangs starting at 25 metres.

### Kanuhuraa Corner ★★

On the outside reef corner are large coral rocks big enough to swim between. At this point there are many reef fish including big-nose unicornfish, angelfish, oriental sweetlip, and schools of fusilier. There are also shells and, if divers look closely, leaf fish can be seen near the corner at 15 metres. On the corner between eight and 22 metres are massive porite corals. Among them are schools of colourful flame basslet.

*Three-spot humbug,* Dascyllus trimaculatus. *Seen around branching coral in lagoons and it is among the first damselfish divers become aquainted with. This fish is an algae feeder and selfishly guards its territory from other herbivorous fish, which usually results in a noticeable increase in coral algae within its boundaries. The fearless males dart out from their protective reef to nip at large fish and divers, especially during the nesting period when defending their cluster of eggs from intruders.*

### Guraidhoo Corner ★★

This is a beautiful reef with healthy coral and an abundance of fish on the reef top. Best diving is on the outside part in depths to 16 metres where large coral rocks and table coral offer protection to nurse sharks and sting rays.

### Maa Giri ★

Maa Giri is shaped like a flower and lies inside Maavaanu Kandu, thus creating a perfect environment for large schools of fish. Here divers are surrounded by hundreds of fusilier and snapper. Divers will also see large numbers of parrotfish, oriental sweetlip and trevally.

The reef slope changes from ledges stepping down like a staircase, to steep walls covered in leather coral. There are also plenty of overhangs and smaller caves. Maagiri also displays the largest gathering of sea anemones in one location.

Somewhere in deep water between Felivaru and Madivaru lies the remains of a seaplane. In 1987 an air ambulance attempted to land in rough seas and nosed-dived into the water. No one was killed and a launch immediately appeared to rescue those on board.

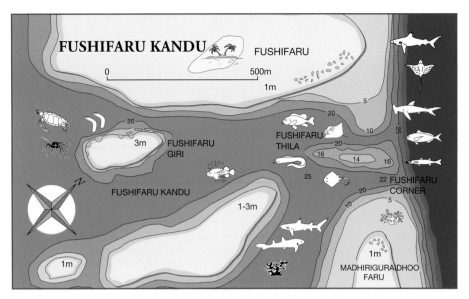

### Fushifaru Kandu ★★★

PROTECTED MARINE AREA

| Location: | Channel east side of Fushifaru Island |
|---|---|
| Depth: | 10m – 20m |
| Fish life: | abundant |
| Coral growth: | excellent |
| Features: | manta rays, reef fish, coral |

The entire channel has been declared a Protected Marine Area. **Fushifaru Thila ★★★** is the main attraction and even the most experienced divers will be spoilt at this site. The thila lies near the edge of the atoll in the middle of a 500 metre wide channel that separates the reefs of Fushifaru and Madhiriguraidhoo Faru. The thila is about 150 metres long and 50 metres wide and rises to about 10 metres at its highest point. At either end, the top is around a depth of 16 metres.

The thila can be dived in two ways. The deeper outside part is the entrance to the atoll at 30 metres. The entrance and the thila can be dived separately or in the one dive. Along the cliff edge, grey reef sharks, hammerhead sharks, barracuda and eagle rays can be seen, depending on the current.

On the top of the thila is an unspoiled reef with brilliant table corals. This layered coral formation offers plenty of protection for morays and shy reef fish. There are cleaner wrasse stations all over the reef and many fish and mantas can be seen at these. Big schools of black snapper, blue-dash fusilier, blue fusilier, yellow-back fusilier and aggregations of oriental sweetlip are common.

The swift currents streaming through the channel give life to beautiful soft corals and they compete for any available space.

Lying on the sand surrounding the thila at 20 metres are white-tip reef sharks and sting rays while around the edges are nurse sharks and turtles.

**Diving hints:** Currents can be extremely strong in this channel especially during the north-east monsoon. An ingoing current provides excellent visibility and enables divers to dive the deep outside rim of the atoll before moving on to the thila. Mantas are more likely to be seen with the current flowing outside the atoll. Care should be taken when diving with an outgoing current. Safety balloons should be carried at all times.

### Fushifaru Corner ★★

A channel and outside reef dive with many interesting variations. It is located on the south east side of Fushifaru Kandu. The gently sloping channel slopes from five metres and bottoms out at 22 metres The reef is liberally covered in green coral trees. The inside of the channel is not very interesting but on the outside, the reef drops away sharply and the steep wall is pitted with small caves and arches. Regularly seen along the wall are grey reef sharks and eagle rays. On the corner between eight and 15 metres is a range of healthy hard corals unaffected by storms or wave action. Oriental sweetlip, lobsters, morays, pufferfish, turtles and leaf fish are found around this coral-rich area. Blotched porcupinefish are common and on a sandy slope on the outside between 18 and 25 metres are sting rays and white-tip reef sharks. Fish life is diverse with big schools of fusilier, unicornfish, red bass, midnight snapper, and many species of butterflyfish. In every respect, this is an excellent dive with many surprises.

### Fushifaru Giri ★★

The north-west side of this 300 metre long reef has the best diving with caves between 12 and 20 metres. There are outcrops of reef and a rugged section with overhangs at the northern end and at the south-west end is a wall with more caves. A sand floor at 20 metres with garden eels, white-tip reef sharks, and sting rays is located midway along the reef. The reef top has healthy table coral with prolific fish life. Napoleon and turtles are major attractions.

*Flame basslet,* Pseudanthias ignitus. *One of many colourful species of basslet to adorn the reefs of the Maldives. Males are more colourful than females and can erect their fins during display and change colour quickly. They usually occur in large schools on the upper edge of reefs.*

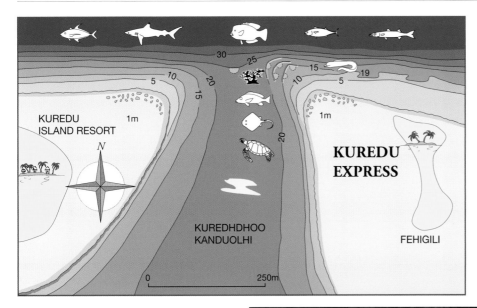

Below Top: *There are many species of fusilier, some yet to be named. In the foreground at centre is a blue-dash fusilier,* Pterocaesio tile, *and behind is an unnamed species with two yellow stripes. The other fish is the yellow-back fusilier,* Caesio xanthonota.

Bottom: *Blotched porcupinefish,* Diodon liturosus. *Like its relatives in the pufferfish family, the blotched porcupinefish inflates with water when frightened. It is covered in spines which point outward when the body is inflated, making an effective deterent against predators. Porcupine fish and pufferfish can become stressed and die if repeatedly handled by divers and forced to inflate themselves.*

## Kuredu Express ★★★

PROTECTED MARINE AREA

Location: eastern side of Kuredhdhoo
Depth: 5m – 22m
Fish life: abundant
Coral growth: very good
Features: overhangs, soft coral, sharks, pelagics

In the first channel next to Kuredhdhoo is one of the most interesting sites in the atoll. It is a long drift dive and covers just about everything divers are likely to see in Maldivian waters. On the steep outside reef are colourful overhangs while on the eastern corner between 10 and 22 metres, the reef steps down with terraces and overhangs. If the current is not too strong,, divers can wait here and let the action come to them. Always present are grey reef sharks, big schools of trevally, black snapper, napoleon, and sometimes barracuda, and eagle rays. Fishermen from inhabited islands often fish in the early morning for tuna at this corner because they are so prolific. The ceilings of the overhangs at 18 metres are covered with soft coral and leaf fish can be found nearby. The channel has small overhangs on the side with plenty of morays. On the sandy bottom, stingrays are a common sight.

# Chapter 8 - Addu Atoll Islands *(Seenu)*

*Addu Atoll lies just south of the equator and is the southernmost atoll in the Maldive archipelago. Gan Island is the most southern island at latitude 0° 42' S. There are four inhabited islands and around 20 small uninhabited islands and sandbars. The atoll is heart shaped and is about 18 km wide and 15 km long. Most of the atoll is surrounded by islands. The islands on the western side, Gan, Feydhoo, Maradhoo and Hithadhoo are connected by a causeway creating a formidable barrier to the rising and falling tides. At the causeway, water levels vary as much as half a metre on either side during the change of tide. Each island is heavily covered in coconut trees and the villages are clean and tidy. The island communities are small enough for incoming mail to be addressed to the houses only. The houses are mostly built of coral and have lush gardens with banana trees bursting with fruit.*

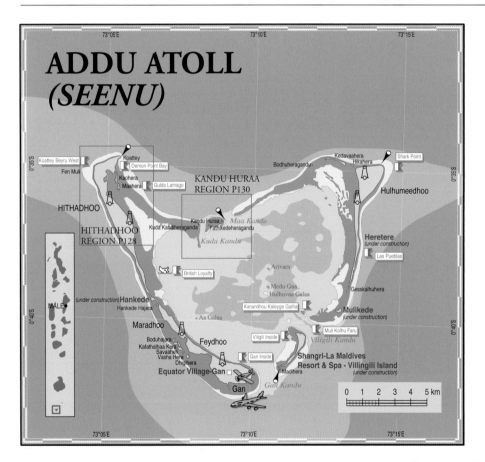

trading and looting in the Indian ocean and the fort, with its good anchorage at Koattey, would have been a secure base for his ships that were being pursued and destroyed by the Portuguese.

On the north western point of the island at Fen Muli are the concrete remains of a British battery built early in World War II to defend the north western side of Addu. About four km south of Fen Muli on the western side of Hithadhoo are the remains of another old fort that has been mostly washed away. The origins of this fort are unknown.

On Hithadhoo in the Thakurufaanu Miskiiy is the grave of Sultan Hassan X (1701 AD) who died in 1765 after 60 years in exile.

**Maradhoo** There are two villages on the island of Maradhoo. Maradhoo and Maradhoo-Feydhoo. To make way for the airforce base on Gan, the population of Gan was moved to neighbouring Feydhoo and the Feydhoo islanders were integrated into the island of Maradhoo. The southern end of Maradhoo island is now called Maradhoo-Feydhoo. A causeway connecting Maradhoo to Hankede Island was first built in 1970 and a new causeway connecting the islands was completed in 2004.

**Feydhoo** was connected to Maradhoo by a causeway in 1970.

**Gan** was cleared of vegetation during World War II to make way for the British airforce base. It is now an international airport and the officers' quarters is the site of Equator Village-Gan, a resort that opened in 1995. It was previously known as the Ocean Reef Club. This resort is completely different from any

**Hithadhoo** is the capital of the atoll with a number of historical features. At Koattey are the ruins of an old fort. Archaeologist, Mr H.C.P. Bell visited the island in 1922 to investigate the ruins, but the origins of this fort are not known for sure. One legend says it was the stronghold of the rebel Maldivians led by Bodu Thakurufaanu who eventually ousted the Portuguese from the Maldives in 1557. According to historians, it is more likely that the fort was built by the 'Lord of Maldives' Kunhali Marakkar, of Malabar, who was trading in the south of the Maldives during the Portuguese period. Kunhali had more than 200 big ships

*The runway on Gan Island was first constructed of steel sheeting in 1941. It was later upgraded by the British in 1957. At its peak in 1960 – 61, it handled 12,500 passengers.*

## BRITISH INVOLVEMENT

In 1887, the Maldives was recognised as a protectorate of Great Britain and the control of the country's defence and foreign relations were vested in G.B. The entire period of British involvement stretched formally up to 1965 when the Maldives gained political independence.

With the outbreak of World War II, the Maldives became an important link in the allied defences against the Japanese in the Indian Ocean. When the British moved into Addu Atoll in 1941, there were 5600 local inhabitants, most of whom suddenly found themselves employed (in 1995 the population was 21,000). Gan Island became secretly known as 'Port T' with the administration of the base initially carried out aboard a navy ship. All the forces, army, navy and airforce, were positioned in this strategic Indian Ocean base. Six months later, regiments from Bengal and India arrived and a base for sea-planes was built at Hithadhoo lagoon, where planes flew in from as far away as Singapore and Trincomalee in Sri Lanka. Underground bunkers for supplies and bombs were constructed at Maradhoo, then covered with trees for camouflage. The first airfield was located on Gan with the runway constructed of steel sheeting.

Almost all the vegetation was stripped and villages flattened to make way for the runway that ran the length of the island. The inhabitants were moved to neighbouring Feydhoo and jetties and buildings constructed. The atoll's defences were strengthened and submarine nets and mines laid across the entrances of the atoll. Also destroyed by the runway were the last remnants of Buddhism on the island.

On March 9, 1944, a German submarine U-183 torpedoed the British oil tanker, *British Loyalty* that was anchored near Villingili in Addu harbour. A man named Mohammed from Hithadhoo recalls:

> About one week before the attack the base was on full alert because of an unidentified high-flying aircraft. Some planes took off to investigate but the enemy plane was not found. Then one week later a submarine just outside the atoll fired a torpedo diagonally through Gan Channel, through the anti-submarine nets, and into a tanker anchored inside the atoll at Viligili. The attack was in the night and the explosion brought everyone to full alert. In the morning there was a big oil slick which the British cleaned up. After this attack the British moved their refueling base to Diego Garcia [in the Chagos Islands].

After it was repaired, the *British Loyalty* was used as a storage hulk and finally scuttled on January 15, 1946 inside the atoll to the southest of Hithadhoo. It was used as a storage hulk and finally scuttled on January 15, 1946 inside the atoll to the southeast of Hithadhoo. When scuttled she had 6417 tons of fuel oil, 43,250 gallons of octane and 105 tons of MT spirit on board. It is a spectacular wreck dive.

After World War II, the British pulled out of Gan but with the independence of India and Sri Lanka after the war, Britain was apprehensive about losing its military strength in the region.

---

other in the Maldives. It is the only one where tourists can mix freely with the local people. A causeway connecting Gan and Feydhoo was opened in 1981 which allows guests to take long bicycle rides through the villages on the western side of the atoll. There is a security checkpoint at the causeway.

The airforce base was solidly constructed and the buildings, roads, workshops, gardens and airport have been well maintained. The roads are lined with tall trees and there is a small post office and a few old shops. The old church has been converted to a mosque. A gun battery was located on the eastern side of Gan Island. The guns of this battery were relocated to the war memorial near the Equator Village-Gan.

Most tourists staying at Equator Village-Gan arrive via Island Aviation Services, which flies daily between Malé and Gan Island. The flight path is directly over the atolls and is a great way to get an aerial perspective of the islands. For a closer view of the islands, adventurous travellers and divers can make safari trips between Malé and Gan. The new international airport at Gan will bring tourists into the southern regions directly from overseas.

Local residents of adjoining islands are allowed on Gan Island during the daytime, but require work permits to enter at night.

**Hulhumeedhoo** There are two villages on this island, Hulhudhoo and Meedhoo. The concrete remains of a World War II battery are on the north eastern point of the island.

**Kandu Huraa** lies in the middle-north of the atoll and is known as Bushy Island. During World War II all the control switches for the minefields around the atoll were located here.

*The British war memorial at Gan is located near Equator Village - Gan.*

In 1952, the British Air Ministry carried out a feasibility survey of Gan Island for the construction of a modern airfield and when the Government of Sri Lanka declared in 1956 that it was not prepared to allow a British military presence on its Trincomalee harbour and Katunayake airport, the Maldives was already on line as an alternative arrangement to link Britain with Australia and the Far East.

An agreement for the use of Gan Island as an airfield and Hithadhoo as a radio-communication centre was concluded and work on the new base began in the second half of 1957, replacing defence facilities in Sri Lanka. When the Maldives gained independence in 1965, Britain retained its lease on Gan. It was initially to last up to 1986, but it was terminated early in 1976 and the British withdrew their forces from the Maldives.

The Gan airbase covered one of the largest aerial search areas in the world and could handle the most sophisticated of RAF aircrafts with the latest navigational and landing aids. It handled some 630 aircraft and 12,500 passengers in 1960 – 61.

Soon after the British withdrawal, Gan Island was reported to be available for lease but the Government, under President Nasir, made it clear that it did not wish to lease the base to any superpower, or others for military purposes. An offer of one million dollars for the lease by the Soviet Union in 1979 for "use by its fishing fleets", was turned down. A garment industry was later established at Gan and tourism is now making inroads into Addu Atoll.

*The North Western region of Addu Atoll is being considered as a protected marine area. It has many natural features- in particular the Eidhigali Kulhi (inland lake)- that is considered an area of special significance.*

Top: *Rocky shoreline Mellon Headed whales. Pond Heron. White Terns.*

Above Pics: *Eidhigali Kulhi.*

**Map (Hithadhoo):**

73°05'E

Koattey
Remains of old fort
Picnic spot

Koattey Beyru West

Tidal area

Fen Muli
British battery
Eidhigali Kulhi

Farming

Demon Point Bay

Bait fishing

Significant bird habitat

Mithadhoo Community

Shallow lagoon area

Kaohera

Sea grass

*Kudhu Kendithan*

Dheerondi

Gulda Lamago

Maahera

Kudhu Maahera

(45m)

Kommuli

**HITHADHOO**

(72m)

73°05'E          Remains of old fort

# Diving Addu Atoll

*Divers who expect an abundance of reef fish may be disappointed with Addu Atoll. But those who want to see wrecks, large manta rays, sharks, turtles and generally big fish all year round, will be delighted with the diving. There are only four kandus in the atoll: Gan Kandu, Viligili Kandu, Maa Kandu and Kuda Kandu. The channels have relatively few caves. Currents are generally not as strong as in the other tourist atolls so the channels can be dived at most times. Depths inside the atoll average around 35 metres but it reaches a maximum of 75 metres in the middle. In the south of the Maldives, there are some differences in language and the kandus are talked about as kandas, farus as faras and giris as galhas.*

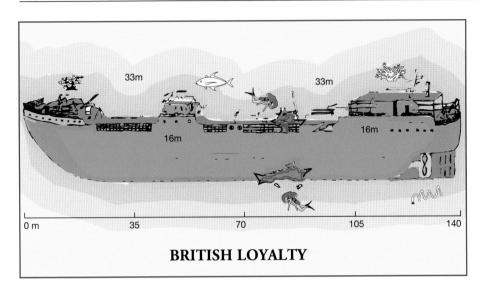

**BRITISH LOYALTY**

### British Loyalty ★★★

| | |
|---|---|
| Location: | south east of Hithadhoo |
| Depth: | 16m – 33m |
| Fish life: | average |
| Coral growth: | very good |
| Features: | wreck, coral |

### History

The 5583 tonne oil tanker, *British Loyalty* was built in 1928 by Palmers Co. Ltd., Newcastle. The ship was torpedoed twice by enemy submarines during the war. The first time was by a Japanese midget submarine in Diego Suarez harbour, Madagascar on May 30, 1942. It was damaged and taken to Addu Atoll in 1943 to be used as a storage hulk. She was torpedoed again in Addu Atoll on March 9, 1944. The German U-183 submarine had ingeniously fired through a gap in the submarine nets blocking Gan Kandu. The ship was damaged but not sunk and

remained there for the rest of the war. The *Loyalty* was finally scuttled on January 5, 1946, before the British withdrew from Gan. According to Mr Mohammed Ibraheem Loutfi, who was a Maldivian liaison officer during the war, the ship was towed by tug to its present location and finally sunk by the guns of a British warship. Mr Husain Didi from Hithadhoo, who was a 15-year-old boy at the time the ship was scuttled, said:

> There were many shots fired into the starboard side and oil floated into the harbour killing some dolphins and fish. The oil continued to come ashore for about 10 years.

### Diving

The wreck lies 30 minutes by dhoani from the Equator Village-Gan between the island of Maradhoo and Hithadhoo. It is lying on the starboard side and the bottom is at around 33 metres. The port side is at 16

metres and the bow points almost directly north. The total length of the wreck is 140 metres and its beam is 20 metres. Coral growth is excellent with large clumps of hard coral all over and a good covering of soft coral. At several places on the railing, big balls of coral look like natural fenders.

The propeller is at 28 metres and originally had four blades made of brass each two metres long. Now the topmost blade is missing but the remaining three are covered in big bushy black coral trees. In front of the engine room, about 60 metres from the stern are two large holes, one on the deck, the other on the keel. These are so big, divers can easily swim through from one side to the other. The holes were most likely caused when the torpedo exploded or when the vessel was sunk. Visibility averages around 20 metres. Schools of blue-fin jack and a large turtle swim around the deck while on the upper side many smaller fish have found a home among the coral.

### Demon Point Bay ★

At Koattey is a small inlet where day trips are made for introductory dives and a barbecue. It is a relaxing dive location with a fine atmosphere.

### Gulda Lamago ★★★

This reef lies to the south east of Koattey and is characterised by a steep slope decorated with hard coral and fine soft coral. There are some caves with lobsters and at about 35 metres the reef undercuts itself to a sandy bottom at about 40 metres. This dive also has a reputation for sharks.

*Anchoring in a crystal clear lagoon for lunch and a swim is the perfect way to survive the heat of the day.*

### Koattey Beryu West ★★★

On the outside reef near Fen Muli are a series of plateaus stepping down at different depths. There is plenty of fish life and between 20 and 30 metres are many white-tip and grey reef sharks. There are also napoleon, schools of surgeon, barracuda and sometimes manta rays. At 30 metres there is a steep dropoff. This dive can only be reached in calm weather and diving is sometimes strenuous due to strong currents.

### Fihal Faru ★★

This is a one km long drift dive along the west side of Kuda Kandu. The reef extends well into the atoll and has big coral heads down the reef face to the bottom at 30 to 35 metres. Fish life includes big red bass, eagle rays, sting rays, and turtles.

### Bushy West ★★

The reef on the west side of Kandu Huraa has a beautiful coral slope dropping to the bottom at 22 metres. There are large coral heads all down the slope and nurse sharks are found sheltering among them. This is an easy drift dive that produces regular sightings of eagle rays, napoleon and turtles.

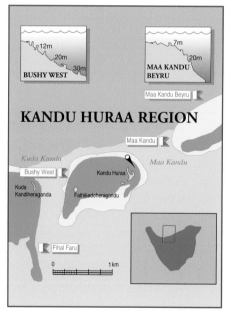

### Maa Kandu ★★

There is a wide reef top on the outside reef corner between five and seven metres which offers a good start to the dive. Many different forms of acropora hard coral dominates the reef here. On the reef slope, which descends steeply from 12 metres, massive coral heads, large brain corals and spongy leather coral are a feature. Big manta rays are regularly seen at the corner.

### Maa Kandu Beyru ★

The outside reef is an easy slow drift dive suitable for beginners with magnificent table and brain corals. Schools of fusilier, turtles, eagle rays, and sometimes mantas make this beautiful reef an absolute joy to dive.

### Shark Point ★★★

On the north east tip of Addu Atoll on the outside of Hulhumeedhoo is a spectacular shark dive. The outside reef drops from five to 30 metres to a sand plateau that is about 30 metres wide. On this sand is the 'shark hotel', where as many as 15 white tip reef sharks and five grey reef sharks can be seen at any one time. On the outside of the plateau, the reef drops to more than 60 metres and when the visibility is good, big sharks are seen swimming in the depths below.

### Las Pueblas ★★

This dive is located on the outside reef of Heretere. It was named after the cliff cities of the natives in the American south west as it has a steep wall with many small caves. The reef edge is at a depth of about 20 metres and the wall drops to around 55 metres to a sand plateau. On the outside of the plateau, well beyond the range of divers, is another wall. Turtles and barracuda feature here but this is mostly a landscape dive.

### Muli Kolhu Faru ★★

The corner into Viligili Kandu is long and rounded with a gently sloping reef from five to 30 metres. Laying on the sandy bottom at about 35 metres is a large hollow steel ball, 2.5 metres in diameter. This was one of the buoys used for supporting the submarine net across Viligili Kandu. Big barracuda, white-tip reef sharks and huge manta rays up to four metres across, are common around the corner. Two hundred metres further into the channel is a large chain starting at a steel anchor point on the reef edge at 15 metres and trailing to the bottom of the channel at about 34 metres. The chain has links 20 cm long and was the main support for the submarine net. Near

*On the reef slopes of Viligili Kandu are the remains of a submarine net constructed during World War II.*

the chain mantas can be seen all year round making this the 'Manta Point' of Addu Atoll. There is also an overhang nearby that is a favourite resting place for nurse sharks. There are more overhangs inside the channel at 30 metres.

**Kanandhou Kaleyge Galha ★**

There is a small reef inside Viligili Kandu ideal for night dives and beginner divers. The reef is half-moon in shape and has a beautiful coral garden on the eastern side.

Coral heads protrude from the reef slope to the sandy bottom at 20 metres.

**Viligili Inside ★**

On the inside southern corner of Viligili Kandu is a finger of reef starting at eight metres and dropping to 20 metres. Divers can spend the whole dive going around this reef. Further south along the reef are shallow bays with pretty coral. At 10 metres is a steel boat about 12 metres long. Cables are also found running into the lagoon on this reef. On the bottom at 13 metres is a large steel ball with a chain that was once a part of the submarine net across Viligili Kandu.

**Gan Inside ★**

Gan Inside is an ideal beginner's dive near the eastern end of the airport runway. Towards the outside of Gan Kandu, there is a small wall starting at five metres. On the top of the reef are wide sandy corridors, sometimes with ten or more resting stingrays. There are also encounters with many hawksbill and green turtles.

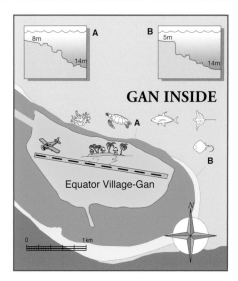

Further inside the channel the reef slopes more gradually to 14 metres. The bottom is sandy with large coral boulders housing a wide variety of marine life. Here divers will find schools of pelagics like blue-fin jack and darts, also sting rays and eagle rays.

*The propellor of the British Loyalty. Inset: The bow section*

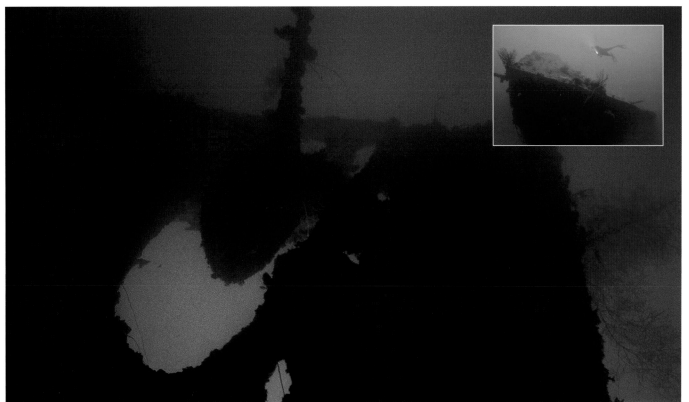

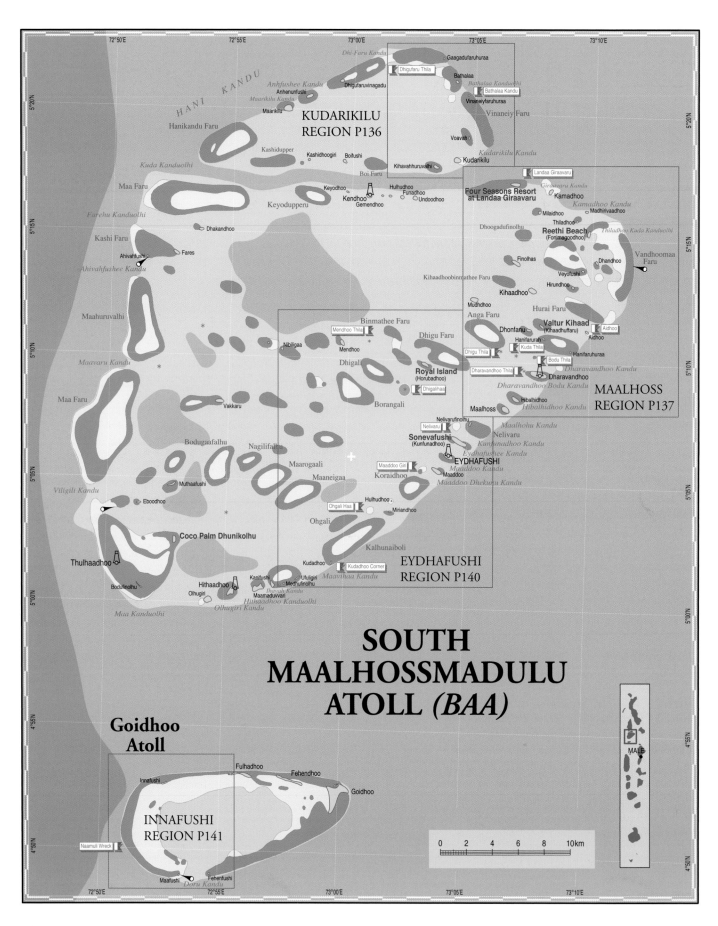

# SOUTH MAALHOSSMADULU ATOLL (BAA)

**KUDARIKILU REGION P136**

**MAALHOSS REGION P137**

**EYDHAFUSHI REGION P140**

**Goidhoo Atoll**

**INNAFUSHI REGION P141**

Dhi Faru Kandu
Gaagadufaruhuraa
Dhigufaru Thila
Bathalaa
Bathalaa Kanduolhi
Anhenunfushi
Dhigufaruvinagadu
Vinaneiyfaruhuraa
Bathalaa Kandu
Maarikilu
Vinaneiy Faru
Anhfushee Kandu
Maarikilu Kandu
Hanikandu Faru
Voavah
Kashidupper
Kashidhoogiri
Boifushi
Kihavahhuruvalhi
Kudarikilu
Kudarikilu Kandu
Kuda Kanduolhi
Landaa Giraavaru
Maa Faru
Keyodhoo
Hulhudhoo
Giraavaru Kandu
Keyodupperu
Funadhoo
Kamadhoo
Kamadhoo Kandu
Farehu Kanduolhi
Kendhoo
Undoodhoo
Milaidhoo
Madhirivaadhoo
Gemendhoo
Thiladhoo
Dhoogadufinolhu
Thiladhoo Kuda Kanduolhi
Kashi Faru
Dhakandhoo
Reethi Beach
(Fonimagoodhoo)
Fares
Dhandhoo
Vandhoomaa Faru
Ahivahfushi
Finolhas
Veyofushi
Ahivahfushee Kandu
Kihaadhoobinmathee Faru
Hirundhoo
Maahuruvalhi
Kihaadhoo
Hurai Faru
Binmathee Faru
Mudhdhoo
Maavaru Kandu
Mendhoo Thila
Anga Faru
Dhigu Faru
Valtur Kihaad
(Kihaadhuffaru)
Aidhoo
Nibiligaa
Dhonfanu
Four Seasons Resort
at Landaa Giraavaru
Mendhoo
Dhigali
Hanifaruhuraa
Hanifarurah
Kuda Thila
Maa Faru
Dhigu Thila
Hanifaruhuraa
Royal Island
(Horubadhoo)
Bodu Thila
Vakkaru
Borangali
Dharavandhoo Thila
Dharavandhoo
Dhigalihaa
Dharavandhoo Bodu Kandu
Bodugaafalhu
Maalhoss
Hibalhidhoo
Nagilifalhu
Hibalhidhoo Kandu
Nelivarufinolhu
Maarogaali
Nelivaru
Maalhohu Kandu
Sonevafushi
(Kunfunadhoo)
Nelivaru
Kunfunadhoo Kandu
Muthaafushi
Maaneigaa
Maaddoo Giri
Eydhafushee Kandu
EYDHAFUSHI
Eboodhoo
Koraidhoo
Maaddoo Kandu
Maaddoo
Viligili Kandu
Maaddoo Dhekunu Kandu
Hulhudhoo
Ohgali Haa
Miriandhoo
Coco Palm Dhunikolhu
Ohgali
Thulhaadhoo
Kalhunaiboli
Bodufinolhu
Kudadhoo
Kudadhoo Corner
Hithaadhoo
Kanifushi
Olhugiri
Maamaduvvari
Ufuligiri
Maavihaa Kandu
Medhufinolhu
Ihavah Kandu
Hithaadhoo Kanduolhi
Olhugiri Kandu
Maa Kanduolhi

Fulhadhoo
Fehendhoo
Innafushi
Goidhoo
Naamuli Wreck
Maafushi
Fehenfushi
Doru Kandu

HANI KANDU

MALE

0 2 4 6 8 10km

# Chapter 9 - South Maalhosmadulu Atoll and Goidhoo Atoll Islands *(Baa)*

*South Maalhosmadulu Atoll and Goidhoo Atoll, or Horsburgh Atoll, as it is called on some European charts, belong to the administrative atoll of Baa. Weaving and fishing are the principal occupations of the islanders. South Maalhosmadulu Atoll is 42 km long and 32 km wide. There are 10 inhabited islands and 41 uninhabited islands. Eydhafushi is the atoll capital. The atoll is separated from North Maalhosmadulu Atoll by a 3.2 km wide channel, Hani Kandu, otherwise known as the Moresby Channel. A 1.8 km wide channel, Kuda Kanduolhi, cuts through South Maalhosmadulu Atoll from east to west. There are 6 resorts in the atoll. Soneva Fushi (Kunfunadhoo), Reethi Beach (Fonimagoodhoo), Valtur Kihaad (Kihaadhuffaru), Royal Island (Horubadhoo) and Coco Palm Dhunikolhu. Four Seasons Resort at Landaa Giraavaru is the most recent resort constructed in 2006. Olhugiri is the most southern island of South Maalhosmadulu Atoll and lies 13 km north of Goidhoo Atoll. Goidhoo Atoll, or Horsburgh Atoll, is 8.5 km long and 17.5 km wide. It has three inhabited islands: Goidhoo, Fulhadhoo and Fehendhoo, known collectively as Goi'fulha'fehendhoo. There are three small uninhabited islands and only one channel, Doru Kandu, in the south of the atoll. The atoll offers a secure anchorage near the islands in the north-east monsoon.*

**Bathalaa** is small and uninhabited with no coconut trees. It has plenty of sand surrounding the island and a long sand bank on the west side. It has a wide, shallow lagoon with an excellent anchorage on the west side only a short swim from the island.

**Vinaneiyfaruhuraa** is little more than a coral and sand islet with no vegetation 50 metres in length on the outside corner of Vinaneiy Faru.

**Voavah.** A small uninhabited island with about 10 high coconut trees and low vegetation. At either end are sand banks and a good beach on the west side. The lagoon on the west side has a deep half-moon shaped bay with good access through the island's outer reef making it an ideal anchorage for deeper drafted dhoanis. Good night diving potential.

**Kudarikilu.** Is an inhabited island with a shallow channel and a marker that cuts through the island reef to a very shallow lagoon on the west side. The island has plenty of coconut trees down to the shoreline. There is an old mosque and cemetery and a prominent *lhoss* tree near the beach on the north side. The old tree is a gathering point for children and islanders passing the time of day. Kudarikilu became known as 'Bomuge Haadhisaa', or bomb island after a floating mine was found by fishermen in 1915 and towed to the island. As the curious islanders gathered around, they could not imagine the tragedy to follow after one of them began striking the strange, spiked object with a steel bar. The mine exploded killing nine people and injuring another 15.

A Lhoss tree on Kudarikilu is a central meeting point for the islanders.

**Landaa Giraavaru.** Landaa Giraavaru has been developed as a Four Seasons Resort. It has a shallow lagoon one to three metres deep surrounding the island. Close by, on the south side is a well protected anchorage with a sandy bottom at 13 metres. Large stands of staghorn coral and coral boulders are spread over the bottom. Near the island, the sand forms a steep slope and rises to three metres. A coral reef forms a protective barrier around the anchorage on the outside. The site is ideal for night diving. Previously the island was used for picnics and had two disused and broken down houses on the island.

**Kamadhoo** is an inhabited island with a stick marking the shallow entrance to the inner lagoon on the west side of the island. There is also a small jetty. Fishermen can often be found repairing dhoanis on the beach or saturating the timbers with fish oil, a smelly practice usually carried out when the wind is blowing the odour away from the island.

**Milaidhoo.** The reef around the uninhabited island of Milaidhoo has some patches of nice soft coral. The island has good snorkelling all round with nice corals on the reef top.

**Fonimagoodhoo** is now a resort called Reethi Beach Resort. It is a thickly vegetated island with a good beach and housereef on the west side. There is a deep housereef three to six metres on the east and north east sides where many rock formations are located with extremely beautiful soft and hard coral. Turtles come onto the island to lay their eggs. There is a good

*Thick vegetation to the waterline is a feature of Horubadhoo. A small number of white-tailed tropic birds nest on the island.*

anchorage at the east side and on the south side a pearl-white beach drops off directly into deep water. Even deep drafted boats can come right on to the beach here.

**Finolhas** is a beautiful uninhabited island, heavily wooded with tall coconut trees.

**Kihaadhoo.** An inhabited island with a shallow channel marked by a buoy on the south west side of the island. It has a narrow fringing reef 50 metres wide with a shallow lagoon around the island.

**Mudhdhoo** is a beautiful, well vegetated uninhabited island with numerous coconut trees, and nice beaches all round. The island was once inhabited and contains the ruins of a mosque, two wells and a cemetery.

**Dhonfanu** is an inhabited island with the anchorage on the north side.

**Kihaadhuffaru** is now a resort called Valtur Kihaad. It is a more sparsely vegetated island with a small number of young coconut trees. It has a beautiful beach all round and is surrounded by a medium sized lagoon.

*Dharavandhoo. An inhabited island but there is no visible evidence of habitation on the south side of the island.*

**Horubadhoo** is now a 200 bed resort called Royal Island. It is a large island thickly covered in lush vegetation to the waters edge. There are many coconut trees, pandanus and a number of 10 metre tall screw pine trees (rare in the Maldives). A small number of white-tailed tropic birds nest on the island. They spend much of their time flying around the island and are clearly identified by their long white tail feathers. The island is surrounded by a narrow beach and a healthy coral reef perfect for snorkelling and diving. The island was once inhabited and the people are reported to have settled at Dhonfanu. There are ruins of an old mosque and a bathing tank among the jungle and a very old cemetery with tomb stones but no writing.

**Dharavandhoo** is a heavily timbered inhabited island with an old mosque and some early remains. The inhabitants of this island, like those from the other inhabited islands in Baa Atoll, produce handicrafts made out of screw-pine leaves such as mats, fans and lampshades for the Malé tourist market.

**Maalhoss.** An inhabited island with friendly people. It has a small lagoon on the western side offering shelter to shallow drafted vessels during the north-east monsoon. A pole with a light marks the entrance. Large schools of herring swarm about the shallows and in the evening the islanders fish for them with a short pole and line. The herring are then eaten or used as bait for larger fish. The eastern side of the island is like a jungle and hidden in the middle is the Huraagandu, or island stone. This 60 cm wide coral stone stood as high as a coconut tree until it broke off one metre from the ground about 20 years ago. No one knows the origin of the stone. A forked 70 year old coconut tree is of special interest. The area around the tree has been cleared and islanders delight in taking visitors to the oddly-shaped tree.

**Kunfunadhoo** is a heavily timbered island 1.4 km long by 400 metres wide. It originally opened as Kunfunadhu Island Resort in 1983, but was later closed, partly because of its isolation. It reopened as Soneva Fushi in October 1995 and to improve comfort and reduce travel time, guest transfers to the island were made by helicopter. Located 115 km from Hulhule airport, it is the only resort development in the atoll, so far. The island is surrounded by a sandy beach and among the jungle areas, bird life, fruit bats and lizards are prolific. Rabbits and chickens have also been introduced to the island.

**Eydhafushi** is the capital of the atoll and the focal point of transportation to Malé for the smaller neighbouring fishing communities. It has been inhabited for many centuries with the main mosque being built during the reign of Sultan Mohammed Mu-eenudheen I (1799 – 1835). The island is clearly distinguished by a large communications tower, visible for great distances at night by its flashing lights. The island has a hospital, school and a good harbour to serve the region.

*In the early morning, fishermen from the island of Maalhoss load their products for transport to the markets in Malé.*

**Goidhoo** is the largest island in the Goidhoo group and being 1.6 km wide and two km long, it is relatively large by Maldivian standards. It is an inhabited island and large deposits of sand and gravel in the centre of the island suggest it has been inhabited for many centuries. It was made the exiles' island in 1962 although some political prisoners and convicts are recorded as being banished here and at other islands in the group, since at least 1602. A strange event occurred in 1963 when thousands and thousands of flying-fish are recorded as having landed on the island.

**Fulhadhoo.** There is a nice white sandy beach and a shallow lagoon with coral heads on the south side of this inhabited island. The island has plenty of vegetation. The *Corbin* was shipwrecked on the reef near Fulhadhoo on July 2, 1602, with Frenchman Francois Pyrard on board. The 40 survivors made it by boat to Fulhadhoo the following day but only four, including Pyrard, are known to have survived the five year ordeal. Many of the survivors were held captive at Fulhadhoo and the other islands in the group during their time in the Maldives. The survivors buried silver from the wreck on Fulhadhoo and one story told is that treasure was buried at the base of a large Nika tree. A group of Frenchmen in search of the treasure are said to have returned to the island many years ago but found no evidence of the Nika tree or treasure.

**Fehendhoo** is similar to Fulhadhoo in shape, it too has a shallow sandy lagoon with coral heads on the south side. On the western end of the island, a long sandbar almost connects Fulhadhoo at low tide. The island is inhabited.

**Innafushi** is a small uninhabited island with some vegetation.

**Maafushi** is little more than a mound of coral with a light tower on the western side of Doru Kandu. There is no vegetation.

**Fehenfushi.** There is little evidence of an island here, just coral rubble on the reef on the eastern side of Doru Kandu.

**Kanifushi.** An uninhabited island with a picturesque sandy beach on the north side. It lies within the same reef system as Medhufinolhu, Ufuligiri and two sand banks. There is a 100 metre-wide barrier reef to cross to get to the deeper inside lagoon. Entrance is at high tide over the unmarked reef on the north side of Kanifushi. Medhufinolhu has about 12 coconut trees and Ufuligiri has some low bushy trees. The islands and sandbanks are connected at low tide.

**Maamaduvvari** is a longer uninhabited island with a close fringing reef on the south west side. It has a beautiful moon-shaped lagoon with a sandy beach on the north west side.

**Hithaadhoo.** An inhabited island lying in the middle of a circular reef. It has a wide lagoon on the south side and the entrance is marked by a post on the north west side of the reef. It is a fishing community and the islanders are well known for their piety in following the tenets of Islam.

**Olhugiri** is the first island to come into view when approaching the atoll from the south. It is quite large, uninhabited but well vegetated and a natural sanctuary for birds and turtles. It has a narrow fringing reef close to the island on the east and north sides with a deep channel close by on the eastern side.

**Thulhadhoo** is home to a number of craftsmen. They produce exquisite hand-carved items with designs of red, black and yellow lacquer work.

Dhunikolhu is a resort called Coco Palm Dhunikolhu. *Dhuni* means bird.

*Fulhadhoo, in Goidhoo Atoll.*

# Diving South Maalhosmadulu Atoll and Goidhoo Atoll Islands

*The north and east sides of South Maalhosmadulu Atoll have many islands, reefs, and channels, providing countless alternative diving locations. The western side of the atoll is characterised by wide channels and big reefs with few islands or landmarks. There are around 20 channels on the eastern side and nine on the western side. A 1.8 km wide channel, Kuda Kanduolhi, cuts through South Maalhosmadulu Atoll from east to west. There are steep dropoffs into this 200 metre deep channel and some interesting diving. Many of the islands have sections of reef with excellent coral growth making them ideal for diving and snorkelling. The inside of the atoll has depths mostly between 30 and 50 metres and there are many thilas, mostly between seven and ten metres. There are excellent sand and rubble zones in the more accessible parts of the atoll floor and many interesting coral heads. This atoll is popular with live-aboards venturing to the northern regions both as a final destination and for stop-overs. There are now five resorts in the atoll spread evenly down the eastern side, and a sixth one on Landaa Giraavaru is expected to open later in 2006. In Goidhoo Atoll, there is only one channel in the south of the atoll, the 2 km wide Doru Kandu, with good diving on the outside corners. On the inside of the atoll, it is deep in the centre but closer to the islands and reefs are wide expanses of shallow sand with many reef flats and coral heads. On the outside of Goidhoo Atoll the structure of the reef is hard and flat as a result of its exposure to rough seas.*

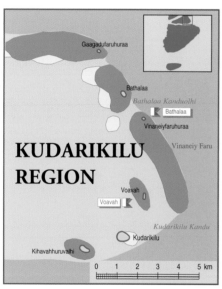

*Pink Coral at Bathalaa*

## Bathalaa ★★★

| | |
|---|---|
| Location: | Bathalaa Kanduolhi |
| Depth: | 6m – 25m |
| Fish life: | above average |
| Coral growth: | excellent |
| Features: | pink coral |

One of the most brilliant sights in the atoll occurs on the outside northern corner of Vinaneiy Faru, where a dazzling display of pink coral clings to the vertical channel wall. The sand islet of Vinaneiyfaruhuraa is on the corner and marks the starting point for the dive. The reef slopes smoothly to a cliff face at 18 metres and then drops vertically to the channel bottom at 25 metres. All along this wall are isolated patches of pink coral interspersed with seafans, black coral and soft corals. There are a couple of pink coral locations inside the channel but the better part of it occurs on the corner over a distance of about 100 metres. The hard coral wall and bottom has many encrusting sponges as well as several gorgonian and black coral species making this wall a kaleidoscope of colours.

**Diving hints:** Take care not break or damage the pink coral when drifting with a current.

## Voavah ★

A secure coral-ringed anchorage on the west side of this small uninhabited island makes this a potentially exciting night dive location. It could well be called 'goby lagoon' because of their vast number and variety, even less commonly seen species. The inside of the lagoon is covered in zoanthids, a small anemone-like coelenterate that appears to have taken over the reef. As a consequence, perhaps, fish life is sporadic inside, although on the outside entrance to the lagoon big schools of blue-striped snapper, red bass, and

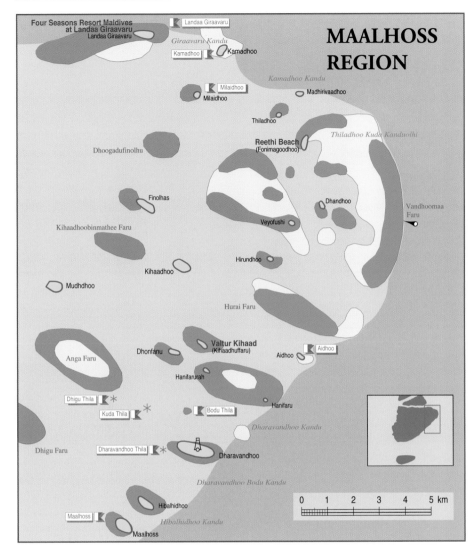

MAALHOSS
REGION

*These zoanthids photographed at Voavah, resemble small anemones. They are colonial and live attached to the reef.*

Above: *White-blotch razorfish,* Xyrichtys aneitensis. *Fairly common around sandy slopes and in seagrass areas.*

life. On the western side are numerous basslet, wrasse, clown triggerfish, blue triggerfish and hawkfish. There are also many sea whips with featherstars attached and on the whips can be seen small shrimps. This dive is a pleasant change and ideal for photographers.

*Slender sponge reef goby,* Pleurosicya elongata. *Found on the underside of fan sponges in Landa Giraavaru lagoon.*

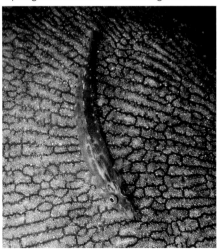

butterflyfish occur. There is a narrow band of seagrass about 50 metres long, in very shallow water close to the island. The white-blotch razorfish can often be seen near this small patch and elsewhere around sand slopes and ridges.

## Landaa Giraavaru ★★

On the outside corner of Landaa Giraavaru is a long narrow reef with very nice hard coral on the reef top. Large fish are prevalent at this site with regular sightings of sting rays and napoleons.

## Landaa Giraavaru Lagoon ★

Diving inside the lagoon from an anchored boat is the perfect way to finish off a day of diving. Safari dhoanis can anchor in 13 metres close to a sand slope on the south

side of the island. Nearby, a coral reef rises to two metres and all over the sandy bottom, coral boulders and staghorn coral attract a wealth of fish life. Some coral boulders rise to three metres. Night diving is excellent and ideal for photographers. Fusiliers, butterflyfish, cardinalfish, snapper and sometimes swarming schools of catfish can all be seen at night. The slopes are peppered with the holes of gobies and flat worms and nudibranchs are more likely to be seen here than at many other places. Much of the coral is covered with thin, floppy fan sponges and underneath are slender sponge reef gobies.

## Kamadhoo ★

A quiet island reef dive with a healthy coral reef top and considerable variation in fish

### Aidhoo ★★

The reef on the north side of the small island of Aidhoo is a great location to view fish of every description including tuna, snapper and napoleon. On the outside reef are large schools of trevally and sweetlip as well as a honeycomb moray and turtles.

### Bodu Thila ★★

This is a very large thila with an interesting landscape and the top around eight metres. There is soft coral on the reef faces and fish life is abundant, including grey reef sharks, large schools of fusilier, sting rays and sometimes manta rays. Turtles are regular visitors and ghost pipefish can be seen among the branches of gorgonians.

### Dhonfanu Thila ★★★ (Kuda Thila)

| | |
|---|---|
| Location: | 2 km south west of Dhonfanu |
| Depth: | 7m — 30m |
| Fish life: | abundant |
| Coral growth: | excellent |
| Features: | reef sharks, tunnel, soft coral, fish life |

A smaller thila with excellent hard coral on the reef top and soft coral on the walls. There are big trevally, schools of blue-striped snapper, and tuna and on the bottom at around 35 metres are sting rays.

### Dhigu Thila ★★★

| | |
|---|---|
| Location: | 150 metres south east of Anga Faru |
| Depth: | 6m – 25m |
| Fish life: | abundant |
| Coral growth: | excellent |
| Features: | caves, overhangs, fish life |

A long, narrow thila about 200 metres long with the top between six and 11 metres. At the eastern end is a sharp dropoff from seven to 25 metres and a large cave at 13 metres with black coral. Around the corner on the north side are a series of spectacular caves stacked vertically down the reef. Nearby and usually visible from the main reef, is a flat topped outcrop of reef 15 metres wide at a depth of 26 metres. Huge schools of red bass, trevally and other fish congregate at the end of the thila and as the current picks up so too does the feeding activity. Along the southern side, mostly between 20 and 25 metres, are big, bright caves with seafans and whips, many grouper, squirrelfish, and lots of smaller fish like white-banded possum wrasse and pipefish. On the sandy bottom around the thila can often be seen black-spotted sting rays. The reef top is covered in fine hard coral with stands of fire coral on the highest point at the eastern end.

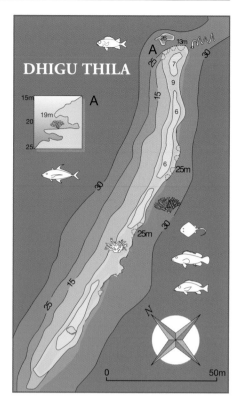

**Diving hints:** The thila lies in an east - west direction and current usually flows the same way. To gain full advantage of the scenery, it may be necessary for divers to start in open water well upstream from the thila when there is a strong current. The options are to dive either the south or north sides with the south side offering the best in the way of caves and scenery. This poses a slight problem if the current is flowing from the east and divers wish to view the caves on the north-east corner. There is not a lot of protection from the current at shallow depths so divers should be fully prepared to make an open water safety stop.

*Snowflake soapfish,* Pogonoperca ocellata. *Rarely seen but has a distinctive skin flap on the chin.*

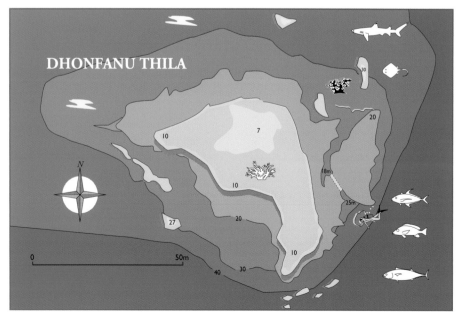

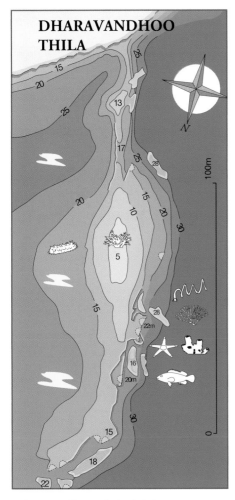

## DHARAVANDHOO THILA

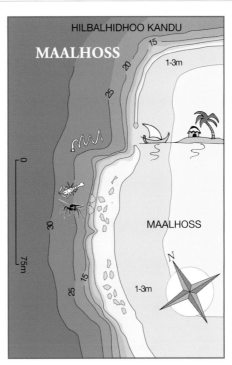

## MAALHOSS

HILBALHIDHOO KANDU

MAALHOSS

*Above : Comet fish,* Calloplesiops altivelis. *Deceives its predators with a false eye.*

*Above top: Cling reef goby,* Plenrosicya micheli.

*Below: Nudibranch,* Chromodoris gleniei *A very distinctive nudibranch endemic to the Indian Ocean, this species appears to be more common in the Maldives than it does in the Seychelles or at other locations. It lives in lagoons as well as on open reef and along drop offs; it feeds on sponges.*

*Bottom: Colour variation.*

### Dharavandhoo Thila ★★★

| | |
|---|---|
| Location: | SW of Dharavandhoo |
| Depth: | 5m – 30m |
| Fish life: | abundant |
| Coral growth: | very good |
| Features: | topography, caves, reef fish |

The beauty of this thila is its unusual features. It begins as a narrow ridge from the island of Dharavandhoo and extends, like a roller-coaster, for over 200 metres with the top between 5 and 17 metres. Along its course it leaves a trail of reef outcrops, steep ledges, colourful caves, sand slopes and narrow crevices. In some crevices and caves are seafans, whips and black coral bushes and some big grouper. There are bright yellow and orange sponges, pink sea-stars, pin-cushions and sea-cucumbers. Also great opportunities for photographers to take stunning landscape shots.

### Maalhoss ★★

| | |
|---|---|
| Location: | west side of Maalhoss |
| Depth: | 3m – 25m |
| Fish life: | abundant |
| Coral growth: | very good |
| Features: | reef fish |

Divers will be delighted with the variety of marine life that is concentrated on the west side of Maalhoss. Twenty metres to the south of the lagoon entrance, the reef wall bends out and drops off to 25 metres before levelling off to a bottom of coral rubble and sand. Caves are liberally sprinkled down the face of the wall. At this point the fish life is interesting. There are many different species of cardinalfish and occasionally a cometfish – uncommon in the Maldives – can be seen. There is black coral and in some caves are lobsters and shrimp. On the deeper slopes among the sand and rubble are many rare species of goby. At this unique location is another rare fish, the snowflake soapfish, Pogonoperca ocellata. At the northern end, in Hibalhidhoo Kandu, the current can be quite strong and attracts schooling needlefish, halfbeaks and herring. This dive is an ideal site for enthusiastic fish watchers.

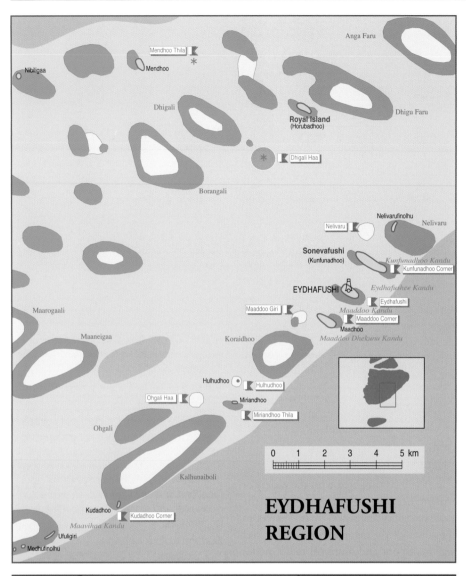

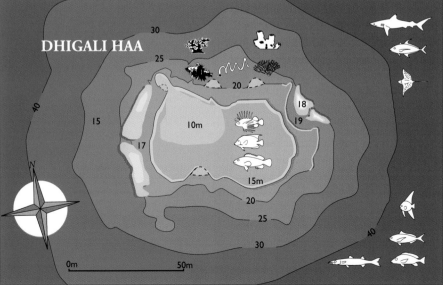

DHIGALI HAA

## Dhigali Haa ★★ (Horubadhoo Thila)

PROTECTED MARINE AREA

| | |
|---|---|
| Location: | 2 km SW of Horubadhoo. |
| Depth: | 10 – 30m |
| Fish life: | abundant |
| Coral growth: | excellent |
| Features: | grey reef sharks, fish, coral, |

This site was heavily fished for shark in the past and is now a protected marine area. It is a good shark viewing location with six or more grey reef sharks circling at any one time. Fish life is varied with blue-fin jacks, fusilier, blue-striped and humpback snapper, batfish, schools of barracuda and eagle rays in the open water. Closer to the reef are lionfish, angelfish, basslets, and trumpet fish. In the caves and around the reef edges are blackcoral bushes, oyster clams, yellow sea fans, sponges and soft corals. This is a small thila, easily circumnavigated in one dive and is a favourite site for shark viewing by Sonevafushi guests. Fish life also includes trevally, fusilier, batfish, small schools of barracuda and sometimes eagle rays.

## Kunfunadhoo Corner ★★

The entrance to Kunfunadhoo Kandu attracts plenty of pelagic action and on the outside corner of Kunfunadhoo is a nice reef featuring a number of napoleon. When the current is flowing into the atoll, a small school of up to five eagle rays often appear near the corner.

## Eydhafushi ★

The outside reef of this island offers the best diving and it is a convenient site for Sonevafushi divers during the south-west monsoon season. Turtles and schools of fusilier are common. The channels on either side of the island are less interesting.

## Maaddoo Corner ★★

The north east side of the island reef offers the most interesting diving. When the current is flowing into the atoll it is more difficult to dive because the water flow splits in two directions around the reef. There are nice overhangs on the corner and very good fish life. On the reef top further inside Maaddoo Kandu are excellent table corals.

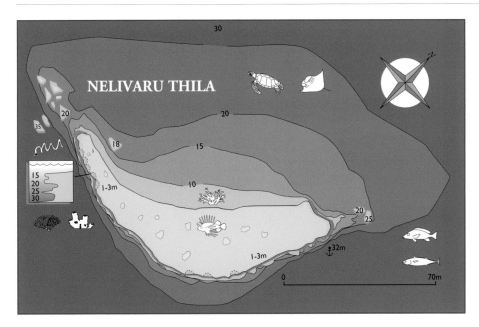

*Many blennies, such as the orange-spotted blenny,* Blenniella chrysospilos, *have a large mouth and appendages above the eyes.*

### Nelivaru Thila ★★

| | |
|---|---|
| Location: | 1 km west of Nelivarufinolhu |
| Depth: | 1m — 30m |
| Fish life: | above average. |
| Coral growth: | very good |
| Features: | reef fish, |

Nearby the island of Nelivarufinolhu, is a large reef with good diving for all levels of divers. There are nice corals, rocks and caves, especially on the north side. Fish life includes snapper, tuna, turtles, mantas. A feature of this site are the scorpion fish. Watch the reef carefully and many can be seen.

### Maaddoo Giri ★

A dive for beginners and experienced divers. On the west corner of the reef is a chimney with the top opening at three metres and the bottom one at 20 metres. Anglerfish, one pink and another black, can be seen if divers are observant and lucky enough. At 30 metres is a large school of blue-striped snapper. East of the corner are large coral rocks, overhangs, and three small pink corals. There is also black coral and sometimes ghost pipefish can be seen among it.

### Hulhudhoo ★★

On the north east side of the island reef are very good soft and hard corals. Napoleon and turtles are regular attractions here.

### Miriandhoo Thila ★★★★

On the south side of Miriandhoo is a small, deep thila for experienced divers only. The top is covered in soft coral and the isolation of the site attracts a diverse range of marine life. Turtles and eagle rays are attracted here.

### Ohgali Haa ★★

A large reef with interesting overhangs on the north east side. There are schools of batfish, some tuna and on the reef top are leaf fish.

### Kudadhoo Corner ★★

At the entrance to Maavihaa Kandu, Kudadhoo corner offers all the usual range of fish life seen at many of the channel entrances. Among them, napoleon, lobster, nurse sharks and turtles.

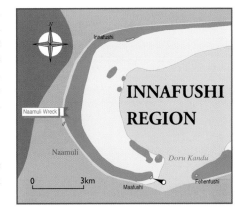

### Naamuli Wreck ★

| | |
|---|---|
| Location: | western point of Goidhoo Atoll |
| Depth: | 5m |
| Fish life: | above average |
| Coral growth: | good |
| Features: | steel wreck |

The reef on the western side of Goidhoo Atoll is called *Naamuli Faru* and literally means shipwreck reef. There is a wide reef flat at the western tip of the atoll and on the top in five metres, lies the flattened remains of an old steel ship. The main body of the coral covered wreck covers a distance of about 30 metres. The steel remains are completely broken up by heavy seas and some rib sections are spread over the reef up to 50 metres away. The highest point of the wreck is at two metres and the deepest at seven metres. Like most wrecks, it offers good protection for fish and attracts many wrasse, surgeon, fusilier, angelfish and emperor. A special feature in little burrows on the reef top are many orange-spotted blenny.

The origins of the Naamuli wreck remain a mystery as there is no known record of the ship available. Even old islanders on Fulhadhoo cannot tell when the ship was wrecked. When it was located some years ago, the wreck was thought to be the remains of the *Corbin* (see p14) and, because of its supposed historical value, divers were banned from going anywhere near it. However, the steel remains indicate it is not that of the *Corbin* and it is hoped further archaeological research will uncover the true origins of the wreck.

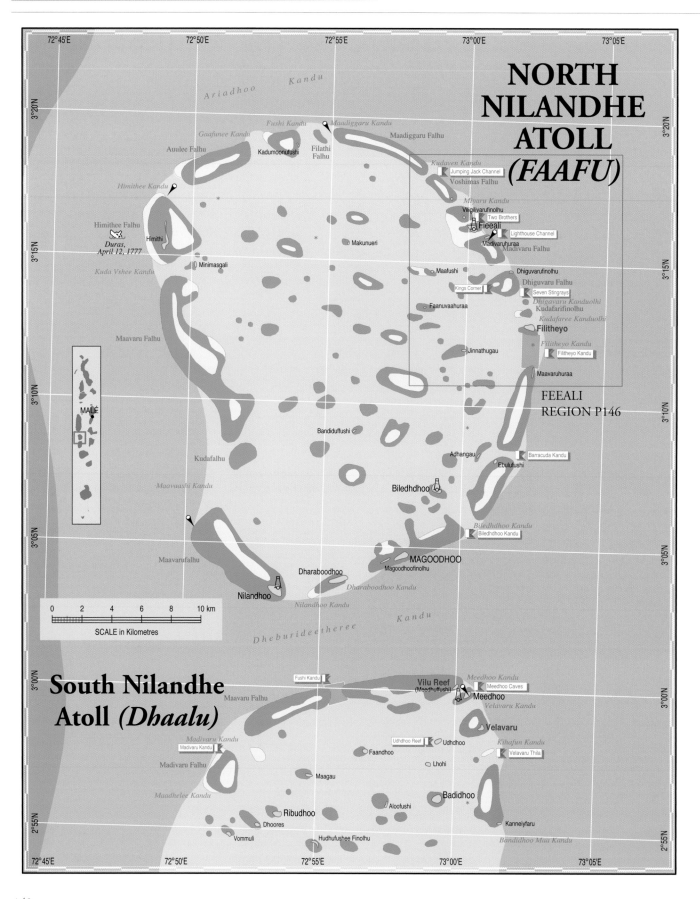

**NORTH
NILANDHE
ATOLL
*(FAAFU)***

72°45'E  72°50'E  72°55'E  73°00'E  73°05'E

*Ariadhoo    Kandu*

*Fushi Kandu*  Maadiggaru Kandu

3°20'N

Maadiggaru Falhu

*Gaafunee Kandu*

Auulee Falhu

Kadumoonufushi  Filathi
Falhu

*Kudaven Kandu*

Jumping Jack Channel

Voshimas Falhu

*Himithee Kandu*

*Miyaru Kandu*

Viiligilivarufinolhu

Two Brothers

Himithee Falhu

3°15'N

Fieeali

*Duras,
April 12, 1777*

Himithi

Lighthouse Channel

Madivaruhuraa

*Kuda Vshee Kandu*

Minimasgali

Makunueri

Madivaru Falhu

Maafushi

Dhiguvarufinolhu

Dhiguvaru Falhu

Kings Corner

Seven Stingrays

*Dhigavaru Kanduolhi*
Kudafarifinolhu

*Kudafaree Kanduolhi*

Faanuvaahuraa

Filitheyo

Maavaru Falhu

3°10'N

Jinnathugau

*Filitheyo Kandu*

Filitheyo Kandu

Maavaruhuraa

**FEEALI
REGION P146**

Bandiduffushi

MALÉ

Adhangau

Barracuda Kandu

Ebulufushi

Kudafalhu

3°05'N

*Maavaashi Kandu*

Biledhdhoo

*Biledhdhoo Kandu*

Biledhdhoo Kandu

Maavarufalhu

Dharaboodhoo

MAGOODHOO

Magoodhoofinolhu

*Dharaboodhoo Kandu*

Nilandhoo

*Nilandhoo Kandu*

*Dheburideetheree    Kandu*

0  2  4  6  8  10 km

SCALE in Kilometres

Fushi Kandu

Vilu Reef
(Meedhuffushi)

*Meedhoo Kandu*

Meedhoo Caves

3°00'N

**South Nilandhe
Atoll *(Dhaalu)***

Maavaru Falhu

Meedhoo

*Velavaru Kandu*

Velavaru

*Kihafun Kandu*

*Madivaru Kandu*

Madivaru Kandu

Udhdhoo Reef

Udhdhoo

Velavaru Thila

Madivaru Falhu

Faandhoo

Lhohi

Maagau

*Maadhelee Kandu*

Badidhoo

Ribudhoo

2°55'N

Aloofushi

Dhoores

Kanneiyfaru

Vommuli

Hudhufushee Finolhu

*Bandidhoo Mua Kandu*

72°45'E  72°50'E  72°55'E  73°00'E  73°05'E

# Chapter 10 - North Nilandhe Atoll Islands (*Faafu*)

*North Nilandhe Atoll is shaped like a kidney and is 30 km long and 25 km wide. There are five inhabited islands, with the capital being Nilandhoo and 15 heavily vegetated uninhabited islands. Filitheyo is the only resort in the atoll and transfers are mostly made by seaplane to Dhiguvaru Falhu, three km northwest of the resort. North and South Nilandhe Atolls are separated by a four km wide channel and regular contact between islanders from the two atolls, links the people closely in family and tradition. It is an atoll of historical importance that once produced the most skilled sailors who contributed significantly to trading within the Maldives and abroad. Travel experiences to these two atolls are rewarding, partly because of the isolation of the resorts, the large number of spectacularly vegetated uninhabited islands and the historical interest of the islands.*

*Nilandhoo island, showing lush vegetation and a small sandy beach with excellent formations of beach rock that underlies the sand and protects the shoreline from erosion.*

*Stonework from the remains of temples at 'Nilandhoo Foamathi' (on Nilandhoo island)*

**Nilandhoo** is the capital island of the atoll and also the most populated. It replaced Magoodhoo as the capital in 1999. *Nila* means blue and could refer to the big blue lagoon within the reef. There is a new harbour and atoll administration buildings on the western side of the island. The island has a fine beach on the southern side. Nilandhoo is a very old inhabited island and archaeological evidence at a 200 metre square site known as 'Foamathi', suggests it was one of the most sacred pre-Islamic sites in the archipelago. *Foa* means areca nut, and many Maldivians chew it, but it also means testicle. According to oral tradition, Foamathi had seven temples that were demolished soon after the arrival of Islam in A.C.1153. The local people refer to the site as Aasaaree Sarahadholhu or Ancient Place and it is believed the people were once Buddhist or maybe even Hindu. At the time of conversion, they were reluctant to give up their old religion, so the first Sultan, Muhammad-ul-Adil, went to the island with soldiers and set up a temporary palace to deal with the strong following of worshippers. One street is called Bodu Ganduvaru Magu, meaning big palace street. All the temples, except the gateways, were destroyed, idols were broken or buried and a new mosque, the second in the Maldives, was built on the site of the seventh temple with much of the stonework coming from the original temples. The mosque has since been rebuilt but some of the existing elaborate coral stones used in the temples are still in evidence. The gateway to the seventh temple still stands in front of the mosque but the remaining six were demolished sometime in the 1950's when little value was placed on archaeological sites.

**Dharaboodhoo** is an island where religious relics have also been found. The island was famous as a breeding place for turtles. One man said that 30 years ago up to 40 turtles would come onto the island to nest every night, but now it is very rare to see them. Islanders are not allowed to kill turtles, but they are allowed to take eggs.

**Magoodhoo** was the first capital of the atoll and used to be called Fonimagoodhoo. *Foni* means sweet.

**Magoodhoofinolhu** is a small nearby uninhabited island.

**Biledhdhoo.** *Biley* is the betel leaf used when chewing areca nut and the island has many betel vines growing on it, as well as Breadfruit trees. The islanders are regarded as good fishermen and a new harbour finished in 1999 offers good protection for the dhoanis. Like most of the inhabited islands, it has long, clean sandy streets, mostly running east and west and telephone booths and streetlights were constructed in 1999. The island office is marked by a flagpole flying the National Flag and is located in the traditional position, not far from the waterfront near the harbour. The island has an old mosque that was built on top of a Buddhist monastery. It was enlarged in 1999 but the small, beautifully built old mosque with its white slabs of coral and intricately carved wooden inner walls, still remains intact within the larger building. The stone foundations of the old monastery can be seen sticking out at angles from the base, as the mosque now faces Mecca and not east/west. The ancient well is lined with coral slabs and the water crystal clear. There are old tombs nearby and a very old bath with steps, now filled with coral and sand. Future excavations should reveal a lot more about the history of the island.

Biledhdhoo mosque.

**Adhangau** is a small uninhabited island.

**Embulufushi** is a small uninhabited island. An *embulu* is a creeper with a small sweet fruit that children like to eat. The plant and fruit is also used as an herbal medicine.

**Maavaruhuraa** is a long uninhabited island located at the northern end of a big reef.

**Jinnathugau.** *Jinni* means fairy and the island name translates as 'the stone which the fairy came and stood on'.

**Filitheyo** is a large island that was once inhabited a long time ago. It opened as a resort in 1999 and is currently the only resort in the atoll. Gravestones and other relics can be found at a small cemetery located 50 metres behind the reception area among the dense vegetation. There are about 10 headstones still visible among the vegetation, including the tomb of "Ismail". He is an unknown person but nevertheless formerly considered 'holy' as many islanders used to leave little white flags and other items at his tomb to bring good luck. There are also the remains of a mosque located nearby but the foundations are now mostly covered in trees and scrubs. The island became uninhabited in the early 1900's, but used to have a flagpole for many years after. When a white flag was flying, it indicated someone was staying at huts on the island. When there was no flag then the island was unoccupied. In 1917 two English officers, Lieutenants Meade and Smith, were on a reconnaissance mission in a seaplane from H.M.S. "Raven" when it ran into difficulties and was forced down near Filitheyo. The officers swam through 2.5 km of "shark infested waters" to reach this island. The seaplane was found floating about Feeali. (See story on page 150)

# The tomb of Filitheyo Ismail

At some time, someone of note was buried on Filitheyo. No one knows for sure who it was, but the tomb of "Ismail" as it became known, has become a part of Faafu legend.

Until recently, people paid their respects and prayed at Ismail's tomb. They made offerings such as food and placed little white flags there to bring good luck. At sunset, travellers from Nilandhoo stopped at the tomb to pray for good fortune during their often hazardous sailing journey to Malé.

One lady from Biledhdhoo said she placed a white flag at the tomb after the birth of her son. She pointed out proudly that her son, then 19, was top of his class at school.

People often make up stories for the deceased and one story about "Ismail" has immortalised his tomb. Some people claim he was a Kanverin, or magician, from Vaadhoo in Gaafu Dhaalu who died while at sea near Filitheyo. The fishing grounds off Filitheyo are well known and large schools of 'Ran Korakali', small golden fish, can be seen there glistening in the morning sun. This picturesque sight is attributed to "Ismail's" magical powers.

As a sign of Ismail's reputation, all dhoanis coming from Malé or elsewhere, steered away from the channels on either side of Filitheyo island, preferring the channels further north or south. This sailing practice is still continued by many fishermen today.

**Faanuvaahuraa** is a small uninhabited island.

**Maafushi** is a small uninhabited island.

**Dhiguvarufinolhu** is a long sandy island.

**Madivaruhuraa** means Ray fish island.

**Viligilivarufinolhu** is a tiny uninhabited island but may have once been inhabited. *Varu* is a group of people or *varu* can also be a place on the reef where waves break.

**Fieeali** is an inhabited island. *Fiee* means rotten while *ali* is a light. The name translates as dim light island. There is a 45 metre communications tower on it and on the south side of Fieeali Kandu is a large light beacon, indicating the channel through which many of the atoll boats pass.

**Makunueri** is an uninhabited island inside the atoll. *Makunu* means monkey and eri means came. In the past, sailors may have arrived at this island with monkeys.

**Kadumoonufushi** means the island on the edge of the channel. It is a small uninhabited island at the northern tip of the atoll.

**Himithi.** This island was inhabited until 1970 and used to be the capital of the atoll. On April 12, 1777, a French vessel the *Duras* was wrecked on this island fully laden with cargo on a voyage to Pondicherry. All the shipwrecked folk met with the kindest treatment from the islanders of the atoll. The passengers and crew were transferred to Malé where they stayed for two weeks before being sent on to India. One of the passengers was the wife of the French administrator of Pondicherry who was preceding him to India. The Sultan of the Maldives, Muhammad Mu'izz-ud-din, salvaged what was left of the ship and with that he built a strong new ship of about 200-tons that continued to sail to the coast of Coromandel and to Orissa for many years.

On Himithi, is the tomb of Shiekh "Boa-huni" Alibay, and the remains of a "thulhu-dhandi", or set of wooden scales that were used in a ceremony to bring good luck to the newly born. Shiekh Alibay's favorite food was "Boa-huni", a sweet made of coconut and honey, so for good luck, the newly born was placed on one end of the scale and balanced by "Boa-huni" at the other. The dish was then distributed to the islanders.

The island of Himithi is constantly 'moving' as heavy erosion and deposition of sand takes place. A story told over previous generations is that a sandbank would one day emerge near Himithi and when it joined the island, the people would leave. This sandbank did in fact form to the north of the island and joined the main island in 1960. Ten years later the island became uninhabited. The story also foretold that the people would one day return to live on the island, but when that happens, the world will end!

**Minimasgali** is a small-uninhabited island near the eastern side of Himithi. It is protected by reefs and was a favoured anchoring place for large vessels that used to operate out of Himithi.

# Himithi Sailors

The island of Himithi was renowned for the skill of its sailors and their teaching of navigation and mathematics. It was here, during his survey of the islands in 1834 that Captain Robert Morseby mentions the island as having a school for navigation. Around this time, there were seven large Odis and Baggalas, 70 to 80 feet long and owned by the Maldivian Government, that sailed to more distant places such as Bangladesh, India, Sri Lanka and Oman. During rough weather, they anchored off the nearby island of Minimasgali, where the reefs offer good protection. One of the most famous mathematicians was Abdulla Ismail Kalafan, whose nickname was Tutu . He went abroad to study in Calcutta and the story told is that he became fascinated with the Almanac, a book used by navigators to study the position of stars and planets. While making his own calculations, he noticed a mathematical error and pointed this out to the English authorities. They were most defensive and ordered him before the Almanac committee to explain his calculations "or he would be shot", so the story goes. After he convinced the committee that an error had been made and showed them the corrections, they all stood up, tilted their hats and called him 'Sir Tutu'. Sir Tutu returned to the Maldives with a lifelong commission and a greatly enhanced reputation after winning the respect of the British.

Another famous sailor was Boduge Hawwaa, a woman of considerable standing in the community because she owned a large boat and was the head of a huge dwelling where 40 people lived. On one trip from Malé to Himithi, her ship was sailing home via Felidhe Atoll - the customary route - when she ordered the boat to anchor securely at Fussaru Falhu. She also ordered a thatched roof built over the boat for protection even though the weather was fine. When the crew asked her why this was being done, she replied: "Don't ask me why. This vessel is mine and you'll do as I say!" Before long the weather turned bad and a violent storm thrashed the boat. As soon as it started to ease, she ordered up the anchors and set sail even before the storm had stopped. Soon the weather was clear again and the ship travelled on uninterrupted to Himithi. The crew were most impressed and stories of Boduge Hawwaa's sailing exploits became legendary.

# Diving North Nilandhe Atoll

*There are many channels on the eastern side of North Nilandhe Atoll, most with reasonably shallow entrances around 20 to 25 metres. They have a number of reefs rising from the bottom to near the surface allowing safe, controlled diving across the channel when the current is favourable. The shallow channels quickly give way to a deeper interior with depths around 30 to 35 metres. In these channels, many big fish like mantas, barracudas, eagle rays, napoleon, white-tip and grey reef sharks, as well as whale sharks in the northeast monsoon, can be seen. Most of the diving is in the northeastern side of the atoll although regular trips to the south are made by Filitheyo resort, the only resort in the atoll. Filitheyo Kandu is wider and deeper than the rest of the channels and is the only protected marine area in the atoll. It attracts a great deal of attention, with many resort divers focusing on the north side of the channel, as well as the more spectacular Filitheyo Thila and Dolphin corner, on the southern side. This atoll offers spectacular and varied diving with a sense of isolation unparalleled anywhere in the Maldives.*

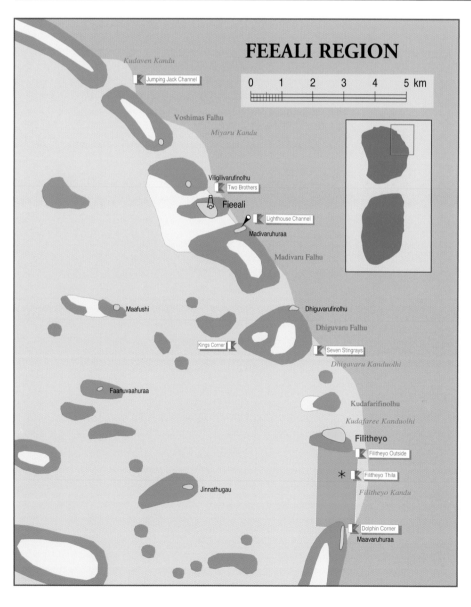

### Two Brothers ★★★

This is a channel dive on the north side of Fieeali with two thilas that attract a wide range of fish. The largest thila lies in the middle of the channel and rises to 5 metres from the channel floor at between 22 to 28 metres. The second and smaller thila is closer to Fieeali and rises to 10 metres. A couple of caves on the inside of the large thila are worth a visit. Usually there are sting rays on the sand and often eagle rays and sharks swimming across the channel entrance. A steep drop off at the entrance plunges from 30 metres to around 45 metres.

### Jumping Jack ★★★

| | |
|---|---|
| Location: | Kudaven Kandu |
| Depth: | 8m to 20m |
| Fish Life: | abundant |
| Coral growth: | good |
| Features: | eagle rays, grouper, sweetlips, jacks. |

This is an exceptional dive that has an underwater ridge across the entrance of the wide channel at around 20 metres. On this ridge are seven thilas with top depths ranging from 8 metres to 12 metres. There are many options for diving this channel, depending on the conditions. With a stronger current, divers can spend the entire dive on the southern outside corner where there are caves at around 30 metres and spend the remaining dive around the first and largest thila with a sand channel at 26

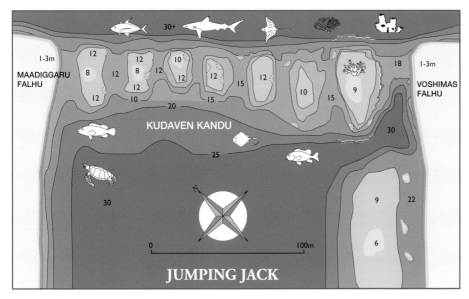

**JUMPING JACK**

### Lighthouse Channel ★★★

| | |
|---|---|
| Location: | Fieeali Kandu |
| Depth: | 4m-25m |
| Fish life: | abundant |
| Coral growth: | good |
| Features: | eagle rays, sting rays, turtles, sharks. |

This is a fascinating exploratory dive with nine thilas that allow many different diving options. These include deep-water drop-offs with caves, different shaped thilas at alternate depths, sand channels of varying length, direction and width, and drift diving with long bottom times. Divers usually start on the south side when conditions are favourable, take a look at the outside drop-off for sharks, eagle rays and big fish and make their way north across the channel, keeping their dive relatively shallow. If the current is flowing strongly in or out of the channel, as it often does, then some protection can be gained on the lee side of the thilas, allowing opportunities in the many sandy offshoots to see stingrays and less obvious fish species, such as scorpion fish and sand gobies as well as invertebrates such as sea cucumbers, soft corals and shrimps.

metres. In the right conditions, divers can cross the entire channel and vary their dive to cross inside the channel at any one of the eight sandy passages. Rounding the corners of these thilas is always a good option to catch large fish, like grouper, by surprise, as well as sting rays and turtles. There are caves at different depths offering delightful interludes to this underwater excursion.

**Diving hints:** If drift diving across the channel, follow the outside line of thilas keeping your depth above 20 metres. Rise to the top of the thilas towards the end of the dive and finish if possible close to the main reef. It's easy to become separated from your group if winding between the thilas, so always carry a safety parachute in case you have to surface in the middle of the channel.

*The island of Fieeali showing Fieeali Kandu (foreground) and adjoining underwater reefs. This dive is known as Lighthouse Channel.*

**Diving hints:** If drift diving across the channel don't go too deep or fight the current, relax and use air sparingly and keep moving across the channel.

*Gold-spot emperor,* Gnathodentex aurolineatus *at Lighthouse Channel.*

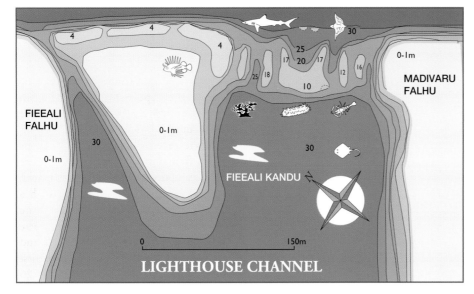

**LIGHTHOUSE CHANNEL**

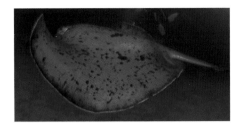

*Sting rays are graceful and harmless unless provoked.*

**Seven Stingrays ★★★** is a channel dive on the south side of Dhiguvaru Falhu, the reef with a shallow lagoon on which seaplanes land. This wide channel has a thila in the middle and when conditions are favourable, it is possible to explore across the channel to the thila. There are good caves on the south west side at 25 to 30 metres and a ridge running parallel with the outside of the atoll. Many fish, grey reef sharks, eagle rays and plenty of sponges can be seen. There are also a number of pipe cleaner black corals and if you take a close look at these bushes, a small commensal black coral crab can usually be seen. There are excellent coral beds on the western edge of the thila around 15m, before sloping down to sand. Sting rays can always be found on this sandy slope and their presence has given this site its name.

**Kings Corner ★**

A good beginners dive with protection from strong currents. It is also ideal for photographers looking for large schools of fish that include blue-stripped snapper, humpback snapper, fusiliers and gold-spot emperors. Angelfish are also prevalent and the occasional sling jaw wrasse can be seen. If you are lucky these fish can sometimes be seen at cleaner stations with their jaws extended. There are six or more coral bombies on the sandy bottom between 12m and 25 metres that are the main area of interest here. Keep a look out for turtles and sting rays on the sand.

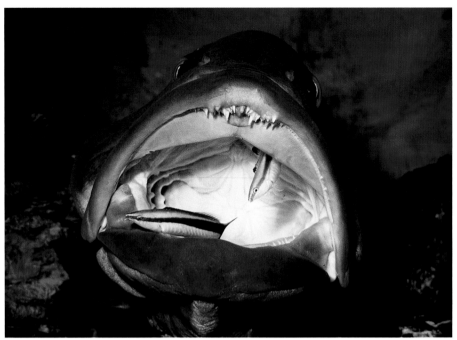

*Blue-streak Cleaner wrasse,* Labroides dimidiatus, *cleaning a large grouper. Groups of these industrious little fish pair together at cleaner stations to pick away dead skin and parasites from the skin, gills and mouth of passing fish. Divers with cuts or peeling skin may also find themselves being cleaned by these fearless fish. When there is a shortage of male fish in this species, the female has the ability to change to the male sex, thereby ensuring the continuation of the species. Cleaner wrasse have a cunning impersonator in the false cleaner, a blenny,* Aspidontus taeniatus, *which has a similar look and size. Once the blenny has gained the confidence of its host, it will enter cavities such as the gills, and take a bite out of the fleshy interior.*

*Emperor angelfish,* Pomacanthus imperator. *The emperor or imperial angelfish, as it is widely known, is among the most exotic species commonly seen in the Maldives. Like other angelfish it feeds on algae, sponges, sea-squirts, and small invertebrates.*

**Filitheyo Kandu**

　　PROTECTED MARINE AREA

| | |
|---|---|
| Location: | Channel south of Filitheyo resort |
| Depth: | 5m to 30m |
| Fish Life: | abundant |
| Coral growth: | very good |
| Features: | batfish, Napoleon, eagle rays, sting rays, white-tip reef sharks, snapper, coral. |

Filitheyo Kandu is a 2 km wide channel with three main dive sites: Filitheyo Outside, Filitheyo Thila and Dolphin Corner. **Filitheyo Thila ★★★** is a shallow "U" shaped reef with a top varying from 10 metres to 20 metres. This reef encloses a sand valley where sting rays are often seen along with large schools of fish. Around the thila are numerous caves, mostly around 20 metres and deeper. Two smaller reef outcrops with a top depth of 10 metres and caves on the outside at around 20 metres are located near the outside reef. They are spectacular sites that attract sharks, napoleon and eagle rays. More caves are located on the outside drop off below 30 metres.

**Filitheyo Outside ★★** is a reef that protrudes steadily down into the channel along a narrow ridge 20 metres wide to a depth of 30+ metres. It features batfish, napoleon, caves and coral outcrops, sweetlips and snapper. **Dolphin Corner ★★** is a similar finger of reef protruding into the channel from the southern side. Divers are advised to start on the steep outside reef and drift to the corner where the reef slope flattens out. Notice the corals, blue-finger sponges, hydroids and featherstars. In a strong current, hold on to dead coral and view white tip reef sharks, napoleon, eagle rays, and schools of fusilier and snapper. With an ingoing current, a good option is to drift over to the protection of the lee side of the reef. There are also two huge mushroom corals on the corner, one at 15 metres and the other at 10 metres. Here many fish gather including moorish idols, blue triggerfish and powder blue surgeon.

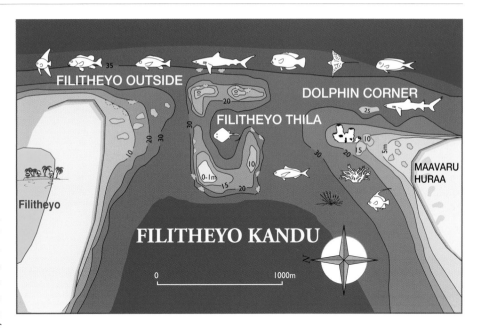

Barracuda Kandu ★★ is a 500 metre wide channel with a depth of around 20+ metres across the entrance. The northern side is the most popular diving section with large coral outcrops inside the channel at 20 metres and a more shallow section at 5 metres on the corner. Large schools of barracuda are seen here as well as eagle rays.

**Biledhdhoo Kandu ★★★** is a one kilometre wide channel with four separate thilas in the middle with depths ranging between eight and 14 metres. Narrow sandy gutters with a depth of 17 to 20 metres separate each thila. The southern side of the channel has a deeper channel of 25+ metres. Sting rays are regularly seen on the sandy bottom and schools of sweetlips make a colourful sight.

*The island of Filitheyo showing the outside reef (right of pic) and the start of Filitheyo Kandu (foreground).*

*Blue finger sponge, Amphimedon sp. Is common on the deeper slopes and gutters in the Maldives.*

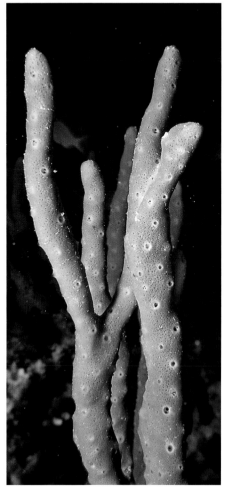

# A Seaplane Adventure

In April 1917, Captain Abbott Meade and his co-pilot Guy, of the Royal Naval Air Service, were sent up late in the afternoon in a new seaplane from their ship H.M.S. "Raven" in the Indian Ocean to reconnoiter the Maldive Islands. They ran into a wind storm and were driven off course and soon found themselves out of radio contact and lost among the myriad group of islands and reefs.

Back and forth they flew until the approaching darkness forced them to land near one of the remote islands. They became stuck on the reef and after the rising tide mercifully carried them off, they taxied around in the dark looking for a channel to take them to the quiet lagoon inside.

They did not find one, so they taxied at high speed over the reef to the quiet waters beyond.

"There was nothing but the lightning to help us beach the machine beneath a bank of white coral sand crowned with coconut trees, which grew right down to the water's edge. We roped her to one of them. Then as the storm increased in violence, we spent a miserable night lying along the lower plane in an attempt to get some little shelter from the driving rain," wrote Captain Meade.

There was no food or water on the island and next day, after consulting their charts, they flew off again at high tide very low on fuel looking for the main island of the group.

In Meade's account: "We used our tunics to dry the plugs and magnetos and left them on the island. It was impossible to go back for our clothes, for our stock of compressed air with which the engines were started was completely exhausted. It was an unpleasant situation, but it had to be faced."

They soon ran out of fuel and landed near the island of Filitheyo, but the wind and tide took them away from the island and onto one of the nearby reefs. With darkness approaching and exhausted from trying to keep the plane off the reef, they set out swimming - stark naked - towards the island, "through a mile and a half of shark-infested water" in an attempt to obtain local assistance.

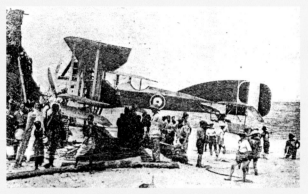

The seaplane on the island of Feeali in1917.

"This may be 'good-bye', old chap," said Guy.

"It may be," replied Captain Meade. "We had better swim apart. Goodbye and good luck".

The pair swam apart and headed towards the shore. Near the island they saw a number of little white flags fluttering in a ghost-like fashion through the gloom. They reached the island exhausted and found a boat without oars and a track leading to three little huts where they ate coconuts and drifted off into a deep sleep. Later in the night there came a flicker of light and they were awoken by voices.

Captain Meade continues: "'Salaam!' Guy said, in his friendliest tones. There was one wild shriek of terror. The crazy lamp was dashed to the ground, where the coco-nut oil flared up for a moment and then died out, and back into the intricate-mazes of the palm-grove dashed three panic-stricken forms."

In the morning, there was no sign of the men and the little boat had gone. The pilots found some filthy linen in the hut, draped it around them and spent the day constructing a raft, while the seaplane could still mercifully be seen floating on the horizon.

Next day, just off the headland lay a small fleet of native fishing boats; the desperate pilots waved and shouted but the boats, although close at hand, sailed off into the distance. However, in fear no doubt of the Sultan's wrath and overcoming their own fear, the boats came back and the pilots swam out to meet them.

As Captain Meade reports the encounter, "A fierce babbling of voices greeted us as we came alongside and hung to the boats. Not a word could we understand, but we took it they were scandalized at our nakedness, for they supplied us with some rags of garments and fed us with dried fish. There followed an infinite amount of jabbering and gesticulation while we endeavored to persuade them to take us out to the distant plane, now nothing but a dot on the horizon"

The little fleet of eleven dhoanis towed the plane to the nearby island of Feeali where it was dragged high and dry onto the beach and later a thatched hut built over it. A series of strange and unreal days followed as Meade reports:

"Some of the bolder spirits became more friendly. Then we took them down to the beach and showed them the plane and our instruments, particularly the wireless telegraph battery, with which we gave them electric shocks. That caused a sensation on the island, I assure you, and Guy and I were regarded with more superstitious awe than ever. But that suited our purpose very well, since it gave them a wholesome fear of the plane."

*The old palace in Malé, The Akoatey Buruzu, early 1900's.*

The pilots were eventually taken to Malé to meet the Sultan. "One morning early, the blue haze of the main island lay before us, and shortly afterwards a little red ensign fluttered from the top of our mast. This we learned afterwards signified that either the Sultan or Englishmen were on board. The Sultan was exceedingly good to us. We were lodged in the palace and given the uniform of officers of his private guard – white trousers with scarlet tunics. A few days later we bade farewell to the intricate mazes of the Archipelago and set sail for Ceylon."

Mr. Mohammed Hassan, a 100-year-old man from Biledhdhoo, remembered how the plane flew north over his island late one afternoon.

"I looked up with the other villagers and we all stared into the sky at this strange-looking noisy bird, it circled around Embulufushi and appeared to go down into the sea on the horizon. Next day my uncle, who was a boat captain, went out with some other dhoanis to look for it," he said. Mr Hassan said the little flags the pilots saw on Filitheyo were most likely those at the tomb of 'Ismail'. "It is a sacred tomb, although no one knows who Ismail was and in those days the flags were placed there by islanders to bring good luck if say the fishing was poor. There was also a flagpole 25 feet high and if a white flag was flying, then it meant someone was on the island. If it was down, then nobody was there," he said.

Mr Zakariyya Hameed, Atoll chief of Faafu, was born in Feeali and remembers his mother telling how the islanders were very afraid of the white people and the strange flying machine.

"Since ancient times the people have been scared of 'kaffaru', or white people. On the islands it is a tradition that when a fishing dhoani has to be pulled onto the beach, then both men and women help. On this occasion when the women folk arrived at the beach to help pull up the seaplane, the men yelled out there were 'kaffaru' so all the women and children rushed home to hide and the children cried. One of the pilots was badly burnt and they stayed for three days before being taken to Malé," he said.

"Four months later a ship came and anchored outside the atoll. Many people, including engineers, came to fix the plane. Before leaving, the pilots gave the people 40 yards of bandages for which they were extremely grateful. All the people were standing around close by until the engines started up. The wind blew sand everywhere, and the people ran away frightened."

*The main bastion in Malé, demolished in the 1960's.*

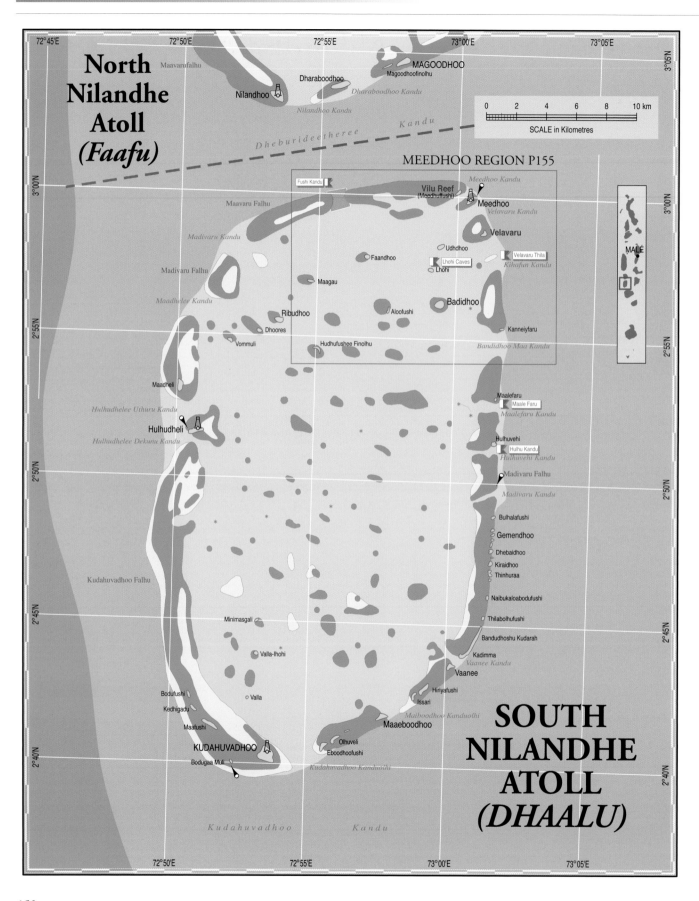

**North Nilandhe Atoll (Faafu)**

Maavarufalhu

Dharaboodhoo

Magoodhoofinolhu

**MAGOODHOO**

Nilandhoo

*Dharaboodhoo Kandu*

*Nilandhoo Kandu*

*Dheburideetheree* K a n d u

0 2 4 6 8 10 km

SCALE in Kilometres

**MEEDHOO REGION P155**

*Meedhoo Kandu*

Fushi Kandu

**Vilu Reef**
(Meedhuffushi)

**Meedhoo**

Maavaru Falhu

*Velavaru Kandu*

**Velavaru**

*Madivaru Kandu*

Udhdhoo

Velavaru Thila

Faandhoo

Lhohi Caves

*Kihafun Kandu*

Madivaru Falhu

Lhohi

Maagau

*Maadhelee Kandu*

**Badidhoo**

Aloofushi

Ribudhoo

Dhoores

*

Kanneiyfaru

Vommuli

Hudhufushee Finolhu

*Bandidhoo Maa Kandu*

**MALÉ**

Maadheli

Maalefaru

*Hulhudhelee Uthuru Kandu*

Maale Faru

**Hulhudheli**

*Maalefaru Kandu*

*Hulhudhelee Dekunu Kandu*

Hulhuvehi

Hulhu Kandu

*Hulhuvehi Kandu*

**Madivaru Falhu**

*Madivaru Kandu*

Bulhalafushi

**Gemendhoo**

Kudahuvadhoo Falhu

Dhebaidhoo

Kiraidhoo

Thinhuraa

Naibukaloabodufushi

Thilabolhufushi

Bandudhoshu Kudarah

Minimasgali

Kadimma

*Vaanee Kandu*

Valla-lhohi

*

**Vaanee**

Hiriyafushi

Bodufushi

Issari

Kedhigadu

*Maiboodhoo Kanduolhi*

**Maaeboodhoo**

Maafushi

Valla

Olhuveli

**KUDAHUVADHOO**

Eboodhoofushi

Bodugaa Muli

*Kudahuvadhoo Kanduolhi*

# SOUTH NILANDHE ATOLL (DHAALU)

*Kudahuvadhoo* K a n d u

# Chapter 11 - South Nilandhe Atoll Islands (*Dhaalu*)

*South Nilandhe Atoll is 37 km long and 12 km wide. There are eight inhabited islands and 35 uninhabited islands of which two are resorts. Many of the uninhabited islands are small and in the northern part of the atoll. However there are a number of small islands over a distance of 12 km on the reef of Gemendhoo. There are many openings in the barrier reef although Kudahuvadhoo Falhu, being the longest reef in the atoll at 29 km, restricts accessibility from the southwest. Like North Nilandhe Atoll, the isolated resorts in this atoll have access to some heavily vegetated islands and other inhabited islands of historical interest.*

*A satellite image of the central atolls of the Maldives.*

**Kudahuvadhoo** is the capital island of the atoll and tradition says the original inhabitants of the Maldives, the so-called Redhin, lived on this island. Remnants of a large Buddhist temple are to be found here. The temple was destroyed when Islam came to the Maldives but the elaborate gateway was left intact and serves as a poignant reminder of the previous religious era. Amidst the elegant decoration on the gateway is a symbol in the shape of a 'Star of David'. This is said to be an ancient symbol 'Suleiman modi', the seal on King Solomon's ring. A mosque was built on the old temple site using many of the handcrafted stones from the temple. The rear wall of the mosque is a fine example of crafted stone masonry. Set into the smooth wall is a stone block, about one square metre, with twelve sides and corners fitting beautifully into the surrounding stones. There is also a very old graveyard with some fine tombstones, two of which are said to be that of the master mason who constructed the mosque. One of them lies at the foot of his grave, the other at the head. Both tombstones are very elaborate and, strangely, they have five points on the top but no one knows why. This is unusual, as Muslim tombstones are usually rounded on top for women and have one sharp point for men. There is a large man-made mound near the mosque, perhaps 25 metres in diameter, known as 'Us Gandu'. No one knows why it was constructed as excavations made several years ago revealed nothing but a heap of sand. Near the mosque among the trees is a bathing tank, once used for the temple worshippers. Some archaeological relics have been found here, including a stone 'head', said to be so big a man could barely reach around it. It was reburied somewhere near the mosque. A stone image of an animal was found in the early 1940's and was sent to Malé, never to be seen again.

**Eboodhoofushi** and **Oluveli** are two small uninhabited islands on the southern end of the reef next to Kudahuvadhoo Kanduolhi. Coconuts are harvested from these islands.

**Maaeboodhoo** is another very old inhabited island and recent rebuilding of the mosque revealed the foundations of an early temple.

**Issari** is an uninhabited island with bushes and trees.

**Hiriyafushi** is another uninhabited bushy island. *Hiriya* means the beautiful, the noble and the honourable presence of a revered guest

**Vaanee** is a very old inhabited island that used to be called Dhiguvaanee. There is a good anchorage in the lagoon and traditionally, dhoanis sailing from Thaa Atoll would anchor overnight here before proceeding north to Faafu Atoll and then across to Malé. The islanders are renowned fishermen.

**Kadimma** is the first of many uninhabited islands on this reef. *Kadi* means the entrance between a lagoon and the outside sea. Access to the inner lagoon can be found just inside the Vaanee Kandu.

**Bandudhoshu Kudarah** is joined to Kadimaa. *Bandu* means stomach and possibly refers to the other island being close by.

**Thilabolhufushi.** *Bolhu* means bend and could refer to the location of the island on the reef, which begins to swerve around towards the north.

**Naibukaloabodufushi** means the Gazi, or magistrate's island. Maybe in the past it was inhabited.

**Thinhuraa, Kiraidhoo** and **Dhebaidhoo** are small, picturesque uninhabited islands.

**Gemendhoo** is a very small but beautiful island where the people have developed a fishing technique that takes full advantage of their unique geographic location. The island lies on a 10 km long reef that has a scattering of 24 islands up the entire outside of the atoll, although some of them are little more than sandbanks with a few bushes. Nearly all these islands are connected at low tide at which time they are surrounded by a wide and exposed reef. Inside the reef is a long, shallow lagoon that stretches the full length of the islands. On the inner atoll side. There are shallow openings across the reef at both the north and south ends of the lagoon. During the SW monsoon season, large schools of Mushimas, a tasty fish and a favourite with the people, swim through these channels to feed inside the lagoon during the day. At night, they return through the channels to get to deeper water. During the afternoon, fishermen lay a long 'U' shaped net on the bottom of these two channels. On the ocean side, is a dhoani with the end of the net and along the channel are three men on each side carrying a long pole between each pair that hangs in the water below each net. When the fish swim through the channel to get to the outside, the first pair of men, lift up their pole and trap the fish inside the channel. The fish are then herded through the channel to the next pair and so on until the end where they are eventually trapped and hauled into the waiting dhoani.

**Bulhalafushi** is a small uninhabited island. *Bulha* means cat.

**Hulhuvehi.** *Hulhu* means big and *vehi* refers to a bushy island. It is uninhabited and mostly washed away.

**Maalefaru** is a small-uninhabited island and its name quite likely occurred because it is from here that many local island dhoanis depart for Malé Atoll.

**Kanneiyfaru** is a small uninhabited island on the edge of the reef. *Kanneiy* means difficult to reach.

**Badidhoo** is an old inhabited island. *Badi* means big gun, like the cannons once seen in Malé from the Portuguese and Dutch eras. Perhaps one of these guns was once located at this island.

**Aloofushi** is a small, uninhabited island named after the potato, *aloo*.

**Lhohi** is an uninhabited island and like many of the islands in Dhaalu, it is blessed with thick vegetation down to the water line and big trees. This is partly because all the inhabited islands in this atoll are large and with a relatively small population there has been no need to cut down the trees from other islands for boats and houses.

**Udhdhoo** is a very bushy uninhabited island.

**Velavaru** is a resort and vela are creeping bushes.

**Faandhoo** is another bushy island. *Faan* means very calm and refers to the waters around the island.

**Meedhoo** is an inhabited island with *Mee gus,* a species of tree that grows very large. There is a passion for story telling that invokes a strong sense of history and rebelliousness among the islanders. One favorite story is told about a rebel countryman from this island, 'Meedhu' Thakur, who was an advisor to the Portuguese during their occupation of the Maldives in the 16th century. In 1573, Muhammed Thakurufaanu led a small band of patriots to overthrow the Portuguese in Malé after a 15-year period of occupation and then went on a trip to the Southern Atolls to check on the conditions there and to strengthen the rule of Islam. He heard Meedhu Thakur was building a ship on this island and furthermore, Meedhu would not allow any Maldivian to follow the religion of Islam. When news spread that Muhammed Thakurufaanu was heading for the island,

Meedhu left secretly on a raft. Muhammed Thakurufaanu destroyed the ship he was building and then pursued him to Faafu Atoll. After five days of searching, Meedhu Thakur was found in the jungle on the island of Dharaboodhoo. When Meedhu realized that capture was imminent, he committed suicide by thrusting himself with a long-bladed knife.

**Meedhufushi** is a small island on the north side of Velavaru Kandu 'belonging' to Meedhoo. It is now a resort called Vilu Reef.

**Maagau** is uninhabited. The name means big stone island.

**Ribudhoo** has a reputation for employing very artistic people. *Ribu* means Goldsmith and the island is still renowned for its gold craftsmen. The inhabitants were formerly the chief jewelers in the Maldives. It used to be a custom that every year the islanders had to pay a small fine of coir rope to be given to the military in Malé. It is believed this custom was introduced centuries ago because the people once rebelled against the sultan. This custom continued until 1940.

**Dhoores** is an uninhabited island. *Dhoo* means tongue and res is 'layer'.

**Vommuli** is an uninhabited island. *Vom* originally meant 'round', but *Voh* also means candleholder, like those found in Buddhist temples and still found in old mosques. *Muli* is a protruding portion of reef.

**Hudhufushi Finolhu** is a long narrow uninhabited island.

**Maadheli** is an uninhabited island that is sometimes referred to as "Temple Island". It was formerly inhabited and contains the ruins of Buddhist temples. This is one island the legendary Redhin were believed to have inhabited. *Maa* is big and *dheli* means charcoal and is also the ink used in pens. The island has a good anchorage in the lagoon during the SW Monsoon.

**Hulhudheli** is an old inhabited island with the remains of a temple washed away on the reef on the west side of the island. One of the first mosques in the Maldives was built here and part of the original building can be seen under the more recent one.

*During the heat of the day a "saturey" gives fishermen shade from the relentless tropical sun.*

# Diving South Nilandhe Atoll

*South Nilandhe Atoll has a number of channels that allow long drift dives, a couple of deep water thilas, and plenty of shallow water reefs ideal for beginner divers, snorkelling and night dives. There are a number of uninhabited islands with excellent snorkelling that are ideal for day excursions. There are 10 channels on the eastern side and five on the western side. Some of the channels, like Fushi Kandu - the only protected marine area in the atoll - are wide and relatively shallow with more than one thila across the entrance. Inside the channel entrances, the bottom is mostly sandy and between 30 and 40 metres in depth.*

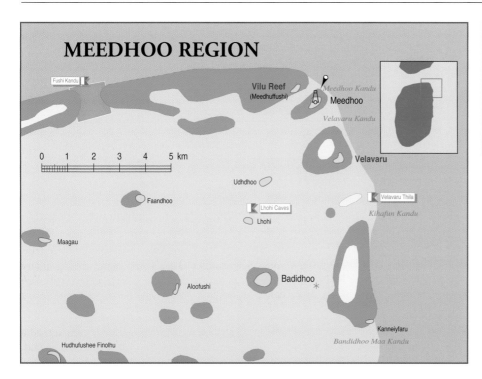

The Spotted eagle ray, Aetobatus narinari, has a duckbill-shaped snout ideally shaped to feed on molluscs and crustaceans.

**Fushi Kandu ★★★**

PROTECTED MARINE AREA

| | |
|---|---|
| Location: | First channel to the west of Vilu Reef resort |
| Depth: | 10m-30m |
| Fish life: | abundant |
| Coral growth: | very good |
| Features: | nurse sharks, napoleon, eagle rays, sting rays, turtles, morays. |

This is an exceptional dive with five thilas across the one km wide channel. The thilas are mostly long and narrow and rise from a sandy bottom of 20 to 25 metres. Depth drops to 30+ metres once inside the channel and the outside ledge drops steeply from 30 metres. Divers can take a look at the outside drop-off for sharks, eagle rays and other big fish and if they return to the thilas and keep a relatively shallow profile, then a leisurely dive across the entire channel can be made. This allows plenty of opportunity to see the sandy channels with stingrays and possibly nurse sharks. The thilas attract many schools of fish as well as moray eels.

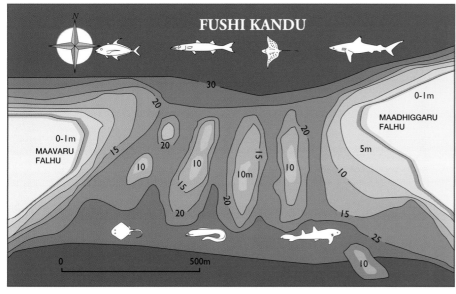

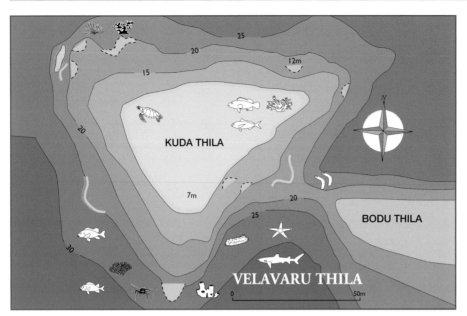

Blue triggerfish, Odonus niger. Also called red-toothed triggerfish. Seen in massive schools on the outer reef. They are shy and dive into holes for cover showing only their scissor-shaped tails.

*Big-nose unicornfish,* Naso vlamingii. *Unicorns are from the same family as surgeonfish and most species have two blades on their tail. Some species of unicornfish have a horn protruding from their head.*

*Sabre squirrelfish* Sargocentron spiniferum

### Velavaru Thila ★★★

| | |
|---|---|
| Location: | First channel south of Velavaru Island Resort |
| Depth: | 7m-30m |
| Fish life: | abundant |
| Coral growth: | very good |
| Features: | schools of snapper, napoleon, black coral, sponges, seafans, turtles. |

Velavaru Thila is made up of three main thilas: Bodu Thila, Kuda Thila and Beyru Thila. Each one can be dived separately or together.

**Beyru Thila** is closest to the outside of the atoll and is a good starting point with an ingoing current. Seas can get quite rough in this wide channel and currents can be fickle, however when conditions are settled, this is an extremely exciting dive with large schools of colourful fish and many, many invertebrates. The top of the three thilas varies from 7 to 10 metres and each one is alive with colourful fusiliers, snapper, fairy basslets, hydroids, sponges and soft coral. Turtles are regularly seen grazing on the reef. **Bodu Thila** is quite large and divers will often start on the north side of this thila and drift northwest across sand to **Kuda Thila**, past sand eels and often resting white-tip reef sharks. Kuda Thila is about 75 metres across and

there are two caves on the southern side at 13 and 25 metres that are full of sponges. There are also harlequin or spotted sweetlips, big-eyes and lobsters. In the deeper cave are two huge seafans as well as soft corals. There are more caves on the northwest and northeast sides at 20 metres with black coral sea whips nearby. On the sandy bottom are arrow dart gobies, sand eels, sea cucumbers and sea stars. This dive has it all and is one of the diving highlights of the atoll.

*A diver lights up a Gorgonian seafan at Velavaru thila.*
*Inset: Gorgonian seafans have polyps with eight tentacles, seen here feeding in the current.*

**Lhohi Caves ★** is a delightful dive with a wide range of invertebrates ideal for photographers and marine naturalist studies. There are a series of caves starting at five metres and descending to 20 metres that are lined with sponges of all colours and size and plenty of stony coral. The caves occur over a distance of about 200 metres and can be comfortably dived at a leisurely pace. Inside are banded shrimp,

*The Sculptured slipper lobster,*
Parribacus antarcticus *is mostly seen wandering about in caves at night.*

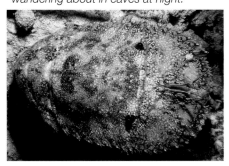

giant spaghetti worms, lobster and slipper lobster, with shells including turbans, tiger cowries and thorny oysters. There are also numerous sea stars, featherstars, urchins and opisthobranchs. This is also an excellent night dive location and can be dived in most conditions.

*The Giant spagetti worm, Reterebella sp. lives in a tube lined with sand and shell grit on the undersides of coral boulders or in holes in rocks, or reef. It has white feeding tentacles that extend up to one metre in length.*

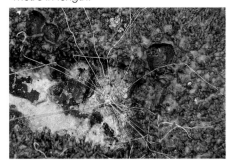

**Maale Faru ★★** is a reef dive off the island of Maalefaru. It features a long, wide thila that extends into the channel on the north side. The top is mostly flat between 16 and 20 metres with some healthy hard corals on the top and on the outside at the channel entrance. There are featherstars, plenty of goatfish, fusiliers and many stands of green coral trees, commonly called midnight coral (Tubastrea micrantha).

**Hulhu Kandu ★★★** is a channel with a ridge across the entrance at a depth of around 15-20 metres. There are a number of small thilas that provide an interesting terrain for divers wishing to cross the channel. This should only be attempted when conditions are favourable as the current can become quite strong here. A recess in the reef on the southern side provides an interesting and slightly protected area with an outcrop of reef inside.

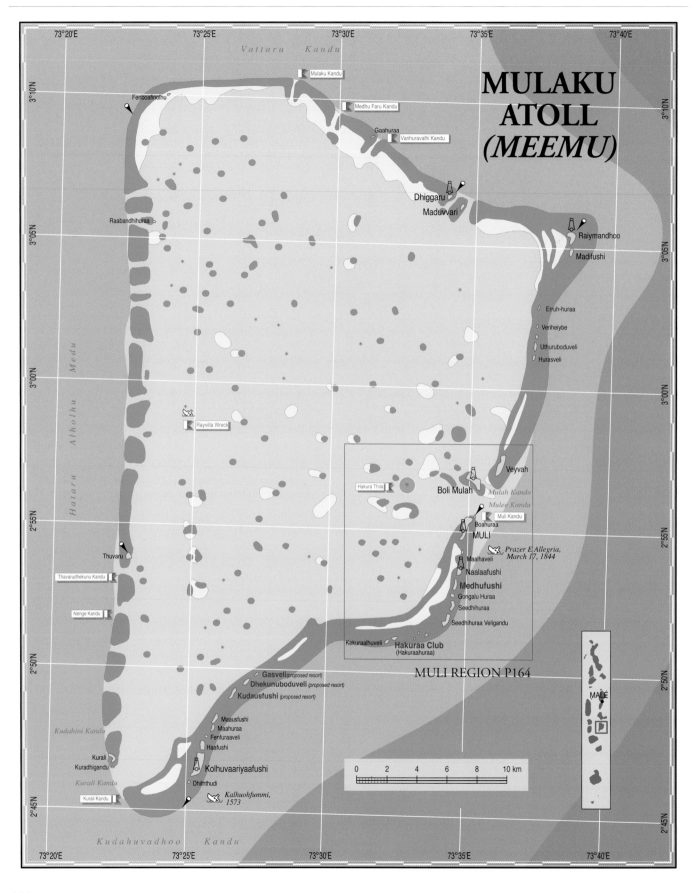

## MULAKU ATOLL (MEEMU)

Vattaru Kandu

Mulaku Kandu

Medhu Faru Kandu

Fenboafinolhu

Gaahuraa
Vanhuravalhi Kandu

Dhiggaru
Maduvvari

Raabandhihuraa

Raymandhoo
Madifushi

Erruh-huraa
Veriheiybe
Uthuruboduveli
Hurasveli

Medu

Alholhu

Hataru

Rayvilla Wreck

Veyvah

Hakura Thila
Boli Mulah

Mulah Kandu
Mulee Kandu
Muli Kandu
Boahuraa
MULI

Thuvaru

Thavarudhekunu Kandu

Nenge Kandu

Prazer E Allegria,
March 17, 1844
Maalhaveli
Naalaafushi
Medhufushi
Gongalu Huraa
Seedhihuraa
Seedhihuraa Veligandu

Kekuraalhuveli
Hakuraa Club
(Hakuraahuraa)

MULI REGION P164

MALÉ

Kudahini Kandu

Gasveli (proposed resort)
Dhekunuboduveli (proposed resort)
Kudausfushi (proposed resort)

Maausfushi
Maahuraa
Fenfuraaveli
Haafushi

Kurali
Kuradhigandu

Kolhuvaariyaafushi

Kurali Kandu
Dhiththudi

Kalhuohfummi,
1573

Kurali Kandu

0    2    4    6    8    10 km

Kudahuvadhoo  Kandu

# Chapter 12 - Mulaku Atoll Islands *(Meemu)*

*Mulaku Atoll is 48 km long and 31 km at its widest point. It consists of 9 inhabited islands and around 30 small uninhabited islands. Muli is the atoll capital and there are two resorts, Medhufushi Island Resort and Hakuraa Club. Another three resorts are proposed, Dhekunuboduveli, Gasveli and Kudausfushi. All the islands lie on the outer reef of the atoll. The principle occupation of the inhabitants is cloth and rope weaving, fishing, some agriculture and employment at the two resorts. The atoll was greatly affected by the December 2004 Tsunami and as a result, it is planned to reclaim land, fortify and build Muli into a "Tsunami safe" island for the region. There are numerous coral reefs inside the atoll and many openings in the barrier reef on the western side of the atoll. There is only one large opening for most of the eastern side. This opening is very shallow and is split into two channels, Mulee Kandu and Mulah Kandu. The northeastern reef of the atoll is 28 kms long and the southeastern reef is 35 kms long. Combined, they form a major barrier to the eastern side of the atoll. The southern reef is unique because the entire length is connected by a shallow and wide lagoon that allows transport and fishing between the islands in traditional style craft specially designed for shallow water travel. These are small dhoanis (bokkuras), canoes (kadubokkura) and rafts (kadufati).*

**Dhiggaru** is a heavily treed inhabited island, more than its close neighbour **Maduvvari**. Fishing is the main occupation of both islands. Dhiggaru has an 80 metre communications tower and is the first island to be seen when travelling south from Felidhe Atoll. There is a 12 mile light marking the west side of the entrance to Diggaru Kandu and a two mile light marks the outside reef of Maduvvari. Maduvvari Kandu is the main channel for boats heading north or south through the atoll.

**Raiymandhoo** and **Madifushi** are inhabited islands with small populations. They are off the main routes through the atoll and are less frequently visited. Raiymandhoo has a communications tower and a 12 mile light. A two mile light marks the eastern tip of the atoll. Raiymandhoo became uninhabited in 1969 but the people went back there in 1975. There are several small uninhabited islands in a big shallow lagoon on the outer barrier reef between Madifushi and Veyvah.

**Boli Mulah** is an inhabited island also called Mulah. It was formerly the atoll capital and fishing and yam growing are main occupations. There is a jetty on the north side of the island that offers good protection during the south-west monsoon. A ferry travels from here to Malé at least once a week. During the heat of the day, islanders gather to sit under trees near the start of the jetty. Anchoring during the north-east monsoon can be difficult and this causes plenty of interest during strong winds. This island has a very shallow and long reef extending into Mulee Kandu. With heavy seas, waves form well out to sea and swells travel up to 500 metres before reaching more shallow water and breaking. At times the waves break early. Boatmen are cautious here.

**Veyvah** is an inhabited island and has a very old mosque built by Sultan Mohammed Ibn Al-Haj Ali (1692-1701 AD). It has a two mile light on its reef marking the northern side of

Mulee Kandu. Close by the light is a "Tsunami tree". Many trees drifted onto the eastern reefs of the Maldives during the December 2004 Tsunami.

**Muli** is an inhabited island that lies at the northern end of a 35 km barrier reef. It is the capital of the atoll and includes the atoll office and a regional hospital. It has a newly reclaimed harbour with a protective outer wall that provides year-round safe anchorage and easy access to the inner lagoon. Boats from Hakuraa Club and Medufushi Island Resort make many of their transfers through this harbour entrance. Coconut trees have been planted around the perimeter of the harbour to provide shade for the many safari boats that stop here during rough weather. Boat building is also a feature of this island with boats up to 100 feet being built. If they are any longer, then the owner has to pay a large increase in fees when landing at Malé harbour.

*The harbour at Muli, damaged during the tsunami, is a safe and spacious harbour for island boats.*

A large part of the inner and outer sides of the island have been reclaimed. On the outside reef, rubble and rubbish from the 2004 tsunami have been pushed into the sea to provide extra space. Muli is being developed as a safe island for the region and a much larger area is to be excavated and reclaimed in the future. The northern end of Muli is a renowned turtle breeding area and a sanctuary is proposed to protect the area from housing development and unwanted intrusion. There is a small island, Boahuraa, located on the northern side of Muli that is accessible at low tide. It is a favourite fishing location for the islanders and humpback snapper are regularly caught by handline off the reef of this island. At low tide, large areas of seagrass are visible and many small shells are seen feeding among it. A 12 mile light on the reef at the end of the island marks the southern end of Mulee Kandu. Following the Tsunami, rubbish of all description covered the reefs of Muli and adjacent islands.

*Many houses on the island of Muli were destroyed during the 2004 tsunami. Following land reclamation works, the atoll capital will be one of four 'tsunami safe' islands in the Maldives.*

A small-uninhabited island, **Maalhaveli**, lies 1.5km to the south of Muli. A ship called the *Prazer E Allegria* was wrecked on the reef near this island on March 17, 1844 with the loss of 11 lives. It is a very picturesque island, about 150 metres long with a good beach on the inner side.

**Naalaafushi**, is a small, inhabited island with a jetty on the inner reef side. A small channel has been cut through the inner reef to provide direct access to the deeper waters inside the atoll. The island has a very old mosque and houses and walls are built of coral stone. There was considerable damage to the mosque during the tsunami, exposing stones with old engravings and inscriptions. Traditional use of log canoes "*Kadubokkura*" and rafts called "*Kadufatis*", are commonly used on the shallow inner lagoons that extend the length of the south eastern reef of the atoll. These are lightweight craft made from breadfruit trees. The women of the island are proficient rope makers. "Roano" or rope, is made from coconut fibre that is first washed in the sea. It is then twisted and joined into long strands.

*Women from Naalaafushi making rope from coconut fibre.*

# Kadufati

The large shallow lagoons in Mulaku atoll mean traditional style mas-dhoanis and bokuraas are often not suitable for crossing the outer barrier reef at low tide. So for this area the islanders developed rafts known as "Kadufati". They are light and made of several logs from the Kadu, or breadfruit tree. They are about 5 metres in length and braced together by means of wooden pegs and lashings. The end of the raft is bevelled upwards and poles propel it through the water. When loaded, the raft rides just below the surface. The Kadufati were also used to catch turtle and to go fishing. They are still used in other areas of the Maldives including Huvadhoo Atoll.

*Kadufatis are used on the shallow inner lagoons that extend for most of the eastern reef of Mulaku Atoll. These lightweight rafts are used for fishing and transport.*

*The island of Naalaafushi looking north towards Muli.*

**Medhufushi** Island Resort is close by **Naalaafushi** and is separated by a shallow narrow channel. There are three uninhabited islands between Medufushi and **Hakuraahuraa** (now a resort called Hakuraa Club). **Seedhihuraa** is a tiny island with bushes and four or five coconut trees joined by a sandbank to a sandy island with bushes called **Seedhihuraa Veligandu**. 300 metres away is a third island with a few coconut trees and bushes but with very little, if any, sand. Another sandbank called **Gongalu Huraa**, appears to be largely washed away. **Hakuraahuraa** is a long island with many water bungalows and a five hundred-metre long jetty crossing a large, shallow lagoon. Windsurfers and catamaran users are fortunate to have access to this large lagoon area.

There are several uninhabited islands between Hakuraahuraa and Kolhuvaariyaafushi. However access to them is restricted by the shallow lagoon and reef. Three of them, **Dhekunuboduveli**, **Gasveli** and **Kudausfushi** are proposed resort islands.

**Kolhuvaariyaafushi** is an inhabited island that lies amid a group of uninhabited islands at the southern end of the atoll. This island was greatly affected by the 2004 Tsunami. Most houses were washed away and at the end of 2005, half the population of 1213 people were living in temporary accommodation awaiting houses to be built, while the other half were living in Malé. Fortunately the island has a good harbour for landing craft. Fishing and yam growing are the principle occupations of the islanders. There were two villages on this island that were joined together in 1962. The main attraction of

*The old mosque on Kolhuvaariyaafushi was badly damaged in the 2004 Tsunami. It was originally built with the remains of Muhammed Thakurufaanu's boat the Kalhuohfummi. (see p162)*

the island here is the old mosque on the southeast corner overlooking the small island of **Dhiththudi**. A long avenue with stonewalls leads up to the mosque. The mosque was originally built with the remains of the *Kalhuohfummi*, wrecked on the nearby reef in 1573 (see story below). It has caught fire once and been rebuilt and was also badly damaged in the 2004 tsunami. Headstones were upended and the roof and stone walls collapsed. This revealed some of the magnificently cut coral stones lying under more recent additions to the mosque. The old woodwork structure inside remained in place.

**Kurali** is one of only five uninhabited islands on the entire west side of Mulaku Atoll. It lies at the southern end and has a tiny islet called **Kuradhigandu** nearby on the same reef. Kurali Kandu is the main channel in the south of the atoll through which boats pass. There is a big shallow reef near Kurali that is a favourite fishing area for local islanders.

The next island north is **Thuvaru**. It was inhabited until 1970 and is now uninhabited, although it is leased and has a house with several workers who farm chillies, bananas and watermelon. Remains of a few houses lie crumbling in the thick vegetation. The island has beautiful sandy beaches, a shallow lagoon and a jetty on the northeast side. For a small fee, visitors from safari boats and the resorts of Medufushi and Hakuraa Club, have picnics here. This island is noted for a flock of about 20 heron, known locally as Markaru. They line the beaches in the morning and evening awaiting prey and at other times they nest in the coconut trees.

**Raabandhihuraa** and **Fenboafinolhu** are tiny uninhabited islands.

# Kalhuohfummi

The *Kalhuohfummi* was the odi of the National Hero of the Maldives, Bodu Muhammad Thakurufaanu (Sultan Ghazi Muhammad Thakurufannu, 1573-1585). It was built on the island of Baarah, in Haa Alifu and on its maiden trip, it was noted that certain fish (kaluoh) were jumping (fummi) out of the water after the boat, hence the name stuck.

In 1573, Muhammad Thakurufaanu led a small band of patriots to overthrow the Portuguese in Malé after a 15-year period of occupation. His odi was renowned for its sailing qualities, having proved too fast for the Portuguese vessels. After defeating the Portuguese, the *Kalhuohfummi* was quickly reconditioned and sailed down to the southern atolls to strengthen the rule of Islam and to confront a rebel islander, Meedhu Thakur.

Muhammad Thakurufaanu defeated Meedhu Thakur and then visited many of the inhabited islands in the southern atolls. He was dismayed at what he found. Many inhabitants could not tell which day was Friday and they knew a lot about charms, black magic and sorcery but little about Islam. He prohibited the consumption of 'toddy', an alcoholic drink, and forbade men and women taking sea baths in the nude. He also separated the areas on beaches where men and women went to relieve themselves.

Muhammad Thakurufaanu also visited the island of Vaadhoo in Gaafu Dhaalu. It is recorded in legend that while on the island he took a Khadaa Walhu, or metal bowl, that was near the house of an old lady. She did not approve of this and became angry and that is why, it is said, his odi was wrecked.

On the return journey back to Malé while travelling between Thaa and Meemu Atolls, *Kalhuohfummi* got caught in a severe storm. It was raining heavily, night-time was approaching and the boat was leaking badly. Muhammad headed towards the nearest island in Meemu Atoll and struck the reef at Dhiththudi near the island of Kolhuvaariyaafushi.

In the morning, they took everything from the boat to the island and went to perform their Fathis prayer. Muhammad Thakurufaanu was disappointed not to find a mosque, so he ordered the *Kalhuohfummi* to be dismantled and all the wood from the wrecked vessel to be used for the construction of a mosque. Various features of the *Kalhuohfummi*, such as the mast and rudder, were displayed, also a sword captured by the Portuguese. When the mosque was finished, Muhammad Thakurufaanu and his crew returned to Malé.

Many years later this famous mosque was burned down in an accident and another was built on the same location with replicas.

# Diving Mulaku Atoll

*Mulaku Atoll has plenty of diving options to choose from with long channel drift dives on the outer reef, small thilas inside the atoll studded with caves and prolific marine life; an abundance of quality inner atoll reefs, many with steep walls and overhangs; outer reefs with an almost continuous source of attractions, including sharks, manta rays and whale sharks; and a splendid wreck dive. Drift diving in Mulee Kandu is a highlight for divers and this channel is within easy range of the atoll's two resorts, Medufushi and Hakuraa Club. For divers making day excursions from the resort and for those on safari boats, there are 15 channels to choose from over a distance of 48 km on the western side of the atoll. Some of these channels are relatively shallow and a few have thilas across the entrance. There are only four uninhabited islands on this side of the atoll and they help to distinguish the nearby channels. In the north there are three channels in a row with very long reefs into the atoll that are excellent locations for drift dives. All have outer reefs with steep drop-offs and interesting corners.*

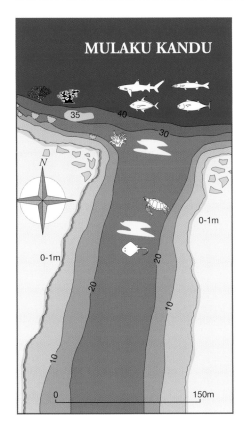

**Mulaku Kandu ★★★**

| | |
|---|---|
| Location: | first kandu north side of Mulaku Atoll |
| Depth: | 5m – 30m |
| Fish life: | abundant |
| Coral growth: | excellent |
| Features: | coral, sharks, eagle rays, sting rays, seafans. |

Mulaku Kandu is about 40 minutes south of Vattaru and is a rewarding dive location accessible only to safari boats or resort excursion boats. Generally the visibility is very good with both ingoing and outgoing currents. The narrow entrance to the channel is at a depth of 25 metres and divers can cross the entrance when conditions are favourable. A blanket of pure white sand glistens on the bottom from the reflected sunlight. Sting rays are often seen here and on both corners are large coral outcrops, which make good starting and finishing points. These rocks are perforated with holes coated in pastel coloured soft coral that conceal sabre squirrelfish.

Currents can be strong in Mulaku Kandu and giant trevally, large tuna, white-tip and grey reef sharks tend to gather around the channel entrance at these times. There are great barracuda and the smaller schooling barracuda and, in the early morning, hammerhead sharks.

The outer reef edge falls abruptly from 35 metres to over 100 metres and on the outside reef edge at 35 metres, large seafans thrive in the conditions. A drift dive inside the channel is a good way to finish the dive, as there are overhangs with superb hard corals that fade away to sand and rubble at 20 metres. Many turtles are seen on the reef edge along with an abundance of reef fish.

**Diving hints:** If current permits, divers will find it worthwhile spending time around the entrance where the combination of clear water, white sand and striking colours creates the perfect atmosphere for an exhilarating dive and the right conditions for stunning photos.

**Medhu Faru Kandu ★★★** is the second channel in the north of the atoll with a depth around 22 to 25 metres. It's a narrow channel so if the current is not too strong divers can cross from one side to the other. There are caves and overhangs below the edge at 30 metres. Large schools of fish are present on both corners, including barracuda, jacks and fusiliers as well as eagle rays and sharks.

**Vanhuravalhi Kandu ★★** is the third channel and is the deepest of the three northern channels. Drift diving along the northern side is a favourite dive beginning at a huge overhang between 12 and 40 metres. Deep inside are seafans and many features so it is a good idea to bring a torch here. On the corner are overhangs and large coral rocks where schooling fish tend to congregate. A short excursion into the channel and back will create opportunities to see sharks, eagle rays and trevally. The channel has a steep wall to 30 metres with overhangs and corals and drifting along the 1.5 km channel is an ideal way to finish the dive. The other side of the channel has many of the same features and is an equally interesting dive.

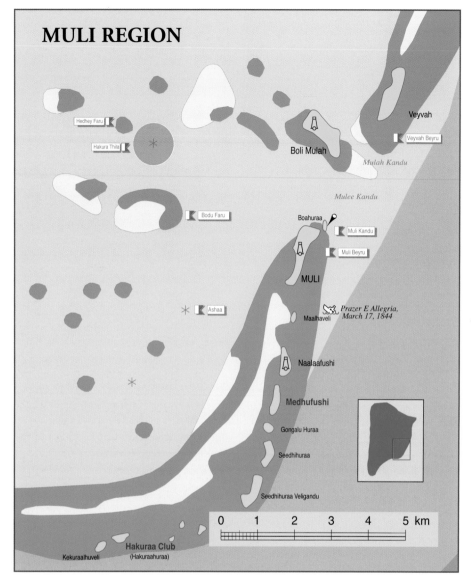

MULI REGION

Hedhey Faru
Hakura Thila
Veyvah
Veyvah Beyru
Boli Mulah
Mulah Kandu
Mulee Kandu
Bodu Faru
Boahuraa
Muli Kandu
Muli Beyru
MULI
Ashaa
Prazer E Allegria,
March 17, 1844
Maalhaveli
Naalaafushi
Medhufushi
Gongalu Huraa
Seedhihuraa
Seedhihuraa Veligandu
Hakuraa Club
(Hakuraahuraa)
Kekuraalhuveli

0  1  2  3  4  5 km

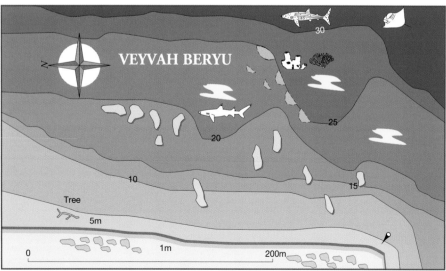

VEYVAH BERYU

N

30

25

20

10

15

Tree

5m

0        1m        200m

## Veyvah Beyru ★★

| | |
|---|---|
| Location: | outer reef near entrance to Mulah Kandu. |
| Depth: | 10m – 30m |
| Fish Life: | above average |
| Coral growth: | good |
| Features: | white-tip reef sharks, manta rays, whale sharks. |

This dive is on Veyvah outside reef near the northern entrance to Mulah Kandu. The channel entrance is marked by a two-mile light near the corner. A 'tsunami tree' further north on the outside reef is a good starting point for drift divers if the current is flowing strongly towards the south. This is an excellent dive that can produce many surprises. The reef top is around five to 10 metres, sloping very gently to 30 metres or more on the outside. Near the channel entrance is a sandy plateau at 25 metres, where a school of white-tip reef sharks range throughout the year, resting mostly during the day and feeding by night. Beyond the plateau is another sand terrace at 30 metres with more white-tips. The two plateaus merge into a wall studded with small caves and drop-offs. A series of small sandy inlets characterise sections of this reef. There are also coral bombies between 15 and 20 metres that act as cleaning stations for mantas during the south-west monsoon season. The regular appearance of whale sharks is an additional attraction of this site.

**Diving hints:** The entrance to Mulah Kandu is at 14 metres and this shallow depth extends a considerable distance out to sea and across into Mulee Kandu. The outer reef at Veyvah Beyru has a wide reef shelf with a gentle slope that drops steeply well out to sea. Further north of the dive point is a 'tsunami tree' where the dropoff is closer to the reef crest and more visible. It is a good place to start if the current is strong but it is helpful for the dive master to consider the strength of the current when diving here. If the current is slight, then it is best to locate the sand terrace first, and start diving here.

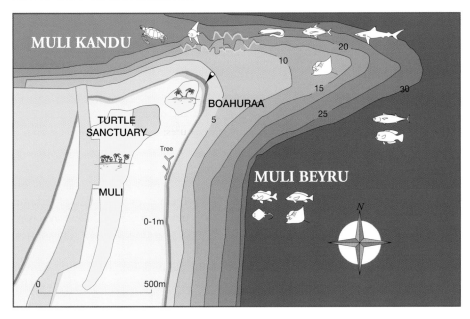

*Giant Trevally,* Caranx ignobilis, *is the largest of the trevally family and often seen solitary or in small schools along the deeper reef slopes.*

### Muli Kandu (Hakura Express) ★★★★

| | |
|---|---|
| Location: | Mulee Kandu, south side. |
| Depth: | 5m – 30m |
| Fish Life: | abundant |
| Coral growth: | good |
| Features: | mantas, turtle, pelagic fish. |

This is a long drift dive along the channel wall off Muli island. It includes the small island of Boahuraa and a finger of reef protruding for more than 200 metres into the ocean. The reef has a rounded top at 15 metres and the outer end of the finger slopes gently to over 30 metres. Near Boahuraa, the reef becomes more shallow and the channel edge becomes more distinct. There is a proliferation of fish life here including black snapper and humpback snapper that swirl in huge schools along with tuna, jacks and trevallies, napoleon, batfish, bannerfish, moorish idol, and fusiliers. There are honeycomb moray on the reef and turtles are commonly seen here. Turtles congregate in the waters off Muli during breeding times, usually around the full moon. They are known as Vela in Divehi and they lay their eggs on the sand at the northern point of Muli. This part of the island has been reserved as a turtle sanctuary. Muli Kandu is one of the best sites in the atoll to view manta rays. These are most frequently seen during the southwest monsoon season between the months of May and December. On the finger of reef between 10 and 15 metres are numerous cleaning stations where mantas circle, allowing long periods of viewing.

**Diving hints:** Mulee Kandu is the only channel for almost the entire eastern side of Mulaku Atoll. Consequently currents can be extremely strong here and should be understood and respected before diving. A strong cross-current can be prevalent on the outer reef finger and a rapid downcurrent is sometimes observed on the channel corner. During difficult times, a quiet dive alternative can be found to the south of the channel at Muli Beyru.

**Muli Beyru ★★** lies on the outside reef of Muli island. This dive starts a couple of boat lengths north of a 'tsunami tree' lying high and dry on the outside reef. There are two big canyons, or blocks, at 22 metres where stingrays gather. Most importantly, there are mantas, black snapper and large schools of sweetlip on the reef at eight to 10 metres.

*White-tip reef shark,* Triaaenodon obesus, *is often seen resting on the sandy bottom by day and usually feeds at night. It has a small home range that it occupies for months or years at a time.*

*Honeycomb moray,* Gymnothorax favagineus, *is white with black spots forming a honeycomb pattern.*

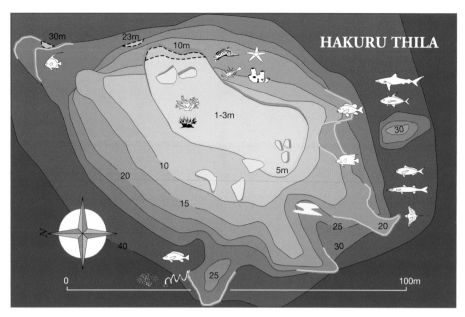

HAKURU THILA

30m  23m  10m  1-3m  10  5m  20  15  40  25  30  25  20  30  25  0  100m

## Hakura Thila ★★

PROTECTED MARINE AREA

| | |
|---|---|
| Location: | Inside Mulee Kandu |
| Depth: | 2m – 30m |
| Fish Life: | abundant |
| Coral growth: | excellent |
| Features: | caves, eagle rays, hard coral, fishlife. |

This is an exceptional thila about 75 metres in length rising to 2 metres with attractions on every side of the reef and is ideal for photographers. On the northeast side is a point in the reef with caves, ledges and overhangs that step down with small plateaus from 5m to 35m. On the eastern side is a big cave between 10 and 15 metres with plenty of invertebrate life. A torch is handy here. On the north side a steady reef slope drops to 30 metres. Further west is a ridge at 25 metres that drops vertically to 40 metres. On the rock face of this outer wall are many seawhips, black corals and seafans. On the western side are three protruding ridges ending in steep dropoffs with overhangs. In between are valleys, one with a sandy corridor. Off the most southern ridge is a lone thila rising from the sea floor at 40 to 30 metres. It can clearly be seen with good visibility. Being inside Mulee Kandu, Hakuru Thila also gets currents that attract the usual array of big fish including grey reef sharks, eagle rays as well as sweetlips, needlefish, jacks and trevallies, snapper, barracuda and fusilier. There are numerous caves to explore where flat worms, sea stars, and sponges in a variety of colours, nudibranchs and cleaner shrimp can often be found inside or around the entrances. Ribbon eels have also been photographed here. On the reef top are plenty of hard corals with table corals spilling over the reef edge and down the side. The reef top is a moving mass of sergeants and damsels, surgeons, butterflyfish, angelfish, basslets and anemonefish.

**Diving hints:** The northeast side of the reef is a good starting point for dives when currents are coming from this direction. The reef point here acts like an arrowhead, splitting the current either side of the reef, giving divers a choice of either side. Divers have the opportunity to explore this reef thoroughly in one dive. If strong currents are present, divers will usually end up at one end of the reef or the other, and both ends have excellent features to spend the entire time.

*Moorish idol,* Zanclus cornutus. *This fish is closely related to the surgeon family. Although it does not have a blade on its tail, it has a similar mouth structure and behaviour patterns. It is seen on the upper reef slope, often in pairs.*

*Yellow teardrop butterflyfish,* Chaetodon interruptus, *often seen on shallow coral reefs singly or in pairs or in small groups feeding on coral, small invertebrates or algae.*

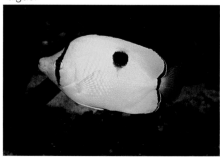

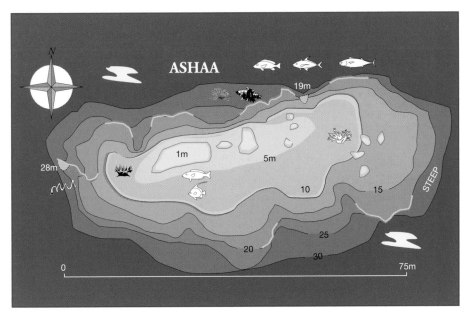

*Bulb-tentacle anemone,* Entacmea quadricolor, *is easily identified due to the swelling a short distance from the tip.*

## Ashaa ★★

| | |
|---|---|
| Location: | Inside atoll near entrance to Naalaafushi. |
| Depth: | 1m – 30m |
| Fish Life: | abundant |
| Coral growth: | excellent |
| Features: | Bulb-tentacle anemone and fish, wall, hard coral. |

This is a small giri about 75 metres in length with the top between one and five metres. It lies inside the atoll in an east-west direction. It is well protected with excellent diving. There is a particularly steep wall on the eastern end at 20m with stunning table and staghorn corals on the reef top that branch over the edge like trees clinging to the wall of a ravine. The western end has an abundance of sea anemones, most noticeable is the brightly coloured Bulb-tentacle anemone with Clark's anemonefish. There is also a cave at 28 metres. The northern side has a continuous wall with caves and overhangs that house a mixed population of marine invertebrates and fish. Among these are black coral trees with penguin wing oysters, thorny oyster clams and seawhips decorated with featherstars. On the top reef are many large and healthy coral blocks. There is an especially big one near a boat mooring rope. It is teeming with blue damsels, basslets, parrotfish, butterfly, angel and damsel fish. In the open water surrounding the reef are rabbitfish, bannerfish, snapper, fusilier, tuna and jacks. The reef drops to a sandy floor from a depth of 30 metres.

**Diving hints:** This is an interesting dive and ideal for beginners. The northern wall offers a good opportunity to work on buoyancy control and the placid waters surrounding the reef gives novice divers the chance to fully appreciate the beauty, diversity and serenity of tropical water diving.

## Bodu Faru ★★

This is a large horseshoe shaped reef with the best diving on the southeast side of the reef between 10 and 18 metres. There are overhangs at 14 metres and a leaf fish can be seen in one of the overhangs. This is a long wall that takes 45 minutes to dive.

## Hedhey Faru ★★

This reef has a small thila at the west end with a top at 20 metres. The depth around the reef is around 35 metres.

## Kurali Kandu ★★

Mantas are frequently seen in this channel during the north-east monsoon. With mantas being seen at Muli Kandu during the south-west monsoon, the two resorts of Medufushi and Hakuraa are ideally located to capture year round viewing of these amazingly gentle and graceful rays. The best place to view them is at two or three coral blocks in a sandy passage at 14 metres depth.

*Suzanne's flatworm,* Pseudoceros suzzanae. *This colourful species is often seen in the Maldives feeding on ascidians. Not to be confused with nudibranchs (shell-less molluscs), flatworms are wafer-thin with many species living under stones and coral.*

**NENGE KANDU**

0                                              500m

White Acabaria, Acabaria sp. Is a gorgonian sea fan that grows like a bramble bush. It has flat-bladed branches with white polyps along each side. Three, four, or five branches grow out from a pink or yellow axis.

### Nenge Kandu ★★★

| | |
|---|---|
| Location: | second channel south of Thuvaru island. |
| Depth: | 5m – 30m |
| Fish Life: | abundant |
| Coral growth: | excellent |
| Features: | wall, caves, soft coral, rainbow runner, |

For a channel that has no name (nenge), divers are unlikely to forget this location once it has been dived. Early morning is the best time and undoubtedly the most memorable highlight is the 200 metre-long vertical wall between 5 and 30 metres on the southern side of the channel. The wall is steep and looks like its been dressed in the colours of the rainbow. Yellow, blue and pink soft corals bend and wave in the current, flashing their morning colours out into the clear water of the channel. There are several big caves on the wall, all lined with soft coral. One is 50 metres long and has a swim-through at 23m. Another at 17 metres looks like a huge mouth and has a pillar inside, like a tonsil, from top to bottom. With an ingoing current, the outside corner is the starting point for this exhilarating dive. Numerous small caves are located here on a steep wall that bottoms out at around 30 metres. Some caves contain long sea whips and black coral while in the open water at the channel entrance, pelagics such as big-eye trevally, giant trevally, long-nose emperor, red bass and schools of rainbow runner, congregate in large numbers. The outside reef and corner is dominated by gorgonian seafans of the "bramble bush" variety, white acabaria. After a long drift through the channel with periodic stop-offs in caves, the remainder of the dive can be spent very quietly and peacefully observing fish and corals around the corner in the shallow depths inside the atoll.

Mauve spiky soft coral, Dendronephthya sp. A spectacular spiky soft coral mainly seen in deeper water on walls and dropoffs.

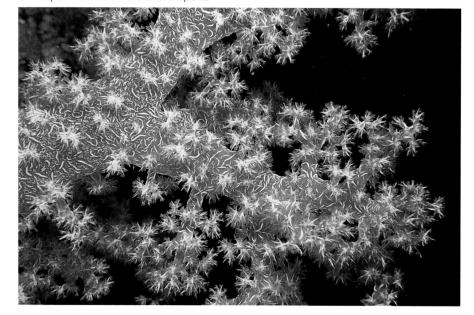

Rainbow runner, Elagatis bipinnulata, a common pelagic species usually found in small to moderate sized schools in pursuit of smaller fish around the entrance to channels.

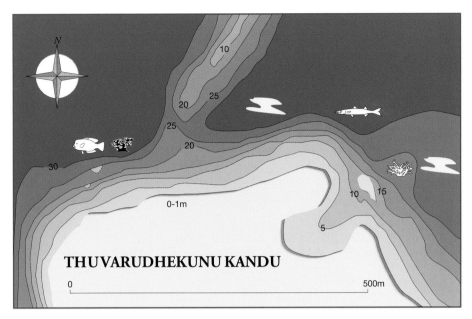

THUVARUDHEKUNU KANDU

0                                                    500m

The reef the Rayvilla struck has
spectacular caves and overhangs.

### Thuvarudhekunu Kandu ★★★

| | |
|---|---|
| Location: | second channel south of Thuvaru island. |
| Depth: | 5m – 30m |
| Fish Life: | abundant |
| Coral growth: | excellent |
| Features: | thila, hard coral, fish. |

Surprisingly, Thuvarudhekunu Kandu is devoid of masses of soft coral, unlike it's neighbouring channel Nenge Kandu, However it has an interesting thila that runs across the channel from the south side. It has excellent hard coral on the top that thrives on the currents streaming through the channel. The coral offers protection for masses of smaller fish. At the channel entrance are a few small caves and a wall that drops to 35 metres. There are some patches of yellow soft coral on the reef while in the open water are napoleon and barracuda. Inside the channel, the wall becomes less steep and the depth rises to 25 metres at the junction to the thila. Sand lies on either side of the ridge and the undulating sandy aspect of the channel continues into the atoll where the bottom is interspersed with healthy coral and rocks. The reef inside the atoll curves back to the south where there is a small inlet with a bottom at 8 metres. This location is ideal for finishing a dive or snorkelling.

**Rayvilla Wreck ★★** lies on the south side of a small reef towards the western side of the atoll. This unfortunate vessel couldn't have gone down at a better location for divers. The 30 metres long wooden wreck was an island transport vessel that hit the reef in 1979 while on a journey to Malé. It lies on the bottom in 20 to 33 metres of water. It allows easy access to its interior where large schools of yellow sweeper make a home as well as moray eels and grouper. The wreck is not the only feature of this dive. After spending time at the wreck, the nearby reef conveniently offers plenty of small caves and large overhangs. The beautiful soft corals and dense schools of fish make this an interesting finish to a memorable dive.

*The island of Thuvaru makes a perfect stopover between dives at Thuvarudhekunu Kandu and Nenge Kandu. There are many unexplored channels to dive in this region as well as the Rayvilla wreck, that lies on a small reef three kilometres inside the atoll.*

*The 30 metre long wooden Rayvilla Wreck lies near a small reef at a depth of 20 to 33 metres.*

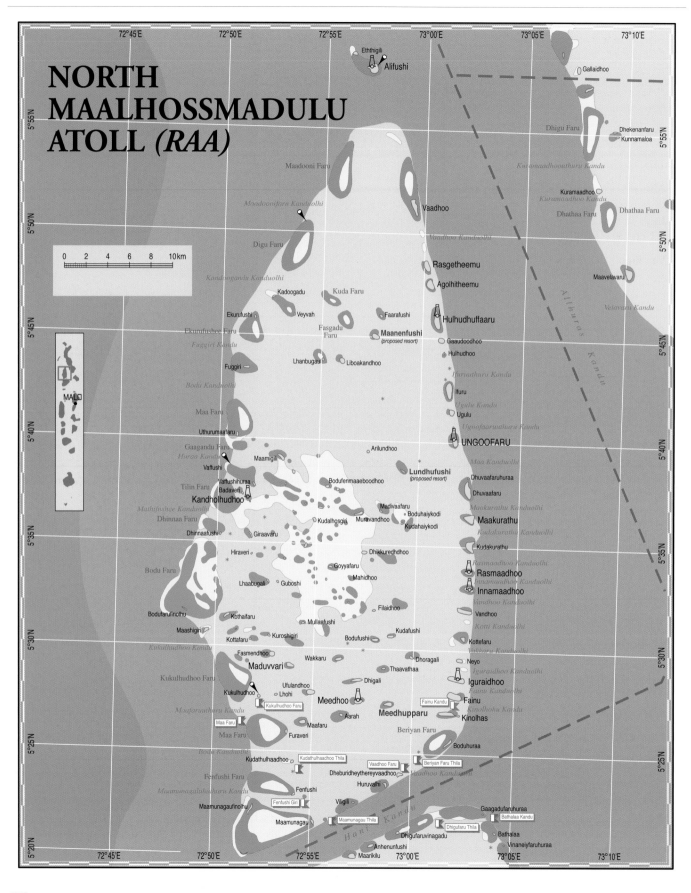

# NORTH MAALHOSSMADULU ATOLL (RAA)

72°45'E    72°50'E    72°55'E    73°00'E    73°05'E    73°10'E

Eththigili
Alifushi
Gallaidhoo

5°55'N

Dhigu Faru
Dhekenanfaru
Kunnamaloa

Maadooni Faru

Kuramaadhoouthuru Kandu

Kuramaadhoo
Kuramaadhoo Kandu
Dhathaa Faru
Dhathaa Faru

5°50'N

Moadoonifaru Kanduolhi
Vaadhoo
Digu Faru
Vaadhoo Kanduolhi

Maavelavaru

Rasgetheemu
Agolhitheemu

Kandroogandu Kanduolhi
Kadoogadu    Kuda Faru
Faarafushi    Hulhudhuffaaru

0  2  4  6  8  10km

Ekurufushi    Veyvah
Ekurufushee Faru    Fasgadu    Maanenfushi
Fuggiri Kandu    Faru    (proposed resort)    Gaaudoodhoo
Hulhudhoo

Allharas Kandu

5°45'N

Lhanbugau    Liboakandhoo
Fuggiri    Ifaruathuru Kandu

Bodu Kanduolhi    Ifuru
Ugulu Kandu
Ugulu

MALÉ    Maa Faru    Ugoofaaruathuru Kandu

Uthurumaafaru    UNGOOFARU

5°40'N

Gaagandu Faru    Arilundhoo    Maa Kanduolhi
Huraa Kandu    Maamigili
Vaffushi    Lundhufushi    Dhuvaafaruhuraa
Bodufenmaaeboodhoo    (proposed resort)    Dhuvaafaru
Tilin Faru    Vaffushihuraa
Badaveri    Madivaafaru    Maakurathu Kanduolhi
Mathifushee Kanduolhi    Kandholhudhoo    Boduhaiykodi    Maakurathu
Dhinnaa Faru    Kudalhosgiri    Muravandhoo    Kudahaiykodi    Kudakurathu Kanduolhi
Dhinnaafushi    Giraavaru    Kudakurathu

5°35'N

Hiraveri    Dhikkuredhdhoo    Rasmaadhoo Kanduolhi
Goyyafaru    Rasmaadhoo
Bodu Faru    Mahidhoo    Innamaadhoo Kanduolhi
Lhaabugali    Guboshi    Innamaadhoo
Vandhoo Kanduolhi
Filaidhoo    Vandhoo
Bodufarufinolhu    Kotti Kanduolhi
Kothaifaru    Mullaafushi    Kudafushi    Kottefaru
Maashigiri    Kuroshigiri    Bodufushi

5°30'N

Kottafaru    Dhoragali    Vilikoi Kanduolhi
Fasmendhoo    Wakkaru    Neyo
Maduvvari    Thaavathaa    Iguraidhoo Kanduolhi
Kukulhudhoo Faru    Dhigali    Iguraidhoo
Ufulandhoo    Fainu Kanduolhi
Kukulhudhoo    Lhohi    Fainu
Kukulhudhoo Faru    Meedhoo    Kinolhohu Kandu
Maafarunthuru Kandu    Meedhupparu    Kinolhas
Maa Faru    Aarah
Maafaru
Maa Faru    Furaveri    Beriyan Faru    Boduhuraa

5°25'N

Bodu Kanduolhi
Kudathulhaadhoo    Kudathulhaadhoo Thila    Gaagadufaruhuraa
Fenfushi Faru    Vaadhoo Faru    Beriyan Faru Thila    Bathalaa Kandu
Dheburidheythereyvaadhoo    Vaadhoo Kanduolhi
Maamunagalithuhuru Kandu    Fenfushi    Huruvalhi
Maamunagaufinolhu    Fenfushi Giri    Viligili    Gaagadufaruhuraa
Maamunagau    Maamunagau Thila    Dhigufaru Thila    Bathalaa
Hani Kandu    Dhigufaruvinagadu    Vinaneiyfaruhuraa
Anhenunfushi
Maarikilu

5°20'N

72°45'E    72°50'E    72°55'E    73°00'E    73°05'E    73°10'E

# Chapter 13
# North Maalhossmadulu Atoll Islands *(Raa)*

**Eththigili** is an uninhabited island at the very north of Raa Atoll. It has a navigation light that marks the beginning of Allhuras Kandu.

**Alifushi** is a very old inhabited island that is famous for its carpentry and boat building. It has a boat building yard and a dredged harbour. It also has good vegetation with banana and other fruit trees.

**Vaadhoo**. *Vaa* is a word meaning jungle but can also be a flying bat. The islanders are regarded as good fishermen and they have access to excellent fishing grounds at the main entrance to the atoll.

**Rasgetheemu**. *Ras* means the beginning or first island and refers to its strategic position at the north of the atoll. Although the island is reputed to have been settled by the original inhabitants of the Maldives, there is no evidence of temples, like on some of the other islands in the atoll. *Rasge,* also means king and *theemu* is an island. The island name is believed to have originated from the legendary story of the founder of the first ruling royal family. His name was Taya-malla ( Koimala' Kalo according to legend), who was the leader of a breakaway group of the Kalabhra people, who made their way to the Maldives from Madagascar in the 12th century AD. Taya-malla wed the Ceylon King's daughter and made a voyage with her in two vessels from Serendib Island. On reaching the Maldives they were becalmed and rested at Rasgetheemu. Learning that the visitors were of Royal descent, they were invited to stay and ultimately proclaimed their king. Subsequently Taya-malla migrated to Malé and settled there with the consent of the original inhabitants of the Maldives, the Giraavaru people. (see H.C.P Bell's, *The Maldives Islands*.)

**Agolhitheemu**. In old writings this name means slave island. According to legend, it is where the servants of the Royal couple who migrated from Ceylon were housed. In local language *agolhi* means the island next to.

**Hulhudhuffaaru**. *Hulhu* means small, *dhuh* means can be seen, and *faaru* (not to be confused with faru) is a wound, or injury. The island was inhabited by Buddhists long before Islam came to the Maldives and there is evidence of ruins. There are also some very big tombs of rich and important people to be seen here. The island has a very nice lagoon and even before the coming of the Portuguese in the early 16th century, many ships trading in cowries and dried fish from Bengal, Arabia and South East Asia were visiting here. The island became uninhabited and was later re-inhabited.

**Faarafushi, Gaaudoodhoo, Hulhudhoo, Lhanbugau** are all uninhabited islands in the vicinity of Hulhudhuffaaru.

**Maanenfushi** is a proposed resort island.

**Liboakandhoo** is an uninhabited island but was once inhabited. There are the ruins of a mosque and bathing tank and also a cemetery.

**Ifuru** is quite a large uninhabited island but it was once inhabited. On the north side of the island are the remains of what appear to have been as small minaret. It was quite common in the earlier days for many people of an island to suddenly die because of sickness and when the population declined those remaining would leave and join other islands. There was no need for permission from the government so islands throughout the archipelago were continuously being uninhabited or re-inhabited.

**Ugulu** is an uninhabited island but was once inhabited. There is a large mound called *Redhinge Usgadu*. The Redhin, much talked about in the Maldives as being the mythical original inhabitants of the islands, were believed to be fisherman from the coastal region of India. *Redhinge* became the Maldivian name for these early migrants.

**Ungoofaru** has been the capital of the atoll for a long time. It has the regional hospital, a youth stadium and two communication towers. Two thirds of the population from Kandholhudhoo displaced after the tsunami were temporarily housed here. Many will be relocated to the newly constructed island of Dhuvaafaru.

**Lundhufushi** is uninhabited but a proposed island resort.

**Dhuvaafaruhuraa.** *Dhuvaa* means moving island. It is an uninhabited island that was once joined to Dhuvaafaru.

**Dhuvaafaru** was once a big inhabited island until a cyclone came and separated the island into two. Dhandehelu, one of the heros of the liberation of the Maldives from the Portuguese in 1573, was born on this island. He was the first mate of the *Kalhuohfummi,* the odi (boat) of Bodu Muhammed Thakurufaanu (Sultan Ghazi Muhammed Thakurufannu, 1573-1585) who led the successful rebellion against the Portuguese. Dhandehelu was a small boy of 12 years when Bodu Thakurufaanu saw him on the beach. He was a very active, cheerful lad who was always busy. During their first meeting, Dhandehelu is said to have been eating with one hand and fishing with the other. He became a devoted assistant of Bodu Thakurufaanu and was later buried in the same mosque in Malé. Dhuvaafaru is being built to accommodate inhabitants of Kandholhudhoo, displaced after the 2004 tsunami.

**Maakurathu** This island is named after the 25th Sultan of the Maldives.

**Kudakurathu** is a large uninhabited island on the outside of the atoll.

**Muravandhoo,** is an uninhabited island that was once inhabited. On the south west of the island there are the remains of a mosque with coral slabs. There are many small, uninhabited islands in the middle of the atoll that are often being eroded or built up according to the seasons. Some of them are: Arilundhoo, Lundhufushi, Bodufenmaaeboodhoo, Hiraveri, Guboshi, Kudalhosgiri, Madivaaaafaru, Boduhaiykodi, Kudahaikodi, Dhikkuredhdhoo, Goyyafaru, Mahidhoo,, Mullaafushi, Filaidhoo, Kottafaru, Kuroshigiri, Wakkaru, Dhigali, Ufulandhoo, Thaavathaa, Kukulhudhoo, Lhohi, Maafaru, Aarah, Maafaru, Kudathulaadhoo.

**Rasmaadhoo.** An inhabited island which is known for its carpenters and boatbuilders. There is reputedly 70 small dhoanis on the island and several large ones, many now being used by Pearl Island Resort.

**Innamaandhoo.** Literally means people living on the island.

**Vandhoo** is a long uninhabited island that used to be inhabited. There are the remains of a mosque with a cemetery nearby. *Van* is a hollowed out coconut tree used for crushing the husks of rice and grain. Two women use one pole each and alternately pound the seed.

**Kottefaru** and **Neyo** are small uninhabited islands.

**Dhoragali** is an uninhabited island meaning stone doorway.

**Bodufushi** and **Kudafushi** were both inhabited in the 18th century and both islands have the remains of very beautiful mosques. The seventeenth sultan of the Maldives is buried on Bodufushi. At the time of his death he was on an official visit to the atoll. At the time, the winds were unfavourable for a return to island capital, so the officials collected nice smelling flowers and screw pine to spread around the boat so they could prevent the decaying body from smelling. The Sultan was buried at the mosque on Bodufushi and his grave marked with a big headstone.

**Iguraidhoo.** Another inhabited island well known for its boat building.

**Fainu** was the first island that the famous Arab traveller, Ibn Batuta, visited when he arrived in the Maldives. There is a good anchorage and in the past, this island was a major trading centre with ships stopping here for trade in slaves, cowries, coir and dried fish. It was the first port of call for ships coming from India during the NE monsoon.

**Kinolhas.** An inhabited island and the last of the bigger islands in the south of the atoll.

**Meedhupparu** is now a resort called Pearl Island. The original name when translated means *"this is the island that someone saw."*

**Furaveri** is an uninhabited island but was once inhabited.

**Meedhoo** has been inhabited for many centuries. The islanders are boat builders and fishermen and enjoy a relatively high standard of living.

**Boduhuraa** is a long uninhabited island.

**Dheburidheythereyvaadhoo** is the longest island name in the Maldives. It means the island of Vaadhoo lays between [Raa and Baa Atolls].

**Huruvalhi, Viligili, Maamunagau, Maamunagaufinolhu** and **Fenfushi** are uninhabited islands at the southern end of the atoll.

**Maduvvari** is an inhabited island. *Madu* means layer, like the layers of planks on a boat and vari means divorce.

**Fasmendhoo** is an uninhabited island but was once inhabited with many people.

**Kothaifaru** is uninhabited but was once inhabited. There are the remains of a mosque with two wells and a cemetery.

**Maashigiri** is a small uninhabited island on the western side of the atoll.

**Bodufarufinolhu** is the most western island in the atoll and has a navigation light on it.

**Lhaabugali** is a small uninhabited island. Lhaabu is the rope, or sling, that toddy toppers (coconut tree climbers) use to climb the trees.

**Dhinnaafushi** is uninhabited and means the island that was given.

**Giraavaru** is uninhabited but was once inhabited. A number of ceramic plates were unearthed on this island in 1980.

**Kandholhudhoo** is not a large island but it was the most populated island in the atoll before the 2004 Tsunami. The population has now been relocated to other islands. *Kandholhu* is a wild lily. The inhabitants celebrated Kuda Eid (just after Ramadan) with a ceremony that reflected Hindu traditions from India and Buddhist origins similar to Burma. The people wore *Kodi* hats or umbrellas that were made on the island of Rasmaadhoo in the same atoll. They also practised water throwing and even went so far as to throw their potential partners into the ocean when they were courting.

**Badaveri** is an uninhabited island. *Bada* means stomach and veri is owner.

**Vaffushihuraa** and **Vaffushi** are uninhabited islands. There is a navigation light on Vaffushi.

**Maamigili** is an uninhabited island that was once inhabited. There are the remains of a mosque and two wells on this island.

**Uthurumaafaru, Fuggiri, Ekurufushi, Kadoogadu** and **Veyvah** are uninhabited islands on the north east of the atoll.

# Diver Information

### Diving facilities.

Every resort caters for scuba divers and all types of international certification are accepted. Divers should bring their log book and C-card and be prepared to do a check-out dive. The cost of a dive includes an experienced guide, the dive, tank and weights. Boat costs are usually extra, depending on distance. Diving boats are required to have a radio, lifejackets, flag, oxygen and medical kit.

Most divers bring their own equipment but regulators, BCD's, computers, masks, snorkels and fins are usually available for hire. International and DIN fittings are optional at many resorts. Safety balloons are an important safety accessory that are not always available at diving schools and should be brought from home.

For those learning to dive, all resorts conduct open water and advanced courses. Many resorts cater for speciality courses and in response to a growing interest in the marine environment, courses such as underwater naturalist and shark specialist have proved most popular. Library and education facilities are becoming more available and dive centres regularly entertain divers with slide and video night presentations.

### Diving prices.

The cost of courses and dives varies with individual resorts. Single dives are offered but diving packages with or without equipment for 10 or more dives are available and give better value for money. Divers should be aware that 'non-limit' diving packages in the Maldives, whether at a resort or on a safari boat, usually includes two dives per day, plus one or two night dives in the course of the package. This is not always the case and divers are advised to check packages and prices with tour operators.

### When to dive.

At resorts, diving is conducted daily all year round and the number of days when diving has to be cancelled are few. During times of strong winds and rough seas, most resorts have a nearby site with protection on the lee side of the reef and only when storms, strong winds and currents affect visibility and diver safety, will diving be cancelled.

The high season is from December to April with the Christmas-New Year period from mid December to early January, and Easter being the most popular. At this time resorts can be fully booked, or overbooked, and prices are higher. In August, the European holidays bring another short 'high' season to resorts. Some of the best diving and greatest value can be had during the low season months between May and November. Smaller crowds, lower prices and top diving regardless of weather are some of the rewards for diving in off-peak periods.

### Diving safaris. What you need to know.

Diving safaris are mostly operated between the months of September and April but some operators continue all year round. The calmest conditions are most likely to be in January, February, March and April but there are no guarantees with the weather and safaris in September and October can result in equally favourable conditions.

There are many boat owners in the Maldives offering their dhoanis for commercial use. Only registered boat owners should be used as they are required to obtain the necessary inter-atoll permits and to meet safety and health standards. Most safari diving operators rent or lease a boat from a registered owner and advertise for their clients abroad.

Up-market vessels have airconditioning, desalination plants, videos and computers. Some of the larger boats are permitted to have bar facilities.

Some safari boats are traditional dhoanis not designed for the diving market. They have limited fresh water, have a separate generator for night time use, are noisy, have limited deck and storage space and are often crowded. Each boat has its own standards in general cleanliness and it is often advisable to check if boats have holding tanks for waste water and sewerage. Once these factors are taken into account, divers can expect to get what they pay for.

To have a successful diving safari, there are a number of questions divers should ask their tour operator. Specific questions such as the capacity of the boat and the number of clients on board, the fresh water capacity for showering and washing equipment, such as cameras, the location of the generator (if it is in the engine room then it is likely to be less noisy) and if there is a backup generator. Also ask about battery charging facilities; electricity supply from generators is generally from 220V to 240V, 50Hz AC using round or square three point plugs but divers may need their own adaptors.

Contact tour operators for availability, prices and services as conditions and prices of boats vary considerably.

### Diving Dhoanis.

Most safari boats are suitable for diving only because they use a separate diving dhoani – a smaller open boat that carries all diving equipment, compressor and tanks – that accompanies the mother boat during the cruise. This makes the cruise more comfortable with less handling of equipment. The diving dhoani is usually slower and makes an early start to meet at pre-arranged dive sites in time. The draw-back of this system if travelling long distances is that the bare minimum of two dives a day may result. It is therefore useful to inquire about diving services on board. Firstly, does the diving package include a diving dhoani? Is there 'unlimited diving' and does this mean more than two dives a day? Are there any night dives? Also check if there is a backup compressor available, if the tanks used are 15 litre or 12 litre and the type of fittings, and if there is spare equipment, oxygen and first aid kit aboard, and so on.

Divers should also inquire about the itinerary of the cruise. Many boats try to cover great distances over short periods of time and dive only at renowned sites. Some divers may prefer to limit the distance, for instance in a seven day safari, to a small area and spend more time in the water diving and snorkelling than travelling between the atolls.

The type of diving varies considerably and divers should ask what type of diving the guide will be conducting and if it is suitable for their needs. For instance, long channel drift dives, thila diving in a current, or deeper dives may be suitable for many, but not, say, for a group of photographers who only wish for a quiet reef with no current and plenty of opportunity to spend time in the water for their favourite hobby. Diving guides are generally flexible and cater for the taste of the majority.

## What to Bring.

Some essential items include suncream, hat, sunglasses, light clothing, a light water proof jacket for the wet season, underwater torch, spare batteries and cameras. A pair of binoculars, compass and a good map are useful additions, especially if on a safari boat.

## Local customs.

When visiting inhabited islands travellers should be aware that neat, conservative dress is required. Women should wear dresses below the knees or shorts that cover the thighs and not low-cut tops and tank-tops. Men should not go bare-chested. Nudity is prohibited but brief bathers and bikinis are acceptable at resorts.

## Visas.

Visitors do not require a visa to visit the Maldives. A 30-day visitors permit is automatically given on arrival. Visitors are required to leave the country before the 30 day permit expires or extend their visa by applying for an extention from the Immigration Office in the Huravee Building in Malé.

## Travel Permits.

Travel permits are required for anyone travelling outside the tourist zone. For divers on a safari trip through the atolls, registered safari operators will obtain the necessary permits before starting. If visiting an inhabited island while on a safari trip it is a good idea to present yourself at the island office. Most islanders are extremely hospitable, but they are more likely to welcome travellers if they are polite and respect local formalities and customs.

## Electricity.

Electricity supply is based on the English system from 220V to 240V, 50Hz AC using round or square three point plugs. Most resorts have multi-use sockets that accept a variety of pin configurations for razors and battery chargers. On safari boats, it is a good idea to bring your own multi-socket adaptor for charging batteries but most boats now cater for all divers electrical needs.

## Health Insurance.

Health insurance is strongly recommended for divers travelling to the Maldives. Some policies do not cover scuba diving so ensure your policy covers the cost of hyperbaric treatment, air ambulances, seaplane transfers and an emergency flight home. The Divers Alert Network (DAN) offers diving accident insurance and world-wide medical evacuation assistance. All decompression cases will be treated, however payment for treatment will be required if insurance cover is not issued.

## Decompression Chambers and Medical Care.

There are two main decompression chambers in the Maldives catering for the general tourist population. The Bandos Medical Centre on Bandos Island Resort caters for divers in the Malé region and the Kuramathi Medical Centre on Kuramathi Tourist Resort in Rasdhoo, caters for divers in the Ari Atoll region. Both centres are well equipped to European standards with trained hyperbaric specialists and nurses on call 24 hours a day.

The Bandos and Kuramathi chambers have space for four people in the main section. One person can be brought into the chamber lying on a special, comfortable bed, built to treat paralysed patients, allowing them to be turned during treatment. Additional services are also offered. Diving medical questions and fitness-to-

dive issues are answered through a special telephone hotline and diving physicians are directly accessible through a mobile phone.

In addition, the centres have beds for in-patients and are equipped with X-ray capability and minor surgery. For rescue operations a portable respirator, ECG/Defibrillator and other necessary medical equipment are available, such as sleds and stretchers. Patients can be brought to the centres by speedboat or sea plane.

## Contact information.

Bandos Medical Centre
Ph: (+960) 6640088
Mobile: (+960 ) 7771086

Kuramathi Medical Centre
Ph: (+960) 6660527
Emergency Mobile: (+960) 7773485

For general health problems, the Indira Gandhi Memorial Hospital (Ph: 3316647) in Malé is the country's main hospital. The AMDC Clinic (Ph: 3325979) and the ADK Private Hospital (Ph: 3324331) offer private care.

## Diver's Medical Check

Before starting any open-water diving course or diving activity, prospective divers are required to fill in and sign a medical statement form. If further examination of conditions is required and the resort does not have a trained diving doctor, then divers can get a full medical checkup in Malé at the AMDC Clinic or the ADK Hospital or at the Bandos and Kuramathi Medical Centres. It is advisable for prospective divers to obtain a diving medical certificate before leaving home.

## Basic Health.

Compared to many other Asian countries, the Maldives is remarkably free of health problems. Resorts are clean and standards of cleanliness are high. In Malé, conditions of cleanliness, especially in Tea Shops, has improved greatly in the past few of years. Most resorts and many inhabited islands, including Malé, use desalinated water for washing and drinking. The water is good and unlikely to cause stomach upsets, but most resorts sell bottled water to clients. Vaccinations against Tetanus, Diphtheria, Polio and Hepatitis A are recommended, though not legally required. Vaccination for yellow fever if coming from an infected area is required by law.

## Health tips.

Drink plenty of water and acclimatise to high temperatures to avoid heat exhaustion. Wear loose clothing and a hat and use a sunblock to prevent sunburn.

Coral cuts and grazes often become inflamed and infected because of foreign material such as pieces of coral, nematocysts and slime. Carry antiseptic or medicated soap to wash and clean the wound and an antibiotic powder or ointment for dressing.

Use 'Aqua Ear' or any other ear wash after every dive to prevent 'tropical ear'. This occurs when the function of the external ear canal has been affected by the removal of the cerumen from the ear, or by divers being immersed for long periods in warm tropical waters. Avoid scratching or using cotton buds to clean the ear.

For serious injuries from stonefish, stingrays or cone shells, bathe the area in hot water and seek medical attention.

When diving continuously over a period of days, do a couple of shallow dives before leaving and allow 24 hours before flying.

# Index of Fish and Invertebrates

(In alphabetic order, grouped by Class and Family)

# Index of Dive Sites

# Further Reading

## HISTORY AND GEOGRAPHY

Pyrard, F. *The Voyages of Francois Pyrard of Laval to the East Indies, the Maldives, the Moluccas and Brazil.* London, Hakluyt Society, 1887.

Tibbetts, R. *Arab Navigation in the Indian Ocean Before the Coming of the Portuguese.* London, Royal Asiatic Society, 1971.

Barbosa, D. *The Book of Duarte Barbosa.* London, Hakluyt Society, 1921.

Huan, Ma. Ying-Yai Sheng-Lan, *The Overall Survey of the Ocean's Shores.* Cambridge, Hakluyt Society, 1970

Pires, T. *Suma Oriental of Tome' Pires.* London, Hakluyt Society, 1944.

Rosser, W.H., and Imray, J.F. *Indian Ocean Directory, The seaman's Guide to the Navigation of the Indian Ocean and China Sea.* London, 1867.

Boxer, C. *The tragic History of the Sea 1589-1622.* Cambridge, Hakluyt Society, 1959.

Davis, J. *The Voyages and Works of John Davis the Navigator.* London, Hakluyt Society, 1880.

Hedges, W. *The Diary of Sir William Hedges,* Hakluyt Society.

Bell, H.C.P. *The Maldive Islands. Monograph on the History, Archaeology and Epigraphy.* Colombo, Ceylon Government Press, 1940.

Battuta, I. *The travels of Ibn Batuta. Travels in Asia and Africa, 1325-1354.* London, Hakluyt Society.

Villiers, A. *The Indian Ocean. A History.* London, Museum Press, 1952.

Godfrey, T. *Atlas of the Maldives.* Apollo Bay, Atoll Editions, 2004.

Ballard, G.A. *Rulers of the Indian Ocean.* Madras, Asian Educational Services, 1998 (First Published London, 1927)

Maniku, H.A. *Changes in the Topography of the Maldives.* Malé, Novelty Press, 1990.

Maniku, H.A. *The Islands of Maldives.* Malé, Novelty Printers & Publishers, 1983.

Farook, M. *The Fascinating Maldives.* Malé, Novelty Printers & Publishers, 1985.

## MARINE LIFE

Anderson, R. C. *Common Fishes of the Maldives.* Part 1, 2, and 3. Malé, Novelty Publication. 1987-92.

Anderson, R. C. *Living Reefs of the Maldives.* Malé, Novelty Publication. 1991.

Anderson, R. C. *Diver's Guide to Sharks of Maldives.* Malé, Novelty Printers & Publishers, 1992.

Debelius, H. *Indian Ocean Tropical Fish Guide.* Hamberg, Aquaprint Verlag, 1993.

Gardiner, J.S. *The Fauna and Geography of the Maldive and Laccadive Archipelagoes, 1899-1900.* Cambridge, 1901-1906.

Coleman, N. *Marine Life of the Maldives,* Apollo Bay, Atoll Editions, 2000.

Kuiter, R. *Photo Guide to Fishes of the Maldives,* Apollo Bay, Atoll Editions, 1998.

Hussain, M. *The Maldives. Home of the Children of the Sea.* Malé, Novelty Publication. 1987.

# Dhivehi (Maldivian) Words and Phrases

## NUMERALS

| | |
|---|---|
| One | *Eheh* |
| Two | *Dheiy* |
| Three | *Thineh* |
| Four | *Hathareh* |
| Five | *Faheh* |
| Six | *Haeh* |
| Seven | *Hatheh* |
| Eight | *Asheh* |
| Nine | *Nuvaeh* |
| Ten | *Dhihaeh* |

## WEEKDAYS

| | |
|---|---|
| Monday | *Hoama* |
| Tuesday | *Angaara* |
| Wednesday | *Budha* |
| Thursday | *Buraasfathi* |
| Friday | *Hukuru* |
| Saturday | *Honihiru* |
| Sunday | *Aadheet'tha* |

## TIME

| | |
|---|---|
| Day | *Dhuvas* |
| Noon | *Mendhuruh* |
| Evening | *Haveeru* |
| Midnight | *Mendhamu* |
| Now | *Mihaaru* |
| Yesterday | *Iyye* |
| Tomorrow | *Maadhan* |
| Morning | *Hendhunu* |
| Afternoon | *Mendhuru fas* |
| Night | *Reygandu* |
| Dawn | *Fathis* |
| Later | *Fahun* |
| Today | *Miadhu* |

## USEFUL WORDS

| | |
|---|---|
| Above | *Matheega* |
| Across | *Hurahah* |
| Again | *Adhi* |
| Anchor | *Nagili* |
| Beach | *Athirimathi* |
| Big | *Bodu* |
| Bird | *Dhooni* |
| Blood | *Ley* |
| Boat | *Dhoani* |
| Cold | *Fini* |
| Compass | *Samugaa* |
| Coral | *Gaa/Muraka* |
| Current | *Oi* |
| Dive | *Feenun* |
| Dolphin | *Koamas* |
| Drink, to | *Boan* |
| Eat | *Kaan* |
| Empty | *Hus* |
| Fish | *Mas* |
| Fisherman | *Masveriya* |
| Happy | *Ufaa* |
| High tide | *Bodu dhiya* |
| Horizon | *Udhares* |
| Hot | *Hoonu* |
| Island | *Rah/Fushi* |
| Lagoon | *Faruthere* |
| Lobster | *Ihi* |
| Long | *Dhigu* |
| Low Tide | *Hiki dhiya* |
| Mast | *Kunbu* |
| Medicine | *Beys* |
| Money | *Faisaa* |
| Moon | *Handhu* |
| Narrow | *Hani* |
| Oar | *Fali* |
| Ocean | *Maakandu* |
| Rain | *Vissaara* |
| Rainbow | *Vissaara dhuni* |
| Reef | *Faru* |
| Rescue | *Salaamaiykurun* |
| Rising tide | *Foodhey dhiya* |
| Rope | *Roanu* |
| Rudder | *Hungaanu* |
| Sandbank | *Finolhu* |
| Shell | *Boli* |
| Shore | *Gondu dhoh* |
| Sky | *Udu* |
| Spring tide | *Foamathi* |
| Stern | *Kolhufas* |
| Storm | *Koligandu* |
| Sun | *Iru* |
| Swell | *Baani* |
| Temperature | *Fini hoonu min* |
| Tide | *Dhiya* |
| Water | *Fen* |
| Waves | *Raalhu* |
| Weather | *Moosun* |
| Wet | *Theiy* |
| Wind | *Vai* |

## USEFUL LOCAL TERMS

| | |
|---|---|
| *Atoll* | A group of islands surrounded by a common reef formation |
| *Cona* | Clear area among corals |
| *Falhu* | Lagoon encircled by a reef sometimes with one or more islands inside |
| *Faru* | Large reef partially exposed at low tide |
| *Finolhu* | Island with few or no coconut trees |
| *Fushi* | Big island usually on the outside reef of the atolls |
| *Futtaru* | Reef where waves break |
| *Giri* | Small patch of coral a couple of metres below the surface |
| *Halu* | Clearing in lagoon |
| *Kandu* | Sea inside atoll |
| *Kandu Olhi* | Channel |
| *Maa Kandu* | Sea outside atoll |
| *Thila* | Coral reef a few metres below the surface |
| *Vilu* | Deep area inside lagoon |

## USEFUL PHRASES

| | |
|---|---|
| When are you going? | *Kaley dhanee kon irakun* |
| Where is it? | *E Kobaa* |
| Where are you going? | *Kaley dhanee kon thaakah* |
| Be quick | *Avas kuraathi* |
| Go ahead | *Kuriah dhey* |
| Go slow | *Madun dhey* |
| How much? | *Kihaa vareh* |
| How are you? | *Haalu kihineh* |
| Thank you | *Shukuriyyaa* |
| Watch out | *Balaathi* |
| What is it? | *Eee kon echcheh* |
| What is the matter? | *Kihineh vee* |
| What time are we going? | *Aharemen dhanee kon irakun* |
| How long does it take? | *Kihaa ireh nagaanee* |
| What is that island? | *E othee kon rasheh* |
| What is the name of this reef? | *Mi farah kiyanee kon nameh* |
| Which way is the current? | *Oi othee kon thaakah* |
| Excuse me I'm sorry | *Maafu kurey* |
| Be careful | *Faruvaa bahattaathi* |
| I see | *Ehen dhoa* |
| Yes | *Aanh/ladda/aadhe* |
| No | *Noon* |
| What time is it? | *Gadin kihaa ireh* |